Revolution in Higher Education

Revolution in Higher Education

How a Small Band of Innovators Will Make College Accessible and Affordable

Richard A. DeMillo
foreword by Andrew J. Young

The MIT Press
Cambridge, Massachusetts
London, England

This book was set in Stone by the MIT Press. Printed and bound in the United States of America.

Library of Congress Cataloging-in-Publication Data

DeMillo, Richard A.
Revolution in higher education : how a small band of innovators will make college accessible and affordable / Richard DeMillo.
    pages   cm
Includes bibliographical references and index.
ISBN 978-0-262-02964-3 (hardcover : alk. paper)
1. Universities and colleges—United States. 2. Educational technology—United States. 3. College costs—United States. 4. Educational change—United States.
I. Title.
LA227.4.D47   2015
378.00973—dc23
2015009376

10 9 8 7 6 5 4 3 2 1

In memory of Chuck Vest

Rather let me say that there are heroes and martyrs, prophets and apostles of learning as there are of religion.

—Daniel Coit Gilman

Contents

Part IV: A Social Contract   265

Epilogue   279

Foreword

I have spent most of my life in the civil rights movement. Even as a public servant, I fought for human rights. Why is a civil rights leader writing a foreword for a book about higher education? The civil rights movement was always about helping poor people, but in the early days, we talked more about ending discrimination than about ending poverty. The reason was simple. We did not think that economic issues would carry the day in the political climate of the 1960s and 1970s. Ensuring the basic rights of minorities was a cause that appealed to fair-minded Americans of all races and backgrounds, so Dr. King made it the moral foundation for a social contract to end discrimination. Nevertheless, our goal was always to erase the triple evils of racism, war, and poverty. That's what I've been doing my entire life.

How things have changed. The country has made progress in ending discrimination, although that progress has to be defended on a continual basis. We see that civil rights in the American South are no different than human rights in South Africa or anywhere else in the world. Basic rights cannot be shared as long as people are excluded. We now know that the triple evils are all about exclusion and inequality, which is what this book is all about.

Inequality cannot be wiped out as long as people cannot obtain a quality education. Quality is important for all schools, but it is especially important in postsecondary education, where economic growth often begins. Unfortunately, in colleges and universities around the world, quality means exclusion. Look at any list of the world's most highly regarded universities. They are highly selective institutions. They are elite. They are prestigious because of who they exclude. The whole idea of quality in higher education is based on inequality.

That was the theme of Richard DeMillo's book *Abelard to Apple: The Fate of American Colleges and Universities*. It was one of the reasons I was drawn to what Rich had to say about the failure of American higher education. It is a theme that he expands on in this book, which describes how higher education will be different if a dedicated group of revolutionaries establish a new social contract. This new contract would ensure that the quality of an institution is judged by how well it serves the people it is intended to serve, not by how many of them it excludes. *Abelard to Apple* was an excuse for me to think long and hard about the failure of American colleges and universities. It is far easier to attack institutions than to look for reasons they are unable to solve their problems, or what they would do if they could. I was intrigued when I heard Rich was writing a book that would tell us what the future might look like. I was even more interested when I found out it might involve a new social contract to democratize education.

Rich and I met a decade ago while serving on the board of the Campus-Community Partnership (C2P), a foundation that pays tribute to Jimmy and Rosalynn Carter's service by engaging college students in social projects. As a result of C2P's work, students from every class and color get introduced to the idea of college. We have been working on expanding access to college ever since, including a unique program called Mentor Walk to make sure that kids from poor neighborhoods actually spend a little time on a college campus and talk to mentors who might be role models.

My own heritage is the American Missionary Association, an outgrowth of the Amistad Rebellion and the abolitionist movement that established more than five hundred schools and colleges after the Civil War. My parents and grandparents as well as Coretta Scott King and my late wife, Jean Childs Young, emerged from this education network. It is no accident that the black middle class of the twentieth century emerged from the civil rights movement or that most of the black leaders in southern Africa emerged from Fort Hare University in South Africa. Nelson Mandela and Desmond Tutu studied there. Fort Hare University also grew out of a missionary movement. When I think of quality in education, I have in mind institutions like these that produce elite leaders and thinkers. That is, fundamentally different from institutions that call themselves elite because of whom they exclude.

Knowledge and truth always inspire change. The question today is whether the way we go about teaching and learning are adequate to the demands of technical and financial aspirations on a global scale. Much of the change in the world was produced by the values and vision of higher education. Change, whether by reform, evolution, or revolution, reminds me of an old Christian hymn: "New occasions teach new duties, time makes ancient good uncouth, they must strive upward and onward, who would keep abreast of truth."

Higher education today is in serious trouble. A small number of wealthy private institutions, which serve a tiny fraction of the people, are becoming more and more remote. Even at public universities, tuition is too high for most families. Completion rates, especially for kids from poor neighborhoods, are too low. Families pile up debt for college degrees that have little value. Meanwhile, university leaders are rewarded, making things even more unequal. A college that rises in national rankings by becoming more selective is considered a success by alumni and donors. *Abelard to Apple* is a kind of "how the leopard got its spots" tale of how inequality crept into higher education. This book looks to the future. It is about what Rich calls a small band of innovators are doing to erase the inequality in higher education. The working title of the original manuscript was *Heroes and Martyrs*. I was a little disappointed that was not the final title. As a preacher, I found the title to be appealing. The idea of heroes in higher education is taken from Daniel Gilman, the first president of Johns Hopkins University. Gilman thought that there were heroes and martyrs of learning just like there were apostles of religion. They are all sent forth into the world to change it. The final chapter is about a new social contract for universities. It has the same universal appeal that the human rights movement had thirty years ago. It is inspiring that so many of the central characters are revolutionaries who turn out to be committed to the same ideals.

What will be different if this small band of innovators has its way? The world will have access to high quality education at lower (or no) cost. The idea of "remedial" education will disappear and be replaced with a more sophisticated understanding of how the brain learns. Remedial education never gets the attention it needs. The idea itself assumes there are two classes of people: those who need remedial coursework because they have failed to learn, and those who don't. Rich believes it is classrooms that have failed, not the students. Innovation can help. For example, he describes classrooms that adapt to the different circumstances that entering students have no control over. Change like this never comes easily. Many in existing institutions fight to maintain their status.

Although this is a book about academia, it is not an academic book. Rich, who was also a dean at Georgia Tech and an executive in industry, writes for those of us who are not insiders. We get to see what's really going on and what challenges the revolutionaries face. *Revolution* is not always easy sledding. Why college costs so much sounds like an easy question,

but the answers are not simple. It takes some patience to make the connections with economics and technology. For every complicated question,
there are hopeful stories, like Mississippi's Jackson State University. While
most historically black colleges and universities look at their mission as a
straitjacket, Jackson State decided to combine technology with its mission
as a historically black university to serve more students.

Actually, it is only partially true that my interest in Rich's work is tied
to high academic and social ideals. I was also drawn by his description of
technology that seems unrelated to education. Rich uses stories to draw
you into more complicated matters, and I was interested in one of the stories near the end of *Abelard to Apple*. After many years as an MIT professor
and entrepreneur, a distinguished engineer named Suh Nam-pyo returned
home to Korea to become president of the Korean Advanced Institute for
Science and Technology (KAIST), often called the "MIT of Korea." Suh was
trying to solve the riddle of how to make KAIST more responsive to the
needs of the Korean economy when he hit on the idea of a "mobile harbor"
that could be used to greatly expand the capacity of deepwater ports with
minimal damage to the environment. This struck me as a wonderful technology that could be used here in Savannah, Georgia, where proposals were
being written for a port expansion that would greatly damage the environment. I decided to pursue the same kind of public-private partnership that
I had used as mayor to build Atlanta's Hartsfield-Jackson International Air-
port and use KAIST's mobile harbor technology to expand shipping ports in
an environmentally responsible way.

As wonderful as this idea was, Suh was an irritant to the existing powers in South Korea and was attacked relentlessly for pushing academic
reforms at KAIST. I had seen this kind of irritant before. When I cochaired
the Atlanta Olympic Committee in the 1990s, I became friends with Patrick Crecine, who was president of Georgia Tech at the time. It was Crecine's idea to use virtual reality technology to illustrate Atlanta's proposal
for hosting the 1996 Olympic games. He also remade Georgia Tech. This
earned him many admirers, but it also made him an irritant, which earned
him many enemies as well. When he passed away, I was asked to make a
few remarks at his memorial. "Pat was always right," I said, "and he always
got people mad." I understood this completely. Dr. King always said that
my role was to be the irritant that kept us focused on the right problems.
The small band of innovators that Rich describes is the irritant that higher
education needs.

I'm looking forward to Rich's next book that I hope will expand on how
education and technology can be used to create jobs. In today's world,

educational opportunity must be joined by access to capital and job creation. The leaders produced by the revolution in higher education have to provide stability and access to food, energy, water, and shelter for the struggling billions of humanity who now threaten chaos because they are excluded from the lifestyles and opportunities that new technology has made available to the rest of the world.

Ambassador Andrew J. Young
Atlanta, 2015

Preface

This book is a companion to my 2011 *Abelard to Apple: The Fate of American Colleges and Universities*, which I wrote just as the global economy was slipping into the Great Recession.[1] I intended it to be a critical narrative of higher education explaining, for example, how American colleges arrived at the chasm that separates their comfortable and privileged past from an uncertain fate. When I started working on *Abelard*, I felt like an outsider, a stranger to the world of policy, economics, regulation, and politics that defines education. But most of the people I knew—even my friends and colleagues who ran schools, colleges, and governing boards—were also outsiders. Few of us—I would discover—understood what was happening to our aging institutions besides what was becoming obvious to anyone who cared to look: they were increasingly costly, inaccessible, and unresponsive to the needs of the twenty-first century. Meanwhile, innovation seemed to be swirling outside the walls of the academy. I hoped that I could help provoke informed debate among the outsiders.

I thought the American system of higher education was in for transformational change of the sort that ancient enterprises rarely experience. I took some care to explain what was in store for the country's colleges and universities, but I believed the events I was describing would take a generation or more to unfold. I badly underestimated the pace and scope that technology-fueled change would have on education worldwide. In amazement, I watched as the magic "Year of the MOOC" (massive open online courses), a crisis of confidence in higher education, and ultimately the kind of systemic changes that transform institutions all began to play out in headlines around the world. By the time *Abelard* appeared in 2011, alarm bells were ringing everywhere. A pile of new books appeared, some decrying and others defending the status quo. News stories carried weekly or daily updates about the "bubble" in higher education. Government authorities started to examine the sustainability of postsecondary education and dig into why, despite decades of investment, so few Americans actually finished college while so many piled up debt that would be difficult to repay. There were debates for and against change. Private foundations that had been traditional supporters of slow and steady progress in academia began calling for projects to test disruptive ideas. A small band of innovators—including some of the same college presidents who I had said should be more open to experimentation—decided that the time was right for change. But for many—even university graduates and others who had spent substantial time on college campuses—change seemed painfully slow. And an amazingly large number of people were simply unaware that change was taking place at all. Much as I tried to do in *Abelard*, I wanted to make this book a simple explanation of what is likely to happen.

Most of what is written about higher education is impenetrable to the average person. Academics write treatises for their colleagues. Politicians and journalists who care to write about universities are dismissed because they are too liberal or too conservative, or because they have axes to grind. Futurists undermine their own narratives with dire warnings of the imminent collapse of institutions that are in no visible danger. If there is one lesson that can be learned it is that modern universities operate with a different set of rules, and you have to be unusually diligent to follow what is going on. And yet innovation is redefining the concept of higher education at an astonishing pace. Those changes will touch virtually everyone. If Abraham Lincoln was correct that creating the future is the best way to predict it, then maybe the best way to predict the future of higher education is to understand what the people who are trying to create it are trying to do.

This book is loosely organized around *Abelard*'s "rules for the twenty-first century," which emphasized the value, technology, costs, academic culture, and need for a new contract with society. This is how I structured my discussions with entrepreneurs, friends, and colleagues—and on many occasions, complete strangers—as I was preparing to write. I wanted to know what the innovators were trying to achieve, and they were remarkably candid with me. Would their work mean the crumbling of entrenched institutions? How would students be better off? What would be an inevitable outcome of their success? To my surprise, the same ideas recurred. It did not seem to matter if I was talking to insiders or outsiders. Nor did it matter where in the world I was. Everyone I talked to described success in the same way. Taken together, their ideas are a road map to a near future being defined by a small band of innovators.

I set out to write a very different book than this one. I thought that knowledgeable observers had figured out what was going on, and that I could simply understand and report their forecasts. I was wrong on both counts. First of all, most people view higher education through a personal lens. If you attended a prestigious research university, you have the idea that every college experience resembles that one. If you attended college later in life, you have a hard time relating to higher education as a place that postadolescents go to mature into adults. Academic insiders have a different understanding of higher education than people who rarely set foot on a college campus. Working on the campus of a research university does almost nothing to prepare you for community college life. Understanding what is going on depends to a large extent on how you relate to a range of experiences that are different from your own. Secondly, I naively thought that there would be little controversy over what the inevitable next steps would be for higher education, particularly once I explained the forces at work and that whatever uncertainty there was would be about timing.

The problem was with the very concept of an inevitable next step. How can anyone know what is inevitable? Even if you believe that the changes coming to higher education are not random, undirected developments—that they are the result of the same drivers of change that have transformed society over the past quarter century—just saying what the next steps are casts you in the role of a fortune-teller. Like Lincoln, however, I believe it is prudent to pay close attention to the intentions of determined individuals who are trying to change things. If they are successful, their goals are tomorrow's inevitabilities. This is a book about the people who are trying to remake higher education and what they are trying to achieve, and why. They are *heroes and martyrs of learning* like the ones that Gilman, in the opening epilogue, called to battle over a century ago.

Acknowledgments

This book would not have been possible without the help and cooperation of dozens of people, many mentioned by name, and whose words, ideas, and visions for the future I have freely borrowed and tried to synthesize into a coherent picture. The many others I have talked with over the last four years include students, professors, deans, provosts, and presidents at a hundred universities. Community and business leaders who have vital interests in the health of higher education also shared their ideas with me. We did not always agree on the problems or solutions, but I am deeply indebted to each of them. The faculty, students, and staff at Georgia Tech's Center for 21st Century Universities tested many of the concepts discussed in this book. Their energy was important as this work took shape. Mike McCracken, my director of online innovation, tirelessly pursued the vision of technology-enabled transformation. He has been my collaborator for thirty years, and his ideas are liberally sprinkled throughout this book. Georgia Tech provost Rafael Bras and president Bud Peterson generously provided financial support and bureaucratic cover for the center's work. Dean Zvi Galil also supplied financial support for the center and an administrative home for our work. Most important, he enthusiastically embraced our message and became our greatest advocate. The Board of Regents and Office of the Chancellor of the University System of Georgia—especially vice chancellor Lynne Weisenbach and system provost Houston Davis—let us infect their strategic thinking and imagine a better way to educate the state's three hundred thousand students.

Ambassador Andrew Young has been generous with his time over the years. My discussion of historically black colleges and universities (HBCUs) would not have been possible without him. It is impossible to live in Atlanta and not feel the presence of institutions like Morehouse and Spellman, but the rest of higher education knows far too little about HBCUs. I regret that I could not tell their story in more detail here. My friends

R. K. and Sue Sehgal along with the other board members of the Campus-Community Partnership Foundation provided indispensable feedback on many of the ideas in this book. The Sehgal's opened their home one remarkable evening to an unscripted gathering of college and university presidents. It was like an informal tribal council, and although I have not directly used their words, their shared sense of mission and concern for the public good infected my thoughts about how this book should be written. Benn Konsynski, Jonathan Cole, Zvi Galil, and Eric Grimson each offered important historical information.

The Lumina and Qatar Foundations also both generously supported my work. I am immensely grateful.

Former MIT president Chuck Vest passed away as the manuscript for this book was being completed. Chuck was one of the heroes mentioned by Daniel Coit Gilman, although when he first explained the idea of Open-CourseWare to me, I suggested that if the initiative went awry, he might be a martyr. When we last spoke, I reminded him of this. He said that when he proposed the idea he was not sure how it was all going to turn out, but he was sure that the world would never be the same.

My patient and supportive MIT Press editor, Marie Lufkin Lee, and the anonymous reviewers whose unvarnished advice reshaped the first, unwieldy manuscripts were unusually dedicated to helping me find a voice for the heroes of this book. My colleague Mark Braunstein made room in his busy schedule to read the final manuscript and root out not-so-obvious errors and defects. Finally, my colleague of forty years, Richard Lipton, and my companion, friend, and wife, Ronnie Martin, generously agreed to review drafts and provide me much-needed criticism. Over the years they have listened to many ideas that in addition to those that found their way into the book, never went anywhere. Despite the generous contributions of my colleagues and collaborators, all defects, errors, and shortcoming are mine alone.

Introduction

I clicked my headset to the on position, and the voice in my ear said, "So this is a big deal, isn't it?" It was not really a question—more like a judgment—and I was supposed to concur. There was no "Hello. How are you?" and if I had asked, "What are you talking about?" the call would have been over, but this was my fifth conversation with a reporter since lunch, and it was only 2:00 p.m. "Yes, it is a big deal," I said. I had the embargoed press release and so did the reporter. She wanted to find out what else I knew. "Does this change everything?" I did not think so. "It's a sign that everything has changed," I replied. The story appeared online Friday. Print versions ran over the weekend. By Monday, there were dozens of sites that ran their own versions of the story and the international press had begun covering the original press announcement. By Wednesday, every major news organization in the world had covered what was being called a revolution in higher education. Everyone I talked to expected that the press would be interested for only a couple of days. A few bloggers would try to keep it going longer, but except for sports, scandals, and an occasional fascination with eccentric geniuses, there had never been a great public appetite for what happens in ivy-covered halls. By next month it would all be forgotten. It turned out to be a bigger deal than I thought—maybe a fascination with eccentric geniuses.

You have to be isolated from the events of the world to not know that colleges and universities are big news. It used to be hard to find a newspaper that had much interest in higher education, but for many months now, it has been impossible to avoid big, boldfaced headlines and breathless investigative reports about the future of universities. It is a global phenomenon. Americans may be worried about rising tuition, low completion rates, unemployed graduates, and the trillion dollars in debt that they have racked up, yet every region of the world looks at its system of higher education, concludes that it is in trouble, and wonders what the future holds in store. Experts are divided on that question, but there is one thing that most of them agree on: higher education is being remade before our eyes.

This is a book about the future of the world's colleges and universities. It is not a book about what I think is going to happen, or even what I wish would happen. It is not a book that defends the status quo, or proposes throwing out a thousand years of history and starting over again. It is not even a book about charting a middle course. It is a chronicle of an agenda for massive, global change. It is an explanation of what some dedicated and inventive people want to accomplish as they set out to remake higher education. It is also about the obstacles along with the opponents arrayed against them. Above all, though, it is about what the result will be if these people succeed.

One thing is certain. If they have their way, everything about higher education will be changed forever. What is happening to the world's colleges and universities is in every sense a revolution. In fact, let us agree at the outset what to call the events that started in the offices of MIT president Charles M. Vest in 2000 and intensified over the next decade until, like a tsunami, they overwhelmed the public's understanding of what a college education means—*Revolution*. If that sounds too dramatic, it is best to keep in mind that history is dotted with other revolutions like this one. Few of us, for example, think of college as a place where students directly pay instructors based on how well they teach, although the first universities were organized exactly that way a thousand years ago. Even the idea that a college degree prepares students for careers was revolutionary in its day. Over the following pages, I will help you keep that history in mind.

What makes this revolution different is the scale of the global enterprise of higher education. There are about fifty thousand colleges and universities in the world, enrolling as many as a billion people.[1] Industrialized nations devote 4 percent of their gross domestic product to higher education. National economies rest on the health of local universities. The times also make this revolution different: it occurs at a nexus of technological, social, and economic change that has never happened before. Everyone who has experienced the birth and adolescence of the Internet knows that the pace of technological innovation now makes possible what was impossible a generation ago. That pace is accelerating, and it is hard for anyone outside academia to understand what is taking place. Even within the academy there is much that is hidden from view.

This book is a peek behind a curtain that is usually drawn. I have chosen an American lens to show what is going on and why. What began as a few Silicon Valley experiments now engulfs hundreds of institutions of higher learning, and tens of millions of students in fifty countries. A small band of innovators—the term comes from Daniel Coit Gilman's inaugural address as the first president of Johns Hopkins University and his imagery of "a small band of well-chosen professors, ... heroes and martyrs, apostles and prophets of learning"—has chosen this path, but it is not a coordinated assault.[2] It would be a mistake to think that the revolution is about a single movement or single technology. It is better to envision the revolution as a set of aspirations about what the world's colleges and universities could become. It is about the intertwined stories of the innovators and what they want to achieve—a series of events that once put in motion, cannot be recalled.

What Makes This Time Different?

This is not the first time that experts have warned of impending doom. Higher education always seems to defy gloomy predictions that the whole enterprise is about to collapse. The academy looks at history, and unimpressed, shrugs its collective shoulders and continues on its way. It was that way when the first European universities were founded a thousand years ago. It continued into the twentieth century with its cycle of calls for dramatic reform—quick and certain action to avoid sinking the entire system—followed by resistance to change.

The challenges always seem grave. "Most planners expect that demographics will lead to enrollment declines, even with other trends taken into account," said forecasts of the 1980s.[3] The system was facing "financial strains of crisis proportions," warned the National Association of State Universities and Land Grant Colleges in 1971.[4] Economist Earl Cheit wrote a landmark report that predicted a new Great Depression in higher education.[5] The gap between Depression-era family income and the costs of higher education alarmed economists in the 1930s.[6] Students' needs were being insufficiently attended to, said critics in the mid-nineteenth century. Wild swings between student apathy and rebellion prompted college presidents to admit that "the collegiate way" might be "too much for vigorous young men to bear."[7] The Second Great Awakening in the early 1800s jeopardized the intellectual nature of a college education with "a torrent of religious piety."[8] Even the famous medieval universities in Bologna and Paris were publicly derided as "moribund homes of outmoded knowledge."

The experts were wrong. In the end, universities emerged little changed from centuries of unrelenting criticism. There was no precipitous drop in enrollment after the last of the World War II baby boomers graduated in the early 1970s. The "depression" that Cheit predicted turned out to be more about inflation and energy prices—problems that had eased by 1985.[9] The land grant movement, curriculum modernization, intercollegiate athletics, and disappearance of dueling from American life resolved many on-campus tensions. Those issues that were not so easily resolved waxed and waned with the social issues of the times.

And so here we are, perched atop the most emulated system of postsecondary education in the world. By most reckoning, the trends in higher education in the United States and most of the industrialized world have pointed upward for a long time. Defenders of tradition and purists would say it was their stubborn resistance to calls for massive change that was key, and whatever ailed American universities was easily treated with patience and discipline, but seldom with help from the outside.

Predictions of disaster have inevitably been followed by rebirth. Every new golden age comes on the heels of such a renaissance. The cycle is so predictable that academics are trained to be cynical about change. There have always been calls to reform. "Everyone says this time is different, but it never is; we have seen all this before," the purists say. Reform is best done slowly and only when it does not disrupt the well-oiled machine that is higher education. And besides, new ideas are few and far between. "Even if we wanted to remake higher education," assert professors and administrators alike, "we don't think there is anything that can replace what we already have." Of course, the fact that in the past everyone claimed "this time is different," does not rule out the possibility that this time really is different.

Why Remake Higher Education?

There is an optimistic narrative of higher education. In it, all downturns are temporary and best endured by appealing to the virtues of the academic endeavor. That optimism vanished with the twentieth century. By mid-2011, problems facing American higher education that had once seemed distant and abstract became suddenly acute with a global economic crisis of historic dimensions. Tax revenues that had subsidized costs for public universities rapidly dried up, and, faced with unprecedented budget cuts, most institutions steered a disastrous middle course of raising tuition and cutting costs. Private universities subsidize costs with earnings from endowments. Endowment income was among the first casualties of the 2008 stock market crash. Many smaller institutions were also forced to raise tuition. Hundreds were driven into chaos, and many more to the brink of financial ruin. Despite this, most college presidents were convinced that things were not so bad. Few made structural changes to adapt to a new fiscal reality.

As a result issues that should have been worked out over a generation quickly became immediate crises. Graduates of respected programs could not find jobs. Default rates on student loans soared. A string of highly critical studies cast doubt on how well universities were doing at their primary job of teaching postadolescents to think critically, reason quantitatively, and communicate effectively. Opportunists were quick to point fingers. Some said it was a bloated administrative class that was causing all the trouble; others thought it was due to a lazy and entitled professoriat. Failure was laid at the feet of an education system that did not prepare high school students properly. Too much infusion of corporate management has destroyed the very ideal of higher education, said those who were repelled by the notion that professors needed to be managed and instead cherished the collaborative atmosphere of academic communities. Too little top-down direction has allowed many universities to lurch from crisis to crisis, pursuing strategies that benefit neither students nor the public, maintained others. As public confidence in higher education began to wane, a major candidate for the US presidency said that the middle-class American dream of a college degree amounted to "snobbery," and many agreed with him. Negative press coverage of the problems facing higher education was relentless. College presidents across the board insisted that they were doing a good job and that restoring lost funds was all that was needed, but the brand of higher education was being damaged by daily, withering criticism. If this was one of those cyclic downturns that shortly would be eased by an improving economy, the signs of reversal needed to appear soon, because the sustainability of the idyllic social, academic enterprise was in doubt.

As I write this—five years after the deepest part of the recession—there is a consensus among knowledgeable observers that American higher education had not been on a sustainable path for a long time. This comes as a shock to outsiders who look at the American institutions at the top of annual rankings of world universities as models to be emulated. US secretary of education Arne Duncan calls them the islands of excellence, yet they are irrelevant islands of excellence to the vast majority of college students who do not have access to them.[10] Unlike their elite cousins, most American colleges and universities are locked in a system that is anything but excellent.

Most American institutions fall into a great *Middle*: the nearly four thousand colleges and universities that lie just below the Élites in the hierarchy of higher education. Élite institutions have global brands and the financial wherewithal to determine their own fate. A degree from an Élite carries with it a promise of considered treatment by employers and strong likelihood of financial rewards. But it is the Middle that enrolls 80 percent of all college students. If you are a recent high school graduate, odds are high that you will attend a college in the Middle rather than an Élite institution. If you are a part-time student, adult retooling for a second career, returning veteran, recent immigrant, or single parent, the odds are overwhelming that you will attend expensive and crowded classes in the Middle. If you happen to be one of lucky 20 percent who actually earns a degree, you will almost certainly find that those classes do little to distinguish you from thousands of other job seekers in a crowded marketplace. When policy makers and political leaders talk about the higher education system, they are really speaking about the Middle.

There are clear signs that the Middle is headed for trouble. It is in financial disrepair. Credit rating agencies say that it is bad bet.[11] There are credible estimates that as many as half of all institutions could be insolvent within fifteen years.[12] Soaring institutional debt and a "cost disease" that causes labor costs to rise at twice the rate of inflation have pushed prices beyond the reach of most American households.[13] Student loan debt jumped past credit card debt, passing the trillion-dollar mark sometime in late 2012. Many students graduate from college with grade-inflated degrees in fields that are in low demand by employers, and many more fail to graduate at all, but are burdened with debt nevertheless. The end result is a soaring default rate for student loans.[14] Forty million current and former students hold federally secured loans, and one out of every seven defaults within two years of graduation. Finally, public confidence in higher education is on the decline.[15] For the first time, the majority of Americans question the value of a college degree. This lack of confidence is expressed in decreased overall spending for public universities and declining applications for many private universities.

As unnerving as these trends are for the Middle, the Élites seem to be immune from their effects. The American model is one in which a handful of institutions—handpicking students and setting prices as high as they wish—become ever more remote. The remaining institutions fight it out over the rest. The "rest" consists not only of average students, both full and part time, but also students poorly prepared for college along with, increasingly, adult learners, first-generation college students, and recent immigrants. These students are less likely to successfully complete college and more likely to take out unaffordable loans. Institutions in the Middle are judged on factors like completion rates and percentage return on investment of tuition dollars, so many of the rest of these students are not the bread and butter that most institutions want to attract.

Higher education in the United States has evolved to accommodate this state of affairs. The system was designed a hundred years ago when relatively few people attended college. To accommodate more students, schools adopted a factory approach to education in which raw materials (students) were sorted by age and ability into batches (classes) to receive uniform doses of content (classes, curricula, and majors). Like defective products on an assembly line, students who did not make the grade were rejected (failed). Factory operations were supposed to be carried out under the watchful eye of managers (administrators and trustees) and quality assurance experts (accreditors). This was an adequate system for many years, but by 2011 it became clear that what was being demanded of higher education had changed. Students had changed. Quality had declined. Most important, the very idea of an educational factory had reached its limits. Without innovation, rising costs would continue to drive a wedge between those who could afford a quality education and the vast majority of American families whose income would rise slightly, if at all. And not just any innovation would make a difference. Productivity would need to be improved, but so would quality.

This kind of innovation had stopped. The factories were not evolving, and it was obvious why. Improving productivity meant that fewer professors would be needed. Institutional missions would be streamlined. More would be demanded for less money. It was time to either fix the factories or replace them with something more suited to the needs of society—and maybe something better. There had never been a more compelling moment to remake higher education. The current path was not sustainable and a new wave of technological innovation provided an alternative to factories, enabling better, more affordable learning for more students. It was an idea that gradually began to infect a group of fearless people who were prepared to do something about it. By 2011, it was apparent what they had in mind.

A Small Band of Innovators

There had been calls for reform before but somehow this time seemed different to a handful of university leaders and Silicon Valley entrepreneurs. For one thing, they realized that they had cheaper, far more effective technologies at their disposal. Many people within academia concluded that the arguments for remaking higher education were ones they had heard before; that there was nothing different this time. But others had concluded the opposite. Higher education had to be remade because it had become unsustainable in its current form, and what made this time different was that there were now tools of change widely available to anyone who might wish to try something new. It was possible to start a revolution when nothing less than a revolution was called for, but who would lead it? Who would tinker with the very idea of a university, and what would higher education look like afterward?

One theory of innovation is that outsiders play a pivotal role, particularly when the innovation disrupts an otherwise-successful venture. Disruption requires an irrational thought: "Why don't we stop what we are doing now, what we have done well, and what has been profitable to us and useful to our customers, and do this new, untested thing that has a good chance of failing?" A rational person would only do that if the old, previously valuable thing was about to disappear—to lose its value to customers or become prohibitively expensive, for example. Even in the rational light of day, there are usually powerful incentives for insiders to avoid innovation. After all, there is ample evidence that the success of innovative disruption comes at the expense of insiders.

In 1934, American populist Upton Sinclair devised a utopian scheme for ending the depression in California. Sinclair's plan was the single platform plank in his failed bid for the governor's mansion. At the height of a surprisingly modern political fight that featured dirty tricks and hostile local newspapers, Sinclair hit on the reason that insiders reject innovation. It takes an outsider, he said, because "it is difficult to get a man to understand something, when his salary depends on his not understanding it!"[16] Higher education is not too far removed from Sinclair's Depression-era politics: there is little good that will happen to academic insiders who embrace the idea that the system is in a state of collapse.

According to another theory, disruptive innovation is a random process: it is impossible to predict where it will arise, and whether it will succeed or fail. Otherwise, insiders would be innovating all the time. In industries like education, health care, politics, and energy, there are many stakeholders with competing interests. Insiders with disruptive ideas are as likely to be advantaged by their own inventions as not, yet these are also the industries that have been the most resistant to change. Resistant but not immune; examples abound. The medical establishment rejected the use of surgical antiseptics well into the nineteenth century despite scientific evidence of their effectiveness. Widespread adoption occurred only as a result of public outcry over the avoidable death of US president James Garfield. Insiders and outsiders often play equally important roles, but it always seems to be a small band of innovators who disrupt the status quo.

In California's Silicon Valley, a financial analyst named Salman Khan had the idea to use a free drawing program to tutor his cousins in mathematics.

He had a knack for making easily understandable explanations of complicated ideas, and when others sought his help, he began to post short videos of his lessons on YouTube to an audience that quickly grew to millions of viewers. Free distribution of educational materials was an idea that had insider help. Some years before Khan started posting his videos, MIT president and consummate insider Charles Vest had made all the university's courseware freely available to anyone in the world with a Web browser. Realizing that students might want to enroll in courses and organize educational content, seven Apple Computer engineers created iTunes U, a section of its iTunes online music store and devoted it to free, downloadable academic content.[17]

At Stanford University, computer science professors Daphne Koller and Jennifer Widdom were experimenting with how to invert the roles of lectures and homework when they came on the idea of using Internet technology to open up Stanford classrooms to an even larger audience. Coincidentally, their colleague Andrew Ng had for several years been intrigued with the notion that classroom time was being wasted and technology could help focus a professor's time on more productive learning activities. When their courses were offered on Stanford's open learning Web site, 150,000 students signed up. Enrollment numbers of that size were unprecedented, and the professors must have been impressed because they quickly decided to form a company to pursue the vision of opening their classrooms to the world. Meanwhile, Sebastian Thrun, another Stanford professor, sent an email to his contacts announcing that he and Google's Peter Norwig would be offering a free version of Stanford's artificial intelligence course using the Web. Again, 150,000 students enrolled in the class (including most of Thrun's on-campus Stanford students), and like his colleagues Thrun was so moved that he publicly announced that he was leaving his Stanford position to devote himself to this new way of learning. A continent away, Professor Anant Agarwal was using MIT's open courseware to teach an online version of his required engineering class to 160,000 students, declaring that he would provide MIT-branded certificates to students who successfully completed the course.

Far from the start-up culture of Silicon Valley, Jackson State University's provost, James Renick, was working on how technology might help the struggling historically black university to reinvent itself when Robert Blaine, a Jackson State music professor, realized that content-authoring tools would achieve two goals at once: they would permit a different kind of pedagogy than competitors were able to offer and would attract a different kind of student. In Canada, George Siemens and two of his colleagues began offering what they called massive open online courses (MOOCs) that enrolled several thousand students who were interested in Siemen's research into learning.

Even the science underpinning educational technology seemed to be accelerating. Armed with the same tools that professional politicians were using to predict the outcome of elections, a new breed of data analysts was using artificial intelligence to sift through tens of millions of mouse clicks, keystrokes, and homework exercises to predict which individual students would need learning systems to adapt to their needs. Cognitive scientists were mapping learning activities to brain functions and using the result to reorganize classrooms to better match how the brain actually learns. And the brain itself was at the heart of a revolution in neuroscience as chemists, computer scientists, and biologists discovered new ways of seeing into the very process of cognition. Nobel Prize winners like University of British Columbia's Carl Wieman were experimenting with how to replace cold and impersonal learning factories with interactive experiences that helped students think like scientists, economists, and sociologists. Wieman had recently taken his passion to the Obama White House where he, along with a cadre of journalists and science writers, began to proselytize the newly rediscovered work of K. Anders Ericsson on the psychology of knowledge acquisition.[18] College presidents wondered openly about how to use pedagogical methods that would have been prohibitively expensive only a few years before. Boards of trustees questioned whether investing in large lecture halls that had changed little in five hundred years was a good idea.

All of a sudden, there was an abundance of interest in pedagogy and educational technology, causing some to hope that the entire system was about to transform itself. But transforming islands of excellence into a system of excellence is a challenging task. It involves the kind of systemic change that universities do not like to make. Despite widespread agreement that change was needed, there were varied opinions about what that change should look like and how quickly it should come.[19] Arizona State University president Michael Crow had been a lonely voice, making enemies by pointing out the obvious failure of research universities that in a quest for prestige had become more exclusive and remote from the people they were supposed to serve. Crow's message was a distant echo of academic chronicler Edwin Slossin's call a century before to judge a university not by how well it scores on self-defined measures of success but instead by how well it serves the people it is supposed to serve. Crow began to create what he called a New Gold Standard for American universities that, like Renick's Jackson State University, would use technology to erase the accidental differences in circumstances among entering students, many of who came from impoverished and underserved neighborhoods—environments in which attending college was regarded as a risk rather than an opportunity. Outsiders like Internet entrepreneur Ben Nelson believed that too much money was being wasted in higher education, and that with a single-minded focus on delivering a quality educational experience, the cost of even an elite education could be brought back down to earth so that the average family could afford it. It was an outrageously ambitious goal, but former Harvard president Larry Summers and Nebraska senator Bob Kerrey, who had served as president of New York's New School, quickly backed it.

In 2011, though, the public view of higher education was pessimistic, and that pessimism was reinforced by each new study showing that academic leaders were by and large more interested in stewardship of an old yet comfortable existence than they were in listening to critics. American Élites had little incentive to change, and change without the active involvement of the top of the academic pyramid was impossible. But then the outsider theory started to crumble. Influential insiders began to say in public what critics had been reporting all along: unequal access was a threat to higher education. Stanford's president John Hennessy said that the cost of maintaining a large faculty was not sustainable and predicted that in the future, there would be fewer professors but they would be using new technologies to teach more students. He then took a minisabbatical—a rarity for university presidents—to acquire a deep understanding of educational technology. University of Pennsylvania provost Vincent Price threw the full weight of his prestigious Ivy League institution behind Coursera, the company that Koller and Ng had founded based on their Stanford courses. Rafael Reif, MIT's new president, declared a kind of moral war on increasingly inaccessible quality education. Georgia Tech president George "Bud" Peterson agreed to use technology to make the university's prestigious computer science master's degree available for 20 percent of the on-campus price. At the University of Virginia, Helen Dragas, the appointed head of the university's governing board, took on an entrenched and entitled culture over the question of affordable access to what she called the "Commonwealth's University."

Most of this activity was hidden from public view, so it was totally unexpected that 2012 would see sweeping change in the United States, and even more unexpectedly, the beginning of a global revolution to redefine the nature and value of universities—a movement offering education to many millions of students around the world who desired it. It was dubbed the Magic Year. A small band had decided to challenge the basic assumptions of higher education. These challenges were not simply to the status quo;

they consisted of projects aimed at changing the way education worked. The innovators had an agenda, and if they were successful, there would be an inevitable change in colleges and universities—and likely education in general. It was to be a revolution that redrew the map of the world, but most everyone involved was unprepared for the national and international reaction to the revolution of that Magic Year.

How This Book Is Organized

What follows is both a chronicle of a revolution and a road map for the future. If successful, the small band of innovators will have changed something important about the way education is conceived and delivered: they will have altered the economics of running a university, culture of academic life, and nature of the contract between higher education and society. I also include a healthy dose of history. This is, in part, because I believe that the future of academic freedom, college affordability, and the value of a university degree is connected to their past as well as the cast of characters who defined the modern university. I include history for another reason: few of the innovators who appear in these pages believe there is anything unique about universities among the panorama of human endeavors and institutions. Politics, finances, society, and individual self-interest play exactly the same role in academia as in other aspects of modern existence. It would be unlikely, for example, that a general economic principle that has been observed over and over again through the decades would—all of a sudden and without cause—cease to apply to higher education. History in one arena might reasonably be expected to inform future events in another. The success of the Revolution counts on this, and so a retelling, however brief, of how things turned out for others sheds light on what we should expect the band of innovators to accomplish.

Revolution

I have divided the chronicle into four parts, beginning with an explanation of what the Revolution seeks to accomplish. The idea that change was afoot for higher education burst on the public consciousness with Thrun's announcement that he had resigned his professorship at Stanford to begin offering free, high-quality university courses to the world. It was a bold statement, but it was only the first. Stanford and MIT announcements quickly followed. Khan became a spokesperson for short-format lectures that would reach millions. Start-up capital poured into research labs and storefront software companies that were more reminiscent of the early days of the Internet than the staid, bureaucratically top-heavy business of running a university. The difference was noticeable and it captured the attention of international media for much of 2012, the Magic Year. Chapter 1 tells the intertwined stories of the key players and their motivations.

The Magic Year was about MOOCs, but it was also about the value of a college education along with the ease with which simple course content could be replicated and distributed to anyone with an Internet connection. To survive in the future, an institution would have to add value beyond a simple recital of information because that was being rapidly commoditized by technology. But even simple survival may not be easy when landscapes shift. Universities are generally conceived as vertically integrated entities, but as soon as families realize that they do not have to pay for unadorned content, the natural question is: "Well, exactly what do I have to pay for?" This is the central concern in chapter 2. Affordable quality is a goal of the Revolution, but it is achieved through an unbundling of a university's value proposition that allows students to pay only for the value they receive. This is an innocent-sounding although in fact dramatic shift in the landscape of higher education.

The Revolution would leave education poorer but for an improved understanding of how to organize the learning process in a way that more closely matches how the brain learns. Chapter 3 explains how learning begins—deep within the brain, where a continual cycle of neurotransmitter production and reinforcement literally rewires neurons as small chunks of learned information move from short- to long-term memory. It is this chemical engine of motivation and reward that new educational technology supports, and if its inventors are correct, the end result will be a different kind of classroom, in which long-form lectures have all but disappeared, replaced by a different kind of learning experience. What will fill the void is an approach called mastery learning, which has been known since the 1980s to deliver superior results in almost every conceivable classroom. Cost has been the principle barrier to the widespread adoption of mastery learning techniques. Without new technology this kind of classroom learning is prohibitively expensive, but the Revolution aims to remove that obstacle.

It is a long way from understanding the principles of improved learning to changing what happens in classrooms—a journey that is described in chapter 4. Educational innovations often face insurmountable hurdles, but the development of technology-enhanced learning is accelerating exponentially. Even from today's vantage point, the outlines of what is achievable are apparent—and they do not resemble the first primitive MOOC technology or faltering business models of traditional online education. "Show me the industry that has withstood the advance of technology," say the innovators—and history usually proves them correct. Artificial intelligence makes it possible to personalize classrooms, even when course content is being distributed to a mass audience. Sophisticated analytic algorithms predict where students are likely to have problems and provide clues to master teachers about how to proceed. Even more important, technological innovation can be used to erase inequalites in circumstances—cognitive ability, social status, or academic knowledge—that plague postsecondary education as it scales to the masses.

If technology-enhanced learning succeeds it will be because of *scale*: the technologies of the Revolution are the technologies of the Internet. That makes them profoundly different from the past. Chapter 5 explains how the Revolution plans to migrate the business of higher education to the Internet, with all the gains in productivity that might entail. Improved classroom productivity means that the structure of academic institutions will change. The number of professors will necessarily decline—a profound shift for an industry that computes the ratio of teachers to students and uses the result as a measure of quality. Teams will form around effective teachers, but they will be teams of specialists. This flies in the face of older models of education, yet it is where the small band of innovators is taking us because higher education cannot continue to expand at the current rate. Conquering the problem of scale will require new kinds of institutions.

Rationale for a Revolution
Part II of this book explains what the Revolution aims to change. What do innovators believe is so severely broken in higher education that the whole venture needs to be remade? No one would start such a wholesale dismantling of a successful enterprise without a rationale, but many inside and outside academia regard dramatic change as an inevitable product of market forces and shifting social priorities and want to make sure that what follows is worthy. Others have far narrower goals: say, changing the course of failing institutions. Still others want to topple institutions in order to redefine what it means to be a university. It is hard to get agreement on whether the failings of higher education justify a Revolution, though there are reasons for doubting that evolutionary forces will make college more affordable or that prevailing, expensive bureaucracies have any meaningful impact at all on educational outcome. The Revolutionaries have seen unfolding events like these before—incumbents bent on preserving their position when the forces of change suggest that their favored status has been undermined. On the other hand, it is apparent that the culture of academic institutions

perpetuates not just meritocracies but also hierarchies of Élites. It is a culture based on costly, self-defeating institutional envy masquerading as strategy. These are the targets for reformers and revolutionaries that part II explains, beginning with the shifting business landscape of higher education.

Understanding shifting landscapes requires a basic understanding of geography—in this case, the *financial* geography of higher education, which is the subject of chapter 6. For most of society, the finances of higher education mean the cost of a college degree. When higher education is heavily subsidized (as it is in Europe and used to be for American public universities), society bears that cost. Otherwise, the cost of a university education determines the price that individuals pay in the form of tuition. Tuition has risen dramatically—alarmingly, by most reckoning—driving a wedge between families and a college degree. Quality college education is rapidly becoming inaccessible. Policy makers and the public are for the most part misinformed about what is behind this rise in college costs, and that is a dangerous combination. Higher education suffers from a cost disease that causes prices to rise, and understanding what leads to the disease is an important first step in seeking solutions. Reformers are betting that the affordability gap—which can be closed by technology or an unbundling of prices—will dominate the economics of higher education for the foreseeable future.

Universities often lose sight of which people they are intended to serve, and this Revolution was launched in part to bring that back into focus. Higher education is hierarchical—a pyramid with a few institutions at the top and the rest defining their value, not in terms of serving their students or communities but rather by which of their competitors occupy a coveted position a rung or two above them. For some universities prestige is all that matters. For them the pyramid is a hierarchy of the Élite in which institutions are not defined by who they serve but instead by who they exclude. For many others—particularly those public universities that cannot be exclusive—rankings are what matter and have become the bedrock measure of academic quality. For all except those few at the top, envy like this is synonymous with strategy. An overwhelming majority of universities promise "world-class" status, even when that flies in the face of common sense and the needs of their students. The next three chapters explain the fixation with elitism, rankings, and strategies based on envy, the ecosystem that promotes the resulting hierarchies, and what will replace them if the small band is successful.

To the Ramparts

Not everyone is happy with the prospect of change, so revolutionaries will encounter stiff opposition. Part III of this book looks at how the Revolution will run headlong into an entrenched and successful academic culture that abhors the kind of change that innovation seeks to bring. University *brands*, for example, will be displaced if some of the innovative approaches to online education are successful. Yet in academia, brands are difficult to establish and hard—but not impossible—to damage. Whether online education can be branded at the same high level as elite education is the provocative question that occupies chapter 10. What happens when a new kind of university decides to concentrate *all* its resources on classroom achievement? Most universities misjudge their own brands, mistaking a longtime monopoly on access to top students for value. Technology has commoditized high-quality dissemination of information, so universities that based their value on guarding access to that information now find their gatekeeper status undermined, bypassed by a new economy. Innovators are counting on this. If their students learn more and are better able to compete in a global marketplace, it will not matter that they do not have the usual badges of acceptance conveyed by academic peers.

Universities are scholarly communities that regard their work as existing on a different plane from most other human endeavors. To succeed, the Revolution has to confront the resistance of academic culture. Chapter 11 takes on the Ivory Tower culture of academia and tendency to regard intrusion into that culture as a moral assault. The course of academic institutions in the last half of the twentieth century has left many irreparable cracks in the Ivory Tower, but the edifice of academic freedom, which the Ivory Tower guards, remains largely intact and well defended by institutions like peer review and tenure. Chapter 11 shows how easy it is to build an Ivory Tower culture in a modern university and how resilient it can be, even when it fails. The relentless onslaught of innovation threatens Ivory Tower institutions such as tenure. "Market forces guarantee academic freedom," say the Revolutionaries. If they are right, the Ivory Tower will crumble. Chapter 11 also examines how the prevailing idea of sharing academic governance among many constituents has become a barrier to technological advances in the universities where it is the strongest.

The question "Who is in charge?" has been replaced in recent years by a more confrontational choice: *labor versus management*. By framing technological change as an assault on justice, an organized labor movement has come to higher education, and it has been responsible for exposing underlying contradictions that must be resolved by opposing forces. These forces clash in dramatic fashion in chapter 12, which pits the concept of legitimate governance against what many who want institutional reform see as the ability of a mob to run roughshod over the needs of students and society. Paradoxically enough, it is the very technology of the Revolution that also amplifies the ability of a small group to promote polarization. The Internet has enabled the rise of empires which maintain their value systems and cultures by exaggerating the consequences of dissent. A resulting clash of cultures came to a head in the 2012 firing of University of Virginia president Teresa Sullivan by a reform-minded board. The events that followed present unresolved questions for the small band of innovators.

A New Social Contract

The central questions facing colleges and universities have not changed much over the last hundred years:

1. Does an institution serve the people it is supposed to serve?
2. Are there among an institution's graduates a sufficiently large number of successes?
3. Successes aside, how well do most graduates do a decade or more after receiving their degrees?
4. What exactly have an institution's graduates learned?
5. How important is an institution to its constituents?

Universities have always been social enterprises, and it is likely that the social contexts and unique circumstances that give rise to particular institutions will continue to be as important as many of the other forces—commoditization of content, economic inequality, failures in governance, and homogenization—affecting higher education. Revolutionaries have already succeeded in making simple delivery of content to distant parts of the globe cheap and simple. Old institutions have lost their privileged status. The Ivory Tower has been replaced by the multiversity. Academic workforces are being restructured. Virtual and physical spaces coexist. But a university must still serve the people it was intended to serve. It must be important to someone or someplace.

Part IV explores the nature of the compact between society and its universities. It is no utopian dream to expect a written compact: in return for funding, trust, and the commitment to respect academic boundaries, universities agree to engage with society. In fact, the world's oldest functioning written constitution says that society has a *duty* to cherish the interests of universities in exactly this way. This is in every respect a social contract, and it has been renewed over time, but it has faded from both public consciousness and institutional missions over the last century. If the small band of innovators succeeds in remaking higher education, it will be because they offer to renew this contract in ways that traditional institutions are reluctant to do. It will be because new institutions rise to the challenge of instilling in their students not only that education has value but also values—virtues for the common good. And it will be because governments consider that to be a duty of society.

Revolutions and Revolutionaries

Higher education is engaged in a global revolution, and like Gilman's apostles of learning, there will be heroes and martyrs among the revolutionaries. Ideas that seem fresh and ambitious today may turn into dead ends that fall to the realities of economics, politics, or the changing tastes of a global public. There may be a new awakening in which the diffusion of knowledge is viewed as essential to preserving modern thoughts and cultures. There may be new agreements that codify a commitment to self-governance, integrity, egalitarianism, truth, and interpersonal trust that define both the responsibilities of society and obligations of members of academic communities. Knowledge may be viewed in the future as a community possession. The global academic enterprise may adopt Andrew Ng's mission of ensuring that quality instruction is a global right. Bright-eyed revolutionaries may cause otherwise-immutable bureaucracies to relinquish their grip on access to education.

No matter what happens, universities in the future will have been forever transformed because of the events that a few fearless innovators set in motion at the start of the millennium. Exactly what that transformation looks like can only be guessed at, although the outlines are made apparent through the lens of history. The reasons that humankind invented universities are eternal, and what we ask today of scholars and their institutions will not be greatly changed by the successes or failures of a few technologies or new ways of doing business. Still, no institution has an entitled position in this vast new landscape. That is how we arrived at a crossroad. My retelling of this journey in *Abelard to Apple* ends with the following exchange with an academic leader who reveled in his institution's increasing selectivity:

He stopped. I pressed him. "Where will those students go in a hundred years? What will the universities that have the capacity for the students you turn away look like?" He realized that I was asking what the university of the twenty-first century would look like. After a long pause, he said, "It will not look like us."[20]

Many people have taken up the mission of answering this question, and among them are heroes who, "possessing no dread of labor, no fear of consequences, no desire for wealth, are carried to success."[21] That is where we begin.

I   Revolution

1 Map of the World

The Magic Year begins not with grand agreements among ministers or presidential flourishes but rather with the almost-imperceptible ceding of territory—a series of small revolts that proceed with breathtaking speed. No battering rams breach campus gates, no pillaging of academic programs, no coups d'état. It begins with old ideas that have never been tested and with genius, ambition, and opportunity. It begins with rare ability to seize the moment.

A Project to Shake Up the World

When Stanford professor Sebastian Thrun stepped to the podium at the 2012 Digital-Life-Design conference in Munich, most people in the audience expected to hear about driverless cars. Some were expecting an update on how real-time photographs of streets and buildings were changing Google's already-booming online mapping business. A few insiders were expecting a preview of new virtual reality technology that could be worn like a pair of glasses and would allow wearers to see the Internet embedded in the real world. Thrun was responsible for all this technology. He ran, in addition to his academic duties, an innovation laboratory at Google called simply X and had free rein to think big. Thrun is a roboticist. He is one of a handful of scientists who have cobbled together this new field that marries engineering, statistics, psychology, design, and computer science. He is a theorist, but it is his engineering skills that have made him a celebrity in the technology world.

No one—perhaps not even Thrun—knew what to expect when actress Maria Furtwängler introduced his talk about a "project that would shake up the world of universities." But instead of describing a project, Thrun chose to tell the audience about a kind of spiritual conversion. "I want to tell you a story," he began, "a story that changed my life in a profound way."

The computer science department at Stanford University is filled with celebrities in a university of celebrities. Stanford is an Élite institution, venerated as much for its liberal arts and humanities programs as for science and engineering. But it was the engineering programs that miraculously bloomed exactly where good fortune dictated that more wealth would be created than at any other place and time. Stanford's history is intertwined with that of Silicon Valley, and that has helped fuel its almost mythical reputation as a birthplace for innovation. Recombinant DNA and the biotechnology industry were given to the world by Stanford scientists. Visionary professors helped Stanford students launch iconic companies like Hewlett-Packard. The pull of Stanford was so strong that along the five miles of Sand Hill Road running through the hills on the northeast border of the campus, one of the world's largest economies set up shop and began investing in Stanford's people and ideas.

These days computer science is one of the fields that dominates Stanford's reputation. John Hennessy, Stanford's tenth president, is a computer scientist often called the "godfather of Silicon Valley." Sergei Brin and Larry Page were Stanford students when they decided to use Lego building blocks to hold the computers that would eventually become Google's first search engine. Ties between Stanford and Google are so deep that it is sometimes hard to say who their respective employees actually work for. Young people, seeking to be close to the hottest ideas and highest fliers and seemingly in the know about who's who at Stanford's computer science department, arrive in flocks—some lucky enough to enroll at Stanford, and others happy to work at the Stanford-inspired companies in Silicon Valley that dot the north–south arteries connecting San Francisco and San Jose.

It is a high-pressure environment—one in which even Thrun had to compete for students. If you were a Stanford student interested in robotics, you were probably also interested in the machine learning courses taught by Andrew Ng or MacArthur prizewinning mathematician Daphne Koller, both stars in the computer science department. Thrun's introduction to artificial intelligence course fared well against stiff competition. It drew about two hundred students at a time—an impressive number—but sometime in early 2011, he became enthralled with Salman Khan and his short videos explaining simple concepts in math, science, and business. With a closet for a studio, Khan had somehow amassed an audience of millions. He called his videos Khan Academy, and Thrun began to wonder whether he was wasting his time teaching to a class of two hundred when there might be a worldwide class of millions who would benefit from his course the same way Khan Academy students benefited from Khan's surprisingly compelling short instructional videos.

Thrun's scientific reputation is based in part on his complete lack of fear in attacking hard problems. You have to be fearless to decide to build and ride in a driverless car that can zip through city streets in traffic with speeds up to forty miles per hour. With that same confidence, believing that he could attract perhaps a thousand students, Thrun and Google scientist Peter Norvig sent a single, precisely worded email to a global list:

Introduction to Artificial Intelligence

Offered by Professors Sebastian Thrun and Peter Norvig

Oct–Dec 2011. Sign up now at ai-class.org

This course is the online version of the Stanford CS211 Introduction to Artificial Intelligence. Students can sign up and take this course for free. All lectures are offered online, and students will have to take the same homework assignments and exams as the Stanford students who take CS211 on campus. Anyone taking the course can interact with the instructors online. Plus, students are graded the same way as Stanford students, so you can compare your skills and knowledge to Stanford advanced undergraduate and graduate students. Enroll (for free) and learn about AI from two of the pioneers in the field. The course starts Oct 2, 2011. Sign up now at http://ai-class.org.

First a trickle, then a flood, of Thrun's online network of fans and followers typed ai-class.org into their browsers to see what was going on. Many of them signed up to take the course. Within a matter of hours, course enrollment shot past 1,000 students. By the next morning 5,000 students had registered, and that number climbed quickly until, for fear of overloading Stanford's Web servers, Thrun and Norvig cut off registration when it reached 160,000.

The Thrun-Norvig online course ran at the same time as Stanford's CS211, in which a full contingent of Stanford computer science students had enrolled. Those students undoubtedly expected to spend the semester in a classroom where Thrun would stand at a lectern for three hours a week, explaining how to build intelligent machines and occasionally quizzing them on their progress. They had not expected to be a small part of a global classroom with 160,000 other students, mostly anonymous, who were following the same syllabus, and had not paid Stanford a penny for that privilege. Eventually 25,000 of the 160,000 finished the online course and were issued certificates of completion. There was great consternation about how quickly the 160,000 registered students were whittled down to a mere 25,000, but that ignored the larger reality: it would have taken 125 semesters in a Stanford classroom to reach that many students.

Among those 25,000 students were 170 of the 200 Stanford students who had paid for and enrolled in CS211, an option that Thrun had given his traditional class at the start of the semester. Thrun was never quite sure what to make of that. On the one hand—since preparing the online course was an exhausting experience—it was a source of great pride that his existing students liked the new format so much that they were willing to abandon the tried-and-true lecture hall. On the other hand, Thrun began to think, "Maybe I am not as good in the classroom as I thought." When he and Norvig started sifting through the final grades, they were in for another shock. The online students who had enrolled in response to Thrun's email had done better than his Stanford students! It seemed only fair that Thrun should send them each a letter to certify their achievements.

The very idea of certificates for online students had put Thrun at odds with Stanford's provost, John Etchemendy. Etchemendy argued that a piece of paper signed by a Stanford professor could too easily be construed as an official university document. The last thing that a university like Stanford wants is to overthrow its carefully administered admissions office—and its tuition invoices, although nobody was saying so—for the Internet-like chaos of an open course. Moreover, bureaucrats at Stanford's accrediting agency (the Western Association of Schools and Colleges) were sure to ask whether Stanford was now assigning actual college credit for a course with no admissions criteria, no requirement to attend lectures in person, and no approved examinations.

Etchemendy and Thrun were at loggerheads. Although Thrun had support and encouragement from many of his colleagues, the Stanford administration would have preferred a less disruptive approach to offering CS211—perhaps something that did not bypass Stanford's existing academic processes. Etchemendy would have much preferred that Sebastian be more like fellow computer scientists Koller and Ng, who were also offering online versions of Stanford courses. Those classes had attracted similarly impressive numbers of enrolled students. Unlike Thrun, however, Koller and Ng had not yet set up their own .org Web sites. Their courses had been advertised on the university's own Web site, Stanford|ONLINE, a university-sponsored portal leading to dozens of free courses.

Three thousand miles away, MIT professor Anant Agarwal was coping with the flood of students who had enrolled in the open, online version of his introductory electrical engineering course. Agarwal had been challenged by his provost to find a new way to reach students around the world. MIT courses were already available through the university's Open-CourseWare (OCW) Web site, so using video and online tools seemed like a natural next step for Agarwal. The MIT course that Agarwal taught was known to be tough, but it was a gateway for the entire engineering curriculum, so demand was always high among MIT students. There would be no MIT credit for students who took the online version of Agarwal's course, but when 150,000 students enrolled anyway, he realized that something had changed.

Open, Online, Massive

They did not know it at the time, but there was a name for the kind of course that Thrun and Norvig had taught: MOOCs. Online courses had been around for decades. For the most part these were prepackaged affairs consisting of videotaped lectures, accompanied by some kind of online test, and offered by moneymaking organizations, including the distance education or continuing education departments of some nonprofit universities. Universities charged full tuition for online courses and offered credit for successful completion. These courses filled a niche—for instance, they allowed students with special circumstances to complete their degrees on time—yet they were not held in particularly high regard. There were notable exceptions, though. England's Open University, for example, was originally a way to offer university credit for courses delivered by radio and television. Once Internet access became widely available, Open University quickly migrated its offerings to the new medium. Western Governors' University in the United States met the same need for a dozen state university systems. Many teachers' colleges, nursing programs, engineering departments, and business schools offered certificates or continuing education training online for "adult learners" who had no need for an in-person classroom experience.

The low cost of online course delivery also attracted a raft of for-profit ventures, like the University of Phoenix, which charged premium prices for canned lectures and personalized services that promised future job opportunities. But these were all approaches that specialized in *content delivery*, not real teaching. In effect, online courses were technologically enhanced, expensive textbooks. If the same material were open—that is, made freely available to anyone with a Web browser—it would undermine the entire business model for online delivery. Yet that is exactly the trajectory for every information-based industry in the Internet age. Open distribution rapidly commoditizes content. A university that staked its future on online courses needed to figure out how to add some value to the content in order to sustain its prices.

By the late 1990s—the dawn of the Internet age—paid content delivery was already under siege by media companies like AOL and Yahoo!, which offered free online news and analysis scraped from the same news services that fed subscription print and broadcast media. So it was not so much a matter of *whether* commoditization would hit distance education as *when* it would happen. The big question was who or what would be bold enough to take the first step. It would have been easy enough for a highly profitable company like the University of Phoenix to offer free versions of its courses to draw an audience to an online curriculum in which most of the classes were behind a paywall, but that is not the way it turned out.

In 2000, Charles M. Vest, the president of MIT, approached the Andrew W. Mellon Foundation with a proposal to put some of the university's high-enrollment courses into an OCW repository that could be freely accessed by anyone from anywhere in the world. The president of the Mellon Foundation was former Princeton president William G. Bowen, a prolific economist with a deep interest in how technology might improve higher education. According to Vest, Bowen said that the idea of an open repository was interesting, but Mellon would only consider funding the project if MIT would put all its course material online. Vest reluctantly agreed. "I was not sure how the MIT faculty would react to this proposal," he later told me. In little more than five years, the MIT course catalog was swept up in a $10 million project called the OCW project. It was a remarkable achievement. For the first time in history, students anywhere in the world could simply "sit in" on courses offered by some of the world's most renowned scholars. An expert observer of technological trends, Vest saw the inevitability of content commoditization. Some worried that the OCW amounted to "giving away the store," but Vest believed that the essence of an MIT education was inextricably bound to the experience of actually attending MIT. He thought that MIT's value went far beyond the mere content of lectures, notes, and quizzes. Vest had another motivation for the OCW. He was moved by his social conscience and belief that there was an explicit contract between universities and the people they serve that compels the sharing of knowledge openly, broadly, and freely. No less a figure than John Adams had said as much 250 years earlier.[1] Whether or not Vest was aware of the contract that Adams had embedded in the Massachusetts Constitution, it was his view that universities had an obligation to share knowledge as broadly as possible. For Vest, it was a sense of mission.

MIT announced the idea of open courses in 2002, but it took another five years before plans were complete to open its entire catalog of eighteen hundred courses. By that time some Canadian educational activists were plotting to make open resources available on an even larger scale, and Web sites like Apple's iTunes U were aggregating and openly distributing high-quality courses. But no one had ever seen 150,000 users from around the world eagerly step-up to the technically challenging courses that had sprung from Stanford. These courses, by anyone's reckoning, were massive. If you knew the hot ideas in online education in early 2012, you would have known that the proper way to pronounce Massive Open Online Course was "MOOC."

Canadian MOOC

The idea of a massive, open, online course was not new. Canadian educators George Siemens, Stephen Downes, and David Cormier had been trying out preliminary versions of these kinds of courses for several years. Siemens was a professor of online education at Athabasca University, Canada's version of the Open University, and Downes was a Canadian National Research Council scholar who concentrated on *open* teaching. Cormier was an expert in software for open learning at Prince Edward Island University. Siemens and Downes had been working on an approach to learning called connective connected knowledge (or CCK) in which students were expected to navigate networks of ideas on their own, exploring pathways and making connections with groups of learners who shared the same interests. They were teaching courses for educators that surveyed the field of CCK when Downes suggested that instead of teaching twenty-five students at a time, maybe they should invite anyone with an interest in new modes of learning to join them online. With the help of Cormier and Jennifer Chesney, the University of Alberta's resident expert in digital product development, it would not cost any more to teach to a large virtual class, and the class itself would provide valuable research data to Siemens. In 2008, Siemens announced the first MOOC based on CCK to his worldwide network of collaborators. He was shocked when twenty-five hundred students showed up. Some were enrolled in the Siemens-Downes courses in online education. Others had been recruited to participate in a study of the effectiveness of online education sponsored by the Canadian Science and Engineering Research Council. Most, though, were simply interested observers.

I was fascinated that a couple thousand students would enroll in a course that promised essentially nothing concrete. Siemens himself acknowledged that many of those who enrolled were not students in the usual sense but rather researchers, teachers, and other educators who wanted to participate in the lively discussions that Siemens and his colleagues inspired. There were no real lectures. Instead, there was a roster of guest speakers who in turn invited participants to an online video forum. Cormier and Chesney had designed a simple chat facility that allowed listeners to carry on parallel conversations (some of which were only tangentially related to the day's topic). After forty-five minutes or so, the guest speaker would throw the whole thing open for group participation with someone—usually Siemens or Cormier—moderating a conference call.

I had been intrigued by the possibilities of the format, although I thought the idea of a course that discussed the course itself—sometimes called self-referential content—was less interesting. When my Center for 21st Century Universities was launched in December 2010 I gave interviews to the *New York Times* and *Chronicle of Higher Education* in which I promised to conduct an experiment of my own using the massive open format. Unlike the Siemens-Downs-Cormier MOOC, I wanted to find a way to offer students Georgia Tech credit for successful completion of the course. I knew how to do it and said so to the reporters. This caught Siemens's attention, and he wrote to me immediately asking whether I would be interested in a follow-on experiment that he was already calling the "Mother of All MOOCs" involving ten thousand or more students.

This new course, which bore the odd title #change11, was still unstructured in a way that I thought was difficult to explain to students, but I had in mind an experiment in conducting online seminars. A seminar is, after all, a learning experience in which there is no fixed syllabus to follow and in which students can pursue their own interests. A colleague and I had just finished offering a traditional seminar on the future of universities that drew twenty or so Georgia Tech graduate students for a weekly discussion of the forces shaping higher education. At the semester's end, students worked in teams to translate classroom material into actions that Georgia Tech might undertake to transform itself in light of the coming changes to the nature of institutions like ours. It was a big hit with both students and faculty, who sometimes outnumbered students at our weekly meetings. The student projects turned into a series of briefings for senior Georgia Tech administrators, including Georgia Tech's new president, Peterson, and Provost Rafael Bras. Students conducted the briefings. To my amazement, Peterson and Bras listened intently, made notes, asked many questions, and shared some of their thoughts with the students on how a traditional university like Georgia Tech might transform itself. We had no problem assigning grades to students who participated, and my first thought was to treat the non–Georgia Tech students who participated in #change11—Mother of All MOOCs—as additional observers in a seminar about how education and learning were changing, much like the one that I had just taught. The course was scheduled to begin September 2011—exactly the same time that the Stanford MOOCs were starting—and would run for thirty weeks. Siemens was hoping that the course would draw ten thousand students over that period of time. The Stanford MOOCs drew ten thousand students within hours after they were announced.

The Mission

It is no accident that Koller, Thrun, and Ng all taught the same courses at Stanford, or that Agarwal had studied at Stanford under John Hennessy. Stanford president Hennessy, who dives into subjects with the enthusiasm of a graduate student, had been closely following developments in online education. In an unprecedented move, he took a six-month sabbatical from his presidential duties to learn as much as he could about the subject. There was every reason for members of Hennessy's informal but vast network of colleagues and students to believe that he was personally invested in exploring the pedagogical possibilities that the new technology might offer. It was a permission slip to experiment. Koller had been thinking about a transformed classroom for a long time and had come to the conclusion that the traditional lecture format would shortly reach a dead end. The main problem as she saw it was that a forty-five-minute lecture was a tremendous waste of time. It was little more than a sermon. She was a masterful preacher, but had little time left to interact with students. How much better, she thought, if all the things she might have mentioned in a classroom lecture were learned somewhere else. A well-written textbook might do the job, but a textbook—which divides knowledge into chapters and sections—is too rigid for most courses. In fact, one of the reasons that a professor delivers a lecture is to adapt and personalize textbooks. How much more interesting, Koller reasoned, if instead of reciting sermons from an idealized textbook, the content-delivery portion of a course were turned into homework. Koller began *flipping* her classrooms, interchanging the traditional roles of lectures and homework.

With the support of the president, Stanford was a good place to experiment with flipped classrooms and other innovative ways of teaching. Stanford lectures were already being recorded by the university's Center for Professional Development. Ng knew how to use these recordings to test the boundaries of teaching. He had noticed, for example, that students would skip class, choosing instead to watch the lectures online. By fall 2011, when

Stanford was just launching open versions of its computer science courses, Ng had already been putting his videos on the university's online course Web sites for several years. One of his motivations was experimentation. "Daphne really influenced my thinking," Ng told me, agreeing with Koller. "A lecture is a terrible use of time."

Ng fires up an iPad app called Dragon Box. It is a card game that teaches the basics of algebra to children. Cards cancel each other out, the screen flashes, and points are given out. The goal is to get two sets of cards to cancel each other exactly. Ng starts turning cards over. "No, this cancels this," he says to himself. He is lost in the game for a minute or so, and then turns to me. "Dragon Box is engaging," he says, smiling. "You think you're playing cards but you are learning algebra." It is a short hop for Ng from a child's game to how engagement might work in the classroom. "We know that when you design a quiz that buzzes or changes color when you get the right answer, it works to help learning. It seems silly, but it works." Once you know the possibilities of the online format, you can turn to what Ng calls the irreplaceable part of teaching: the skill that the instructor brings to a classroom.

Those are the skills that Ng wants to experiment with. "Teaching is a physical skill in the same way that baseball is a physical skill," he says. "You see a student slouching in his seat and you have to be in the moment—ready to react. You can't read about it. It's all practice." Critics who recoil in horror at the notion of using video to replace live lectures have it exactly wrong. "Professors are irreplaceable mentors," explains Ng. "Your favorite professor cannot be replaced by a computer, but your favorite professor is spending most of her time doing other stuff"—like broadcasting content.

Ng and Koller won over Widdom, Stanford's computer science department chair. "Class time could be made more enticing for students and instructors alike," Widdom wrote in a 2012 blog post.[2] Noticing that students actually preferred video, she asked, "Why not purpose-build better videos: shorter topics, specific segments, punctuated with in-video quizzes to let watchers check their understanding?" The Stanford professors set out to create what Koller now calls "Hulu™ for Education."

They realized that the software they needed did not exist. What they needed was a *platform*—a way for instructors to load videos, homework, and exams on to a Web server; connect students to tutors and teaching assistants; and collect data, including test results. Course instructors did not want to be bothered with the details of the technology, and students would be tough critics if the video quality was bad or there were too many different software tools to juggle just to make it all work. As Koller, Ng, and Widdom were building the precursor to the first commercial MOOC platform at Stanford, and Thrun was imagining what it was like to peek through the window to another way of teaching, Stanford alumnus Agarwal found himself in hot water at MIT.

Agarwal was director of the famed Computer Science and Artificial Intelligence Laboratory at MIT, and in summer 2011, he had been called into a meeting by Rafael Reif, MIT's provost. Reif was worried about MIT's growing commitment to international programs. "What is that experience like?" Reif asked. For several years, MIT had expanded its partnerships with leading institutions around the world. There was already a major investment in Singapore that resulted in faculty exchanges at several of its growing research laboratories. Plans were nearly complete for a new public university called the Singapore University of Technology and Design that would make substantial use of MIT's OCW materials.

"Why bother?" Agarwal recalls asking in response. "We teach exactly the same thing as in Cambridge." Agarwal then suggested, "Why not use MIT's OCW as the basis for online versions of those courses for flipped classrooms?" On-site mentors could after all do a better job of personalizing commoditized content for their specialized needs. "I left the meeting with the distinct impression that I had just volunteered to refine MIT's international experience," Agarwal recalls. It was not something that he had intended to volunteer for.

Reif had been observing the events in Palo Alto, California, from a continent away but, when he visited Etchemendy that fall, he saw firsthand the reach that Stanford had achieved with just three courses. However, Stanford was still trying to work out its differences with Thrun. The concept of a Stanford certificate of completion may not have been popular among the university's leaders, but it was an opening for MIT. Reif must have felt some urgency about planting the MIT flag in the new landscape. Within weeks MIT issued a press release to announce the creation of MITx, an open educational Web site through which MIT courses—the material for which was readily available online as part of the MIT OCW repository—would be offered in a format that would re-create the MIT classroom experience. Even more important, MIT would issue certificates to students who successfully completed MITx courses. The natural candidate to kick off MITx—a prototype, they called it—was Agarwal's introductory electrical engineering course, circuits and systems, called 6.002 in the university course catalog. Circuits and systems is a required course for many engineering degrees—a so-called gateway class—and it was already wildly popular. Reif seemed to have few doubts that 6.002x, the MITx version of 6.002, would fail to be a runaway hit.

MIT's announcement had made it clear that students who successfully completed MITx courses would receive certificates backed by MIT. There was no mention of credit, but MIT officials did little to tamp down speculation that one day students would be able to receive credit for completing MITx courses. In the meantime, the strength of the MIT brand would establish a market for MITx certificates of completion. Stanford was not ready to go that far. Etchemendy and Stanford president Hennessy were not fans of accrediting agencies like the Western Association of Schools and Colleges, which they regarded as a colossal waste of time and money for an institution like Stanford. Any Stanford activity—even one that was disguised on a separate Web site—that might invite further scrutiny was not to be encouraged. Unlike Etchemendy, Reif seemed to have few reservations about blurring the lines between MIT and possible online incarnations.

Meanwhile, forty miles north of Palo Alto, entrepreneur Nelson was plotting to dethrone the Élites with a degree equivalent in stature to an Ivy League degree and was offered completely online. Nelson's idea, which he called the Minerva Project, was to offer elite quality at an affordable price. He reasoned that there was a market for bright and self-directed students who could not get access to Harvard or Princeton. Among these students were Americans who did not want to settle for what Nelson called "a no-brand public university degree." But Nelson also knew that there was a growing wave of international students, many of them in China and emerging nations in Africa, who simply could not afford to attend an Ivy League school. If there were as few as two hundred thousand students in that market, Minerva would only have to attract 5 percent of them to thrive.

It would have seemed like a long shot to success but for Nelson's backers. Former Harvard president and US Treasury secretary Summers had agreed to chair Minerva's advisory board, and former US senator Kerrey was recruited as executive chair of the Minerva Institute. Kerrey, whose background included the presidency of New York's New School, had been a vocal and influential advocate of change in higher education. It was Kerrey who made sure that the national media paid attention to Nelson. Minerva's advisory board included former leaders from Princeton, Columbia, and Stanford— the very universities that Nelson was trying to dethrone.

Largely unnoticed in the rest of the world, start-up capital had started to flow into a dozen new education ventures. Benchmark Capital invested $25 million in Minerva's first round. John Doerr, the legendary partner at the Palo Alto venture capital firm Kleiner Perkins Caulfield & Byers, was quietly rounding up support for a $25 million investment to turn the Koller-Ng MOOCs into a platform called Coursera. Thrun raised $21 million in funding from Andreessen Horowitz, Charles River Ventures, and Silicon Valley entrepreneur Steve Blank to fund his vision. He called his new company Udacity and set it up in a storefront at the edge of the Stanford campus, just a few blocks from the Institute for the Future. The symbolism would not be lost on visitors.

MIT was using its clout differently. Senior administrators and alumni approached Harvard about joining forces to create a nonprofit entity that might be funded with a $60 million package of gifts from private donors and foundations. And Khan's academy—the closet-based studio that launched three thousand instructional videos and attracted ten million subscribers—had no problem raising $16 million in funds from billionaire backers with social consciences like Doerr's wife, Ann, Bill Gates, and Google chair Eric Schmidt.

It is hard to imagine more unlikely warriors, yet that is how the Magic Year began. Remarkably, everyone involved still articulates the same ideal: to bring high-quality, affordable college education to the world. It is as if they have all agreed on Vest's mission. I asked Doerr what he thought the conclusion of all this disruption might be, and he stared at me for a long time. "We're not in this for the short term," he said. "Google was a good idea, but did we think it was going to turn out as it has: the curator of the world's knowledge?" He shook his head slowly. "Education is changing, and I may have ideas about where it's going and who will be important," he began and then let the sentence hang there. Andreessen Horowitz's Peter Levine said that the "aim is to democratize education."

Ng, who is so quiet that you sometimes have to strain to hear, does not shy away from the question. "We have a Mission," he says. "Whatever happens to Coursera, we will maintain that. These courses will always be available to the entire world for free. That is our Mission."

Peeking through a Window

By the time Furtwängler turned the Digital-Life-Design 2012 podium over to Thrun—who had self-funded his artificial intelligence course—he had decided that there was no turning back. His conflict with Etchemendy must have weighed on him. He had been thinking for some time about ways that YouTube could rearrange education, and seeing Khan's success was probably great motivation to get on with it. Or maybe it was as simple as what he later said:

Now that I saw the true power of education there is no turning back.... I won't be able to teach 200 students again, in a traditional classroom setting. I've just peeked through a window into an entirely new world, and I am determined to get there.[3]

Whatever inner turmoil led to it, there was no mistaking Sebastian's intention:

I can't teach at Stanford again.... [A]s much as I love Stanford, it's impossible.... I've seen Wonderland.... You can make education free for the world, accessible everywhere, help people in the developing world to become much better and much stronger. I've given up tenure at Stanford and I'm launching my own online platform.[4]

US newspapers lit up almost immediately:

Stanford Professor Gives Up Teaching Position, Hopes to Reach 500,000 Students at Online Start-Up.[5]

The US edition of Reuters emphasized that this announcement was about the future of online universities.[6] It took a while for the real importance of Thrun's announcement to register. This was about all universities, and in modern times universities are under the control of professors. If Thrun could successfully reshape the future of all universities, professors would be caught in the wake. They were a powerful force but, in the minds of many, it was the tendency of universities to base strategy on what is good for professors that was a root cause of the problems facing higher education.

Almost as an afterthought, Thrun had said that he wanted to "stop empowering the professors and start empowering students." But courses and professors define a university, and a MOOC that empowers students by delivering better courses from a storefront studio in downtown Palo Alto is a university of a different kind. It is a global university. The Western idea of a university—campus, buildings, laboratories, offices, and libraries—is what defines higher education in most of the world, but a new kind of university might look quite different. It is a dangerous thought for an enterprise that accounts for a trillion dollars of global economic output. If you stop empowering professors, what empowers the university? And, if the university is not empowered, where does it derive its value? It is with questions like these that revolutions are started.

The Magic Year

Three days later, I was having breakfast in Palo Alto with an unusually ebullient Sebastian Thrun. If he was feeling any trepidation about the path he had chosen, he was not showing it. He was surprised by the amount of press coverage that his Munich announcement had received. Public interest had been aroused by the *New York Times* announcement of MITx a couple weeks before.[7] The timing of the MIT press release still chafes for some. "Who makes an announcement like that a week before Christmas?" asked one observer. "It's almost like a preemptive media strike." The effect, however, was electric. MITx might have been the first act, but Thrun's Munich performance was a strong second act.

The historical analogies came tumbling out. "What was drama like before the invention of film? You had to go to the theater to see a play performed. That was a fundamental limitation. If you did not live near a theater or you could not afford to travel to one, you were just out of luck," he said. He did not think you could judge what direction MOOCs would take because the technology was just beginning to be understood. "The first movies were made by pointing a camera at the stage." He thought the video capture of a lecture is like that. "It took a long time for people to master the art of making a motion picture. A movie is a completely different art form than a stage play." He wondered where the next Steven Spielberg was going to come from.

In another breath: A MOOC is a textbook, a democratizing force, a more realistic way of learning, something that is more closely tuned to how the brain operates. "Khan was right," he said. "I can't believe that such a wonderful thing is possible," he noted, quoting from the hundreds of emailed responses to his course. "This serves a basic human need."

It was January 26, 2012, an unusually cold and wet New Year in Palo Alto. January 25 was a Tuesday, and I had spent the day at Google's Mountain View campus a few miles south of Palo Alto. I prevailed on my Google host, Jeff Walz, for a conference room, so that I could conduct my segment of the #change11 MOOC. It was not a satisfying experience. The Mother of All MOOCs that Siemens had imagined was fizzling badly. The ten thousand or more students that we had hoped to see never materialized, largely due to the wandering and somewhat-diffuse nature of the course. By the time my week rolled around, some twenty weeks into the course, the two thousand enrolled students had been whittled down to a much smaller number— how much smaller is impossible to say because there was no direct feedback from students to the instructors. Many had already selected smaller and more specialized subgroups to follow. The course had also failed to attract Georgia Tech students who wanted credit. One of my assistants was responsible for documenting the outcome of the experiment, but the open-ended student comments told the story. Even when a course is free, students by and large expect to learn something, and this course—which had been planned a year before on a seemingly different planet—had failed to deliver on that basic promise. The experiment quickly became the furthest thing from my mind. Whatever was going to happen in 2012 would be all about *change*, but it would have little to do with #change11.

I was already focused on that change. I was scheduled to give a talk in Google's authors@google lecture series, right after my #change11 session. My hosts were buzzing about my talk and what it meant for the future of universities—and Google. Google was also awash that day with talk of Khan's academy. I had spent most of the previous evening in my hotel, comparing one of Khan's ten-minute calculus videos with the ninety-minute videotaped lecture on the same subject that was available on MIT's OCW site. The MIT lecture was a virtuoso performance, but the main point of the lecture was buried, nearly lost in a sea of irrelevant technical detail, administrative discussions, and digressions. The Khan Academy video was by contrast a polished gem. Nearly devoid of notational complexity and irrelevant context, Kahn got to the heart of the matter within seconds. It was a revelation. Much like Thrun, I too felt I had peered through a window and set out to tell him about it. He was ahead of me.

"Let me show you what the students say," said Thrun. He opened his laptop, and we scrolled through dozens of email messages from students from all over the world. Some of them were simple thank-you notes from appreciative students:

First, thanks for the work going into the AI course—it's very much appreciated!

Also wanted to thank you for extending the midterm dates; for some of us that will be a very big help!

Others took more time to digest:

I'm completing the course from remote areas of Afghanistan, and often don't have great Internet connectivity. Or electricity. Or Internet connections that don't block YouTube.

I spent the last few days under incoming mortar and rocket attacks, dodging checkpoints under questionable legal status to exfiltrate a war zone to a third world air field until things settle down. I have about an hour of fairly solid Internet connectivity to be able to get the assignments done and still managed a respectable score. This is a typical week here for me.

I had already made up my mind that my experience with the Canadian MOOCs had nothing to do with this kind of change when Thrun said, "Coursera has email just like this." I did not know what Coursera was, but I knew who had founded the company. A few weeks later I found myself in a conference room at the offices of Kleiner Perkins Caufield & Byers with Brook Byers, Doerr's associate Lila Ibrahim, and Koller. "We are still called DKandme," said Koller. "It's a very different model than Sebastian's," she said. "Sebastian wants to disintermediate the university out of existence. Our goal is to gather the best university teaching in the world and make it available to as many people in the world as possible."

We were only a few miles away from DKandme's offices in Mountain View, so Koller hastily arranged a tour. Tucked into a Menlo Park building, which they shared with several other early stage technology companies, these offices looked nothing like Udacity's storefront. There was room to grow, but now the space was eerily empty. Ng's office consisted exclusively of a single workstation. It seemed to me that DKandme would have to catch up quickly if it was going to compete with Udacity and MITx. Udacity was already offering courses. MITx had quickly refurbished Agarwal's 6.002 circuits and systems course. DKandme, which was changing its name to Coursera, did not have plans to produce any courses at all. Coursera instead would rely on a network of distinguished university partners and serve as a value-added distribution platform, but no one had signed a partner agreement. Although there were rumors and whispered discussions among a small group of universities, Koller was closed mouthed about the potential partners, yet I had already decided that Georgia Tech would be among the first. In a deal that Stanford endorsed, Coursera's platform would be based on Widdom's software. Then Koller asked me, "Do you want to read some of the open-ended comments from students about the Stanford courses?"

The Udacity and Coursera emails blend together. They could have been written by a dozen happy students, but they were not. Between the two companies, there were hundreds of messages. Some were funny. Many were sad. Almost all were moving. Both Thrun and Koller encouraged me to spend as much time as I wanted. The messages read like this:

[This course] feels more "intimate" than most of the lectures I attended in the past. I felt that you both were personally tutoring me.

And this:

I'm literally overwhelmed at the possibilities after taking this class. I'm sure it's going to be people like me who will make the world a whole lot better.

There were comments from teenagers in Bangladesh as well as their parents and grandparents, Canadian senior citizens, and teachers in rural Indiana. There were comments about how different these courses are from "weeder classes," which set people up to fail, or classes where everyone gets an A+. Students knew about using college classes to stratify winners and losers. In the end, regardless of what they have learned, everyone moves on.

Ng later described for me the surprises hidden in his "A/B" tests that are used to evaluate design alternatives—the difference, for example, between sending an email saying, "Your homework is due Saturday," and one saying, "You did a good job on last week's assignment, and by the way your next assignment is due on Saturday." At some basic level, the difference is due to a neurochemical buzz. "The second email is a more pleasurable experience," he speculates. Here is how that difference affects a student:

I work 40+ hours a week, I'm a single mother of 2, and my younger child is only 7 months old. I have no time to concentrate, or to dedicate, and I've still been hanging onto the class by my fingernails, wanting to learn, and to feel a sense of accomplishment.

Just before Homework 5 was due, I suffered another series of great, chaotic difficulties in my life. My job has been threatened by the economic climate. My personal life kind of exploded. I'm on my own with the children. The baby has been sick, a family member is suddenly sick, another losing their home, the list goes on and on.

Why am I telling you way too much personal stuff? Because on November 13, I gave up. I told myself that I was ridiculous to think I could justify continuing this class, taking this time, given all the other problems that surrounded me.

And then that Monday morning I checked my email and saw the note you sent Saturday. And I stared at it for a while. And then I sighed, and told myself, "I can't quit now."

I took the midterm this weekend, mostly while holding a teething infant. None of my other issues have gone away. But I feel more determined than ever to see this through … for myself.

Later on, Anant Agarwal, said to me, "Sit down and read these emails from MITx students, but by that time, I did not need to read any more of the comments. I already knew what they were going to say. By the summer of 2012, sixteen internationally renowned universities had signed agreements with Coursera, a dozen more had agreed to participate in a Harvard/MIT platform known as edX that was an expansion of MITx. Udacity was in trials with a half-dozen colleges to embed MOOCs in traditional classrooms. My own center at Georgia Tech had signed agreements with Coursera and Udacity to produce twenty MOOCs, with plans to produce another twenty in 2014. By January 25, 2012, Georgia Tech had enrolled a handful of students in the #change11 MOOC. MOOC enrollment at Georgia Tech jumped to twenty thousand by August. It climbed steadily, and by the end of the year was nearing two hundred thousand. I have now read hundreds of comments from Coursera students.

To understand this revolution, you have to first get outside the system of higher education and look at it as you would look at a map in an atlas. To an observer on the ground, the distant horizon may be indistinct and possibly unreachable, but there are, in the immediate vicinity, choices, risks, and rewards that are much more concrete. That is what drives the missionary spirit of the professors who have chosen to participate. This is not a mission to win converts; that battle is over. Rather, it is a mission to minister.

"I was able to touch lives," said one MOOC professor. It is no accident that St. Ignatius of Loyola, founder of the Jesuits, sent his priests to build the network of universities that would bear the name of the order by telling them, "Go forth and set the world on fire."

Inevitabilities

What is propelling the Revolution? There seems to be inevitability about it. If that is true, what exactly is inevitable? Let's ask the people who are trying to change the world. The chapters of this book will explore what is in store for the fifty thousand or so universities in the world—and millions of people who depend on them—if a small band of innovators, the revolutionaries, are able to remake higher education. For American universities, it is a matter of sustainability: costs continue to rise, public subsidies continue to decline, and family incomes remain flat. American higher education has a growing gap between what it wants to do and what the average American can afford. Sooner or later systems like that fail. Americans will eventually have to choose between preserving a system designed to serve the public good or becoming resigned to a new kind of system for just the privileged few—a permanent state of unequal opportunity. Whichever choice is made, the result will be a new kind of higher education in the United States.

The map of the world of higher education is being redrawn. Harvard and MIT are partners. Coursera is now a network that links over a hundred of the world's most highly regarded universities, thousands of their professors, and millions of students. New alliances spring up every week.

Whatever the political, economic, and social forces at work, they are not uniquely American phenomena. Yet that was not apparent in December 2012, when I returned a call from *New York Times* higher education reporter Tamar Lewin. MIT was ready to announce the creation of MITx, a credential-issuing venture that would offer certificates to students who successfully completed MOOCs. I had seen the press release. I picked up the phone, and the first thing that Lewin said was, "This is a big deal." There were more phone calls and more reporters as the day wore on. By two o'clock, I knew what to expect as I clicked my headset on: "Yes, it is a very big deal." Over the coming months there would be many more phone calls and interviews, as it became obvious that the battle had been joined.

David Brooks called it a tsunami,[8] but it was Revolution. It was global, and it would not only "shake up the world of universities," as Furtwängler had predicted, it would redraw the map of the world. By the end of the Magic Year, the outline of a new approach to higher education was being sketched by a small band of troublemakers. They did not speak with one voice, but they all spoke with missionary zeal. A year after Thrun's dramatic announcement in Munich, he took the stage in Davos, Switzerland, where world leaders gather annually at the World Economic Forum. Koller, Reif, and Agarwal joined him. This time it was not Thrun who said he had peeked through a window. It was Khadijah Niazi, a twelve-year-old from Lore, Pakistan, with a schoolgirl's enthusiasm for physics. She explained that a revolution had taken place that had let her peer through that same window. Davos attendees are the movers and shakers of the world; presidents, ministers, and chief executives of all sorts, they take great pride in anticipating the next big thing. The state of the world's universities is a topic that comes up often in Davos, but it seldom goes beyond a general lament for the declining state of higher education. The Davos crowd was subdued by Niazi. They were silent, and many of them were moved. Without ministerial signing ceremonies or the flourishes of power, a Revolution had engulfed them. A world map had been redrawn. This new atlas was not yet visible to most people, but soon it would be.

2 Shifting Landscape

The window that Sebastian Thrun peered through that January morning opened on to a vast landscape. By most measures, his goals had remained modest throughout most of the Magic Year. If a Revolution was coming, there were no great preparations being made by either side. Entrepreneurs like Thrun were focused on building software and creating courses. With few exceptions, traditional institutions ignored what was going on in places such as Silicon Valley. If there was change coming, it would be a concern of the MITs and Stanfords of the world—and perhaps others who could afford the Mission. Yes, more people around the world would have access to quality courses, but Thrun had no secret plan that would greatly alter the landscape. Even the prospect of content commoditization did not set off alarms in higher education.

There were good reasons to be blasé. The specter of commoditized content had been raised over and over again since the founding of the first European universities. Medieval universities had wrestled with the problems posed by the widespread availability of printed texts and found accommodations. The first Jesuit universities realized that they could not possibly produce the quantity of course materials that had been in use for many decades at civic universities. That presented a dilemma to new colleges that wanted to concentrate their meager resources on teaching, not on textbook publishing. "It has been said in town that we do not have a method for teaching," Father John Paul Nicholas explained in 1558 to the bishop of Perugia, who had asked why Jesuit instructors were reluctant to adopt Latin grammar textbooks. It so happened, said the bishop, that there was an adequate text, written by a professor at the University of Perugia named Christopher Sasso. John Paul replied, "If we use Sasso's book, they will say what our students have learned, they learned from Sasso, not from us."[1] Universities had survived crises like these before, and there was no reason to think that MOOCs, which many considered to be simply a new form of textbook, would be any more likely than Sasso's grammar book to alter the landscape of higher education.

The founders of Udacity, Coursera, and edX believed that their technology was more than an electronic textbook. MOOCs were entire courses, and their success depended to a large extent on how students experienced them. If MOOCs turned out to be a better, cheaper way to experience courses, then traditional universities needed to figure out how to add value before students found out. Even if the new format was only effective for some courses, its success was bound to have an effect on the business of running a university. Students (and their parents) would quickly realize they were paying a hefty price for quality instruction they could get free online. Price-conscious consumers might ask whether a full four-year residential campus experience was worth it when two or three years were just as good and considerably cheaper. College administrators might feel compelled to start unbundling their offerings, which paid—critics argued—unnecessary attention to an expensive, outmoded classroom format that had not changed much over the centuries.

These were architectural changes that would alter the landscape, but traditional universities seemed firmly in control. Thrun's Udacity seemed best positioned from a commercial standpoint. Like a textbook publisher, Thrun only had to sign up individual professors, but that in itself was unlikely to threaten established institutions. edX was a consortium for Élites, and Agarwal thought he could gradually build internal support in much the same way that Vest had built support for the OCW. In any event, universities like MIT and Harvard, which did not recruit price-conscious students, were never going to have much incentive to unbundle either their tuition or curriculum.

On the other hand, Coursera was completely dependent on university partners. The company did not create its own course content. It was also the most threatening. EdX was a nonprofit and would distribute its courses on behalf of its members, but Coursera was a for-profit company. It intended to make money by distributing courseware that its partners had produced at great cost. What kind of university would agree to such an arrangement? Perhaps a struggling liberal arts institution or two would add some courses to Coursera's catalog—much as they had done with iTunes U a few years before—for marketing purposes. But that was not the Coursera plan. Daphne Koller and Andrew Ng needed the enthusiastic support of the universities that seemed to have the most to lose if Coursera were to succeed: highly ranked research universities. They needed the support of the few insiders who had recognized that a consequence of MOOC success would be a great unbundling of higher education. They needed allies from the same conservative universities that had never wanted the landscape to shift too much.

Advancing Pedagogy

University of Pennsylvania provost Vincent Price was watching the Silicon Valley developments throughout fall and summer 2011 with keen interest and perhaps even some impatience. Price was the chief academic officer at this Ivy League institution. Despite its name, Penn, as it is usually called, is a private university—one of the Élite. Its president, Amy Gutmann, was a long-serving and popular leader of a university with a long waiting list of applicants and $7 billion endowment that had allowed it to weather tough times during the worst of the recession. Penn students won Fulbright awards and Rhodes Scholarships. Penn faculty included Nobel laureates and Pulitzer Prize winners. There was every reason for Penn to chart a conservative path for its future, to be classical, to be elite in every sense. But Gutmann was impatient and, although she had great appreciation for Penn's heritage, she was not its hostage.

Recent history invites comparisons to the University of Virginia, another institution with a venerable heritage.[2] Founder Thomas Jefferson is always resident on that campus—a visible and revered presence. In 2012, the University of Virginia was the subject of unwanted international headlines when trustees briefly removed President Teresa Sullivan from office. At issue was Sullivan's steadfast refusal to consider the kind of change that had enveloped peer institutions like Stanford and Penn. It was a position that the board thought put the university and Commonwealth of Virginia at a disadvantage. Virginia's trustees believed that Sullivan was captive to an overly conservative view of the university's heritage. It was a course that somehow seemed out of step with Jefferson's devotion to reinventing higher education in the United States.

Benjamin Franklin founded the University of Pennsylvania, but it carries his values in a different way. Like Jefferson, Franklin believed in a natural aristocracy based on virtue and talent, yet in matters concerning education, Franklin was a pragmatist, a practical man who believed in self-education and experimentation, though not in classical European schooling. Franklin wanted graduates of his academy to have "an Inclination join'd with an Ability to serve Mankind."[3] Franklin was also an impatient person.

This was the point on which Gutmann's 2004 inaugural address turned. It was not a speech that, like so many inaugural addresses, promised only stewardship of a sacred reputation. Her speech was a modern echo of Horace Mann's 1859 sermon to Antioch College graduates: "Be ashamed to die until you have won some victory for Humanity."[4] It was a promise "to use knowledge to serve Humanity," and it was the origin of the Penn Compact, a commitment to increase access as well as engage both locally and globally.

Gutmann was herself a former provost and, when Ronald Daniels stepped down as provost to assume the presidency of Johns Hopkins University, Gutmann turned to Price, communication professor and associate provost, to take over on an interim basis. Price had been a professor at Penn for eleven years when he was selected for the interim job. Shortly thereafter, he was named provost. Price would have enormous responsibility for implementing "this new beginning ... worthy of our boldest aspirations."[5] The Revolution brewing in Silicon Valley touched on those aspirations. Technologies that enabled Penn to reach around the globe to students spoke to the democratic ideals that the Penn Compact embraced.

"I watched the origins of Coursera in the fall of 2011," Price told me, "and my general feeling was that this was an unprecedented opportunity to advance pedagogy and to meet students where they are." He had spent enough time with Penn students to understand that their needs were evolving. In fact, he had regular meetings with a student committee on undergraduate education that had been advocating for open courses and investigating new modes of learning that did not necessarily depend on lectures. The pace of change was remarkable, as were the opportunities, but Price was aware of the pitfalls. Coursera was, after all, a for-profit company, and thus a potential challenge for academic purists who might be distrustful of any alliances with commercial enterprises. If there were going to be hurdles, he wanted to know as soon as possible. He told me, "I put the matter in front of deans and faculty members as quickly as I could."

He was pleased and somewhat surprised with the welcome reception that the idea encountered. The deans thought that Penn had the potential to become a leader in exploring learning and experimenting with new models. "They felt they could use a test bed," Price said. He invited Coursera cofounders Koller and Ng to Penn to meet with key faculty members and administrators. It was a faculty-to-faculty conversation and greatly smoothed the way for a broader discussion on campus. At times, there were difficult discussions and some anxieties that the university might be moving too quickly but, even among "deep skeptics," there was a feeling on campus that these conversations were necessary and overdue.

The MIT announcement of MITx in December 2011 rattled Koller and Ng, but it convinced Price and Gutmann that they should move quickly.

Since it was unlikely that Penn would strike out on its own, the question was who to approach about partnerships. MITx—which was quickly evolving into a pending MIT-Harvard partnership known as edX—was perhaps one possibility, but according to Price, "the Penn calculus was different from what MIT was considering." Price began to talk to his colleagues at peer institutions—among them Princeton, Michigan, and Stanford—who were also mulling over a possible partnership with what would soon become Coursera. "It was invigorating to talk to people at the highest levels of those institutions about striking out in a novel direction," he recalls. Confident from his consultations on and off campus that Penn should step forward, he called Koller and said, "Yes." Price had committed Penn to Coursera. His high-level discussions at the other institutions paid off, because most of those universities also signed agreements with Coursera. Koller says, "It was a pivotal moment. I am not sure we would have been launched without Vince Price." Once Penn made the decision, Price wanted Penn to be as energetic, public, and visible as possible in its support of its new open learning initiative. "When Coursera was launched, I wanted to have Web pages university-wide to display publicly the exciting range of things we do."

Coursera's public launch in April 2012 eclipsed the MITx, edX, and Udacity press announcements, as first a half dozen, then a dozen, and then a rolling wave of highly regarded universities began to produce courses. It was, according to several *New York Times* articles, "a tsunami," but Price regards it differently, as something potentially transformational that would nevertheless not sweep everything away that came before any more than motion pictures completely displaced stage drama. "The long-form lecture can be powerfully effective as an art form. There will always be gifted performers and performances," he explained. "It's just that they may not be the cornerstone of most courses."

Still, if courses are more than lectures, then perhaps a curriculum is more than the sum it its courses. "If the architecture of higher education really shifts," says Price, "then efficiencies can be realized, faculty resources can be redeployed, and some courses might be delivered at less cost. Ultimately, the marketplace decides. But I want to see faculty out in front of that marketplace and not behind it, defining new, more effective ways of teaching and learning." It is what Koller says, too. "It doesn't matter whether we professors think it's a good thing or not. The marketplace will decide."

In order for Penn or anyone else to offer courses for less it has to be prepared to say with some certainty what it costs to offer a course in the first place, but that is not as easy as it sounds. Not only is the academic marketplace a complicated network of students, teachers, institutions, bureaucracies, and employers, but universities lump many services together into an aggregate cost. The students who line up to enroll at the University of Pennsylvania look at that aggregate cost and believe that it represents an aggregate value, yet the rest of the higher education marketplace may not behave that way. The marketplace may want students to know exactly what they are paying for.

Pace of Change

A year after the launch of Coursera Georgia Tech announced that it would partner with AT&T and Udacity to offer a MOOC-based master's degree in computer science for under $7,000. The media lit up at the announcement. MOOCs had been in the news for a year but, as the academic world tried to figure out how technology had really altered the landscape, the international conversation about the future of higher education had become muted, more measured, and more technical. Problems with individual courses, dissenting voices, and a deafening lack of enthusiasm from university presidents became as newsworthy as another batch of university partners for Coursera or edX. The Georgia Tech announcement reversed that trend overnight. There was above-the-fold coverage in the *New York Times*, followed by *Wall Street Journal* editorials, CBS and Fox News reports, and hundreds of print and online articles. President Barack Obama mentioned it in speeches. Most of the coverage zeroed in on the same point: this was a high-risk bet that higher education was going to change radically.

Shortly after the Georgia Tech announcement, I received an email from Steve Mintz, the man who directs the Institute for Transformational Learning for the University of Texas System.

I felt the entire landscape of higher education shift. For truly the first time, the disruptive potential of MOOCs was realized: A high-demand program from a leading institution is available for a degree at an affordable price.... The future is here. From now on, the pace of change will only accelerate.

Mintz is responsible for finding the pockets of educational innovation in the massive Texas system and then investing to make them successful. "Anything that really improves learning is interesting to me," he once told me, "but I suspect that students are going to vote with their feet for digital knowledge." In 2012, he put the weight of his position behind an investment in edX, betting that the MIT-Harvard-led MOOC consortium would be an efficient way to create an environment for rethinking pedagogy.

It was a hard sell for the many Texas faculty members who had been reading about all the disruption that was in store for them. Texas governor

Rick Perry's embrace of a low-cost, $10,000 bachelor's degree and seven "breakthrough" university reforms emanating from the conservative Texas Public Policy Foundation had raised the specter of a major research university reduced to measuring faculty worth by simplistic formulas and consumer feedback. Although Texas was often at the center of ideologically fueled fights about the nature of a university education, Perry's proposals were actually and openly the product of a network of politically conservative policy think tanks. Other states had moved well beyond the planning stages. Florida governor Rick Scott had engineered a $10,000 bachelor's degree program. Another conservative, Wisconsin governor Scott Walker, who triggered a recall election by picking a fight with public employees, announced his own set of reforms. In many states with newly elected Republican governors, concern over ever-rising tuition and low completion rates had turned, in the eyes of many, into an assault on the entire enterprise of higher education.

Mintz risked being lumped together with misguided and politically motivated reforms in the minds of the very Texas faculty members whose support he needed in order to succeed. Widely circulated blogs accused him of working for moneyed interests and being a "corporatist." He worked hard to convince hundreds of professors at the fifteen member institutions in the University of Texas system that he was one of them—not only to demonstrate that his motives were pure, but even more important to carry the message that change was coming and they would be better off designing an agenda themselves rather than having one imposed on them by an outsider. Selling colleagues on his academic bona fides was not Mintz's problem. A social historian with impeccable credentials, Texas had plucked him from Columbia University's Graduate School of Arts and Sciences. His problem was to find a way to help his colleagues imagine a different way of learning. The Georgia Tech announcement must have seemed for him like providential good fortune.

Columbia University is an unlikely incubator of revolutionaries. After all, it is home to the core curriculum, a reaction to the modernization in American universities that started in the 1860s. When the first colonial universities were formed, compulsory, classical courses of study had been borrowed whole cloth from their better-known European cousins. By the end of the Civil War, social and economic forces had begun shaping a different kind of university—one that was more in tune with the needs of a growing nation and changing nature of students.

Starting in 1862, the Morrill Act, which established the American system of land grant colleges, added practical subject matter to classical studies by requiring the new universities "to teach such branches of learning as are related to the mechanic arts … in order to promote the liberal and practical education of the industrial classes."[6] In 1869, Harvard, which John Adams had regarded as the Oxford of the New World, inaugurated Charles Eliot as president. No doubt Eliot had been selected in part because he pledged to address growing concerns about Harvard's unmotivated students, whose "individual traits of different minds have not been sufficiently attended to" by the existing compulsory, prescriptive course of study. Eliot's solution was a radical reformulation of the very idea of undergraduate education. Over the next twenty years, Eliot removed nearly all of Harvard's subject requirements. It is hard to appreciate today how radical Eliot's reforms were. The landscape had shifted, but change comes reluctantly to higher education. Later critics would charge Harvard with the abandonment of its soul.

In the early years of the twentieth century, Columbia was the largest university in the country and aware of its influence. Columbia College's "Introduction to the Masterworks," a vision by a Columbia professor named John Erskine, was perhaps an attempt to retrieve what had been lost at Harvard by refocusing undergraduate education on Western classics. By 1919 Erskine's curriculum, which required courses in Western civilization, art, music, and science, had become the Columbia Core Curriculum. Even when progressively radical student movements in the 1960s attacked the core curriculum for being Anglocentric, Columbia soldiered on, oftentimes appearing as the lone, stalwart defender of a more conservative approach to higher education. Columbia was not a university to threaten the status quo.

It was into such an environment that Jonathan Cole was installed as Columbia's provost. Provosts tend to stay in their positions for relatively short periods of time. It is the ultimate staff position in a university. With no budget, a provost frequently has few tools with which to get things done. It is a notoriously ill-defined position, often serving as catchall for those tasks that a university president cannot—or does not want to—perform. Provosts tend to either burn out or move on to presidencies. Cole held the provost's position at Columbia for nearly fifteen years. He had none of the earmarks of a troublemaker. A distinguished sociologist and expert in science policy, he was a defender of traditional academic values, but some of his actions at Columbia were not exactly consistent with conservative stewardship. They were, in fact, radical.

For example, Cole hired economist Michael Crow from Iowa State University. Crow's considerable administrative skills propelled him quickly through positions of increasing responsibility at Columbia, but it was when Cole called on him to help develop and launch an online course platform called Fathom that Crow became a committed revolutionary. Crow, who as president of Arizona State University figured prominently in *Abelard to Apple* for his single-minded pursuit of the new American gold standard for public universities, was even in those days devoted to the idea of broad access to high-quality university education.[7] When I asked Cole what had inspired him to hire Crow, he simply said, "Michael believed in what he was doing."

Fathom was an interactive Internet portal with features like online forums and multimedia content that were years ahead of their time. Although Fathom.com was a for-profit corporation that intended to charge upward of $500 for its for-credit courses, much of the content was offered for free. It took much longer to produce content than planned, and successive revisions of the original business plan opened the platform to other universities, which many thought thus diluted the Columbia brand. Costs quickly outstripped income, and despite Cole's commitment to the idea of expanded access, Fathom.com closed in 2003. By that time, Crow had accepted the presidency at Arizona State, but he had already imprinted the spirit of rebellion on his colleagues.

One of those colleagues was another Cole protégé, Israeli computer scientist Zvi Galil. Galil was chair of Columbia's computer science department when Cole selected him to be the dean of engineering. At most Ivy League universities, engineering does not occupy center stage. That is a position reserved for the classical training expected to launch careers in business, law, diplomacy, and policy. In 1995, Columbia was no exception. The School of Engineering occupied cramped space in the center of campus, and the engineering faculty seemed content to pursue traditional scholarly careers. Despite close ties to Bell Labs and a considerable endowment, there were few visible forays into the Internet and other new technologies that appeared to be infecting many other leading engineering schools. I was told that Columbia undergraduates by and large avoided engineering, and that the dean of engineering needs to concentrate on things that matter to Columbia's students. It was an admonition to keep one's head down while the big names in the arts and sciences slugged it out.

Galil was an ideal dean for the Columbia environment. He came from the mathematical side of computer science—a scholar's scholar who was less concerned with competing with the much larger engineering schools at places like Illinois, Berkeley, and Georgia Tech than he was with keeping Columbia's reputation as a home for quality scholarship intact. It was a successful strategy. Columbia's engineering faculty disproportionately included a large number of members of the National Academies of Science and Engineering, and the graduates of its PhD program wound up on the faculties of the most highly regarded universities in the world.

As if to make the point, Galil eschewed most of the trappings of technology. He did not profess much interest in the Internet or advances in applied fields like software engineering. His professional and personal associations ran toward the sciences and arts. Outward appearances aside, though, Galil was becoming a radical.

He was close to Crow, and because Crow was instrumental in pulling together Columbia's many centers with large social agendas to form the Earth Institute, he also came in frequent contact with many of Columbia's larger-than-life, high-profile academics like Jeffrey Sachs who were not shy about imagining the future. Galil quietly began using the untapped power of the Internet to reach the people who mattered most to him: Columbia students.

"I was the email dean," he says proudly. His daily—and sometimes hourly—missives were broadcast to a large mailing list. There were announcements of comings and goings along with awards won by faculty, students, and alumni. There was simply not that much news to send, so many of his email messages were jokes, aphorisms, and—because his English is colored by an Israeli accent—an occasional malapropism. The hundreds of email messages were, of course, the pulse beats that let Columbia students know he was there and thinking of them. He was the email dean.

The personal ties that the email created between Galil and Columbia's undergraduates were remarkably strong. When in 2007 he was tapped to lead Tel Aviv University, his final commencement was memorable because the entire graduating class rose and said, "Please don't leave us, Dean Galil!"

He was also close to Cole. The engineering school had been operating a distance education program called Columbia Video Network (CVN) since the late 1980s. CVN reached thousands of students, but by the time Galil was named dean, the program was losing money. Galil's predecessor had wanted to shut down CVN, but Galil convinced Cole that it should not only be saved but also should convert from videotape distribution to Web-based courses. The turnaround was dramatic. CVN rapidly began generating millions of dollars—funds that were much needed by the little engineering school hiding in the center of Columbia's massive New York City campus.

We Could Be Doing More

By the time Galil was named my successor as dean of the College of Computing at Georgia Tech, Revolution had turned into hard work. The Threads

Program, a redefinition of a college degree that allowed students to tailor the undergraduate curriculum to suit their interests and needs while retaining enduring academic values, had been operational for several years.[8] Students and employers loved it, and although there were pockets of resistance among the faculty who missed the more rigid boundaries of the old core curriculum, almost everyone else involved in computer science at Georgia Tech took special satisfaction in the number of times the program had been adopted around the world. Galil embraced Threads, although he was clearly looking for a way to make his own personal mark on Georgia Tech. "One of the first things I did," he said "was to let everyone know that Threads made our students unique among computer science graduates, but it seemed to me that we could be doing more."

What shape "more" might take was less clear. Galil had been an enthusiastic backer of Georgia Tech's MOOC agreement with Coursera, yet he remained troubled by the institute's vision. "It was wonderful to see hundreds of thousands of new learners drawn to Georgia Tech instructors," he said, but he had learned from Crow's experience with Fathom that sooner or later, someone would have to pay for designing and producing these courses. "I was also concerned that Georgia Tech's MOOCs were not being offered for credit," he recalls. "I saw what happened at Columbia when Fathom started spending money on noncredit courses." He was determined to not make the same mistakes. On the other hand, CVN, which granted not only credit but also led to actual degrees, had been a great financial success—and financial viability was one of Galil's top priorities.

In spring 2012, I was in various negotiating stages with Coursera, Udacity, and edX to produce and distribute MOOCs. Faculty and administrative support for this new course format were important. There were already powerful voices around the country trying to scuttle the new technology before it had a chance to be evaluated. Charges that MOOC providers were out to decimate the ranks of traditional faculty members or that students would be shunted to impersonal, ineffective videos versus high-quality classrooms were common. Alumni were worried that large pools of enrolled online students would dilute brands that had been carefully built over a hundred years. No one wanted to be forced to jump to an entirely new form of instruction that apparently bypassed human interaction. Most of the issues that Eliot had to contend with at Harvard in the 1860s were suddenly dusted off and applied to MOOCs.

The poor quality of many MOOCs did not strengthen the hand of early enthusiasts. Although Thrun had a clear pedagogical vision, Koller and Ng had decided early that Coursera would not enforce standards. The first edX

MOOCs were simply videos of actual classroom lectures. There was an understanding that these first-generation products did not fairly represent the potential of the medium, but that message was often lost on critics whose arguments depended on the current state of the technology, not its rapid rate of improvement. The growth of the Internet in the 1990s was the model for rapid feedback and revision, but it was at best an abstract argument. The first courses varied wildly. Thrun's Udacity implemented Benjamin Bloom's mastery methods in which fifty-minute lectures were replaced by several ten-minute learning modules interspersed with quizzes. A student had to demonstrate mastery of the previous material by passing a quiz before moving on to the next module. Although it had been known for thirty years that this was a superior way of organizing a classroom, it was expensive and required a great deal of work on an instructor's part to redesign traditional courses to conform to this new format. Coursera's vision was to bring entire courses to the world, and there was little appetite among the partners for a standard template of the kind that Udacity demanded. As a result, some courses were rigorously developed using mastery learning (ML) techniques, but others were of the point-a-camera-at-the-podium variety.

It seemed to many who were already using MOOCs that critics were at times patently unfair. For example, sometimes strength would be portrayed as weakness. When an astute reviewer caught an error in a Udacity statistics course, there was a media frenzy about the poor quality of MOOCs. An anonymous blogger who claimed to be a college math professor but was known only as Delta "felt compelled to survey one of these courses, so as to assess their general quality, advantages, and disadvantages." The assessment was devastating:

The course is amazingly, shockingly awful. It is poorly structured; it evidences an almost complete lack of planning for the lectures; it routinely fails to properly define or use standard terms or notation.... I personally got seriously depressed at the notion that this might be standard fare for the college lectures encountered by most students during their academic careers.[9]

Message boards were flooded with calls to correct the errors. Defenders of academic quality said that problems like this one were the inevitable result of mass-market approaches to education, ignoring the obvious: every course—online or not—is riddled with errors. Whether the problems with statistics 101 were as severe as critics maintained, it is a unique advantage that online courses allow instructors to catch and correct errors without going through layers of academic bureaucracy. Within hours, Thrun responded. "I agree with the author of this article.... [T]he course can be improved in more than one way." He promised that unlike traditional university courses that are often not revised for several years, statistics 101 would be revised right away:

In the next weeks we will majorly update the content of this class, making it more coherent, fixing errors, and adding missing content. I believe that Udacity owes all of our students the hardest and finest work in making amazing classes. We are very grateful for any feedback that we receive. These are the early days of online education, and sometimes our experimentation gets in the way of a coherent class.[10]

There were other bandwagons that critics could jump on. The fraction of students who successfully completed MOOCs—often less than 1 percent—seemed alarmingly small. Males outnumbered females by a wide margin, which some said indicated gender bias in the selection of topics, courses, and instructors. Credit-bearing MOOCs seemed like a remote prospect for institutions such as Georgia Tech. Many people thought that was a good thing since cybercrime was on the rise, which raised the specter of widespread cheating. And there was a chorus of critics demanding to know who would pay for "free" MOOCs.

Unlike many other universities, Georgia Tech's online strategy was not being defined by the administration. Groups of faculty, like the members of the Center for 21st Century Universities, would have to make the case to their colleagues if the MOOC experiments were going to be successful. There was an advantage to this approach that no one had anticipated: MOOC instructors (who had started calling themselves "MOOC faculty") formed an informal community for improving the quality of online teaching, which they were quick to point out also improved the quality of their traditional lecture courses.

A computer science professor named Tucker Balch was teaching a Coursera MOOC on applied statistics when he noticed that many of the problems identified by MOOC critics were based on anecdotes, not actual experience.[11] Balch took advantage of a new Coursera feature called "Signature Track" under which students who paid a small fee could receive certificates of completion if they performed well in the course. He noticed that 99 percent of the students who paid the Signature Track fee completed the course. This was a startling contrast to the 5 percent completion rates that MOOC critics were citing. Even more surprising was that the completion rate for Signature Track students was nearly 25 percent higher than the full-tuition-paying Georgia Tech students who took the same course on campus. Virtually every aspect of Balch's course offered similar surprises.

Other MOOC faculty had noticed differences as well. Knowing of Thrun's experience with statistics 101, one professor reviewed dozens of online forum messages every day, searching for suggestions for how to change course materials. The ability to change content "on the fly" was an advantage that MOOCs had over traditional courses, where changing lectures or exams might involve many committees, and take months or years. Almost by accident, MOOC-based courses had enabled a rapid feedback mechanism—a pedagogical tool with such a strong influence on learning that it stands as one of the pillars of modern instructional design.

Finally, the deeply personal stories that students told affected even a tough, no-nonsense instructor like former physician Mark Braunstein, whose course on health care informatics drew students from around the world. "The two from Africa are the ones that I'll never forget," said Braunstein. "The first one (a physician from Benin) came in almost immediately after the course launched the first time. I had to look up where it is!" These were slightly older students than the ones who signed up for introductory courses, but the impact on their lives was no less profound. Braunstein received dozens of messages like this one from a physician who was using the course to transform health care delivery:

I wish every physician ... could watch some of your presentations to have a better idea of why quantitative data is an important key in the [health care] process.

Braunstein was moved as he saw the effect that his course had on hundreds and then thousands of students who would never set foot in a Georgia Tech classroom. These experiences with Coursera had convinced a small band of professors that MOOCs were not only interesting experiments but they also were actually a good way to reach an entirely new population of students with a better mode of instruction—one that incidentally improved classroom teaching as well. As stories like these circulated through the MOOC faculty, support for the idea of credit-bearing MOOCs gradually grew at Georgia Tech. Thrun agreed to help out, and over the next several months held informal discussions with on-campus groups. During one of his many visits to Georgia Tech, Thrun mentioned that he thought a high-quality master's degree in computer science could be offered for $1,000 if most of the courses were in MOOC format. He believed that this was a way of hitting the ball outside the existing system. "If you did this," Thrun said, "you will end up educating the most people in the world, and the university that educates the most people becomes the most important university in the world." Galil was at that meeting and agreed that it was a compelling vision. But he also knew that once all the university's expenses were aggregated, a $1,000 degree was impossible.

The $1,000 Degree

It seems like an easy arithmetic problem. Each credit hour is worth $500 for graduate credits and $350 for undergraduate credits.[12] Students who try to allocate their personal educational budgets in this way run into immediate problems, however. Universities charge students to enroll in courses, not to complete credits, and the price that a student pays to enroll in a three-credit graduate course is often not equal to $1,500. There are many ways that this seemingly straightforward calculation can go awry.

For example, students who are enrolled in a degree program pay a certain minimum tuition, regardless of how many credit hours their courses add up to. It also matters which curriculum a student enrolls in. At many schools, for example, enrolling in a business curriculum is more expensive than the humanities. In general, part-time students do not pay prorated prices. Certain graduate degrees carry a premium price tag, a sort of surcharge on the price per credit hour. And then there are fees: technology fees, student fees, international fees, and athletic fees; fees for enhanced information services, library usage, and parking. There are also fees for nonresidents, fees for the international experience, and a separate charge for health centers and counseling. Professional degrees frequently are more expensive than traditional academic ones. Credit hours delivered online may be just as expensive as credit hours consumed in a physical classroom, where the costs of instructors, teaching assistants, lights, heating, and physical security have to be taken into account. Students enrolled in research universities often find that their tuition invoices are higher than their friends who are attending four-year colleges.

It is tempting to view enrolling in and paying for a university class as a commercial transaction in which a service (one three-credit-hour course on US history) is offered for a price determined by the cost of offering the class (the fixed cost of the instructor and assistants plus all the variable costs associated with class size). If that were true, then higher education would constitute what is called a *single-sided market* in which a seller sets a price for a product or service that a buyer is either willing or not willing to pay. In reality, higher education institutions do not work that way.

Universities link more than buyers and sellers of credit hours. They connect buyers and sellers of entertainment services like intercollegiate athletics and performing arts, public information services such as newspapers and radio stations, and health services like university hospitals and clinics, housing and hotel services, parking services, retail stores, food services, and research services. Each of these groups uses a university to service an independent market need, and since many of these groups have conflicting interests, there is often competition among them for resources. Higher education is a *multisided market* that links these groups together, aggregating costs, prices, subsidies, and cross-subsidies. Businesses that operate like this are frequently called *platforms*. In the Internet age, platforms are common. eBay, for example, is a platform that links buyers, sellers, and payment processors. In order for Georgia Tech—or any research institution—to offer a $1,000 master's degree, the university would have to sever some of those links, to disaggregate its costs—a challenge for any platform that depends on discounts and cross-subsidies to offer low prices to one side of the market at the expense of another side. Technological innovation usually spurs this kind of disaggregation. It often leads to widespread disruption.

The newspaper business is an example of a multisided market that has gone through significant disruption. Newspapers link together print subscribers, buyers of classified advertising, and display advertising. Prior to the Internet, classified advertising was an enormously profitable business for local newspapers—so profitable that it enabled newspapers to underprice subscriptions. Cheap subscriptions increased circulation, which made it attractive for buyers of display ads to pay premium prices for ad space that would be seen by many readers. Local newspaper executives reasoned that classified advertising was by definition a local product that could only be offered by a local newspaper, an assumption that allowed them to keep their classified ad rates high. Craigslist, an online classified ad service offering free local ads, allowed buyers and sellers of used cars, babysitting, and dozens of other goods and services to communicate directly with each other, bypassing the classified advertising pages of local newspapers and depriving classified ad managers of revenue.

The result was a downward spiral that threatened the extinction of the local newspaper business.[13] The loss of classified ad revenue meant that subscription prices had to be raised to compensate. Rising subscription prices meant that fewer readers were willing to subscribe, and fewer readers meant that display ads could not command the high prices of a large circulation newspaper. The loss of revenue from display ads meant an even steeper rise in subscription prices. Robert Seamans and Feng Zhu describe the effect as follows: "The impact of entry by an online competitor on the classified-ad side propagates to the subscriber and display-ad sides."[14]

This is exactly what can take place in universities if technological innovations like MOOCs disrupt other sides of the higher education market. Here is how market disruption might work in public research universities, for instance. A public research university has at least four sides: faculty members, who are paid market rates to conduct research and teach students; students, who pay tuition and fees; a state budget that subsidizes overall costs to keep student tuition low; and sponsors, who pay the university to conduct basic and applied research at attractive prices, in effect underpricing their research services.[15] In fact, the rates paid by research sponsors are kept artificially low by cross-platform subsidies. Who subsidizes low research prices? Professors who both teach and conduct research allocate some of their time to teaching, but must also keep enough time in reserve to meet the demands of research sponsors. A professor who does little research can spend more time in the classroom and therefore appears to be a more productive teacher. A professor who is also paid to do research can offer to maintain the same high level of teaching productivity, but that is rare. More often than not, research funds are used to reduce a professor's teaching load to free up time for research. This allows a university to hire a replacement classroom teacher. If research services were priced to take this into account, then the cost of hiring the replacement would balance income from research sponsors. But in reality, universities underprice research. Research sponsors pay considerably less than the actual cost of the research, so universities must pay not only for the replacements to teach courses but also for the portion of the professor's time not paid for by sponsors. Administrators hope that in the aggregated costs of running the university, some other side of the business will make up the difference.

Since research affects teaching productivity, there must be some flexible source of funds to absorb the losses. When faculty researchers are in high demand, the only sides of the higher education market that have significant pricing flexibility are students (through higher tuition and fees) and government (through increased state budgets) or endowments (through increased earnings). Figure 2.1 shows teaching productivity trends at five types of institutions.

It is obvious that the number of courses taught per semester, which is a rough approximation of teaching productivity, is lower at universities that conduct research, and that the number has gone down over the last twenty years. The decreases virtually track the increased workload by program officers at federal funding agencies like the National Science Foundation (NSF), which, since staff spending at the NSF has been stagnant for at least twenty years, is really just a measure proposal submissions.

Why does productivity drop at research and doctoral institutions? According to an NSF study, the tendency in most NSF program offices is to deliberately underfund project proposals.[16] Over half the researchers surveyed reported that their budgets had been cut by 5 percent or more and

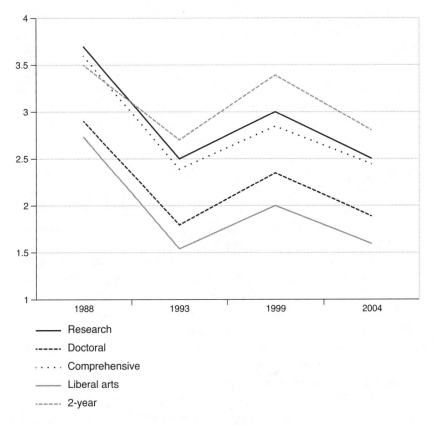

Figure 2.1
Courses taught per professor by institution type
Source: National Study of Postsecondary Faculty, 1988–2004, in Lewin 2013.

that their grant duration had been slashed by 10 percent or more. There is little room for padding an NSF budget, so these are real cuts in funds that are needed to successfully complete a research plan. Budget-cutting aside, there are real costs associated with a winning research proposal. The same study reported that the principle investigator's (PI)

estimate of the time it took for them and other people—for example, graduate as- sistants, budget administrators, and secretaries (not including time spent by institu- tional personnel)—to prepare their FY 2001 NSF grant submission was, on average, 157 hours, or about 19.5 days. It should be noted this is the time for just one pro- posal that was successful.[17]

Since the NSF success rate is currently around 25 percent, that's about eighty days just to prepare a winning proposal. Add to that the time needed to conduct the research that goes into every proposal submission and you get a rough idea of what needs to be funded just to make research pay for itself. This is lost productivity, and it all shows up in reduced faculty teaching loads.

The trends at comprehensive, liberal arts, and community colleges measure something slightly different: each of these institutions sees climbing the reputational hierarchy represented by research funding as important to their missions. For example, the NSF awarded $350 million to community colleges in 2011. The lion's share of these funds went to projects to train technicians, broaden participation in the sciences, and support research experiences for returning veterans. Individual awards for some of these programs start at $200,000, and solicitations for larger proposals are encouraged. Like their research cousins, community colleges reduce classroom productivity to compete for federal research awards. An institution with an undergraduate research mission can easily get drawn into a system it cannot afford and the data support that. For the period covered in figure 2.1, proposal submissions from these institutions have increased almost in lockstep with lost classroom productivity.

Teaching workload is not the only way to measure productivity, nor is increasing teaching workload the only way to increase productivity. It is possible, say, that a technological innovation could allow an individual professor to teach more students. If that could be accomplished without affecting the amount of time a professor could devote to research, the benefits could flow to students. It could conceivably enable a university to offer a $1,000 master's degree by disaggregating the costs of participating in a multisided market. That was the calculation that Thrun was counting on.

Not an Experiment

Galil had heard the idea of teaching the world before. Columbia's Crow had tried to use Fathom to offer free high-quality courses. Galil's own CVN had greatly expanded the reach of Columbia's engineering program, but it was priced out of reach for most of the world. His own advisory board at Georgia Tech had wanted him to explore ways to teach computing to the world. He even had the backing of Provost Bras and President Peterson. Bras had been deeply involved in negotiating a Coursera-like agreement with Thrun's Udacity, and Peterson had just returned from the World Economic Forum in Davos, where Thrun, in a reprise of his 2012 Digital-Life-Design conference address, had made an impassioned plea to expand the reach of higher education to the rest of the world. Peterson was moved, which was a good thing.

When Thrun suggested a $1,000 master's in computer science degree, "I immediately liked the idea," recalls Galil. "But I told him that $1,000 will not do." Galil suggested $4,000, but even that "was based solely on intuition." Galil believed that universities would be going through some fundamental changes. "This was an opportunity to put our mark on the future of higher education," he says. MOOCs were an interesting experiment, but Galil maintained that without credentials and degrees, they would not change much. "I thought about it in the following days. There were really two reasons to do it: we should and we can."

Like Price, Galil had to let faculty members come to the conclusion that such a plan was a good thing without a lot of interference. "I told Sebastian [Thrun] that I will need some time, and I told the faculty that we would only do it if they were behind the idea." The entire process took almost seven months. Thrun came to the campus to meet with faculty groups and answer questions. "It turned out this was a very smart move," says Galil. Although there were deeply skeptical critics among the computer science faculty, sentiment moved steadily in the direction of approving the degree. Reporters who later acquired minutes of faculty meetings tried to cast unfiltered discussions as rampant dissent, but the facts were quite different.

By January 2013, Thrun and Galil had rounded up $2 million in philanthropic support from AT&T. Over the course of several months, the outlines of the online master of science degree (OMS) began to emerge. AT&T was restless and wondered aloud why it was taking so long to agree to a program. In the end, the program won the support of 75 percent of the faculty. Peterson and Bras were both supporters. Bras made the final presentation to the board of regents, which approved the OMS in less than an hour. There were ruffled feathers among some on-campus committee members who thought their voices were not being heard, but the faculty vote was what mattered.

Although Galil knew that the degree would cost closer to $4,000 than the $1,000 that Thrun suggested, saying how much more would require costs associated with the degree to be disaggregated in a way that no university had ever tried before. Bras asked me to work with financial officials to develop some alternative business plans. The only criteria were that the courses had to remain free and open to non–Georgia Tech students and that enrolled students should get the benefit of the disaggregated costs. Skepticism was pervasive in the finance offices, yet one by one the costs were peeled away. OMS students would not need to pay athletic fees. Their use of on-campus facilities would be limited. On the other hand, new counseling and support services should be paid for as core services for OMS students, not as a charge that was spread among all Georgia Tech students.

In the end, it was the underlying cost of course production and distribution through Udacity that determined the program's price. How many students were required to make the program viable? How many hours of tutoring help would be needed per student? Who was providing and training the teaching assistants? Was there a simple multiplier that could be applied to yield the tuition? What was the cost of ensuring that OMS students received the same high-quality education as residential students? Admission requirements were to be as stringent as on-campus admission requirements. It was to be what Bras called a "full-service degree."

The shifting landscape that Mintz felt was real. It was, in one step, a transition from individual noncredit courses to a curriculum that led to an accredited degree. Obama's Council of Science and Technology Advisors said that "it could begin the process of lowering the cost of education and lowering barriers for millions of Americans."[18] But only if it works. Galil himself admits that there are many unknowns. "I love to do things that have never been done before," he says. "We want to prove that it can be done. What is important to me is to make a high-quality degree at an affordable price." Starting with master's students "made a lot of sense," explains Galil. "They are more mature and they have different expectations than eighteen-year-old freshmen."

The one word that is never used for OMS is experiment. "An experiment is something you can walk away from," says Tech president Peterson. "We know we cannot walk away from this." Peterson is an engineer. He thinks of the OMS as a prototype. "We will tweak it, improve it, redesign it even," he says. It is the one condition he placed on the program. "We do not think of this as an experiment. This is a pilot."

3   Levity, Brevity, and Repetition

New York Times columnist Thomas Friedman, speaking to a gathering of Coursera partners in early 2013, told the audience that "if it can be done cheaper and better, then someone will find a way to use technology to do it." It was not the lesson that critics wanted to hear, but it is what gave a sense of inevitability to the Magic Year. So much public attention was paid to "cheaper" it was easy to forget that—lost in a tumble of announcements and op-ed articles—making education better was at least as important to the Revolution. It is where traditionalists always thought they had the upper hand. Upset with the prospect of robots replacing human instructors, many *Chronicle of Higher Education* readers asked, "What video can replace the impact an inspired teacher has on the lives of students?" They invoked images of Mr. Chips ("Brookfield will never forget his lovableness"), or the passionate John Keating and his Dead Poets Society (whose members greet him with "O Captain! My Captain!").[1] "But passion alone," as even the most committed supporters of traditional classroom instruction will tell you, "is empty, even dangerous," especially when it is divorced from the kind of work that real learning requires.[2]

A live instructor has no intrinsic advantage when it comes to teaching. Even beloved Mr. Chips had "begun to sink into that creeping dry rot of pedagogy ... giving the same lessons year after year,"[3] before he learned how to become inspiring. The real question is not whether there is a live classroom lecture but instead what exactly students learn in class. And in order for learning to take place at all, what takes place in classrooms has to have some relationship to how the brain actually learns. The real question is whether traditional classroom instruction promotes learning, or even whether the classrooms themselves—often the deliberately "dark, airless, ugly places" imagined by the designers of American public educa-tion—actually discourage learning.[4] Science supports the idea that there is a secret to learning. A complete understanding of how learning works is still decades away, but if you were determined to design a method that would discourage it, you would invent the college lecture hall and its fifty-minute lectures crammed with hundreds of piece of information, ineffective testing, and a tyranny of content that promotes students who have not yet mastered material. That is the pedagogical architecture that University of Pennsylvania provost Price wanted to replace with something better.

If Price and his colleagues were going to change the architecture, it would have to be the result of science. It would be the culmination of decades of research into how teaching might be made more quantitative. Neuroscientists, cognitive scientists, and educational psychologists have been filling in the details for fifty years. Although the picture was still incomplete, by 2011 it was clear that the traditional lecture format did nothing to promote learning. The brain likes to learn in stimulating short bursts, with frequent assessment to test mastery of concepts along with a tightly coupled feedback loop between teachers and students. The only thing standing in the way was cost. Teaching like this was prohibitively expensive. In other words, the problem was teacher productivity, but that was the kind of problem that technology is meant to solve.

What Happens When the Brain Learns?

The best place to begin discussing the technical foundations of higher education is where education begins: it begins with the brain because that is where learning occurs. Learning changes the brain, and without learning education does not make much sense.[5] At first sight this does not seem like a controversial position to stake out, but—despite near universal scientific agreement that brain rewiring takes place during learning—there are huge battles being waged between educators and scientists over exactly this proposition. There are good reasons for the battles.

Educators and the scientists who study the brain and cognition—neuroscientists and cognitive scientists—sometimes seem to live on different planets. "Education research is concerned with entire people, not just their neurons," the educators argue. There are so many factors—environmental, societal, and developmental—that laboratory experiments that do not take the whole person into account are meaningless in the real world. Even if there were a credible biological explanation for a specific learning event, how would you know how to design instruction that triggers such an event? What neuroscientists hear in the educators' objections is fear that they would lose control if teaching were reduced simply to biology. There has always been tension between the knee-jerk defensiveness of educational researchers and what can appear to be the arrogance of the elite on the part of the more established and quantitative sciences. To neuroscientists, the questions posed by educators are miscast as all-or-nothing propositions. To educators, the neuroscientists are trying to impose a simplistic, reductionist worldview.[6]

The middle ground between education and neuroscience is fertile for mischief. Teachers who have little understanding of or experience in neurobiology are easy targets for peddlers of products and services whose effectiveness is grounded in cherry-picked data or misrepresented scientific research. The Internet is filled with brain-based learning methods, video games that exercise your brain, incomprehensible curriculum design methods based on neuroplasticity, and bogus policy proposals allegedly based on the latest results of neuroscience.[7]

My intent here is to skirt as many of these controversies as I can. One consequence of the Revolution described in chapter 1 is a renewed interest in pedagogy—literally, an interest in the study of teaching. There are many like Coursera founder Andrew Ng who believe that teaching is in part a physical skill that must be acquired through practice. Ng's view is not necessarily at odds with many others who think that the time is right to look for the principles that would turn teaching into a quantitative, predictive science. International research projects on brain mapping are picking up steam; neuroscientists are able to probe more deeply into brain structure and function than ever before; cognitive scientists who span traditional psychological research, computer science, and artificial intelligence are with increasing precision able to model cognition; and massively scaled online courses have created the world's largest education laboratory. The growing number of research universities investing in laboratories devoted to understanding how the brain learns is an indication of how seriously the idea is being taken. Some of the best scientists in the world are shifting their attention from physics and chemistry to education. To understand where the science of teaching is heading, you do not need to have an understanding of exactly what it explains about learning; you only need to understand that there are well-understood connections.[8] The reason this is an important place to start is that those connections tell us what to pursue and what to avoid, although they may not at the moment shed light on anything more. This might be the safe middle ground between educators and scientists.

There are many examples in the history of science where this process of braiding scientific knowledge with practical advances was exactly the right pathway to follow. In the mid-eighteenth century, cancer patients regularly died not from the disease itself but rather from a combination of ghastly operating room hygiene and unnecessary trauma caused by radical surgery. It would be many decades before a detailed understanding of the human genome led to more effective cures for cancer. Nevertheless, a surgeon who washed before operating on an unconscious patient saw an improvement in surgical outcomes.

Think of this chapter as a short primer on how to wash your hands before you start learning about learning and teaching—how to do no harm.

Learning takes place when the brain moves information from working to long-term memory. By information I mean facts, rules, procedures, movement, images, or just about anything else that someone would want to recall for later use. Working memory is concerned with handling memories that are not long-term, and because there is no hard-and-fast rule that tells you when information has been tucked away in long-term memory, it is best to think first of short-term memory.

Most information processed by the brain consists of the observations and fleeting memories that are stored in short-term memory for at most a few seconds, but there are things that you can do to maintain those memories for many seconds or minutes. Still more attention allows information to be stored in long-term memory. In that process, the neurons in the brain change. Animals somehow know how to devote the kind of attention to working memory that causes changes to the brain's neurons. They know how to learn. Human beings not only know how to learn, they appear to think about how to learn and get better at it over time.

Because short-term memory is refreshed so frequently, it does not need to be able to store much information. In the early 1990s, American psychologist George Miller conducted a series of experiments to determine how much information can be stored there. Miller's results suggested that short-term memory can accommodate about seven items.[9] Later research indicates that about four pieces (what are sometimes called chunks) of information can be stored in short-term memory. Around short-term memory there is a whole system of processes called working memory that examines, organizes, and reinforces short-term memories, gradually moving some of them to long-term memory. Yet if working memory receives too many chunks too quickly, the entire process of moving information to long-term memory becomes less efficient. It slows down and some chunks are ignored.

Learning takes place, when neurons in the cerebral cortex change so that information can be stored in long-term memory.[10] No one knows for sure how different kinds of learning produce these changes, but it is known that both the structure and function of the neurons change. The changes themselves seem to be developmentally related. Infants and college students, for example, exhibit different changes. Sometimes the changes are highly directed so that new neurons and new connections are produced to handle the learning task at hand. At other times the brain overproduces an abundance of new structures so that learning carves away unwanted pieces like a sculptor forms a figure from a solid block of marble.

But in all cases learning requires a change in the neurons themselves. In fact, there is a specific change common to all learning: a change in the chemicals (called neurotransmitters) that stimulate nearby neurons (Figure 3.1 [inset]). Some neurotransmitters activate neurons while others deactivate them. This is one way that neurons create and delete links with other neurons, producing the lacy networks that constitute the body's nervous system (figure 3.1).

Motivation and Reward

Babies learn to satisfy basic needs without a lot of motivation, but academic learning is different from learning how to breathe, hunt antelope, find a suitable mate, or avoid a hot flame. There is no basic need that the classroom satisfies—academic learning, for instance, does not satisfy our need for food or sex—so it is hard to imagine what intrinsic motivation human beings might have to learn music or philosophy—except for one. Human beings are motivated by social rewards.

Academic experiences lead to social rewards. Virtually everyone has ready examples. Classroom friends made in elementary school are frequently friends for life, so there must be a reward system associated with these and other school-related social interactions. Academic learning is often a source of praise, which increases a person's sense of self-worth. Higher social status is a reward that is often a result of academic performance. These, like most other social rewards, involve some measure of satisfaction. They are for most of us pleasant experiences.

Pleasant experiences trigger what is called the reward-attention-motivation cycle. The important neurotransmitters involved in learning include the chemicals acetylcholine, dopamine, and serotonin, all of which are also important for regulating the body's sense of well-being. Deep in the brain is a structure called the amygdala, which senses pleasant experiences and in response triggers the production of dopamine.[11] The cerebral cortex, where functions like memory and planning reside, contains dopamine-sensitive neurons. The connection between dopamine and learning has

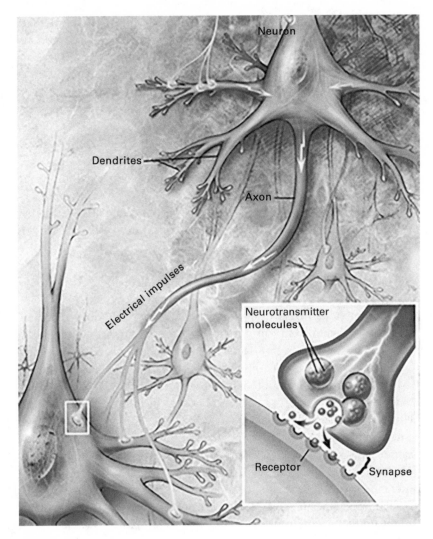

Figure 3.1
Neurotransmitters and network of neurons

been demonstrated in the laboratory. Experiments show that when dopamine is artificially reduced in this area, learning performance suffers, so in a sense, dopamine *is* the reward for learning. The cerebral cortex seeks out activities—some, like playing the piano, are positive, and others, like using cocaine, are harmful—that increase the reward.

Maintaining this reward cycle is critical to learning. It has to be constantly reinforced with new stimuli. There is nothing to suggest that the brain learns how to reward itself in the absence of stimulus. Although many researchers have tried to find a way for the rewards to be transferred from one learning cycle to the next, they have failed. Furthermore, there is no specific transfer from one task to the next. Learning how to add does not make it easier to learn long division. Nor is there any general transfer: much to the dismay of my middle school teachers, learning Latin has not made me a better learner in general. There is, for example, an elaborate theory of multiple intelligence that claims there are several specialized ways of learning, and that within those different kinds of intelligence learning can be transferred more easily. This theory has been the basis for a number of experimental schools, but like most constructions that try to explain brain function via bypassing the stimulus model, it is a fiction. The evidence points toward a general intelligence factor that describes the efficiency of the working memory cycle, but the reward cycle has to be activated for each new learning task.

Furthermore, memory is unstable and must be reinforced. Even something as simple as recalling a recent face or name is a new act of learning. The human brain is not wired like a computer with facts and figures stored in long-term memory simply awaiting a demand to recall them. In fact, the very act of recalling a memory results in rewiring the network of neurons associated with the memory. Each act of recall is a reconstruction that reengages the dopamine-based reward cycle.

Armed with this simple understanding of how the brain functions, researchers know there are actions that promote and inhibit the transfer of information from working to long-term memory. Repetition and emotional excitement, for instance, both change the amount of neurotransmitters that are produced at the connections between neurons, which in turn increases the number of connections among neurons. There are factors, like diet, that promote learning, and others, such as sleep, that consolidate learning, but most of them are beyond the control of classroom teachers.[12]

Teachers, however, can control repetition and excitement. Effective teaching almost always involves doing something to redirect a student's attention in ways that change how the brain works. Public speakers, when they first embark on their speech-making careers, are often given the following advice: "The secret to a good speech is levity, brevity, and repetition. Let me say that again."

It is an often-repeated joke, but I don't think there are many professional speakers who realize the deep connection with brain science. Of all the factors that influence classroom learning—and that are so poorly understood today—the repeated stimulation of the reward cycle by redirecting attention to small learning tasks is one that we are sure matters. Like eighteenth-century surgeons, we stand in awe of a human brain that we only vaguely understand, yet that is no reason for inaction, even if the action is—like the washing of hands before surgery—to do no harm.

The Case of Lecture 14

Time is fixed in an academic year. It is measured by a calendar divided into semesters and courses, and by a syllabus that dictates exactly what topics should be presented in each interval of time. For most of the last thousand years, lectures have connected the beating pulse of a college curriculum to learning. College courses are divided into a fixed number of classes—meetings at which a professor faces an audience of students to give a speech. The lecture is the one thing that a university professor can control in the classroom, and it is even today a fiercely guarded prerogative of faculty members to dictate exactly how lectures are to be carried out. But there have been major battles waged over the purpose of a lecture and, most important, who the lecture is designed to benefit.

In 1229, the liberal arts faculty members of the University of Paris decided that the lecture was primarily for their own benefit when they enacted the following statute:

The masters of philosophy [must] deliver their expositions from their chairs so rapidly that, although the minds of their audience may grasp their meaning, their hands cannot write it down.... Henceforth in any lecture, ordinary or cursory or in any disputation or other manner of teaching, the master is to speak as in delivering a speech, and as if no one were writing in his presence. A lecturer who breaks the new rule is to be suspended for a year.[13]

Students had little say in the matter. The statute prescribed a one-year suspension for any student who complained by "shouting, hissing, groaning, or throwing stones." The masters at the University of Paris were worried that transcripts of lectures, quickly copied and sold, would undercut their own value. Although the Paris faculty eventually rescinded this statute, the faculty-centered preoccupation with the lecture formats still exists.[14]

Today lectures are likely to be syllabus centered. A syllabus maps course content—lectures, quizzes, and exams—on a class-by-class basis so that students know what material is being covered each day. It is a convenience for students and a kind of script for instructors—a teleprompter that tells them to speed up or slow down. A syllabus may be designed once and used for years, every time a course is taught. Sometimes a syllabus is designed by a committee for use by many different instructors, each with a distinct approach to teaching. But however conceived, a syllabus is a tyrant. In fact, that is the whole point: a syllabus is hard to change and nearly impossible to personalize. The problem is that since courses must cover a certain amount of material, they can easily become controlled by a syllabus. It is a tyranny of content in which professors teach material, not students.[15] The calendar, not what students learn, dictates what is taught.

Here is how the syllabus-centered lecture for one of those courses works for one actual class taught by one particular professor. This professor, who has a pleasant lecturing style and receives high marks from students who have taken his course, is one of the world's foremost experts in his field. Like the vast majority of undergraduate required courses at research universities, this one is delivered as if from a theatrical stage in thirty-two lectures that last approximately fifty minutes each. There is nothing special about this specific course. I chose it at random from a sample of hundreds of other general education courses. Lecture 14 is especially interesting to me because of its subject matter, which I always considered wondrous. The lecture itself is flawlessly delivered. There are perhaps twenty distinct ideas that are mentioned, including some interesting applications of the main idea and some equally intriguing alternative formulations.

Lecture 14 also includes some material from lecture 13 that there was not time to cover and some background material for lecture 15. In total, the classroom session for lecture 14 requires students to remember perhaps thirty different concepts. The instructor helpfully provides homework assignments for lecture 14. Those assignments are not due until lecture 19, by which time an additional ninety topics will have been introduced. There is no indication of when the graded homework was returned to the students, but in the most optimistic scenario, students would not have received instructor feedback on their understanding of lecture 14 for six weeks. Between lecture 14 and the assignment due date is an examination on the material. Most important, a mastery of the material in lecture 14 is required for understanding lectures 15–17.

How does a student experience lecture 14?[16] First of all, a student has to be present in class to experience the lecture at all. According to a university student survey, 10 percent of the respondents said that they attended only half their classes, so it is a good bet that a number of students were simply not in class that day. After an initial settling in of perhaps five minutes, students appear to be ready to pay attention to the concepts that will come their way at the rate of one every two minutes. At the five-minute mark, there is a noticeable increase in the number of students whose attention has lapsed.

These are short lapses of perhaps a minute or so. At the eight-minute mark there is another burst of lapses, followed by another at ten minutes and so on throughout the lecture, increasing in frequency throughout the period, until by the end of the lecture, everyone's attention is lapsing every couple of minutes. The consistent pattern is that many of the students who attend lecture 14 hear only two-thirds of the material that is being presented. The opportunities for learning concepts that are not heard are limited.

Presumably, the professor sees a sizable number of students "zoning out" and realizes that they are not actively engaged in learning, because he makes frequent reference to the homework assignment for lecture 14 and the lecture notes that will be published online. It is unknown whether these stimuli have any effect on the learning that takes place in the classroom the day that lecture 14 is delivered, although given the realities of a packed calendar that will examine students on material before their homework is graded, it is hard to imagine what that effect might be.

Brevity is nowhere to be seen. Except for occasional interludes about homework, the entire lecture is delivered as a seamless performance that requires sustained attention to details on the audience's part. The other two factors that we know for sure affect learning are repetition and excitement, and they are also absent that day. There is no time for repetition, because lecture 14 has been carefully engineered to accommodate exactly the thirty concepts that are covered. Nor is there room for excitement. No change-up to reset the attention clock, no pop quiz to redirect a student's attention, and no donuts for more primal stimulation. Unless the instructor can maintain an audience in a continual state of dramatic anticipation for the entire fifty minutes, there is simply no room for anything to flood neurons with dopamine. Tyrannical content has won the battle for lecture 14, although neither the professor nor his students will know that until after lecture 19.

Lecture 14 is a dramatic improvement over the faculty-centered lectures of thirteenth-century Paris, but it is teaching that focuses on the material, not learning. Might there be learning that takes place despite the short-comings of lecture 14? There are bound to be students—competitive, self-directed learners—who have already figured out that they need to create their own personal syllabus and learning plan. They will be the ones who line up outside the professor's door with questions, form study groups, and have assembled their own framework for learning. Paradoxically, many of those students are not in class to hear lecture 14 in person. Students reported that they decide whether to attend lectures based on the lecturer's ability to engage and entertain along with the availability of the same material elsewhere.

Some of those students have stumbled on to Web sites like that of Khan Academy, where the main point of lecture 14 is covered in one sixteen-minute video.[17] There is no time limit for viewing the video, and students whose minds wander can always replay the portion that they missed. There is a little quiz at the end, and students who have missed the mark are advised to go back over the material again. Once the main concept has been mastered, students can earn "points" posted on a subject dashboard that they can choose to share with classmates in a video-game-style competition or they can simply use their point totals as a way of keeping track of their own progress. Khan Academy is free.

I attended a meeting in 2012 with the president of one of the top-ranked American research universities and its board of trustees. The purpose of the meeting was to discuss how the sudden appearance of new technologies like MOOCs was changing not only classroom practices but also the entire approach to spending. Newspapers were extensively covering Khan Academy and MOOCs along with the question of whether the traditional lecture actually does damage to how the brain learns. I expected fireworks because university presidents spend much of their time raising funds for new buildings, and this particular president was a superstar when it came to campus expansion. What happened next shocked me: the president asked the head of the board of trustees, "Why are we building expensive lecture halls, heating them in the winter, and filling them with students who are only 30 percent successful at learning what is being taught?" What he said next stopped the meeting cold: "Why would you ever approve another new building?"

If lectures disappear—as this president believes they will—or if, as some believe they become an art form practiced by virtuosos rather than a common form of classroom engagement, it will be because the beloved classroom itself has been replaced with a different kind of space—one in which the traditional roles of lectures and homework have been interchanged or "flipped." What takes place in a flipped classroom is active engagement. Quizzes are given, problems are solved, groups hold discussions, and topics are repeated as necessary. Dopamine-producing events are everywhere. What are these students discussing? They may be talking about that sixteen-minute Khan Academy video and their dashboards. They may be participating in MOOCs that are offered by edX. Whatever else takes place in a flipped classroom, it is surely different from the live performance of lecture 14 given in a darkened theater to a passive audience.

At the end of the semester, there will still be an accounting. Certain material has to be covered over a thirty-two-week period. A flipped classroom does no harm to the learning process, but even flipped classrooms cannot withstand the tyranny of content, because at the semester's end, exams will be written, and students will pass or fail. But with increasing frequency, being passed on to the next course is what happens. For many European-style universities, passing or failing an individual course is a meaningless concept because examinations are given only at the end of a program. For American-style universities in which letter grades are assigned based on final examinations at the semester's end, there are data that paint a frightening picture.

A 2012 report by the *Teachers College Record* bears the ominous title "Where A Is Ordinary," and documents the systematic long-term trend toward inflation of grades in public and private universities.[18] The results are summarized in figure 3.2. By 2008, two-thirds of the students at 135 public and private universities were receiving As or Bs. A student earning an A or B in a first-year math course should have mastered skills that are required, for example, in a sophomore statistics course. That is not what happens. The best predictor of subsequent grades are the SAT scores of entering students, but SAT scores do not predict that two-thirds of the students who are successfully passed on from their first year will have mastery of first-year material, which is what a grade of A or B should signify. In other words, student success in the sophomore year is better predicted by general aptitude and knowledge prior to entering college. This means that whatever was taking place in the first-year lecture hall did not have much of an influence on a student's ability to improve beyond that year. The average second-year student arrives in the fall having successfully completed thirty-two hours of lecture—not because of what they have learned, but rather because that is the pulse beat of life on a college campus.

Invisible, Changing Brains

Is it a fleeting achievement when a skilled instructor moves a classroom of motivated students to master a concept or demonstrate a newly acquired skill? Teaching may be, as Ng suggests, a physical skill that is acquired by practice, but there are nevertheless two problems that effective teaching has to overcome. The first is that most of what takes place when the brain learns is invisible to teachers. The second is that human brains change. The changes from one year to the next may be imperceptible, but over twenty years or so, the effects are large enough to measure. What is effective in one generation may completely miss the mark in subsequent ones.

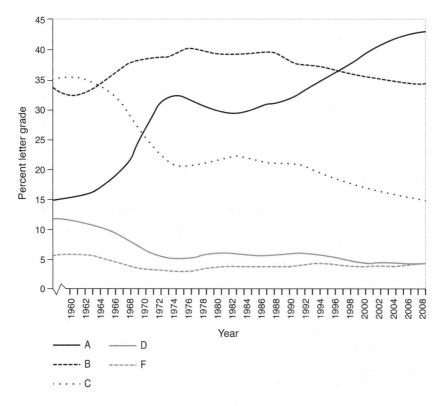

Figure 3.2
Distribution of grades at American colleges and universities over time
Source: Rojstaczer and Healy 2012.

Measuring cognition is hard enough in laboratories, but in classrooms it is nearly impossible. Teachers cannot actually monitor brain functions, but, if they could, there might be indicators that a student finally grasps the significance of a particularly difficult passage in *Finnegans Wake*. When an electroencephalograph (EEG) is connected to the parietal lobes of a normal human subject—the same portion of the brain involved in the stimulus-response-reward cycle—a wave pattern called P300 appears whenever the subject experiences a cognitive event that is sometimes called the "ah-ha!" moment. For example, when a subject is shown photographs of people she doesn't know and a picture of a close friend is slipped into the pile, there is a moment of recognition—the moment at which the subject says to herself, "A-ha! I recognize that face!" At that moment EEG electrodes record a positive change in voltage that lasts roughly three hundred milliseconds—the delay between visual stimulation and a recognition response. The P300 event is a universal response to recognition. It has been repeated thousands of times in laboratory tests, and does not vary with age, gender, race, or geography. It is such a reliable response that courts now regard EEG responses as a kind of brain fingerprint that is admissible along with other forensic evidence.

If there is a corresponding response to a learning event, it has not yet been discovered. Even if there were a repeatable change in brain activity, a classroom full of electrode-wearing students, each of them hooked up to a recording device, presents many other problems. But that may be unnecessary.

If learning takes place online, for example, keystrokes and mouse clicks can be automatically recorded in very large numbers, effectively creating a laboratory database of learning activities that can be analyzed and mined to determine when a particular event has occurred. Several new companies like Knewton are rapidly creating a field called *learning analytics* that allows instructors to monitor the learning pathways that students take in college courses.[19] In Knewton's case, the courseware is analyzed by teams of experts who break the content into small units called atomic concepts. Several universities have developed these concept maps for their online courses. Algorithms that track progress from one atomic concept to the next monitor overall student progress, and then display the results in dashboard fashion so that instructors can adapt to the needs of a particular student.

There is also evidence that cognitive functions change significantly from one generation to the next—an effect that some psychologists have characterized as getting smarter. It is called the Flynn effect, referring to the 1984 discovery by James Flynn of a consistent, continual rise in IQ scores over the last hundred years. Test scores have increased around the world, and the increases can be seen in all standardized methods for testing intelligence. There is no way to directly measure intelligence, so a rise in test scores does not actually signal a global rise in intelligence, but it does signal a change in cognitive ability over time. The increases are significant. The Wechsler Intelligence Scale for Children, for example, records an increase of about three IQ points per decade, which means that there is a sustained increase of nearly ten IQ points per generation. In an interview with the editors of *Scientific American*, Flynn was asked whether that meant our ancestors with an effective mean IQ of seventy were mentally retarded.

Of course they weren't. They could use logic on the utilitarian and function perfectly well in the concrete world. But we, thanks to use of logic on the hypothetical and our propensity to classify, can attract a much wider range of problems.[20]

According to Flynn, the changes seem to be a result of modernity. A brain at birth looks much the same from one generation to the next, but an autopsied modern brain shows that it has been used differently than three generations ago. One way this shows up is in the ability of children to do more abstract problem solving than their parents. One experiment—which I have tried using my daughter and mother as unwitting subjects—is to show a two-year-old and her grandmother how to use a computer mouse to "press a button on the screen." Children grasp the idea immediately, but the first inclination of a grandparent is to actually pick up the mouse to press it against the screen. This ability to spontaneously create impressive abstractions has been documented, for instance, by educational researcher Sugata Mitra, who placed primitive computer kiosks in rural Indian villages. Mitra discovered that not only did children teach themselves how to use the computers; they began demanding more powerful computers.[21]

It is unlikely that educational experts two generations removed from current high school students are going to have a clear idea of what their technology expectations might be. Georgia Tech president Peterson says that he sees differences in each new first-year class. "It's one of the reasons I was drawn to the idea of MOOCs," he told me. "We don't know whether our students are going to prefer iPads, online courses, and social networks over the kind of instructional environment I grew up with. What is new and foreign today will be commonplace tomorrow." Current online courses like MOOCs may be primitive and may not resemble learning environments two generations from now, but in Peterson's view, "We are going to be better off with the option of evolving our understanding. I would hate to look back and regret that we did not jump on that opportunity when we had the chance."

What Matters Most

Amid public concern about student loans, the high cost of a college degree, poor completion rates, and whether or not college equips you for a better job, the impact of better learning tends to get lost in a sea of policy and budget proposals, political debates, and hundreds of new ideas about how universities should be organized—none of which would have a direct influence on learning. The factors that directly impact learning are pushed to the sidelines because they are the most difficult ones to solve with the stroke of a pen. But they are the ones that matter most.

What are the direct influences? They are the factors that we know have a cause-effect relationship on the quality of learning: student aptitude, the nature of classroom instruction, and the environment in which the student lives. We know that these are the most important factors, in part, because in 1994, Margaret Wang, Geneva Haertel, and Herbert Walberg analyzed fifty years of education research in an attempt to determine what directly influences student learning. From a knowledge base of eleven thousand statistical results, they were able to aggregate findings spread across many studies to arrive at a consensus view of the most significant influences on learning.[22]

Not only do their findings point in a different direction than the one advocated by policy experts and politicians today, they complete the story that began with squabbles between education theorists and neuroscientists. In fact, the smallest influence was found in factors like class size, institutional governance, and state-level policies that seem to occupy much of the public debate over higher education today. Figure 3.3 shows the average impact of each type of factor.

A teacher has to teach to a classroom full of students with different innate abilities and aptitudes, and there is nothing that can be done to change those characteristics. Likewise, a student's individual circumstances are beyond a teacher's control. A teacher may have some say over program design and school organization, but it is hard to argue that an instructor has control of those factors. Governance is even further removed from teacher control. Of the direct influencers, the only one that an individual teacher actually controls is what happens in the classroom. If traditional lecture-style methods of instruction fail the test of doing no harm, is there a way of conducting a class that is more aligned with how the brain learns? This was the question that occupied University of Chicago educational psychologist Benjamin Bloom for the last half of his career. In 1984, he announced that the answer is "Yes!" Not only is there a better method of instruction, but it is so much better that traditional methods of instruction should be dropped immediately and replaced with what Bloom called ML. In a landmark paper

Types of influence	Average influence
Student aptitude	54.7
Classroom instruction and climate	53.3
Context	51.4
Program design	47.3
School organization	45.1
Government/system characteristics	35

Figure 3.3
Influences on learning
Source: Wang, Haertel, and Walberg 1993/1994.

titled "The 2 Sigma Problem," Bloom and his students presented the case for ML by comparing it to the traditional classroom.[23] ML is so superior to all other modes of instruction that if you add it to other factors that directly influence learning, you can consistently raise the achievement level of even large classes so that average performers will demonstrate a mastery of the course material. Bloom's results do not depend on student age and ability, subject matter, or geography.

The sigma in the title of Bloom's paper refers to the statistical concept of a standard deviation, which measures the amount of variability in a set of measurements, like the distribution of examination scores in college classes. If, for example, you plot the frequency of test scores and the resulting chart looks like figure 3.4 (the classic bell-shaped curve), test scores cluster around an average, whose value is represented by the Greek letter mu (written μ) in this diagram, and taper off to the left and right depending on how far a given score is from μ. A single standard deviation above or below μ, represented by the lowercase Greek letter sigma (written σ), indicates how far above and below the average you have to go before you have accounted for 68 percent of all the test scores. Another standard deviation (2σ) above and below μ accounts for 95 percent of all scores. If you were "grading on a curve," scores that were 2σ above the average would probably be graded A. Bloom's two sigma discovery states that ML is capable of moving the average student in a traditional classroom up two standard deviations to the upper 2 percent in terms of what has been learned.

Here is how ML works. In the ML classroom an instructor presents identical class material in the same format as in traditional classrooms, but rather

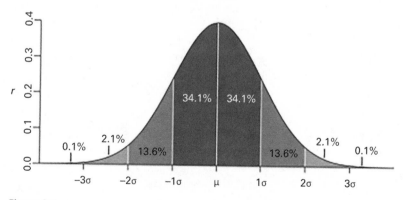

Figure 3.4
Normal distribution with standard deviations

than using tests to sort students into passing and failing grades, the tests are used to provide feedback to teachers on what students have learned and not learned. Teachers continue to explain and provide additional practice about those concepts that have not been adequately mastered until students demonstrate mastery of the material on a test. There is an improvement to ML called 1–1 tutoring in which a tutor rather than a classroom teacher offers the instruction followed by the feedback-corrective instruction-retest cycle that characterizes ML.

Bloom and his students discovered that ML, all by itself, moves the average student in the traditional class by 1σ. ML plus 1–1 tutoring moves the average student by another σ. In a real sense, it moves an entire traditional class to the ninety-eighth percentile. Figure 3.5 shows how Bloom visually represented his results.

Bloom and his students were also able to discover the relative impact of altering certain aspects of classroom instruction (figure 3.6).

The effects of these variations are measured by their standard deviation σ, so, for example, the effect of tutorial instruction was 2σ. But the

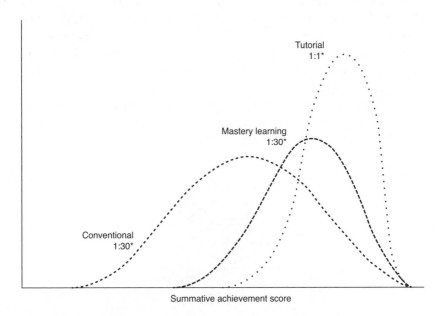

Summative achievement score

* Teacher-student ratio

Figure 3.5
Achievement distribution for students under conventional, ML, and tutorial instruction

Effect size	Percentile	Strategy
2.00	98	Tutorial instruction
1.20	86	Reinforcement
1.00	84	Corrective feedback
1.00	84	Cues and explanations
1.00	84	Student classroom participation
1.00	84	Student time-on-task
1.00	84	Improved reading/ study skills
0.80	79	Cooperative learning
0.80	79	Homework (graded)
0.60	73	Classroom morale
0.60	73	Initial cognitive prerequisites
0.50	69	Home environment intervention
0.40	66	Peer and cross-age remedial tutoring

Figure 3.6
Relative impact of altering classroom instruction

1.2σ impact of reinforcement was almost as great. Simply returning graded homework to students moved the average 0.8σ to the seventy-ninth percentile. Other direct influences from the Wang, Haertel, and Walberg studies were also present in the Bloom data. The innate ability of students (0.6σ), while important, was less crucial than corrective feedback (1σ). Overall, what Bloom and his students uncovered was a direct link to the significance of repetition and stimulus—how the brain learns.

For almost thirty years, planners and administrators have known that by simply organizing classrooms to reinforce the factors that are most closely related to how human beings are known to learn, student performance can be lifted to the ninety-eighth percentile. Why has ML not been uniformly adopted in education? Was this a conspiracy to maintain approaches to teaching that were vastly inferior? Would the current model in which students are grouped into cohorts by age or ability for efficiency be damaged by an approach to classrooms in which individual students are treated as individuals? Or were Bloom's results somehow too simplistic and deterministic? Was future evaluation and experimental testing needed before this research could be applied to actual classrooms and actual students?

Bloom almost certainly recognized the importance of his discovery, and wondered in print about how to reap the benefits of ML and 1–1 tutoring:

The tutoring process demonstrates that most of the students do have the potential to reach this high level of learning. I believe an important task of research and instruction is to seek ways of accomplishing this under more practical and realistic conditions than the one-to-one tutoring, which is too costly for most societies to bear on a large scale.[24]

The answer for Bloom and an entire generation of education researchers was, "You can't do that!"

The Revolution that started in Silicon Valley laboratories for the first time makes it feasible to teach students to learn like the brain does. Technology is endlessly creative at stimulating minds and is tireless, so there is no measurable cost to personalized repetition. There is no reason that a course has to last exactly thirteen weeks if students want to proceed at a faster or slower pace, so the tyranny of content can be put to rest. We cannot look inside the brain as it learns, but artificial intelligence software can create a personalized experience, and billions of keystrokes can be mined to discover better ways of teaching and learning. The Flynn-affected modern human mind adapts to a concept like online social networking, and instantly recognizes it as a tool for creating communities of mentors and learners. ML moves every population of students to higher levels of learning, but is so costly that an entire generation of educators came to believe, "You can't do that." Like so many other problems, technology has removed the "You can't" barrier.

4 Technology Curves

One persistent myth about educational technology is that it consistently overpromises learning improvement. Critics are quick to point out the many failed experiments in educational technology that had little or no impact on learning.

Fortunately for humanity, the number of failed scientific experiments has no bearing on the march of progress. It is equally misleading to discuss technological innovation in isolation from business innovation, since each enables the other. Seen in that light, major educational innovations have been on an accelerating growth curve for a thousand years. At the start of the Renaissance, colleges in southern Europe disrupted the business models of civic universities and, enabled by the sudden availability of relatively inexpensive textbooks, provided a way for effective teaching to chip away at state-run monopolies. It took only two hundred years for slate blackboards to transform classroom teaching styles and less than a hundred years for a disruptive American business innovation to overthrow the classical European university curriculum and begin the process of massification. When you think of technological change, you need to think beyond MOOCs.

This chapter is about the pace of technological change, but since it is not always obvious which technologies will matter in the long run, it is best to think about the forces that drive all technological change. It took several centuries, but cheap and effective transportation allowed students and teachers to travel increasingly large distances with relative ease, gradually changing the character of local universities. It took about a century for radio and television to extend the reach of central campuses to the masses, enabling Great Britain's Open University to eventually enroll three hundred thousand students. The transition to computer-mediated instruction—although it was accompanied by many expensive missteps—took less than fifty years to complete. The transformative power of educational technology is on display almost everywhere. The International Digital Children's Library project at the University of Maryland has digitized nearly five thousand children's books and made them available to millions of readers around the world who would otherwise not have access to them.[1] The Internet has irretrievably altered the idea of a university library—a trend that Google's ambitious effort to digitize all books in print has only accelerated. That transition took less than a quarter century. The widespread use of online courses was accomplished in less than a decade, and it took only five years for flipped classrooms and other innovations to become acceptable substitutes for long-format lectures.

Large-scale warehouses for educational data are being deployed as I am writing this book, and learning analytics will certainly be in widespread use by the time it is published. Each advance occurs on an accelerated timescale that halves the time between major innovations. That is exactly the pace of change in technology.

Technology improvements follow an exponential curve that doubles capability every eighteen to twenty-four months. Futurist Ray Kurzweil has plotted the intervals between major innovations and found that the pace of discovery is accelerating at the same exponential rate.[2] It would be remarkable if discoveries in teaching and learning did not keep pace. Even if only a fraction of the new ideas bear fruit, technology curves are exponential, which means that important educational innovations also happen at an exponentially accelerating rate. That is what the innovators are counting on.

From Teddy to TED

Zen and the Art of Motorcycle Maintenance begins, "What is in mind is a sort of Chautauqua, like the traveling tent-show Chautauquas that used to move across America."[3] Teddy Roosevelt called them "the most American thing in America." They were intended to "edify and entertain, improve the mind and bring culture and enlightenment to the ears and thoughts of the hearer." Depending on one's point of view, Chautauquas were either revolutionary—William Jennings Bryan said they were a "potent factor in molding the mind of the nation"—or, as William James found them, "depressing from [their] mediocrity." Chautauquas were part vaudeville and part theater in which a single actor might play all the roles in a reenactment of the works of Charles Dickens. But there were also lectures on serious topics like Maude Ballington Booth's 1902 lectures on prison reform, replete with descriptions of prison life so wrenching that she could "bring her audiences to tears."[4] A Chautauqua—the name comes from the lake in upstate New

York where the movement started in 1874—was a kind of educational summer camp—a movement that spread through rural America until the 1930s, when the automobile and new technologies like radio and film brought adult education within practical reach of small-town America which no longer had to rely on live summer performances in brown tents to find out the latest thinking on the important cultural issues of the day.

It would be more than a century before the brutality of prison life would move another Chautauqua audience to tears. "I am stunned," said Alicia Greenall after hearing psychologist Phillip Zimbardo's twenty-three-minute lecture *The Psychology of Evil*. "I cried, laughed and at the end I left feeling hope."[5] The Stanford prison experiment—in which realistic role-playing had transformed otherwise-normal, sane subjects into sadistic "guards" and depressed, passive "prisoners"—had been Zimbardo's project in the early 1970s, but *The Psychology of Evil* was not about role-playing in a fake prison. It was about the horrors of Abu Ghraib prison in Iraq. And like Booth, Zimbardo moved his audience to tears. No one knows exactly how many people heard Booth's lectures, but it could not have been more than a few thousand. On the other hand, we know how many have heard *The Psychology of Evil*—slightly more than 3,537,000 as of this writing.

Zimbardo is a popular performer in a modern, technology-amped Chautauqua called TED, which stands for technology, education, and design. Of course, TED does not conceive of itself in that way. TED was the Silicon Valley brainchild of an architect and polymath named Richard Saul Wurman. Wurman is the author of eighty-three books, most of them self-published. "The first thing [publishers] said was that we'd have to change the size of the title. As soon as I heard that, I knew I'd be wearing shoes that don't fit," he explains. "The projects that I do come from this passion of mine that stems from not understanding something that I find interesting," Wurman says. "The project is actually a journey from ignorance to finding out about something." Wurman organized a gathering of technologists and designers to have a "conversation." Conversation, he believes "is the most remarkable thing human beings do." TED was conceived as a way "to put a balloon around that."

"Packaging conversation" may have been Wurman's inspiration, but it took some time before he found a financially viable format. The annual TED conference quickly outgrew its five-hundred-seat home in Monterey, California, and in 2008 moved to the three-thousand-seat convention center in Long Beach. What started as conversation had become performance. It is the unique nature of TED performances (they are called TED Talks) that makes TED a rightful heir to the sometimes-sweaty summer Chautauqua shows that moved from town to town a century ago. By the time TED relocated to Long Beach, Wurman had handed the franchise off to a social entrepreneur named Chris Anderson, who promptly branded TED Talks as "Ideas Worth Spreading." Anderson called himself a *curator* and began building a media-distribution empire for freely spreading the TED Talk ideas. A typical TED speaker walks on to a bare stage—there is seldom even a podium—armed only with an earpiece fitted with a boom mic and a large projection panel onto which compelling images—never PowerPoint—help connect the ideas to real life.

TED Talks are well-coached morsels. Speakers are trained to deliver their material in no more than eighteen minutes of punchy, dramatic speech making. TED Talks about death are common and as dramatic as you might expect, ranging from a graphic depiction of what the brain experiences during death—filled with long pauses that allow an audiences to catch its emotional breath—to artist Jae Rhim Lee's plea for a "cleaner, greener Earth," delivered in the mushroom burial suit that she hopes will help her become one with the environment, postmortem. The recruiting pitch for speakers includes a lengthy description of what is expected and how much work it will be, even for experienced public speakers and teachers, to fit a complex idea into an eighteen-minute distillation that somehow fills the large, bare TED stage and touches the audience.

TED Talks may be viewed for free, but attending a TED Conference is decidedly not free. An annual membership fee of $6,000 entitles a subscriber to attend the yearly conference and access the various networking tools that TED provides. The format was so successful—there have been over five hundred million viewings of TED Talks—that Anderson began licensing TED to independent organizers of TEDx conferences. TEDx speakers must follow the same format as the annual TED speakers, and they must agree to allow TED to edit, market, and distribute their talks. There are TEDMED conferences for health and medicine, a TEDWomen series, and an international conference called TEDGlobal.

There are those who claim that the lecture is dead, but like a modern Chautauqua, TED is a place where lectures thrive.[6] There are thousands of hours of recorded lectures available at TED.com to anyone with a Web browser. TED's Open Translation Project crowdsources translations of TED Talks into ninety-seven different languages. Each TED Talk is a perfectly honed lecture, a piece of performance art that—although it aims to edify and entertain—does not "put a balloon around" conversation as Wurman once imagined. Despite many efforts to incorporate TED into classrooms and curricula, they are not connected to larger conversations and are prey to the same criticism that plagued Chautauqua. Author Nassim Taleb calls TED "a monstrosity that turns scientists and thinkers into ... circus performers."[7]

Because they are so stylized, TED Talks are prone to parody. In 2010, comedian and satirist Sarah Silverman staged an elaborate send-up of TED Talks by accepting an invitation to speak at the annual conference. What followed was a caricature of TED-inspired speeches that are long on overwrought emotion and short on meaningful content. Silverman's TED Talk veered crazily from a bizarre, repellent adoption scheme—complete with pauses for applause for the plan's "awesomeness"—to a deadpan ode to human bodily functions accompanied by technographics. The ensuing social media flap between Silverman and Anderson—who had by that time blocked access to the video—drew many tens of thousands of viewers into the joke, and allowed Silverman, with barely concealed delight, to air her bitter disappointment on social media and late-night talk shows.

Wurman himself jumped back into the conversation business to "once again reinvent the business conference," with something called the WWW. WWW conference, a series of improvisational conversations "with a hundred of the world's greatest minds having a conversation, two at a time." He calls it "intellectual jazz" without speeches, slide shows, or tickets.

The Minerva Programme

A few years before the Great Depression brought Roosevelt's "most American thing" to a sudden halt, and well before the Internet-enabled rebirth of Chautauqua made TED-style lectures available to villages around the world, a former schoolteacher named Jack Stobart was joining the fledgling British Broadcasting Company (BBC) as director of education. In a 1928 speech to the British Association for the Advancement of Science, Stobart proposed that wireless technology be used "in the service of education." What he had in mind was a series of performances and lectures "selected so as to give an understanding of current problems in politics, economics, etc. and to keep listeners in touch with progress and achievement in every line of human activity."[8] This Minerva Programme, as Stobart called it, would essentially operate as a new network, but there were already forces under way in England to supply adult education to the British public.[9] A 1928 report had determined that the BBC could "widen the field from which students are drawn" and "provide a means of education for those beyond the reach of other agencies."[10]

By 1930, BBC adult education broadcasts had become university-like in their organization.[11] There were three twelve-week terms per year, with content defined by a syllabus. The programming from spring 1930 promised adult education fare ranging from language talks (fortnightly) in French and commercial Spanish to Cyril Burt's weekly (8:00 p.m. in Daventry only) lecture entitled "The Study of the Mind." It was an impressive offering to the British public, but it was still something of a Chautauqua movement. There were no universities willing to give credit for following a BBC adult education curriculum, and no degrees were awarded. Despite a postwar call to expand higher education to increase the supply of scientists and engineers, British universities were elite institutions. By the late 1950s, only 4 percent of eighteen- to twenty-four-year-olds attended a university, and most of them followed classical curricula in the arts and humanities. While students in the United States were pouring into colleges and universities, the percentage of young people who went to college in Great Britain rose only slightly.

Stobart's proposal had not been forgotten. The Institute of Electrical Engineers called for a Teleuniversity that would combine broadcast lectures with on-campus residency at traditional universities. By the early 1960s, the BBC and politician Harold Wilson's Ministry of Education were discussing a "College of the Air" that bore a striking resemblance to both Stobart's Wireless University and Lord Michael Young's proposal for an "Open University." The Open University began operations in January 1971 with lectures broadcast over radio and television. By 1980 there were seventy thousand students enrolled in the Open University, and the numbers continued to grow over the next twenty years, first to a hundred thousand then to nearly two hundred thousand, most of them nontraditional students who would otherwise be locked out of university educations.

There is a strong sense of social responsibility behind all the efforts to provide widespread access to high-quality educational material, but except for the Open University none have had the backing of a figure like Young. Although Young was a baron, he was born into poverty and chose to become a social reformer. He argued that IQ exams in schools divided society in a more insidious way than old class-based systems. His masterwork *The Rise of the Meritocracy*—although it was taken by the conservative elite as a call for establishing a new order based on accomplishment—was actually a satire in which one kind of elitism is replaced with another, only slightly less unsavory kind. Young wanted to democratize institutions and give the people a stronger role in their governance. Equality, diversity, and a dedication to social justice are Open University core values to this day.

Openness

The word open in Open University does not refer so much to technology as to open learning—the idea of encouraging "learning in your own time by reading course material, working on course activities, writing assignments and perhaps working with other students." Open also means open access, which implies low—usually nonexistent—barriers to locate and use course materials. The term open in MOOC is also used in this sense. A MOOC is open because anyone can follow it for free. Sometimes open has a technical meaning that implies a degree of interchangeability of parts. Courses that are delivered by video are sometimes uploaded into a special format that is only used for that purpose; that is the opposite of an open architecture that would allow users to use whatever video formats they want.

But above all, open is a code for a democratizing principle—the same one that consumed Lord Young. It is no accident that the OpenCourseWare (OCW) movement took root at MIT. In the 1990s, MIT was home to the two technology movements that changed the face of an entire industry. The first was the result of Richard Stallman's moral crusade against proprietary software. Stallman was a programmer in MIT's Computer Science and Artificial Intelligence Laboratory in the 1970s, at a time when software was becoming an economic force and engineers began choosing sides between commercial software developers, whose restrictive licenses prohibited the free sharing of computer codes, and a new "hacker" culture that believed proprietary software to be part of a value system that was antidemocratic and therefore immoral. Stallman's GNU General Public License (GPL) was an agreement that committed software developers to not only freely share their own creations; it also bound them to treat any programs on which they depended as if they were covered by a GPL license. Finnish programmer Linus Torvalds, the developer of the open-source Linux operating system, later joined Stallman's open-source software movement. The MIT intellectual underpinnings of the open-source movement ran deep. Stallman's first appointment at MIT was as a research assistant for computer science professor Gerald Sussman. In the ensuing years, Sussman maintained a personal involvement in Stallman's free software crusade.

In the early 1980s, Sussman began collaborating with his colleague Harold Abelson on an introductory computer science course based on the idea that the logic and methods of computer programming could be applied to any formal field. It was a long-term partnership that led to an entirely new way of looking at physical systems, including the basic biological building blocks of life. Sussman and Abelson served together on the Free Software

Foundation board, but Abelson took things one step further when, in 2001, he joined forces with Internet activist Larry Lessig to found Creative Commons, a group advocating for the expansion of intellectual property rights. Creative Commons licenses allow creators of otherwise-protected work to specify exactly how they want to share their work, which rights they want to maintain, and the extent to which they wish to allow others to incorporate licensed material into new works.

Abelson was cochair of MIT's Council on Educational Technology (CET) in 1999 when Provost Robert Brown asked the group to consider ways in which digital technology might change the face of universities. Brown and MIT president Vest had been watching while Columbia mounted the ambitious, for-profit Fathom Project for online education and knew that other leading institutions were also investing in the future. MIT, Brown explained to the CET, needed to be thinking bigger. Vest had become convinced that MIT had not found its place in the online world and the Internet would soon have a major impact on the university. The CET dismissed the idea of using the Internet to generate a new revenue stream for the university, but there was a strong feeling that since the MIT classroom was known for the quality of both instructional faculty and course content, opening a window into the MIT classroom would allow people around the world to see for themselves what MIT was really like. The committee recommended that certain course materials, including lectures, notes, and exams, be made available to anyone for free. Abelson was at the forefront of an international movement aimed at open access to intellectual property, and both he and Sussman had thought deeply about pedagogical problems. That was a rare combination. The CET had one important reservation: there should be no traditional, credit-bearing courses involved. The committee was clearly uneasy about offering free access to regular courses, fearing it would dilute the brand.

Vest was excited. He explained to me at the time how making courseware readily available to anyone reset the bar for higher education globally. "Information should be available to everyone," he said. "That's what the lectures and notes are." Figuring out how to share information was what Vest considered the revolutionary idea in what he had started calling the OCW project. But open access, open software, and open architecture were already part of the MIT culture. Creative Commons would solve most of the licensing problems: anyone would be free to use, modify, and build on MIT courseware provided that they attributed the work to MIT and agreed not to use it for commercial purposes.

MIT had credibility in the world of open Web access. The World Wide Web was the foundation of an open architecture, and the OCW plan was to use the communal nature of media sharing on the Web as its information backbone. Not coincidentally, MIT was the host institution for the World Wide Web Consortium, whose mission it was to define the open and free technologies that would keep the Web from becoming a proprietary product for any one company (or country). Open access for educational content presented some new technical challenges. For example, it was not obvious how to distribute OCW video because the first-generation video-coding algorithms were proprietary. That problem became less important as YouTube became a ubiquitous—and open—tool for user-generated video distribution.

There was still the issue of how to fund an initiative that—from its inception—would involve expenses but no offsetting revenue. Vest started making calls on technology companies and philanthropic foundations. He visited me at Hewlett-Packard—where Abelson was also employed as a consultant—and others in Silicon Valley. I had just shipped a truckload of Hewlett-Packard servers to Egypt at the request of MIT professor Mike Hawley for the new digital Library of Alexandria. Vest's project also interested me. He made the rounds of foundations that were focused on higher education. One of those was the Andrew W. Mellon Foundation, whose president, William G. Bowen, was a noted economist and former president of Princeton University. Bowen had been interested in the impact that digital technology would have on higher education. He also liked the idea of online education, yet was deeply suspicious of attempts to turn online education into a moneymaking venture for Élite universities.

"Bowen was intrigued," Vest recalled, but he thought the interest was lukewarm. "What would really be interesting," Vest said, relating a later conversation with Bowen, "is putting the entire Institute on OCW." Bowen was suggesting exactly what the CET had recommended against: diluting the MIT brand by making its entire course catalog—all eighteen hundred courses—available online for free. Vest knew the risks, but he managed to convince Brown and the university leadership of the central value proposition for OCW: the value of an MIT education is not in the information transmitted during a semester but rather in the experience of interacting with MIT faculty and students, participating in the unique intellectual life of MIT's Cambridge community, and establishing lifelong networks of friends, colleagues, mentors, and collaborators. It was the deciding factor for Bowen along with William and Flora Hewlett Foundation president Paul Brest. Each foundation put up $5.5 million to fund OCW's start-up phase. The $11 million grant would eventually grow to more than $15 million.

Apple's iTunes U and other content platforms soon enabled other universities to make their courseware available without the massive investment that MIT had been able to secure. Apple Computer was not a company that easily opened its technology, but that was the price of admission for the new open-courseware movement. Apple reviewed each new proposal for an iTunes U site carefully to make sure that courses were of high quality and represented the actual university course catalog. Once that review was complete, Apple made authoring tools available at no cost to the universities. By 2010, when iTunes U was at the height of its popularity, it was a portal into 350,000 different offerings from over 800 universities. By 2012, there had been over a billion downloads of iTunes U lectures. Unlike OCW, however, iTunes U was a clearinghouse. In addition to MIT, Stanford, and Oxford, iTunes U hosted courses from community colleges, trade schools, and distance education programs. Most important, it fit with the ethos of Apple Computer under Steve Jobs: provide the simplest, most compelling user experience to the maximum number of users.

Yet for all the success of the Open University, OCW, and iTunes U, courses were still like a series of TED Talks. They were Chautauqua performances. Most consisted of lectures captured on video—sometimes by literally pointing a camera at the front of a classroom—without the possibility of interacting with instructors. There were some specialized certificates in areas like nursing or special education, but the vast majority of these open courses carried no credit, did not constitute a curriculum, and did not lead to a degree. It was only a matter of months before technology enhanced the Chautauqua. Interaction was destined to allow the replacement of online lectures in which information was broadcast in one direction only—from the speaker to an audience—with something else entirely.

Interaction and Achievement

There is a persistent belief among educators that personal interaction between teachers and students has a strong influence on learning outcomes. What happens in the classroom has an enormous influence on learning, so it is not an unreasonable belief. But the lack of personal interaction in online courses has been used like a cudgel to beat down the suggestion that online instruction can be effective. "Cold and impersonal" is how online instruction is described by skeptics. Other critics claim that the "passive nature of watching a video" is no match for the excitement and engagement of a face-to-face encounter with a great teacher. If that were true, then there would be little point in going beyond simple lecture capture as a tool for online education. Perhaps the OCW will put high-quality materials in the hands of great teachers, but without a human teacher (the argument goes) it will have little effect—or it will have an overall negative effect because it will be used as an excuse to pull human teachers out of the classroom. "Look at our test scores in reading, math, and science," said one respondent to the question of the cost of replacing personal interactions with technology. "Our children spend more time strengthening their thumbs than learning the skills to be competitive on the world stage."[12]

Criticisms like these fall away on closer examination. In fact, the available data support exactly the opposite conclusion. There are many things that matter in education, but even among those things that matter, some affect student achievement—the demonstrated mastery of concepts and skills—and some that while crucial for learning, have little bearing on what students achieve.

Personal immediacy is one of the factors that affects learning. It represents "distance" between instructor and student. Its effects can be observed, for example, when students are asked to rate feeling or emotions related to a classroom experience. Students tend to feel better about instructors who remember their names or recall previous encounters. Instructors who are never available for one-on-one meetings are invariably rated less effective than ones who acknowledge engagement by providing cues like listening or responding that increase a student's enthusiasm for learning. Immediacy is one of the things that people mean when they talk about the impact of face-to-face instruction on learning, and it is one of the things said to be sacrificed in online instruction.

There is overwhelming evidence that immediacy matters. It affects a student's attitude toward both a teacher and a course.[13] It reinforces positive learning experiences. The effect of immediacy is so strong that it is readily identifiable in almost any classroom setting. On the other hand, immediacy has almost no noticeable effect on achievement. In other words, experiments designed to determine whether or not immediacy changed what students actually learn and how well they do so show that the effects are negligible. Education researcher John Hattie characterized the situation in more dramatic fashion: the impact of teacher immediacy is so low that, compared to other statistical variables, an observer would be more likely to notice a height variation of 1 percent among students than variation in student achievement due to teacher immediacy.[14]

Similar results are found for other aspects of face-to-face instruction that skeptics find lacking in the online world. Mentoring, for example, is based on the idea that supportive relationships with older people are important for personal and intellectual growth—an environment that would be difficult to achieve online.[15] Mentoring does indeed have some positive effect on student attitudes, but it also has almost none on achievement.[16]

What does have an effect is feedback. The effect of feedback is stronger than almost any other single factor on student achievement. It is easy to confuse immediacy and mentorship with feedback.

The mistake I was making was seeing feedback as something teachers provided to students.... It was only when I discovered that feedback was most powerful when it goes from student to the teacher that I started to understand it better.[17]

This effect is so strong that it improves achievement in almost every conceivable situation. Almost as strong is the effect of testing that is spaced out appropriately over time as opposed to a single, cumulative test. In fact, the frequency of testing alone accounts for most of the variation in learning outcomes, and when the outcomes of frequent tests are used by teachers to change what they do in the classroom the effects are the most dramatic. These *formative evaluations* are effective across nearly every student population and instructional style. How feedback is presented to teachers seems to matter as well. Simply recording data has less effect, say, than visually graphing it.

Why is research like this important? Because unlike traditional classrooms, technology-enhanced learning makes it more likely that feedback and formative evaluations along with a dozen other techniques that are known to have a major effect on achievement will be carried out. Personal immediacy may matter in a small classroom, but modern classrooms are not small, and the sheer effects of size are bound to counterbalance whatever small advantage comes from immediacy.

Carl Wieman, the 2001 Nobel Prize winner in physics, began thinking about these problems when, as a young assistant professor, he noticed that students were not reacting as he expected to his "brilliantly clear and clever explanations." Most of his students simply did not get the material: "For many years this failure of students to learn from my explanations remained a frustrating puzzle to me, as I think it is for many diligent faculty members."[18]

Because of experiences like this, Wieman started to consider how to approach teaching like a science. That meant applying the methods that have made scientific advancement possible to teaching itself, basing teaching pedagogy on cognitive psychology and educational research.

Take, for example, the question of whether individual attention in the classroom can be achieved without individual interaction between a teacher and student. Wieman and Louis Deslauriers, a postdoctoral fellow at the Science Education Initiative at the University of British Columbia, measured the achievement of physics students in a large class when the traditional lecture format was replaced with simple technology: an electronic clicker that made it easy for students to signal interactively. Students were guided through activities that had been shown in previous studies to enhance achievement. Students, for example, were divided into small groups that had to reach a consensus in solving complex problems. The clickers were used to provide *student-to-teacher* feedback. Students in the interactive format scored nearly twice as well on standardized tests as the students in a traditional lecture. Clickers are primitive though effective tools for interaction. Web-based courses allows for much more sophisticated methods.

The Power of Peer

In late summer 2010, a scientist at Hewlett-Packard's Indian research laboratory in Bangalore announced on the Internet that he had solved a long-open mathematical problem:

Dear Fellow Researchers,

I am pleased to announce [a description of the problem followed] which is attached in 10pt and 12pt fonts.... Comments and suggestions for improvements to the paper are highly welcomed.

It was not just any old mathematical problem that the Hewlett-Packard researcher had claimed to solve. It was a *Millennium Prize Problem*, one of seven problems that the Clay Mathematics Institute in Cambridge, Massachusetts, had identified at the start of the new millennium as having historical significances should they be solved. A mathematician solving one of these problems would receive a $1 million prize. In keeping with standard scientific practice, the researcher's paper was being circulated to a small group of colleagues before submission to a mathematical journal. There an editor would review it for appropriateness before assigning it to somewhere between three and ten reviewers, chosen from a catalog of mathematicians—peers—who were known to be experts in the field, and whose background and reputations suggested that they could offer detailed and unbiased assessments of the paper's correctness.

This is how science works. Peer reviewers have the usual professional and personal conflicts and complex motivations as everyone else. Some of the reviewers might be jealous, wishing that they had found the solution first. Some might have thought that the author did not deserve the $1 million.

Still others might have had personal or professional grudges that colored their opinion of the author or their employer. It rarely matters. If a reviewer recommends the rejection of a paper, there must be specific reasoning to back up the recommendation. By the same token, a recommendation to publish a paper has to convince the editor that the paper is correct, original, and worthy of publication. Superficial, glowing comments are summarily discarded. Some articles are rejected after this first round of reviews, but the most common outcome of this elaborate process is a set of questions that the editor relays to the author. The author is supposed to respond by fixing, explaining, or revising some aspect of the write-up. This continues until the editor senses that there is a consensus among the reviewers. The same method is applied to tens of thousands of scientific articles submitted annually for publication around the world. It is a spectacularly successful method that goes awry so rarely that it is front-page news when it does. One drawback to peer-reviewing scientific articles is that it is time-consuming, so when the "Dear Fellow Researchers" email hit a few dozen mailboxes on August 7, 2010, everyone expected that it would be months—perhaps years—before the world would know whether the paper was correct. What actually occurred was a complete surprise.

My colleague Richard Lipton, who a few years before had begun a rather technical blog called Gödel's Lost Letter (or simply GLL), was one of those who received the email. Lipton briefly looked the paper over. "At first glance it is a long, well written paper by a serious researcher," he wrote in GLL.[19] "My first thought is who knows—perhaps this is the solution we have all been waiting for." It was a somewhat-chatty posting of a newsworthy event. "But first there is the small issue of correctness. Is his paper correct?" Lipton and his blog are unlikely Web stars. The GLL postings are frequently long and complex, filled with notation and argumentation that makes sense to professional mathematicians but few others. Nevertheless, GLL has an unexpectedly large and loyal following. There are many postings that attract upward of ten thousand readers, and the discussions are often carried out over several weeks with dozens of comments. So when Lipton wrote, "I suggest you look at his paper to see his own summary … and of course the details of his proof," he thought he was inviting perhaps several hundred dedicated followers to look at the paper. He even provided a short summary of the key ideas so that a nonspecialist would have an easier time following along.

Something quite different happened. A small army of math bloggers began pointing toward GLL. Hundreds of comments poured in. One person said,

Note that the n-th digit of pi can be calculated in $C*n^3*\log(n)^3$ time.

Another person asked,

Does the paper seem to imply anything stronger?

Lipton's coblogger and State University of New York professor Ken Regan wrote,

Having seen this only since 5:30 this (Sunday) afternoon, here's my attempt at a somewhat more fleshed-out description of the proof strategy, still at a very high (and vague) level.

When someone offered the comment, "There is one thing which really surprised me: Page 44 (so 47 of the pdf …) he gives 'succ' relation," Regan quickly responded,

I think you mean Page 44 of an earlier 63-page version of the paper (with more condensed lines) which corresponds to page 67, not 47, of the present 102 –page version.

Over the next two weeks, a hundred thousand reviewers visited GLL over a million times. Within two days after the first posting, Lipton had organized a worldwide project called the "Group" to work with the author:

The Group has decided for now to let things go along in the current ad hoc fashion. If and when [the author] wants help, we are prepared to help in any way that we can.

By August 12, Lipton had published an update titled "Fatal Flaws?" Meanwhile, the author was busily trying to fix problems with the paper, hoping to "resolve the issues raised about the finite model theory portion of the proof." Within a month, the excitement faded. The author still claimed to be working on fixing the article, but there was a consensus among the thousands of reviewers that the result would not withstand further reviews. Of the episode, Lipton recalls, "There was this real electric feeling. Here was a possible breakthrough and people put time and effort in a selfless manner to try and resolve whether the paper was correct or not, including some who were famous, some who were professional mathematicians and some who just wanted to try and help." A process that might have taken years had been shortened to just a few days by the power of a crowd. Lipton sees "a future for this type of online work," for accelerating the pace of scientific discovery, yet there is a larger lesson to be drawn.

Crowd-powered peer reviews are effective at more than uncovering errors in scientific papers. They are a powerful approach to many different kinds of assessment. Computer systems are often reviewed to determine whether their security measures are vulnerable to attack. A team of four or five reviewers has a 20 percent chance of finding those vulnerabilities, and doubling the number of reviewers only raises that likelihood to 50 percent. But as more and more reviewers are added—that is, as the reviewers begin to resemble a crowd—something interesting happens. Fifteen reviewers raises the probability of finding a flaw to around 80 percent, and by the time there are twenty-five or more reviewers all engaged on the same task it is nearly certain that security flaws, if they exist, will be uncovered.[20]

One prominent drawback of large online courses is that hand-grading homework and exams is prohibitively expensive. Yet online courses have an abundance of peers to act as potential reviewers. The question is whether peer assessments, like the crowd-powered reviews of GLL or security reviews of computer systems—can be used in place of instructor's hand grading their assignments in online courses. The answer seems to be yes; just as crowd-powered reviews of scientific research actually improve the process, peer assessment probably improves on human grading in a wide variety of settings, ranging from engineering design to writing.[21] The demographics of a peer community vary wildly from serious experts to unskilled novices, but the number of evaluators has a critical effect on the usefulness of the outcome. Even for tasks that involve reading and understanding large amounts of text, nonexperts can perform as well or better than expert counterparts.[22]

Peer assessment is only one aspect of technology-mediated learning. MOOCs like those offered through Coursera and edX encourage students to use an associated online group to pose and answer questions, lead discussions, and network with other students. When Lipton invited online comments in GLL, the Group quickly formed to facilitate and lead the rest of the reviewers. The same thing happens in the discussion forum of an online course. A forum might consist of a handful of self-appointed leaders and a much larger number of more passive participants, but before too long a hierarchy of learners begins to emerge. At the top of that hierarchy are those who have the ability to become *coteachers*.

A company called OfficeHours set out to recruit such groups in a directed fashion. OfficeHours staff members were given the opportunity to recruit the highest-performing students from an advanced mathematics MOOC to act as "teaching assistants" the next time the course was offered. No compensation was offered, and although they were given strict quality guidelines to follow, the teaching assistants were given no other rewards for volunteering. Sixty-five former students agreed to participate, including seven PhDs, a software engineer from Google, a researcher at the Central Bank of Argentina, an environmental scientist in China, a curator of the Museum of Mathematics in New York, several professors of mathematics and engineering, a Wall Street investment analyst, and a professional ornithologist. OfficeHours cofounder Jeff Levy estimates that "this is a talent pool of TAs that you will not find on-campus at any university in the world."

The emergence of groups of peer tutors is more than an artifact of Internet technology. It is closely related to observed learning achievement levels. In effect, enabling groups of peers to serve as coteachers actually *improves* learning, and the effect is not incidental to learning. As John Hattie noticed after analyzing 767 different studies involving 2,676 students, "The overall effect is quite powerful."[23] Arranging the peer-tutoring group so it contains a range of ages has the most dramatic impact on learning. The effects are quite different from simply increasing the number of designated teachers. Adult tutors raised overall achievement levels only slightly, and if there is no age or authority stratification among the peers, the results are not much better. But a group of peer tutors who span several age groups improves the overall performance of the group by 50 percent. The learning effects also seem to be spread among all ages and ability levels. The impact on the tutors is as strong as on those who are tutored. Student control of the peer-tutoring process—of the kind that is commonly found in MOOCs—is consistently more effective than tutoring that is under the control of an instructor.

There are emerging technologies that make use of these results. NovoEd, another Stanford University spin-off, is based on the power of peer. Like its competitors, NovoEd offers familiar short video format courses, but also makes it easy to "create a connected, engaged and collaborative learning experience for students at web scale," adding tools like reputation management and calibrated peer review to the peer networks.[24]

Personalized Learning and the Power of Data

Nell sat in the corner, opened the book and started to read. She did not know all of the words but she knew a lot of them and when she got tired the book would help her sound out the words or even read the whole story to her, or tell it to her with moving pictures.

—Neal Stephenson, *The Diamond Age*

By far the largest influence on learning is formative assessment. When instructors can observe students directly and modify their approaches, they can systematically improve the performance of an entire class by nearly two standard deviations. In fact, formative assessment can be used to achieve the Bloom two sigma effect, but most studies of formative assessment were conducted a decade or more ago—well before the availability of new technology capable of *personalizing learning*.

Neal Stephenson's dystopian novel *The Diamond Age* is often mentioned by people who believe we are rapidly approaching a tipping point in personalized learning. "*The Diamond Age* had a big influence on me," says Arizona State University president Crow, "mainly because I realized that the *Primer* is an individualized learning device." The *Primer* that Crow refers to is the *Young Lady's Illustrated Primer*—one of the novel's important plot elements. It creates a highly personalized learning experience for its owner. Crow thinks that there are things that can be done right now to move education in that direction. "We see ourselves as that kind of platform," he says, "an aggregator." Universities like Arizona State that admit capable students from backgrounds that make learning difficult have long struggled with what many see as the central problem of mass education. Of the top fifty factors that influence student achievement, the individual circumstances of income, status, family, and environment are currently off-limits to a classroom teacher.[25] Crow wants to work on what he thinks of as "all three dimensions" at the same time. "The exciting thing is that we may finally be able to attack unfairness in the system by overcoming the limits of culture and individual circumstance." It is technology that Crow sees empowering the platforms, "but the effects would be incredible," he predicts. "Can we take kids from any background that have a certain capability and 'net out' their individual circumstance?"

Massification—a model of higher education in which students are grouped by age into cohorts that move in lockstep through from one class to the next—is the opposite of personalization, yet it is the educational model that has enabled institutions to accommodate rapid increases in student enrollments over the last fifty years. Mass education is a kind of factory.[26] Michael Horn, who cofounded the Clayton Christensen Institute for Disruptive Innovation, says that even as a factory, it does not make much sense. "Just imagine," he explains, "that at every point along the assembly line, you conduct a quality control test, but instead of correcting defects, you just pass them along to the next point." That is the only way that massification scales to the numbers of students pouring into the world's higher education institutions. "A grade of C is a passing grade," Horn points out, "but a C means you did not master a concept that is needed for the next course." Bloom's ML model is fundamentally incompatible with the educational version of a factory assembly line, because students have to achieve mastery before attempting to learn the next concept.

In personalized education, there are many possible outcomes of a learning event—so many possible outcomes that *Diamond Age* technology is needed to keep track of it all.

Learning Analytics

When it comes to personalization, technology-mediated learning has one overwhelming advantage. It is possible to capture everything that a student says or does, and relate that information to both the outcome for that particular student and also the outcome for every other student who is trying to learn the same concept. For instance, a student who is viewing short-format digital videos instead of physical lectures leaves behind traces of learning activities. The amount of dedicated time (the time on task) devoted to viewing lectures is easily recorded, as are the number of times the video is repeated, the time between viewings, and biometric or cognitive indicators like stress, eye movements, keyboard and mouse clicks, and delays between successive viewings. Quizzes can be tailored to personalized student profiles and administered as many times as needed. Pretesting students is no more expensive than posttesting, and because it is more effective to space tests of concepts out over time rather than combine many concepts into a single assessment, test results can be related to the amount of delay between lectures and assessments.

In one study researchers from Carnegie Mellon University used these parameters to group students based on the number of hints they requested from an automated tutoring system, the number of errors made, the time before a first hint was requested, the number of errors made before the first hint was requested, and the time taken to exhaust all available hints.[27] These groups or *clusters* reveal how students learn. One cluster, for example, groups members who request a moderate number of hints and make a moderate number of errors. A second cluster contains students who are not shy about using the tutor's resources. They make errors but also request many hints. One group is called "Confident." They request few hints and make few errors. "Stubborn" students, on the other hand, fail to make use of the tutor's resources, and although they may perform adequately, they do not request help from the tutor when they make mistakes. There are no simple calculations that predict the kind of learning approach that an individual student will adopt. The more students there are, however, the more these groups can be used to predict an individual student's learning strategy. They can also be used to identify individual cognitive traits. One of these traits might be the condition of cognitive overload, which can be addressed by adjusting the timing of interactions. These are students who fall into clusters in which many hints are requested early in problem-solving situations. Being able to predict cognitive overload would be a way to adapt to the needs of an individual student. But large amounts of data are required in order to make predictions like that.

Every consumer who uses online banking or a grocery store loyalty card knows the effect that large of amounts of data have on a merchant's ability to predict behavior. The more data there are, the more exact the predictions are. In some applications like online banking, algorithms are so sophisticated that banks can predict when an individual account holder is considering changing banks. Consumers who regularly use online stores like Amazon.com are often surprised at the accuracy of recommendations for related projects or services. Imagine how much more accurate predictions might be if there were a thousand or million times more data available to tune the mathematical models. Educational technology generates a hundred million times more data than other e-commerce technology. Users of online consumer applications seldom remain online for more than a few seconds or minutes (as long as it takes to swipe a loyalty card, pay a bill, or complete a purchase). Educational applications are in a completely different category. Students spend many minutes—sometimes hours—on a task and frequently return to the same task. Furthermore, students are active when they are online, and each basic online action is composed of mouse movements and clicks, keystrokes, and latency periods of varying length. The multiplicative effects are large. The amount of data available for educational personalization is several orders of magnitude larger than almost every other online application. Researchers have a ridiculously simple way of talking about such extreme amounts of data and the accuracy of the predictions they enable: they call them simply *big data*.

Arizona State University has organized this kind of big data into a warehouse. Data warehouses are often used in commercial applications because their contents can be *mined* to uncover statistical patterns that would not be noticeable on a smaller scale—patterns that are predictive of future behavior. In 2008, a former executive at Kaplan, Inc., the for-profit education and testing services provider, analyzed learning data to prove that online tests administered by the Educational Testing Service were vulnerable to cheating. Along the way, he realized that the amount of educational data available was growing much more quickly than had been previously imagined. Jose Ferreira had a unique background for an entrepreneur in education. He had a Harvard MBA, and had worked as a derivative trader on Wall Street and political strategist for John Kerry's presidential campaign. When he founded Knewton, he knew that big data would become an important part of online education. If big data could be used to predict when and where an individual student would have trouble mastering a concept, that information could be fed back to instructors in time for them to *adapt*, thereby channeling time and resources to serve the needs of individual learners. It was an ideal application of what educators had known for years about formative feedback and ML.

Knewton found a willing partner at Arizona State. The university was already offering blended versions of many of its courses, in which technology and in-class interaction were combined in a single course. Arizona State was not an adopter of MOOCs, but there was an adequate supply of short-format videos for science and math courses, and Crow had set up an educational innovation center to experiment with blended learning. Knewton had hired some of the same analysts that Ferreira had worked with at Kaplan to analyze online exams—people who knew how to create graphic representations of the concepts for certain subjects that should be mastered before moving on to a new topic. These maps of "atomic concepts" could be used to determine how well students were progressing through material based on the successful completion of tasks versus the amount of time they were spending in class.

At Arizona State University, Knewton's methods were first applied with the aim of implementing ML for developmental math students. These students' readiness to move on to college-level math courses was currently being assessed as if they were all moving forward in unison. The Arizona State University–Knewton Math Readiness Project created atomic concept hierarchies so that many different personal learning paths were possible. Instructors for the first time had the ability to adapt in real time to how students were performing. The results were evident immediately. After two semesters and two thousand students, withdrawal rates dropped from 16 to 7 percent, pass rates rose from 64 to 75 percent, and nearly half the adaptive learning students finished four or more weeks early.

The kind of big data analysis carried out by Knewton is sometimes called *learning analytics*. Knewton is just one of a growing number of companies that has started to develop interfaces with learning management systems, online platforms, and academic back-office systems. Others have engaged in public discussions of similar plans, and more traditional technology suppliers have clear commercial interests in the development of learning analytics tools based on big data approaches that aggregate massive amounts of shareable, individualized learning records in a data analysis pipeline.

Georgia State University (GSU) vice president Timothy Renick had been carefully following ASU's experiments with Knewton. A large urban university, GSU had in recent years seen the number of poor students rise by over twenty-five percentage points. That demographic shift matched almost exactly the rise in minorities in GSU's student body. These were students who often stumbled in their first college courses and never recovered. He knew that first-year problems led to low graduation rates. Eighty percent of the GSU political science majors who earned an A in freshman comparative politics graduated with degrees in political science. The graduation rate dropped to 25 percent for C students, and only 6 percent for students receiving a D or F. Renick reasoned that, if learning analytics could be used to track student progress, perhaps with enough data it would be possible to predict when students were veering off track. Prediction would mean earlier intervention, and the earlier the problems were identified the better the chances were of either matching students to more suitable majors or identifying additional resources that would improve their chances of success.

Renick set out to gather ten years of student data and nearly 2.4 million grades from university information systems and to build a system that would track over seven hundred alerts for student risk factors. Predictive analytics was a rarity in higher education, but nightly feeds from academic systems and daily alerts to advisors gave Renick some assurance that his models could predict student success in individual majors and courses. He watched, first as the number of student visits to the university advising center jumped to over 42,000, then as the first-term retention rate began to creep up from 83 percent in 2010 to almost 90 percent in 2013. Just as important, minority students began zeroing in on majors much more quickly. In 2010, African American STEM majors had accumulated 151 credit hours by the time they graduated, which was almost two semesters more than required for graduation. By the end of 2013, students were averaging 140 credit hours, a direct effect of predictive analytics that directed students toward the most suitable majors earlier in their studies.

GSU tools were developed in conjunction with a Washington, DC, education research organization called the Education Advisory Board (EAB). Knowing that the more data there is to mine, the more powerful predictive analytics engines become, EAB encouraged collaborative sharing among institutions, but sharing student data raised new problems. For instance, Renick had wisely not included race or other demographic information in his risk factors, but with widespread data sharing there was no guarantee that others would not be able to reconstruct such profiles in the future—even if that was not intended.

The shareability of student data is a key element of big data in education because the mathematical approaches that can be usefully applied become more powerful when many analytic tools can be brought to bear on data warehouses that have well-defined, open interfaces. In effect, learning analytics enables the global sharing of private data. Sharing at this scale may involve storing student data in large shared data centers— "in the cloud" is how information technology professionals describe it—but there are also institutional approaches in which hundreds of millions of transactions are stored in local data centers, and made available to administrators, professors, academic staff, government agencies, families, and institutional researchers. Candace Thille, who led learning analytics at Carnegie Mellon University's Open Learning Initiative before moving to Stanford's Graduate School of Education, calls it nano-level data and has begun to think about how it might be shared, at first, between research centers, but ultimately between learning environments like classrooms and MOOCs: "Providing meaningful, actionable information to all stakeholders in the education system will require building agreements on the technical processes for sharing data that are collected across multiple levels and multiple systems."[28]

Inevitably, individual learning records will be combined with external data sources such as location data, social media, financial records, and electronic health records. It is currently beyond the state of the art to share such data while simultaneously limiting the disclosure of private data to unauthorized individuals and ensuring data utility.[29] The combination of personal information with large external data sets can be used to create "new facts" that had not been adequately anticipated by system designers.

Privacy threats in this kind of environment are still emerging, but even casual observers have already identified major vulnerabilities that would compromise privacy.[30] Cloud storage and other data-warehousing methods incentivize both the creation of more data and longer retention time for it. Both trends increase the opportunities for compromising privacy. There are no currently practical approaches to ensuring the accuracy or consistency of stored data.

Marching at a Different Rate

In virtually every known category of learning, technology appears to be driving improvements in learning achievement. As one university president said to me, "Human beings are not going to get much better at what they do in the classroom, but technology seems to be marching at a different rate." In fact, even modest improvements in technology can have a big impact on learning because those improvements occur one on top of another, every few months. But, even if technology successfully enhances student achievement, the university workforce is not necessarily designed to accommodate it. Universities are designed so that there are many professors teaching relatively few students—indeed, that's one of the ways that a university's reputation is established. What happens when even better results for even more students can be achieved by hiring *fewer* professors?

5 Internet Scale

Higher education suffers from a cost disease—an incessant rise in costs at about double the rate of inflation—because education has been extraordinarily resistant to the kind of productivity increases that technology brings.[1] Family incomes have been flat or declining for a decade or more, and there are few economists who predict that they will begin rising in the near future. The result is a steadily growing college affordability gap that acts as a wedge driven between those who can afford a college education and those who cannot. I will explain what causes this gloomy gap in part II, but regardless of why it arises, inequality makes the current system of higher education unsustainable.

All paths to sustainability require increased productivity on the part of colleges and universities. It does not matter whether the Revolution succeeds or fails; the number of professors that it takes to educate college students is too high. Either the number of students must decline—an unlikely prospect since there are more students entering the college pool than ever before—or the productivity of classroom teachers must be substantially improved. Productivity can be forcibly improved by simply slashing the number of professors, leaving institutions to sort out the consequences for educational quality. A 50 percent cut in spending would do the job, but the result would be chaos. On the other hand, productivity can be improved by making structural changes—putting productivity-enhancing tools in the hands of classroom instructors and advisers either improve teaching at lower cost or make much more efficient use of a student's time on campus. Josh Jarrett, former head of higher education innovation programs at the Bill and Melinda Gates Foundation, quantified this challenge for me: "Obtain 120 percent of the quality at 80 percent of the cost." No amount of spending cuts achieves this goal. It can only be achieved by changing the scale at which quality instruction is carried out or by reducing student demand on scarce resources. In chapter 4, I described how Georgia State University used a predictive analytics model to reduce the number of credit hours that students have to earn before graduation. Other approaches change scale by expanding the number of students that an individual professor can teach. Still other approaches reduce the amount of remedial time that students need by insuring consistency of learning outcomes. But whatever happens, enhanced productivity means that the number of professors will decline. How that decline takes place is a matter of scale.

There have been calls to reform higher education in decades past, and technology has often been at the heart of those reforms. It is unfair to say that technology has always failed, but educators have learned to be skeptical of marketing claims. "Overhyped" is what some have said of the Magic Year, typically citing "setback after setback," but failing to mention success after success.[2] The setbacks are often as not the same two or three examples—a failed San Jose State University experiment, the importance of which is amplified in the retelling, or a highly visible professor who, overcome with guilt, decides to chuck it all and return to the comfort of a lecture hall.

On the other hand, hype is not always a bad thing. It generates investment and spurs further innovation, for example. Those innovations are focused squarely on productivity, and if they are successful, it will be because they have taken advantage of scale. There may be great uncertainty about exactly which technologies will succeed, but there is no uncertainty about how students will approach college. They will use Web browsers and Internet tools. Higher education has become an Internet business, and to understand how to change the scale at which quality instruction is carried out, you have to understand the idea of Internet scale.

Dismal Failure

Much as Benjamin Bloom lamented that society could not bear the cost of a two sigma improvement in learning, the landscape of educational reform is littered with a host of ideas that are untried and unimplemented because everyone seems to know "You can't do that!" Technology should be used to remove "You can't," but it has seldom worked that way in education.

Every few years, a new technology is launched with great fanfare as an educational breakthrough. A new wave of educational reform brings a new cohort of inventors, entrepreneurs, and earnest tinkerers who either see a buck to be made in an underserved marketplace or believe that a better mousetrap is just around the corner. Virtually all these innovations are ill-fated. Many fail a fundamental test for educational technology: they do not directly influence learning. But others do have a direct impact on classroom practice. They may generate excitement and trigger more investment, but they are eventually cast aside, not because they are uninteresting or uninspiring, but because they lack another basic ingredient. They do not make possible something valuable that could not be achieved without them.

The connection between media and educational technology has always seemed compelling. Thomas Edison predicted that motion pictures would revolutionize teaching. Radio and television broadcasting was the next logical step, but despite the success of distance education, these are technologies that have had little measurable impact on classroom learning. Nevertheless, the idea that machines could improve human learning was a tantalizing prospect. The appearance of computer technology gave advocates of machine-based learning a name for such an approach: *programmed learning*.

Inspired in part by behavioral psychologist B. F. Skinner's idea that learning could be reduced to small, self-paced, programmed steps, the advocates of programmed learning seemed to have hit on a better way of aligning what happens in the classroom with how the brain actually learns. The problem was that except for relatively unsophisticated subjects, programmed learning required special workbooks and other materials along with nearly constant grading of tests. It was complex and costly to administer, but perhaps this was a teaching method in which automation might help manage complexity. Computer manufacturers jumped on the opportunity. Skinner thought that programmed instruction offered through machines would enable students to learn at twice the rate as traditional classroom methods. Despite a rush of new companies and investment capital to the educational technology market, the number of programmed learning titles peaked at about seven hundred in the mid-1980s and then fell dramatically over the next five years. Others, like the ambitious PLATO project, which was launched at the University of Illinois in the 1960s, combined the most advanced technology of the day with programmed learning to replace human teachers with computer-based instruction.[3]

A billion dollars went into PLATO's networking, computing, and display technologies and into the development of PLATO courseware. There were some early promising signs, but then as project costs began to grow it was clear that PLATO would need more than the bootstrapped business plans of university laboratories to be successful. It would need professional product management. What began as a university research project was transferred in the 1970s to the now-defunct Control Data Corporation (CDC), whose CEO William Norris was convinced that half the company's revenue would come from educational services based on PLATO courseware hosted on CDC supercomputers. Unfortunately, encouraging results from university prototypes do not always lead to business success. Independent studies failed to find any improvement in learning due to PLATO. Even more important, CDC could only make a profit on PLATO courses by charging $50 per hour per student, which was many times the cost of human instruction. Furthermore, each student required both a computer terminal and access to a CDC data center to use the system at all, which meant that there were no economies of scale for schools that wanted to adopt the technology. By 1986 CDC left the education market—and PLATO with it. Although elements of PLATO were eventually translated for use on personal computers, the damage had been done and the technology never reemerged as a serious possibility for computer-aided instruction.

PLATO's failure aside, investments in computers in the classroom and universal Internet access have been cornerstones of educational technology policy since the late 1980s, but the results have been dismal.[4] Throughout the 1960s and 1970s, computers in the classroom were thought to be the next great educational idea. The failure of massive technology spending to alter classroom performance is used to promote the proposition that since overhyped educational innovations have failed to deliver in the past, the next innovation is also bound to fail:

The cycle began with big promises backed by the technology developers' research. In the classroom, however, teachers never really embraced the new tools, and no significant academic improvement occurred. This provoked consistent responses: the problem was money, spokespeople argued, or teacher resistance, or the paralyzing school bureaucracy. Meanwhile, few people questioned the technology advocates' claims. As results continued to lag, the blame was finally laid on the machines. Soon schools were sold on the next generation of technology, and the lucrative cycle started all over again.[5]

To underscore the point, critics often argue that since there is no good evidence that computers significantly improve teaching and learning, computers in the classroom must be "over-hyped flim-flam aimed at prioritizing computer and new media skills" over the study of European history, biology, chemistry, and physics, dealing with social problems such as drugs and family breakdown, learning practical job skills, or reading John Steinbeck and Ernest Hemingway.[6] The argument seems to be that where education is concerned, hype alone disqualifies an idea from further serious consideration.

The academic marketplace, which has seen failure after failure, is deeply distrustful of technological innovation:

Today's technology evangels argue that we've learned our lesson from past mistakes. As in each previous round, they say that when our new hot technology—the computer—is compared with yesterday's, today's is better.[7]

It is a problem for early adopters and investors alike because there is no real guide to tell you when the crash that inevitably follows hype will happen. In education, as in most other industries, we are told that a rational stakeholder will steer clear of technologies that radiate this kind of exuberance.

Being wary of hype is a good, safe strategy, but it is one that only makes sense if you don't look too deep, because there are many counterexamples. Apple Computer was launched with the following mission:

Apple is committed to bringing the best personal computing experience to students, educators, creative professionals and consumers around the world through its innovative hardware, software and Internet offerings.

But sometime in the 1990ss, Apple's vision was revised to remove specific mention of education or educators. Some have seen this as a retreat from educational technology on the part of one of the world's most innovative companies, but as Audrey Watters points out, *success* is a better interpretation.[8] Beginning with Macintosh computers, and then iTunes, iPods, and iPad tablets, Apple products have been runaway hits with consumers. But educators and student are consumers also, and they love Apple products. By 2001, Apple laptop computers had captured 26 percent of the education market. By 2010, iPad tablets had become a de facto standard for electronic textbooks, which began eating away at traditional textbook sales, prompting publishers to either partner with Apple or develop online distribution strategies of their own. As early as 2001, Apple CEO Jobs—who had a lifetime interest in applying computer technology to the arts—was publicly explaining how that was going to happen: "Rather than bringing students to the computer, the new way is bringing computers to the students."[9]

Apple's success seems hard to reconcile with the "it's all just hype" dismissal of educational technology. Maybe the key is the way that Apple insinuated its products into daily life. Georgia Tech professor Gregory Abowd's Classroom 2000 was an ambitious experiment in the seamless integration of ubiquitous computing technology into classrooms and learning spaces, but by 2002 there was scant evidence that educators knew what do to with all that computing power. Some years later, Abowd described it to me as a "living laboratory filled with innovative gadgets that unfortunately remains more a dream than a reality." Abowd has applied the same ideas to health care and other fields, so I wanted to know what was different about education: "There was lots of technology, but much of it was in the aid of the presenter of the material and not for the students who were struggling to keep pace with the increased flow of information."

The fact that technologies are hyped, it turns out, has virtually nothing to do with their eventual success. The last classroom innovation to be universally adopted was the blackboard.[10] That was in 1801, yet even the humble blackboard had a rocky road to acceptance.

The Brief History of Hype

There was a lot of hype surrounding the introduction of blackboards. Manufacturers rushed these strange products into the new marketplace, but as late as 1841, there was no agreement about how to use them. The situation was so severe that Josiah F. Bernstein was moved to publish a user's manual:

Although the black board for the primary school is strongly recommended in many works on education, yet none of them furnish examples and illustrations showing in detail the methods of using it. It has been thought that a manual, prepared with reference to this deficiency, would be acceptable to teachers. As such the following pages are offered, believing that they will prove to be an aid in making the black board what it was designed to be—a **luminous** object in the school.[11]

Part of the problem with blackboards was that they were only functional when accompanied by an array of accessories that were not yet readily available but should certainly include "brass holders for the crayon or chalk," and a pointing stick, which "should be a suitable one and used only for this particular purpose."[12] Even more important, just fastening a large writable surface to the wall did nothing to help teachers integrate the new technology into old pedagogical methods: "Instead of confining the youngest scholars to the printed page, it is earnestly recommended to teachers that they frequently take six or eight of them at a time to the black board."[13]

Blackboards obviously survived the hype curve—a proof that such inventions are sometimes useful and necessary. Victory was so complete that later improvements, like erasable whiteboards, write-on projection transparencies, and even Microsoft PowerPoint were readily accepted and soon completely replaced the older technologies.

PLATO promoter Norris was not the last corporate leader to try to ride the hype curve.[14] As late as 2001, John Chambers, CEO of the Internet company Cisco Systems, was proclaiming "e-learning" as the next major killer application,[15] but in reality, most computers-in-the-classroom products have failed. Many critics of the technology revolution that began with the introduction of MOOCs in 2012 have been quick to seize on the parallels.[16] Critics claim, "All this is just hype. The rush to online, open courses is just playing us all for suckers." They ask, "What is different this time?" It's a good question, yet it's also one that is easy to ask, because most innovations fail. So why should this time be different? Despite the hype, blackboards did not fail. Just because things are frequently not different does not rule out the possibility, that this time, things really are different. The deciding factor for blackboards was a realization in the 1840s that they allowed teachers to replace the lockstep progress of a solitary, passive student with group interaction that was variably paced and allowed for immediate teacher feedback. This was so valuable that the technology took off. The 1840s, it so happens, was a good decade for hype.

I can imagine that sometime in the mid- to late 1840s, there was a young investor prowling a back alley outside London's Capel Court stock exchange asking a purveyor of dubious scrip how to honestly make £10,000 in railways. The 1840s marked the end of a technology hype cycle that began with demonstrations of new locomotive technology in which the modern-day equivalent of $2 trillion was pumped into railroads. It is not surprising that the first rail lines connected major centers of commerce. Once those cities were linked, the only opportunities for later entrepreneurs often lay in connecting desolate and economically insignificant outposts. In the end, the hype-fueled railway mania of the 1830s was responsible for 2,148 miles of railway, but most of that capacity had little economic value. The conclusion that most people draw from this story is that the early investors in British railway companies were played for suckers. The reality was somewhat different.

The mania probably started with an announcement in the May 1, 1829, edition of the *Liverpool Mercury* that offered a premium of "£500 (over and above the cost price) for a locomotive engine which shall be a decided improvement on any hitherto constructed." The competition drew enormous interest. Contestants used everything from horses on treadmills—an idea that came to ruin when one of the animals crashed through a wooden floorboard—to more sophisticated lightweight steam engines that could reach uphill speeds of twenty-four miles per hour. It did not hurt the innovators' cause that Queen Victoria declared herself charmed by the winning steam technology.

Business innovation—ticketing, first-class seating, and agreements allowing passengers to change carriers midtrip—was rapid and fueled as much by intense competition as by a chaotic, frenzied stock market in which valuations soared beyond any seeming sense of proportion, causing observers in the middle of the decade to despair, *"The more worthless the article the greater the struggle to attain it."* When the market crashed during the week of October 17, 1847—in no small measure due to crop failure and potato famine—financiers were exposed as swindlers. The Scottish essayist Thomas Carlyle demanded public hanging for the bankers.[17]

The collapse in expectations is not the end of the story. Between 1845 and 1855, an additional nine thousand miles of track were constructed. By 1915, England's rail capacity was twenty-one thousand miles. British railways had entered a golden age. The success of British railways teaches an important lesson.[18] There is a pattern to the cycles that inevitably accompany technological revolutions. Innovation enables technology clusters, some of which transform the way that business is done. Early successes and intense competition give rise to new companies, grossly inflated expectations, and an unregulated free-for-all—all of which lead to a crash. Collapse is followed by sustained build-out during which the allure of glamour is replaced by real value, leading to a golden age that results in more innovation as lives are structured around the new technology.

What really happened to all that investment in the 1830s? Andrew Odlyzko at the University of Minnesota has analyzed the British railway mania example and concluded that the early investments did quite well.[19] According to Odlyzko, a rational investor, who does not know the course of future events, stays away from hyped inventions. But that almost uniformly ignores or misrepresents periods of tumultuous change, like the large investment mania of the 1830s, whose nature does not fit the rational investor pattern. Most people focus on the disaster of the 1840s, yet that ignores what real value was created during the 1830s.

After all the speculative excitement died down, there was a period of about a half-dozen years during which investors kept pumping money into railway construction. This was done in the face of adverse—and occasionally quite adverse—monetary conditions, wide public skepticism, and a market that consistently told them through the years that they were wrong. In actuality, the end result of the wildly speculative exuberance of the 1830s was the *"creation of a productive transportation system that had a deep and positive effect on the economy."* Furthermore, investors saw great returns. An 1841 shareholder in London and South Western Railway who paid a total of £97.50 would have watched the investment double in less than three years, defying most rational forecasts that kept telling the investor that the London and South West Railway venture was a mistake.

British railway mania has been used for years as a template—an illustration of the innovation cycle and dangers of hype—but it is one that leads markets and investors astray because it misrepresents actual patterns. There are many more examples of dead-end ideas that once generated irrational enthusiasm than instances like the British railway mania. There is no shortage of failed ideas that can be used as risk-averse templates for rejecting sales pitches that start out "This time is different!" But that does not mean it is never different. This is a crucial lesson for educational technologists because although the underlying technology changes, the underlying economics does not, and this time is different.

The Scale of the Problem

What makes today different from programmed learning or PLATO? The difference is *scale*, and scale changes everything. As recently as 1997, management icon Peter Drucker—on whose words CEOs and professors alike base entire strategies—was hyping the coming collapse of universities and their replacement by recorded lectures: "Thirty years from now the big university campuses will be relics. Universities won't survive. It's as large a change as when we first got the printed book."[20]

That seems unlikely, but not because Drucker was mistaken about the forces shaping higher education. He was right, for example, that "uncontrollable expenditures, without any visible improvement in either the content or the quality of education, means that the system is rapidly becoming untenable."[21] The cost disease is a long-term trend and, despite much handwringing, large research universities prospered until the onset of the 2008 recession. Drucker died at age ninety-five in 2005 and therefore missed the developments that make this time different.

Higher Education Is an Internet Business

Unlike calls to reform higher education in decades past, there is no uncertainty today about where to meet students: they are online. Highly selective institutions have been at the forefront of Internet-based course delivery and that trend will accelerate, which would mean that an increasingly large number of students from Élite institutions will use the Internet for at least some of their coursework. But this accounts for only a small fraction of all college students. By far the largest number of students worldwide will come from developing countries. In nations with the highest expected student growth, Internet access will dominate, continuing trends that are visible today. Less well known are new studies indicating that even in the United States, access will be the primary factor influencing college choice. Despite initial reports that people who enroll in MOOCs tend not to be the kind of serious students who are likely to successfully complete courses, high-quality Internet delivery will attract a disproportionate share of high-achieving college students.

A 2012 study by Stanford economists Carolyn Hoxby and Christopher Avery concluded that "the vast majority of very high-achieving students who are low-income do not apply to any selective college or university." The reason is access. Unlike students in densely populated areas, these "income-typical" students "come from districts too small to support selective public high schools. There is no critical mass of fellow high achievers, and students are unlikely to encounter a teacher or schoolmate from an older cohort who attended a selective college."[22] The best source of information for these students remains the Internet. As Internet-enabled course offerings are made known, those students would be expected to convert their online searches for suitable colleges to online course enrollment for at least some of their undergraduate requirements. This is the pathway that new schools—like those planned by Nelson's Minerva Project, which "aims to help high-performing students succeed"—are banking on. As Nelson told me, the much-discussed value of a "residential experience for undergraduates" is hard to document in practice. "We believe in the residential experience," he said, "but the market is not there." It is a uniquely American practice to go away to college, but, as Nelson points out, "even in Massachusetts, 50 percent of the students drive to classes."

As traditional institutions scramble to find niche applications for MOOCs and short-format video (about which most presidents and provosts remain skeptical), they overwhelmingly plan to expand further into online course delivery. According to a Gallup survey of college provosts, "[Eighty-seven] percent will focus on funding programs aligned with their mission, and a similar proportion of [chief academic officers] say they will emphasize expansion of online programs at their institution over the next year."[23] Aside from courses, a veritable ecosystem of services will draw more Internet traffic to higher education. From assessment and credentials to online textbooks, tutoring, and analytics, the services most likely to be successful are those that can be delivered to users with a Web browser, and do not depend, for example, "on the geographic concentration of high achievers."[24]

Scale Favors Everyone on the Internet

The ability to *scale up* or *out* is a consistent theme in Internet economics. The lacy diagram in figure 5.1 is a map of the Internet.

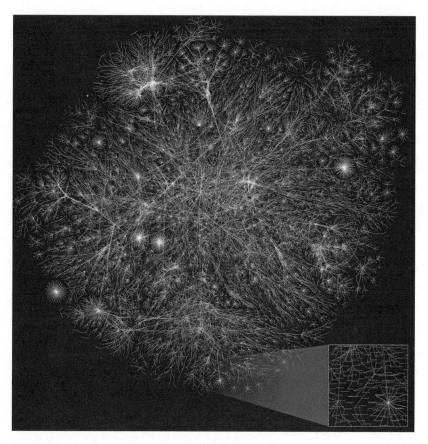

Figure 5.1
Map of the Internet

Each dot corresponds to a *host*: a Web page, computer hosting many Web pages, or complex Web site like yahoo.com. Lines connect the dots when there is a connection between hosts. For instance, if a Web page contains an embedded link such as http://whitehouse.gov, then there would be a line from the dot for that Web page to the dot corresponding to the White House's home page. Some dots have many connections because they correspond to popular Web pages that are referred to often. Other dots are less popular; although they may refer to several other Web pages, they themselves are referred to infrequently. In this way, the map of the Internet forms a network of *hubs* and *spokes*. Hubs are popular hosts that have many spokes connecting them to other hosts.

There is another way to look at Internet popularity. In a list of all Web pages ordered by popularity, the most popular Web sites are referred to about twice as frequently as the ones that are the next most popular. By the same token, the third most popular Web pages are half as popular as those in second place, and so on down the list of hundreds of millions of Web pages. A plot of popularity of rank-ordered Web pages would look something like the curve in figure 5.2, called a *power curve*, or *Pareto distribution*.

At the left of the curve are the extremely popular Web sites and Web pages, like google.com. Although they are very popular, there are relatively few of them. Most of the word's Web pages are not all that popular. They appear far to the right of the diagram in what is called the *long tail* of the distribution. Internet search engines like Google and Bing make use of this model to decide which search results users might be most interested in seeing first. Google, for example, assigns to a Web page a number called a *page rank* that represents how many other pages refer to it. When a user searches for a phrase such as "hammer and saw," search engines display those pages containing "hammer and saw" that have the highest page rank first—in this case, those happened to be the Web pages containing the nonsense verse, "I see said the blind man as he picked up his hammer and saw," as opposed to, say, any of the thousands of hardware stores that might sell hammers and saws, or handyman Web sites that use hammers and saws as logos. The same distribution can be observed in the rank-ordered appearance of words in texts (where it is called Zipf's Law), or populations of cities, citations

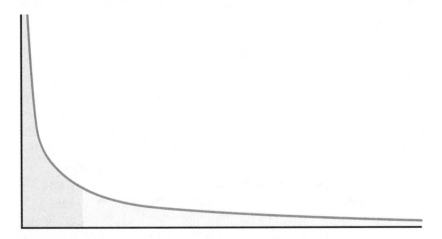

Figure 5.2
Power curve

to Internet blogs, frequency of stocks transactions, readership of newspapers, or popularity of universities. In Internet economics, power laws rule supreme. Internet businesses that ignore the logic of hubs and spokes have scant chance of success. Underpinning that logic is the concept of scale.

Scaling Up Millions upon millions of users visit the most popular Internet hubs. In fall 2013, the US government launched healthcare.gov, a Web site that Americans were supposed to use to register for health care exchanges under the new national program called the Affordable Care Act. The Web site crashed when hundreds of thousands of people tried to access it simultaneously. The ensuing chaos damaged the brand of the Department of Health and Human Services along with the contractors who were involved in constructing the Web site, and gave ammunition to political foes who seized on the Web site's failures to cast doubt on the viability of the program itself. This was a failure to scale up to the amount of traffic that the most popular Internet businesses are able to handle. Aside from a few enterprises, like Open University and the University of Phoenix, higher education institutions have rarely had to scale up. MIT's OCW and Stanford's MOOCs changed that, but scaling up is costly, and without structural changes to institutions, it is impossible.

Scaling Out Internet businesses in the long tail would be impossible to sustain without technology. Before the Internet, the creation of a national broadcast television station required massive capital investment. Studios, equipment, and the creation of a national broadcast network were so prohibitively expensive that in the entire United States, only four networks were economically feasible. Those networks depended on such large audiences that finding time in a crowded schedule for topics that interested only a few viewers was virtually impossible. A national broadcast network consisting entirely of humorous videos about household pets would have been out of the question. YouTube provided a platform for a channel for funny cat videos. Specialty digital magazines, retail stores that serve niche markets, and Salman Khan's academy of short video lectures all succeed because they have solved the problem of scaling out on the Internet. None of those examples relies on assembling all the components of a large-scale business. Instead, they tap into the power of platforms for services that are not core competencies. Businesses in the long tail make it easier to personalize services. Mass customization is the name given to marketing strategies that carry out personalization at Internet scale. A college or university that decided to focus on a narrower mission might easily become a long tail Internet business, but that would mean a smaller faculty, fewer laboratories and lecture halls, and less expensive academic services like admissions and alumni relations. A college that successfully scales out might be impossible without the same kind of structural changes that are required for scaling up.

Key Technologies Have Matured Simultaneously

The current hype cycle in higher education might also be different because, like the British railways of the 1840s, key technologies are all maturing at the same time. Drucker certainly knew the potential that video held for off-campus offerings, but in 1997 the Internet was not yet mature. The problem of scaling—whether up or out—was yet to be solved. PLATO required expensive integration of technologies that made it difficult to deliver personalized educational services because network technologies were immature and supercomputers were needed to run PLATO courseware. The only way to distribute interactive video to more than a handful of users at a time required dedicated video servers. Social networks did not make an appearance until 2004, so establishing online communities of users was not feasible. Learning analytics required special-purpose facilities to gather data, and even then only meager amounts of data could be captured.

Personalization technology did not arrive until the late 1990s, and advanced "big data" algorithms would not be discovered until 2002. If there is a technology threshold for delivery of high-quality instructional services, the present time is different because all of the required capabilities are now of acceptable quality, and technology curves tell us that they will improve rapidly.

There Are Reasons to Adopt New Technologies

Prior learning technologies were interesting experiments, not strategic necessities, but—due to decreasing affordability—the cost of higher education today is not on a sustainable path. Public confidence in the value of a university degree has eroded at the same time that demand worldwide for education is growing. Public investment that subsidized growth in prior years has dwindled for educational institutions. Wealthy private institutions may see a rebound, but as recently as early 2014, a growing number of private colleges and universities in the Middle are unable to attract enough students to continue operation, even with a steep discounting of tuition. This time is different because there are now compelling reasons to look toward new technology to solve deep structural problems.

The Structure of Academia

In the decades immediately preceding and following the American Revolution, Harvard College graduated an average of forty students annually. The entire Harvard faculty prior to 1776 consisted of a president, two professors (mathematics and theology), and four tutors. By 1800, one professor of Hebrew was added to Harvard's faculty.[25] Of the quality of instruction, Henry Adams, grandson of US president John Quincy and great-grandson of President John Adams, did not speak kindly: "The method of instruction had not changed in the interval, being suited to children fourteen years of age; the instruction itself was poor, and the discipline was indifferent."[26]

Despite "the spirit and vivacity of the coming age [that] could not be wholly shut out," Harvard at the end of British rule resembled not a modern university—or even the brand-new institutions like the University of Virginia or University of Pennsylvania—but rather a medieval relic, "a priesthood which had lost the secret of its mysteries, and patiently stood holding the flickering torch before cold altars, until God should vouchsafe a new dispensation of sunlight."[27] Adams may have thought them medieval relics, but the first three universities in America—Harvard, Yale, and William and Mary, which regarded themselves as European in the style of Oxford or Cambridge—bore a stronger resemblance to "the independent grammar schools of Elizabethan England or the dissenting academies after 1662 than to the medieval universities."[28]

Nevertheless, change eventually overtook Harvard. When Charles Eliot was inaugurated as president in 1869, Harvard enrolled 120 students—not much changed from colonial times—who were instructed by 19 faculty members.[29] By the time Eliot's plan to abolish all required courses was complete in 1892, Harvard's enrollment had increased tenfold to nearly 1,200. The size of the faculty, however, had grown to 600—a thirtyfold increase resulting from the loss of efficiency of a common, compulsory curriculum.

From 1870 to the outbreak of World War I, the average ratio of students to faculty at American universities hovered around 9.8:1, even during periods of rapid growth. The growth of the faculty remained in lockstep with student enrollment, until a post–World War II surge swelled student ranks by a factor of ten. During that period, the ratio of students to faculty doubled, and professors absorbed the increased workload. That ratio has grown at a small but more or less constant rate ever since, although the rate of increase at public universities has been larger than private universities. Student-to-faculty ratios at research universities in Europe, Asia, and Latin America are not vastly different from American institutions. Undergraduate institutions are more variable. At selective colleges, like Williams, Harvey Mudd, and Olin, there are between 7 and 9 students per faculty member. At less selective institutions and community colleges, the ratio can be as high as 50:1 or more.

None of the historical trend lines for traditional American universities support scaling up for large universities or scaling out for smaller institutions in the Middle. According to the Center for Educational Statistics, 3.4 million students were added to American institutions of all kinds between 2006 and 2010.[30] The number of instructional faculty members grew by 167,000. On an annual basis, enrollments have grown about 1 percent faster than faculty. Virtually all this discrepancy is attributable to growth in the number of students outside the eighteen- to twenty-four-year-old population in the United States, which averages about 1 percent per year. In other words, the source of the growing workload gap is also the source of the scaling problem for colleges and universities: hubs are operating at near institutional limits, and there are not nearly enough schools in the long tail that are capable of scaling out.

The picture at for-profit universities tells a similar story. Despite their reputation as diploma mills, most for-profit universities use exactly the same structural metrics of program quality. Historically stable student-to-faculty ratios for private, for-profit institutions have grown dramatically from less than 12:1 in 2006—before the recession—to nearly 16:1 by 2010.

Public perception is that traditional universities have tried to manage this growth in times of declining revenues by hiring more *contingent* faculty members—instructors who are not part of the full-time, tenure-track faculty. Many contingent faculty members are paid on a per course basis, often without access to health care or other benefits that full-time workers enjoy. Because they have little bargaining power, contingent faculty members are frequently portrayed as an exploited class of workers. The American Association of University Professors (AAUP), whose membership is increasingly drawn from the ranks of contingent faculty, claims that in 2013, the majority of university faculty members were contingent. This statistic, however, lumps together the many kinds of instructors who fall in the contingent professor category to paint a misleading picture of institutional forces.

The definition of contingent faculty is the problem. In the first place, not all non-tenure-track professors are part-time. Many are full-time instructional faculty members who enjoy the same job security as other university employees. Second, many contingent faculty members are actually full-time business or government employees who have volunteered to teach a course or two at a local college. Finally, many contingent faculty members are retirees, full-time parents, or others who are not interested in full-time teaching jobs. The AAUP's own data support this analysis. Not only do contingent faculty members who desire full-time employment constitute a small minority, the remaining instructors are already employed elsewhere:

Part-time faculty [who do not desire full-time teaching jobs] is disproportionately represented in the fields of business (10 percent) and education (13 percent). Almost 90 percent report that their other job does not involve teaching, and 71 percent report that their other job is full time. The typical member of this group appears to be a successful midcareer nonacademic, working in either business or education, who earns a more than adequate salary at a different, primary job and thus is willing to teach a course or two in addition to his or her main employment.[31]

The Scaling Problem

With current methods of instruction and staffing, it is unlikely that the structure of academic institutions can be made to accommodate the kinds of large increases in enrollment that will be faced in the coming decades. Even contingent faculty and other nonstandard instructional ranks do not appear to change the economics of providing a quality educational experience to large numbers of new students. This is a problem that is so important to future road maps for higher education that I want to give it a name: the Scaling Problem.

> The Scaling Problem: One professor, teaching several large lectures, even with the help of a small army of teaching assistants, can touch at most a thousand students at a time.

Increasing labor costs make this unsustainable. A single professor must be able to touch tens of thousands of students at a time. Either universities have to abandon the kind of personal attention that has been the hallmark of traditional classroom instruction or the very structure of the university workforce has to change: the student-to-faculty ratio at hub institutions has to increase a hundredfold with improved levels of learning and achievement. Gains through big data, artificial intelligence and other emerging technologies do not solve the Scaling Problem.

Teams and the Rise of Super Professor

"Our goal," says Arizona State University president Crow, "is to evolve our workforce of two thousand tenure-track professors, so that each of them is an enhanced super professor." Crow, like many other university leaders, sees a dramatic expansion of scale and scope without a dramatic expansion of the professoriate. The appearance of super faculty, in Crow's vision, becomes "an expanded, powerful, intellectual force within the university. That means twenty-five thousand graduates per year, a hundred thousand online students, and $750 million in sponsored research, all with the same size faculty." That kind of university cannot be achieved without solving the Scaling Problem. That solution involves structural changes that affect everything from increased compensation to the use of technology-enhanced teaching. "You cannot extrapolate from where we are now to this," says Crow.

Stanford's Hennessy agrees with this analysis. "We're going to have to improve productivity," he observes. "Some people have taken that to mean student-teacher ratios." But just making large classes is no solution. "Quality goes down, learning goes down, and graduation rates go down." Hennessy is frank in the face of the scaling problem: "I think the cost disease is real." Georgia Tech's Peterson sees the rapid growth in applications from students who want to study there, but says that the existing business model cannot support a rapid expansion of the faculty. "We will admit more students, we will expand our staff to do that," he notes, "but we will not dramatically expand our tenure-track faculty."

Productivity improvements like this are not unprecedented, and many of the methods for achieving them are well known. College instructors operate in *silos*—vertically integrated mini-enterprises that are responsible for design, delivery, advising, tutoring, assessment, and all matters related to the use of educational technology. *Deskilling*, the process of replacing high-cost, highly skilled workers with automata and lower-skilled workers to increase productivity and profits, is a concept that has been roundly criticized by economists like Harry Braverman and Shoshana Zuboff for its dehumanizing effect on workers, but there is a new definition of deskilling that does not fit any of those models.[32] Deskilling can also mean removing tasks from a highly skilled profession that do not require that particular skill, and delegating them to other professionals with different training and skills. Many people who look at the productivity problems in higher education see deskilling as a way of solving the scaling problem.

Cancer treatment centers are, in many ways, parallel and instructive labor markets for higher education. Like higher education, demands for services are increasing much faster than the existing health care system can accommodate. Like tuition, cancer treatment costs are rising at twice the rate of inflation. Concern over the quality of care is rising. It is also a system in crisis. In September 2013, the Institute of Medicine of the National Academy of Sciences issued a report on how cancer treatment might move beyond the current economic impasse.[33] The recommendations are strikingly similar to Michael Crow's ideas about how to structure the academic workforce. The solution is to replace siloed medical care with a technology-augmented, team-based system. In this model, a patient care team is led by an oncologist who is responsible for planning and organizing treatment. But team members include psychologists, radiologists, nutritionists, and family counselors:

The report recommends ways to respond to these challenges and improve cancer care delivery, including by strengthening clinicians' core competencies in caring for patients with cancer, shifting to team-based models of care, and communicating more effectively with patients.[34]

In cancer care, the productivity improvements come from the inherent efficiencies of teams, enhanced technology utilization, and optimizations like skill sharing among teams. One nutritionist, for instance, may be shared among two dozen patients at significant savings, while a lead oncologist, the most senior and highly compensated member of the team, may expand the number of patients by a factor of ten or more. And since all team members participate in patient care, duplicate tests or redundant paperwork are far less likely.

Team-based models of care make a great deal of sense in higher education. Early experience with MOOC production suggests that professor-instructors are uniquely unsuited for some of the most scalable tasks in course delivery.

Instructional Design: Strange as it may seem, most professors are not skilled instructional designers. The long-form lecture format has trained generations of college professors to give speeches, but not necessarily to structure courses in the most effective way. That job is increasingly the responsibility of an academic professional known as an instructional designer. A typical instructional designer can easily participate in four or more courses.

Technology Management: Technology choices abound in MOOC production, yet professors are generally not knowledgeable about underlying technology. An uninformed technology decision can be disastrous to an online course, driving up costs and degrading student learning experiences. An educational technologist who is familiar with the specific needs of a course and the delivery platform can participate in fifteen to twenty separate course teams.

Video Production: A combination of producer and director, video production specialists schedule studio time, manage video recording and editing, and serve as financial consultants to keep expenditures within budget. These are skills that are far outside the interests or capabilities of most professors. A single video production specialist can manage a half-dozen projects simultaneously.

Advising and Tutoring: Advising and tutoring services, particularly if they are Internet based, have great leverage. Three advisers and three tutors per thousand students are sometimes sufficient. Start-ups like Atlanta's OfficeHours allocate as many as ten tutors per thousand students. Advisers and tutors can be shared among many teams. When used in conjunction with predictive analytics, advisers can be efficiently assigned to students who need intervention the most, which provides still another productivity boost.

Assessments: Despite the fact that professors have been designing exams for hundreds of years, there is no evidence to suggest that tests have improved in quality. The science of assessment, on the other hand, has benefited from a better understanding of cognition and improvements in computing that facilitate detailed analysis. There are academic specialists who are experts in test design and interpretation. They work closely with instructional designers and lead professors, but since their work is scheduled sporadically, they can also be shared among many—perhaps dozens—of teams.

Data Analysis: Experts in the algorithms that are used to interpret the massive amounts of learning data that universities generate, analysts work with other members of the team to ensure that lead professors have a current and useful picture of student status and progress. Analysts are typically shared among many teams.

Business Development and Marketing Skills: In traditional courses, professors are responsible for determining the number of students who are interested in a new course and developing the business plan. In reality, this is a haphazard process that results in courses that have marginal value or are more costly than required to achieve an educational outcome. At Internet scale, ineffective planning results in a massive waste of scarce resources. A single specialist in marketing and business development might serve an entire curriculum, and be shared among a hundred courses.

These are real teams, and they share information because team members are shared between courses. "A single professor and a half-dozen teaching assistants might be able to teach a thousand students, but five teams like this, can teach five hundred thousand students," says Mike McCracken, director of online innovation at Georgia Tech's Center for 21st Century Universities. Exactly this kind of team approach was used in planning the Georgia Tech online master's degree. Two additional faculty members were needed to manage an increase of nearly nine thousand students.

Crow is realistic about the challenges of moving to this new model. "We are running in the face of the pure model," he says. "Student-faculty ratios do not matter, because we are building a different kind of institution." The older conceptualization gave us education as a commodity, but Crow admits, "we cannot continue to expand at the same rate. We have to find a way to partner and enhance what our faculty are capable of doing."

II Rationale for a Revolution

6 Accessibility

If current trends continue, there is a date in the not-too-distant future after which half of all states in the United States will budget nothing for their public universities.[1] Within sixty years, most American public universities will have disappeared, replaced by something more closely resembling private institutions that draw their income from student fees, scholarships, federal aid, and gifts from wealthy alumni. From that point on, tuition for most Americans will rise at twice the annual rate of inflation. The situation is similar in Europe and Japan, where in spite of heavy government subsidies, the amount that students pay for degrees is also on the rise. Nearly four hundred thousand Canadians, who had become accustomed to paying about 20 percent of their annual income for college tuition—the lowest in North America—took to the streets of Quebec in 2012 in response to a planned 75 percent increase in tuition.[2] In France prominent humanities professors say—despite being "poor as church mice"—their universities are better off avoiding the American dream of producing skilled workers because "knowledge is immaterial, abundant, communicable, and not automatically mercantile."[3] It is not completely incidental to the discussion of higher education that one of the best-selling books of 2014 was a weighty, dense academic treatise on the nature of economic inequality, whose French author argued that the growing gap between the rich and poor was pathological, and could lead to social chaos.[4] Economic inequality is also the fate of higher education systems left alone to follow their current paths.

A primary rationale for the Revolution is the spreading realization that current trends make higher education unsustainable. The rising cost of running a traditional university drives a wedge between those who can pay and those who cannot. There are limited options for closing this gap. Governments could somehow be convinced to shoulder a larger burden of costs that appear to be rising uncontrollably (twice the rate of health care cost increases in the United States, for example). Another possible solution is for society to collectively decide that unequal access to a quality college education is fine. Neither of these options is realistic, and even clever combinations in which government carries the costs only for those least able to pay do little to help. Every other option involves knowing what happens when prices are more than what people are willing to pay. Traditional universities are incumbents—institutions that once had entitled status. What has loomed so suddenly to threaten them? Have they been wasteful squanderers? Are the incumbents so fragile that their positions can be undermined by simply asking about their economic value? Exactly how would a technology-enabled revolution affect the economics of higher education? It is hard to progress too much further in explaining the rationale for this Revolution without a basic understanding of the finances of modern universities, which is what this chapter is about.

In every revolution there is an incumbent to be displaced—an old order that is being replaced by a new one. Change can be gradual—for instance, like evolutionary change—so that old regimes have time to reform, grow, shrink, and adapt. Gradual change offers incumbents the hope of surviving or even prospering later on. Radical change, however, holds out few options for incumbents. An incumbent can offer to voluntarily turn things over to a newcomer and then retire. Revolutions await all other incumbents, and revolutions have uncertain outcomes.

The Fate of Incumbents

It may seem that the future of the higher education world is being redrawn by a small handful of Silicon Valley technologists, but there are some who have seen the road maps and think that evolution is the most likely outcome. "Anyone who has seen the numbers knows where we are headed," says Arizona State University president Michael Crow. "And it's always about the numbers," he adds quickly. When Crow says "numbers" he means costs, or more precisely, the difference between how much money a university is required to spend and the amount that it can be reasonably expected to take in as revenue. But even starting a conversation about the numbers is a remarkably hard thing to do in higher education. Crow is often attacked for wanting to replace faculty labor with something that costs less—"I mean really excoriated as a corporatist," he says. "It is a Marxist reaction." In his twelve years as president of the behemoth public university just outside Phoenix, Crow has done more to demonstrate the power of change in higher education than almost any of his peers. On the day he was inaugurated as Arizona State's sixteenth president, he vowed to create a "New American University" that was rooted in a different set of values than he saw being pursued by other large public institutions. It was an agenda that valued fairness and inclusion as a pathway to greatness, and it was ideally suited to Arizona's diverse population and struggling economy. It also made Crow a controversial figure.

The corporatist appellation does have a Marxist ring to it, but it is not a new charge and it is not hurled only at Crow. As you will find out in part III, there are those who have staked the labor (versus management) claim for higher education in such a way that almost any exercise of administrative authority in a college or university is met by cries of "corporatism!" They know how to get their message out, and reformers like Crow are frequently the target.

Most research universities—including Arizona's other research institution, the University of Arizona—sought a different route by imitating prestigious Élite public and private universities. Prestige meant becoming more and more selective, but that would have excluded exactly the people of Arizona that Crow was determined to serve. Setting high standards for admission without imposing a limit on size was an idea that had been tried only rarely. Crow thought that Arizona high school students who had a B average in a challenging curriculum and reasonable test scores—roughly the same admission requirements that the best public universities had in the 1960s—should have a place at Arizona State. Anything else would have defined the university by who it excluded rather than by its successes.

The only way to realize what Crow liked to call the New Gold Standard was to find a way to fund massive expansion. It was a strategy that many of his colleagues said was doomed to rapid and dramatic failure, but today he is one of the longest-serving presidents of any public institution, outlasting University of Arizona president Robert Shelton, one of his most vocal critics. But Crow has equally vocal support from presidents like Stanford's Hennessy, who says Arizona State has a great mission: "[It is] the university that graduates the highest proportion of at-risk kids." The biggest risk, according to Hennessy, is trying to do everything at once.

At times Crow does appear to be swimming against a strong current. At a recent summit on higher education sponsored by *Time* magazine, former Princeton University president Harold Shapiro accused Crow of not understanding the underlying economics, and former Harvard president Derek Bok claimed that any conversation about cost was an affront to quality. "You're undermining the entire enterprise," he said.

Is a University a Business?

To the presidents who want to paint him as out of touch with the economic realities of running a university, Crow declares, "Not likely!" His rapid rise through increasingly important leadership positions at Columbia and professional association with the social economists of the Earth Institute have given him a rare perspective on large systems like American higher education. But the conflict does illustrate why the fate of the incumbents is hard to predict. The public looks at a university as an obviously commercial enterprise. A university collects money to operate, and uses those funds to dispense services according to both a budget and mission. This is the very definition of what it means to engage in commerce. It seems self-evident that a university is a business, and thus needs to be run like one lest it overspend its budget or fail in its mission.

"Not so fast!" say a large number of traditionalists. "A business is managed hierarchically. It sells its wares to consumers and is subject to the whims of a sometimes-fickle marketplace. Our students are not consumers. If there is a marketplace involved, it is a marketplace of ideas, not dollars. Most important, businesses exist to make a profit. We are not a business, and we object to using the language of business to talk about what we do." Traditionalists object because using the language of business is demeaning and, like Bok, they believe that it undermines the entire enterprise.

Setting aside the counterarguments that there are many, many businesses that are neither managed hierarchically nor for profit, it would help the conversation along if there were some basic agreement about what kind of business a university might be engaged in, if it were in fact a business.

Submitting one's work to an economic marketplace is what seems to be the sticking point for those who do not believe that higher education is a business. For them it is the dividing line between being a business and not, and there is a wealth of writing on exactly why it would be disastrous for academic institutions to be thought of as a business.[5] The alternatives have been less well thought out. Economist Anthony Downs, whose knowledge of what makes large organizations work has been tapped by US presidents going back to Lyndon Baines Johnson, is especially interested in enterprises that match the following profile:

1. They comprise many full-time employees
2. There are clearly defined management lines of authority for more efficient command and control
3. Hiring, promotion, and retention decisions are based on criteria for assessing performance (rather than, say, membership in a class)[6]

Universities clearly have these characteristics. Generally speaking they are large organizations. Most universities are likely to have many employees—more than the average person would be able to come in contact with on a daily basis. Universities are organized into faculties, disciplines, laboratories, schools, and colleges with defined leadership roles for academic and administrative tasks as well as decision making. And it is a hallmark of academic life that hiring and firing decisions are made on the basis of achievement and merit. The entire system of tenure and promotion depends on this fact. If a university's outputs were evaluated by markets, Downs would say it was a business. For many academics, the idea of being associated with a business is cause for recoiling in disgust.

If a university is not a business, then what kind of organization might it be? According to Downs, it is a bureaucracy. It is an organization that has the three characteristics listed above, but one for which "the major portion of its output is not directly or indirectly evaluated in any markets external to the organization by means of voluntary quid pro quo transactions."[7] But these are the defining characteristics of a bureaucracy. Few academics want to admit to being bureaucrats. Academics tend to heap scorn on bureaucracies and commercial enterprises in equal measure. It is an uncomfortable position.

A clever dodge is to change the subject. Some say that the business of a university is to help eighteen- to twenty-four-year-old postadolescents over the hump from childhood to maturity. Others say that the university is primarily there to promote economic development, cement social ties, conduct research, serve the needs of its faculty, or provide a backdrop for intercollegiate spectacles. Most insiders—at least those who might acknowledge that universities are engaged in business—would probably agree with philosophy professor Robert McCauley, who argues that "the business of the university is inquiry and inquiry is its definitive task."[8] This cannot be correct. In fact, John Henry Newman, the nineteenth-century British philosopher who founded University College Dublin and had enormous influence on the shape of modern universities, said just the opposite: "If its object were scientific and philosophical discovery, I do not see why a university should have students."[9] There is hardly a university in the world for which educating students is not its primary mission. Whatever else a university might be empowered to undertake, the business of every university is education.

It also cannot be the case that simply talking about the business of running the university undermines the educational enterprise. Costs are going up so much more quickly than the revenue to cover them that refusing to talk about costs is irresponsible. In the United States, where that cost falls increasingly on families, the blanket refusal to discuss costs involves a certain amount of arrogance. You can almost hear *The Music Man*'s Harold Hill on his way to River City to convince townsfolk that no price is too great to pay for trombones and band uniforms.[10]

There also seems to be a reluctance to talk about cost versus quality. Quality occupies much academic writing about higher education, but putting a price on that quality is another thing altogether. When pushed, traditionalists do not seriously offer the argument that putting an economic value on quality is an affront. Cardinal Newman himself maintained just the opposite: "Life is not long enough to expend upon interesting, or curious, or brilliant trifles."[11] In other words, there are so many worthwhile things to pursue that choices have to be made about what to study and what to exclude, but the very act of making these choices assigns value. It is an economic decision. In every human endeavor that I know of, quality comes at a cost. Usually—but not always—a willingness to pay a little more improves quality.

The result is sometimes modeled by an S-curve (figure 6.1) that shows how quality changes over time. In the beginning, most of the money spent on a new product or service goes to fund start-up activities, but eventually a well-run organization uses its resources to increase quality. Quality may rise for a long time, but eventually the quality curve flattens out. Adding unwanted but expensive features to a mature product or gold-plating services that no one asks for are examples of what happens when the quality S-curve plateaus. Spending more at this point may increase prices, but it does not necessarily increase quality.

What happens when people lose confidence that an increase in quality is worth the increased price? Sometimes prices just keep going up, and people find ways to pay. That is what happened in the housing bubble that led to the 2008 economic collapse and global recession that followed. Many people have argued that at least in the United States, higher education is another economic bubble. The evidence for this viewpoint is compelling. College tuition may have risen much faster than inflation, but there has been no corresponding increase in the percentage of students who graduate on time or find gainful employment if they do graduate. Nor does higher tuition affect what college graduates know, how well they perform their duties, or how much money they make. When the public decides that there is no benefit—either personal or economic—from increased prices, the bubble collapses.

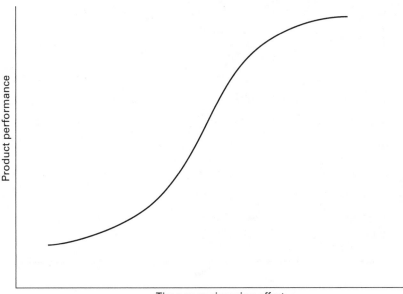

Figure 6.1
A single S-curve

Discontinuities

Another possibility is that higher education sits on the cusp of a disconti-nuity—a transition between ways of doing business (figure 6.2). When a marketplace decides that increasing costs are not worth it (curve A in figure 6.2), new ways of doing business sometimes appear and customers adopt a lower cost alternative (curve B in figure 6.2). The new alternative may not have the quality of the higher-priced incumbent, but quality gradually improves to an acceptable level because the new alternative has its own S-curve. The transition from curve A to curve B is a discontinuity that is often powered by technology.

For Arizona State and its president, technology is a means to attack unfairness. "It's an unbelievable moment to be around," says Crow. "We are at the early stages of the emergence of these empowering technology platforms." Crow's aim is to find a way to attack unfairness in the system using technology, but in order to do so he has to find a way for his faculty to be more productive, and that means a new way of doing business.

It is the same conclusion that a handful of other presidents have reached. For Jackson State University president Carolyn Meyers, it means

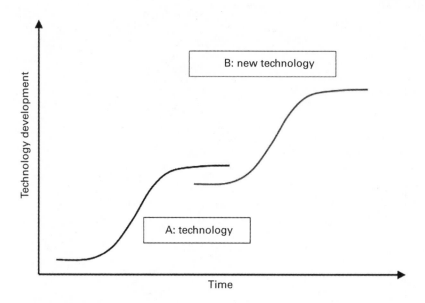

Figure 6.2
Dual S-curves with discontinuity

using technology to turn the limitations of her mission at an HBCU into a platform that makes her institution unique. For Southern New Hampshire University president Paul LeBlanc, it meant jumping to curve B (figure 6.2) to invent a new kind of college experience and turn a struggling two-thousand-student, private institution into a thirty-thousand-student, data-driven enterprise. LeBlanc uses technology to underprice competitors and serve what he says is the sweet spot for higher education—the 80 percent of all college students—most of them older than twenty-five—for who a degree is a pathway to the middle class.

Not everyone is so excited about the future, especially one that involves MOOCs. Nearly 60 percent of all college presidents view MOOCs negatively.[12] Even more important, they see little reason to change: by an overwhelming 64 percent majority, presidents believe that higher education is already going in the right direction, and 84 percent believe that the higher education system already provides value for the money spent by students and their families.

Incumbents apparently see little reason to embrace change, particularly technology-inspired change that disrupts their business models. For them to be right, higher education would have to obey economic laws that do not apply to the rest of the world, but no industry has emerged unscathed in the face of technological innovation. University presidents—who have an interest in protecting their current business models—by and large believe that innovation will come from within, yet that would require them to know what kind of innovation matters. That would defy history. Hennessy has seen this before:

> I remember the music industry guys telling me they were not going to change. They wanted to continue to sell plastic discs for $16 that had twelve songs on them. If only university research could help them shut down piracy so they could go back to their business. Of course their business was going to end. Steve Jobs saved them because their industry was going to collapse. And by the way, Jobs redefined Apple in the process, so that it was no longer a computer company. That is a lesson for higher education.

That is what incumbents face: an innovation from outside their industry that disrupts the way they do business. The list of incumbents who did not survive that kind of disruption is long (table 6.1). When there is a revolution—when technology surges—there will be newcomers who threaten the existing order, and when that happens it is hard for incumbents to survive.

Table 6.1
Table of Incumbents in Times of Technological Change

Encyclopedias
Rail transport
Mobile discount operators
Catalog stores
Mainframe computers
Minicomputers
Navigational maps
X-ray imaging
Netscape
Vertically integrated steel mills
Cathode ray tubes
Telegraphy
Sailing ships
Offset printing
Chemical photography
Newspapers
Bookselling
Universities

The Power of Tuition

First, let's look at the numbers. Sometime in 2012 the total indebtedness due to loans made to American college students topped $1 trillion, surpassing credit cards and second only to home mortgages as the major source of indebtedness. The principle reason that students took on debt was a dramatic rise in the cost of attending college. It is a complicated pathway from the check that families write for the privilege of attending college to the quality of their educational experience. Tuition used to be a concept that was unique to North America, Japan (where the majority of colleges and universities are private), and India (where storefront colleges offering training in marketable skills are common). But as the economics of higher education shifts worldwide, the idea of a "free" college education is rapidly being replaced by something that more closely resembles the American system.

Figure 6.3 shows the relative rise in college tuition from 1982 to 2005. College tuition is currently growing at four times the rate of inflation and nearly twice the rate of increase in the cost of health care. From 2005 to 2012, tuition rose at an annualized rate of 8 percent. It is a breathtaking climb, and because family incomes rose hardly at all during the same period, it meant that students had to borrow unsustainable amounts of money to fund their education. Not all those loans are paid back. From 2000 to 2005, the default rate for student loans actually fell from 6 to 5.5 percent, but by 2011 it had nearly doubled.

Such facts are fodder for cable television talk shows, political speeches, and a considerable number of faux populist attacks on the very idea of a college degree. Ideas about how to control college costs abound. In the United States, the Obama administration challenged colleges and universities to control costs with initiatives that focus to a large measure on affordability. The conservative and liberal wings of American politics are sharply divided on the issue of college affordability. Many conservative politicians say that it is the ready availability of federally backed loans that is driving cost increases. Liberals say that the same cultural factors that drove banking abuses are also driving the disparity between who can afford a college education and who cannot. There is little evidence that either statement is true, and considerable evidence that neither is.

Take the question, for example, of whether student loan availability has an effect on tuition. Former US secretary of education William Bennett, a vocal small-government conservative, claimed just that: "College costs and prices rise and will continue to rise far above the rate of inflation (as has

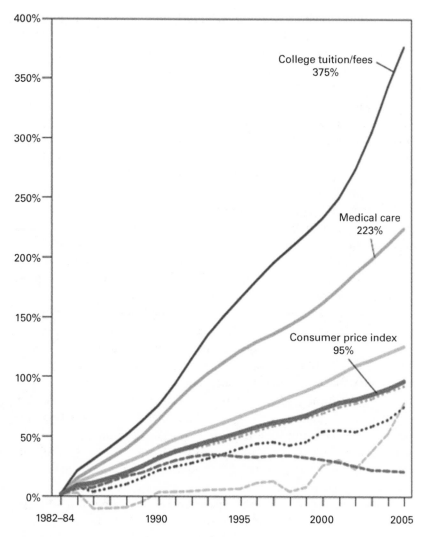

Figure 6.3
Rise in tuition

been the case for decades) because (a) many colleges are greedy, (b) families will pay anything to get their kids into some colleges, and (c) the federal government endlessly subsidizes these increases."[13]

It is true that tuition has risen above the rate of inflation for many years and much of this has been driven by increased costs, but the availability of federal grants and loans has little to do with it. If federal loans influenced tuition at greedy institutions by inducing students to attend college regardless of the price, then the availability of more federal loan funds should drive up both the cost of college and number of students enrolling at these inflated prices. In fact, just the opposite occurred.[14] In 2007, the US Department of Education raised the cap on the maximum amount that could be borrowed under the Stafford Loan program, the most common form of federally guaranteed student loans. After the change in loan limits, "the price and the numbers of undergraduate students enrolling in the nation's institutions of higher learning increased at a rate generally consistent with prior years." In particular, there was no surge in the number of students borrowing more than the previous cap. Those who did take advantage of the increased caps, did not use their loans to attend the high-priced Élite schools, as Bennett imagined, but rather to attend lower-cost public institutions.[15]

Tuition is used by institutions for something that is not readily apparent from the outside. It is one of only two levers that can be pulled to keep the financial ship afloat. The first lever controls what a university does or does not do. It is entirely within the scope of administrators and faculty members to choose which academic programs to offer, the number of faculty and administrative staff members, how many students to admit, the number and kind of buildings that will be needed, and whether to expand the institutional mission to include research or intercollegiate athletics.

The US Department of Education issues a regular report on the financial health of degree-granting colleges and universities. When I started tracking the course of these institutions, there were about 100 nonprofit colleges that failed the test. By 2008, that number had risen to 127. By 2010, the *Chronicle of Higher Education* was reporting that 150 nonprofits had failed the department's test.[16]

Almost in parallel with the US Department of Education report, Moody's Investor Services issued a report on the liquidity of public universities.[17] The median level of debt for two-hundred-plus public institutions rated by Moody's grew by 31 percent between 2005 and 2009. How would public institutions—whose average total financial resources grew by only 15 percent-- service this kind of debt? By 2010, the debt per student exceeded financial resources per student by $1,200. State subsidies were on a steep decline due to falling tax revenues. The market crash had gutted many endowments. But according to Moody's, "Most public universities will be able to raise tuition to help absorb the revenue gaps."[18] That is the power of tuition, the second lever.

P = MC

How do colleges and universities determine what price to charge their students? Does the *total amount due* on a student's tuition invoice have anything to do with the cost of educating that student? Universities are in competition with each other for students, faculty members, and brand recognition that comes from a winning football season or a high *US News and World Report* (*USNWR*) ranking. They all offer the same degrees. In fact, the entire accreditation industry is built on the idea that credit hours and degrees mean more or less the same thing regardless of which university grants them. Higher education certainly *seems* like a competitive industry, but in a competitive industry, price should equal marginal cost—P should equal MC.

What is the additional cost to a university of enrolling the next student who walks in the door? The classrooms, dormitories, labs, and common spaces are already built; the professors have already been hired, and so have the teaching assistants, secretaries, and maintenance staff. The next student has almost no incremental impact on heating, lighting, or water. Those are all marginal costs, so for all practical purposes the marginal cost of teaching that extra student should be zero.

Yet the marginal costs are not zero. For one thing, students do not arrive one by one. They arrive in cohorts, and an increase in the number of cohorts has to be matched by an increase in classes and therefore an increase in faculty size. There are other, less obvious marginal costs as well. Institutions do not market degrees like interchangeable commodities. No one would expect a student to check the sticker price at one school and then drive down the road to the next one looking for a better deal, although that would be a perfectly reasonable thing to do since accreditors ensure that degrees from different institutions are comparable. In higher education, marginal cost is not the cost of letting one more student in the door. The real marginal cost is often the marginal cost of all those other things that universities do to compete with each other. For instance, there are marginal costs of being known internationally, fielding a nationally competitive football team, and winning federal research contracts. In parts of Europe, universities have numbers, not names. Is there a marginal advantage to a T-shirt that proudly displays the seal for Paris 6 or Paris 8? In the United States and many other parts of the world, names of universities are brands emblazoned on pants, pennants, and paraphernalia. There is a marginal cost to being known as the University of Nebraska. Those costs are not zero, and they have a large impact on the price of admission.

For-profit institutions aside, you would think that there would be a straightforward relationship between costs and prices since, after all, the name of the budget game in a university is to take in just enough revenue to offset the costs of operating programs and facilities. You would think, for example, that costs were simply passed along to students in the form of tuition and fees, which are components of the revenue side. There is a final wrinkle to complicate the discussion of college pricing. The published tuition—the sticker price—is not the price that most students pay. Neither is the discounted price: the amount that a student has to finance after various charges—institutional aid, grants, gifts, endowments, state support, and discounts—are written off. Total tuition can be far less than the cost of operating an institution—a situation that would not last long in the business world. The system is only viable because of the prevalence of subsidies: state appropriations in the case of public universities, and earnings from endowments and gifts in the case of private institutions. These subsidies are supposed to keep pace with rising costs, but they have been dropping since 1975. During tough economic times state tax revenues and endowment earnings decline sharply, yet even during boom years, subsidies from all sources have been either flat or shrinking.

Prices Unbundled

Status in American higher education is achieved through exclusion, and that has a profound impact on the price that a university can charge. The combined undergraduate enrollment of the top ten nationally ranked universities is 57,364.[19] Unranked Miami-Dade College alone enrolls almost as many students (54,100), although its student population is in turn small compared to the 320,000 students enrolled at the for-profit University of Phoenix, which is also unranked. The average tuition at the top-ranked universities is $44,163. Tuition and fees at Miami-Dade College total $11,309 annually. The University of Phoenix charges $10,440. Except for the University of Pennsylvania, which enrolled nearly 2,500 first-year students in 2013, the top-ranked universities each enrolled approximately 1,200 new students. On the average, 4 percent of the students who apply to the top schools (about half of all students accepted) actually matriculate as freshmen.

The prices of the top-ranked universities are not sensitive to demand. They already receive ten times more applications than the number of students that they can accept. Demand is growing, but these universities could probably set their prices as high as they want and there would still be a line of students anxious to get in. Their prices are determined by prestige, and prestige is by and large determined by how many applicants are rejected. It is a vicious cycle: status draws applications in large numbers; a fixed number of positions are available and so only a few applicants can be selected; and selectivity increases status, which increases their desirability.

Highly selective universities are able to set their prices high precisely because they gain status through exclusion. "High market elasticity points allow you to drive up faculty salaries," is how Crow explains it. Everything about prices at the top of the reputational pyramid is determined by this line of reasoning, but the $7,000 price tag for the Georgia Tech online master's degree is an illustration that prices—even for elite degrees—can be determined in a different fashion if an institution is willing to disaggregate its prices by effectively allowing students to pay only for the services they want (table 6.2). Those services are predominantly instructional services provided by professors and teaching assistants. Unlike tuition for traditional programs, economies of scale mean that the total cost of those services is unlikely to increase much over time.

Cost Disease

Tuition rises because variable costs rise, subsidies decline, and universities expand their missions to include new programs and activities (or cling to previously subsidized activities when the subsidies disappear). Most of the cost of running a university is tied up in labor costs, and most of the labor

Table 6.2
Classification of University Services

Type of service	Examples
Instructional	Classroom instruction, research, public service, libraries, and computing
Administration	Personnel management, financial and clerical services, human resource management, institutional data gathering and analysis, and auditing and legal services
Student services	Counseling, advising, admissions, and registrar
Buildings, maintenance, and operations	Utilities, janitorial services, groundskeeping, repairs and building maintenance, and fleet management
Scholarships and student aid	Grants in aid, student loans, scholarships, and fellowships
Auxiliary services	Dormitories, food services, parking and event management, bookstore operations, and campus police

costs are due to faculty salaries. This one factor alone accounts for about half of all tuition increases.

In good times and bad, college costs rise at about twice the rate of inflation. This is often cited as a central issue in higher education, but in fact the labor cost increases in higher education are not unusual. When compared to the price of automobiles or personal computers, higher education looks like a bad bet. Even health care performs better than higher education. On the other hand, college tuition rises at about the same rate as the price of legal services, dentistry, or symphony orchestras. Indeed, over time the price of a college education behaves about the same as the price of any service offered by highly educated professionals. The reason seems to be that these industries are all particularly resistant to automation. Lawyers still take about the same amount of time to read a contract as they did a hundred years ago. A violinist needs fourteen minutes to play a Mozart string quartet. And despite many attempts to improve the productivity of college professors, it still takes fifty minutes to deliver a lecture to a class of three hundred students.

When a technological innovation sweeps through an industry like manufacturing and dramatically increases the productivity of skilled professionals, companies need fewer of those workers. Therefore, their overall number goes down. But as that skill become scarcer, those remaining professionals who possess it become more valuable and thus can command higher salaries. Many of the most valuable skills are fungible—they can be applied in several industries—even those industries that have been resistant to productivity increases. As a result, compensation rises for all professionals who have that skill.

Higher education is no exception. In order to compete for highly educated engineers, accountants, writers, and architects, colleges and universities have to raise salaries. Since there are no offsetting productivity improvements to keep overall costs down, prices rise.

The analysis behind this principle was carried out in the 1960s for the performing arts by the economists Bowen and William Baumol, and subsequently applied by Bowen to the economics of higher education.[20] The principle is today known as the cost disease:

Markets dictate that, over time, wages for comparably qualified individuals have to increase at roughly the same rate in all industries. As a result, unit labor costs must be expected to rise faster in ... education than in the economy overall.[21]

"The cost disease is real," insists Stanford's Hennessy, "and unless there is something to close the gap between rising college costs and affordability, higher education is headed for trouble. The only way out of this dilemma is to increase the productivity of individual professors. Productivity increases like this generally require technological innovation, but these are exactly the innovations that produce discontinuities like the one in figure 6.2. These are the innovations that foment revolution.

Gatekeepers and Bypasses

This is a chapter about incumbents, evolution, and revolution. Like the cost disease, the effect that technological disruption will have on higher education has its roots in economics. Joseph Schumpeter, an early twentieth-century economist, charted the course of economies that undergo change.[22] Schumpeter was interested in what happens to the normal flow of economic affairs when entrepreneurs who try to introduce innovations are perpetually destroying the equilibrium. A successful introduction of an innovation disturbs the normal flow of economic life because it forces some of the already-existing technologies and means of production to lose their positions within the economy. Innovations like that are disruptive. Schumpeter was concerned about the incumbents during times of disruption. Would they adapt and evolve? Or would they be overthrown?

For most of their history, universities have functioned as gatekeepers. Schumpeter's economic equilibrium depended on the fact that all paths to a college degree required the approval of a gatekeeper. The economics of higher education worked because access was inexpensive and fair. The boundaries between entities were clear and well understood. MOOCs, the Minerva Project, proprietary universities, an explosion of new institutions in India and elsewhere in Asia, and the sudden ascendance of schools like Southern New Hampshire have put the gatekeeper role of traditional universities in jeopardy. As boundaries are destroyed the pent-up demand for postsecondary education will bypass the incumbents.

Harvard economist Shoshana Zuboff and James Maxim studied the emergence of bypass economies. Their work describes the "chasm that separates individuals and organizations."[23] It is a dangerous and subversive guide for revolutionaries. "It is also a guide," Zuboff told me, "for what will happen to universities if they do not evolve. People have changed more than the organizations they depend on, and the new breed of individuals will find a way around the gatekeepers." Zuboff listed for me the unmistakable signs that boundaries are being destroyed:

1. Services are desired by many, but affordable by few

2. Trust between stakeholders and service providers has fractured

3. Business models are concentrated and have high fixed costs that could be distributed

4. Organizations can be replaced with outside networks with hidden assets

5. Organizations do not have all the assets they need

6. Stakeholders have needs that have not been imagined, and there is no way to learn about their needs

Each of these signs appears repeatedly throughout this book, because the wedge that is driven between the cost of college and what the public can afford is an inescapable economic pressure that fractures trust and leaves the door open for disrupters. If universities—the incumbents—do nothing, then a new generation of innovative, responsive, and affordable individuals and organizations will find each other and collaborate to dismantle boundaries. They will build a bypass economy.

7 Pyramids

The story is told by nineteenth-century philosopher William James: one of his former students at Harvard, who had otherwise-impeccable credentials, was appointed to teach literature at a local college when the awful discovery was made that he was lacking a PhD degree. Claiming that the appointment had been made by mistake, the offer was promptly withdrawn and the candidate was advised to procure the Harvard degree as quickly as possible. Harvard's faculty took great care to point out that the lack of a doctorate in philosophy had no bearing whatsoever on his ability to teach literature, and that "he was of ultra-Ph.D. quality and one of the strongest men with who [they] had ever had to deal." It was a futile cause since "the quality per se of the man signified nothing in this connection." The only thing that mattered was the degree: "The College had always gloried in a list of faculty members who bore that doctor's title, and to make a gap in the galaxy and admit a common fox without a tail would be a degradation impossible to be thought of." The story ends happily for the student, who—after several false starts—"passed a first-rate examination, wiped out the stain, and brought his College into proper relations with the world again."[1]

Advanced degrees were a novelty in 1900, but American universities already had staked out their positions in a hierarchy—although their outlines could barely be seen—with academic titles that appeared, according to James, invented to "ape aristocratic titles ... to dazzle the servants of the house of one's friends."[2] It did not take long for the hierarchy to solidify. Those at the top made sure that their positions—almost always tied to outward signs of prestige and wealth—were securely established. Political columnist Nicholas von Hoffman added corporate capitalism embodied by Andrew Carnegie and John D. Rockefeller to the list of forces destroying higher education, dispensing money to institutions, von Hoffman noted, "on the condition that [they] changed themselves to fit a new national system of interchangeable academic parts." It has made the institutions impervious to change:

"Student complaints of the last decade have had absolutely no effect on the administration and organization of the university," wrote von Hoffman. "No university has seriously asked itself whether it might be able to do the same job or a better one for less money by reorganizing itself."[3]

The academic hierarchy is held together by the veneration of outward symbols of status, slavish adoption of bureaucracies (like the testing, classifying, and accrediting regimes that are the modern legacy of Carnegie and Rockefeller), and autonomy from economic and political control. Clark Kerr once pointed out that these are also the characteristics of the seventy-five existing institutions that are enduring and unchanged since 1520. Among those institutions are the Catholic Church, parliaments of the Isle of Man, Iceland, and Great Britain, governance structure of Swiss cantons, Bank of Siena, and sixty-one universities that are "mostly in the same locations with some of the same buildings with professors and students doing much the same things, and with governance carried on in much the same way."[4]

It is a devastating attack. The hierarchies of higher education have been protected by the Élite and have persisted through the centuries because universities have been impervious to any major technological changes. They are protected by incentives that reward individual achievement and respect for status. To understand the rationale for this Revolution, you have to have a basic working knowledge of the mechanics of the academic world. The workings of academia do not change much from place to place and they have not greatly changed much from time to time, but institutions have grown protective armor. It is this armor that will be removed if the Revolution succeeds. Academia depends on pyramids—hierarchies in which there is a pinnacle at the top. Great battles are waged below.

Hierarchies

American psychologist Abraham Maslow is best remembered for creating a "hierarchy of needs" that describes how human beings ascend from preoccupation with satisfying the fundamental requirements of life such as food, sleep, and sex to a state called self-actualization (figure 7.1). Self-actualized people are able to focus their attention on morality, creativity, and problem solving. They live in a psychological state in which there are frequent "peak experiences" characterized by feeling that horizons are limitless. The catch is that self-actualization is only possible after more basic needs have been met. And conditions have to be right before the needs at the first four levels can be satisfied. An individual needs certain freedoms like freedom of speech, for example, to satisfy more basic needs.

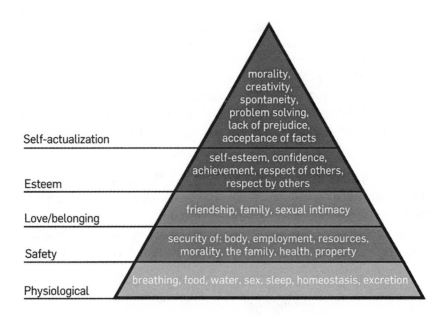

Self-actualization

Esteem

Love/belonging

Safety

Physiological

Maslow's Hierarchy of Needs

Figure 7.1
The Maslow hierarchy of needs, published under the creative commons license

I want to use the Maslow hierarchy as a metaphor for how universities around the world view themselves.[5] Academics seem to imagine two, sometimes-opposing ideals for how the higher education enterprise works, but they are both based on hierarchies. One is optimistic, inspired, and somewhat romantic, premised on the high-minded aspirations of pure and unfettered scholarship. It is Daniel Coit Gilman's ideal of "heroes and martyrs."[6] The other is base and strangely mechanical—almost predatory—and is more authoritarian than optimistic, more susceptible to mob rule than reasoned discourse. A century ago, Max Weber warned young scientists that it is political in the extreme and prone to cause "spiritual damage."[7] That these two inconsistent concepts can thrive side by side is strange enough, but stranger still is that century after century, the trappings of academic success and reward have expanded to embrace both worldviews with equal enthusiasm. What unites these two wildly different views of the same enterprise is the pyramid—an aspirational hierarchy in which the pinnacle confers such favor that thousands of universities are willing to sacrifice anything to reach it.

At the top—the pinnacle of the heroic pyramid—is the modern research university, a self-actualized, problem-centered, autonomous organization. Driven by the scientific needs of the developed world, research universities are an almost-exclusive creation of the world's industrialized economies. It generates controversy in academic circles that the humanities and liberal arts are sometimes left out of discussions of the nature of research universities, but research universities exist largely because of a worldwide network of science and technology collaborators that provides funding and economic incentives.

Humanities faculties are aware that they have been on the sidelines and have even fashioned the state of their field as a crisis—a "seamless garment of crisis," according to the president of the Modern Language Association.[8] The Association of American Universities in calling for "Reinvigorating the Humanities" painted a stark contrast between how differently the sciences and humanities see the research enterprise: "While 1,200 pages of Science and Engineering Indicators are published biannually, data collection in the humanities is still at a primitive stage…. Currently there is no national data set for the humanities."[9]

It does not help that many in the sciences are "troubled by the apparent decline in the standards of intellectual rigor in certain precincts of the American academic humanities," view research in the humanities and liberal arts with suspicion, and find their journals unintelligible, intellectual mishmashes of "self-indulgent nonsense."[10]

Bitter intra-academic feuds aside, research universities are distinguished from other institutions of higher learning by their commitment to a particular form of knowledge creation. Laboratories and other infrastructure are important, but equally critical is openness in both the creation of knowledge and publication of research results in peer-reviewed journals. Most colleges and universities expect their faculty members to engage in scholarly activities to keep current with crucial developments in their fields, yet to succeed as a professor in a research university, simple scholarship is not enough. Faculty members must make contributions to the body of knowledge that defines fields of study.

The idea of research as a component of academic life came relatively late in the history of universities. Medieval universities were made of up of scholars from different fields, but their primary purpose was to train clerics, lawyers, and physicians. Whatever knowledge creation took place must have happened by accident, and sometimes to the embarrassment of an ecclesiastical hierarchy that suddenly found itself confronted by the writings of scholars like Galileo Galilei and Nicolaus Copernicus that were in bold contradiction of church teaching. The very curriculum of early universities—with an emphasis on liberal arts along with the relegation of science and mathematics to a little-studied curriculum—seemed designed to avoid these sorts of controversies.[11] The idea of training students for a career was so ingrained in Western education that curricula were prescribed by law. Professors became civil servants whose purpose was to ensure that university graduates had been properly instructed and examined on the required concepts.

It was not until the nineteenth century, when the German scholar Wilhelm Humboldt imagined a university in which professors did not so much instruct students but rather supervised their independently conducted research, that the research university took recognizable shape. Just like Maslow's hierarchy demands freedom to climb to higher levels, so does a university faculty require freedom to be able to conduct research that might take an investigator down unknown and potentially dangerous pathways. For the next century German research universities defined academic scholarship, and they were much copied by the other great university-based research centers in England, France, and Denmark.

For all the success of German research universities, it was an American institution that realized the ideal of a university devoted to the creation of knowledge. Gilman was the first president of a new university endowed by Quaker philanthropist Johns Hopkins. Gilman was quite clear about the goal of higher education:

First, it is the business of a university to advance knowledge.... [N]o history is so remote that it may be neglected; no law of mathematics is so hidden that it may not be sought out; no problem in respect to physics is so difficult that it must be shunned.[12]

Johns Hopkins University was founded in 1874, a period of literally explosive growth in American higher education. By the end of the nineteenth century there were dozens of universities, public and private, that had cast themselves in Gilman's mold. While hundreds of others were wrestling with more basic needs like self-esteem, the research universities of Western Europe and the United States had climbed to the top of a pyramid. At the start of the twentieth century their vistas indeed seemed to be unlimited. Like the self-actualizers of developmental psychology, they were able to exert moral, creative, and unbiased influence far outside their normal spheres. They were destined to be among the most prestigious institutions in the world.

Pinnacle

By the dawn of the twentieth century, the sheer number of new American universities had overwhelmed the ability of policy makers, philanthropists, and the public—and even school administrators themselves—to manage the labyrinth of definitions, certifications, and seemingly endless bureaucratic demands that were being heaped on them. It was not at all clear, for example, that a high school diploma from Illinois had the same meaning as another from Ohio. The implications were staggering. If college admissions officers could not count on the meaning of a credit of high school math, how were they to fairly compare the academic records of students from Chicago and Dayton? The answer seemed clear to philanthropists like Andrew Carnegie whose donations were helping to fuel the growth: standard tests should be given to graduating high school students and used as yardsticks to determine what students knew. Working under a congressional charter, the Carnegie Foundation for the Advancement of Teaching became the most influential philanthropic organization in higher education. In 1947, it joined forces with two other nonprofit organizations, the American Council on Education and College Entrance Examination Board, to create the Educational Testing Service, which today operates the Standardized Achievement Test (SAT) and a dozen other widely administered standard exams.

By the late 1960s, armed with an impressive record of successes, the Carnegie Foundation tackled the two principle problems that policy makers thought would be facing higher education in the decades to come: the number of enrolled students and kinds of institutions they would be attending. The foundation enlisted the support of Kerr to chair a commission whose job it would be to develop a classification "to assist research on higher education."[13]

After Gilman, Kerr was certainly the most important figure in the development of the modern research university. As chancellor of the University of California, Kerr presided over the unprecedented growth of research at Berkeley after World War II. It was Kerr who tied together the many disparate missions of Berkeley's multifaceted programs, bringing graduate and undergraduate education, professional schools, and athletics and other revenue-producing activities along with research sponsored by industry, civilian agencies like the NSF, and military research offices all under one roof. He even invented a term for universities that support such diverse missions: *multiversities*.

It was with multiversities in mind that Kerr led the first Carnegie Classification of Institutions of Higher Education, but in the long run, the effect was not what Kerr and the other commissioners had intended. The Carnegie classification was a hierarchy—a pyramid that placed doctoral granting institutions at the top, and two-year colleges and other institutes at the bottom.

Although the Carnegie classification aimed to be a simple summary of empirical data that in 1969 captured the identities of the 2,800 institutions of higher learning in the United States, it was actually a statement about quality, prestige, and market position. Even the names of the classification categories carried value judgments with them. If you were going to be a

Doctoral-Granting Institutions
Research universities I
Research universities II
Doctoral universities I
Doctoral universities II
Comprehensive Universities and Colleges
Comprehensive universities and colleges I
Comprehensive universities and colleges II
Liberal Arts Colleges
Liberal arts colleges I
Liberal arts colleges II
Two-year colleges and institutes
Professional Schools and Other Specialized Institutions
Theological seminaries, bible colleges, and other religious institutions
Medical schools and medical centers
Other health professional schools
Schools of engineering and technology
Schools of business and management
Schools of art, music, and design
Schools of law
Teachers' colleges
Other specialized institutions

Figure 7.2
The first published Carnegie classification

Doctoral University, wasn't it better to be a number I rather than a number II? And why would a liberal arts or teachers college not jump at the chance of be labeled Comprehensive? Before too long, presidents, boards of trustees, and even professors began to ask themselves whether their respective positions in the Carnegie classification were something that could be corrected with a more ambitious plan and a little hard work. If the classification was a pyramid, then wasn't it better to be at the pinnacle?

Part of the difficulty with Kerr's commission was a naive view of the future. Kerr's commission had assumed a static system, in which few new students and few new institutions would be introduced to spoil the underlying truths of the classification. The commission clearly did not anticipate enrollment increases that would cause the existing institutions to burst at their seams. They had projected that under the most aggressive scenario, US college enrollments would at most double by the year 2000. In reality, enrollments increased by a factor of four. Growth undermined the idea of a static system. After all, the commission had recommended "holding steady the number of universities."[14] In 1970, there were between 150 and 200 PhD-granting universities, and the commission concluded, "We find no need whatsoever in the foreseeable future for any more research-type universities granting the Ph.D."[15] But by 2000, that number had jumped to nearly 400.[16] Like human beings climbing the Maslow hierarchy of basic needs, virtually every institution of higher learning began to climb the Carnegie classification—from Doctoral to Research, from II to I, from specialized to comprehensive. This had consequences that in retrospect, even the Carnegie Foundation acknowledges: "A special irony of the Carnegie Classification ... is the homogenizing influence it has had, as many institutions have sought to "move up" the classification system for inclusion among "research-type" universities.[17]

If the Carnegie classification were a closely held secret, available mainly to researchers interested in the analysis of institutional capabilities for research purposes, it would be one thing. But that was never the case. Everyone involved in higher education and a fair number of people who are interested observers are acutely aware of where their colleges rank in the pyramid.

That was in large part because professors' salaries are tied to Carnegie designations. Professors at Research I universities (which in the trade are called R-ones) tend to earn much more than their colleagues at Doctoral and Comprehensive universities. Those salaries are in turn much larger than pay in corresponding ranks at community colleges. There is also a widely held belief that the best students tend to congregate at the R-ones, even though most undergraduates—who after all are mainly interested in degrees that put them in the best position for employment—have little interest in the research missions of such schools. In fact, exclusive liberal arts colleges that refuse to play the Carnegie hierarchy game provide almost as many students to graduate schools around the world as the R-ones.

The Carnegie Commission also recommended resisting homogenization by "increasing the diversity of institutions," but just the opposite occurred. With few exceptions, university presidents and boards believe there is more room at the top of the pyramid, and that they will be rewarded for looking more like whoever is that the top. Those who manage to climb the pyramid find themselves enmeshed in still other hierarchies. There is competition for prestige, influence, recognition, and financial gain. These are hierarchies that attract the attention of policy makers, business leaders, and heads of state, so there are incentives for polishing reputations beyond basic educational needs. Von Humboldt wanted research universities to enhance Germany's scientific development. It became a national goal. At the top of the Carnegie hierarchy, university reputations are measured by the number of patents and publications, awards earned by faculty members, and memberships in exclusive academies. At the top of the pyramid there are Élites that attract wealthy donors and large research contracts. Even today, there is a price to be paid for nations whose universities are not near the pinnacle.

Meeting Local Needs

Leaders of developing economies are keenly aware of the benefits of Élite universities, but agendas aimed at climbing the pyramid don't always serve local needs. In 2010, a group approached me that wanted to establish a Western-style research university in one of the former Soviet republics. It was to be, in the words of the government officials, a showcase to demonstrate how a modern, American-style research university could rejuvenate both the culture and economy by focusing on areas like innovation and entrepreneurship. A survey of potential students and recent graduates demonstrated that enhancing theoretical knowledge through hands-on practice was the top priority, followed closely by providing credentials that would enhance prospects for employment in a knowledge economy. State-owned universities had been held in high regard for turning out skilled academicians before the collapse of the Soviet Union, but afterward government support quickly evaporated, foreign students left, and quality quickly declined. Existing local universities were hopelessly mired in local bureaucratic struggles. Expensive, new facilities were under construction, yet they had the look and feel of Soviet-era factories with large, dimly lit classrooms and laboratories that were obviously intended for obsolete technology. Even more alarming was their location. Large, drab buildings were being placed in former industrial zones. It was apparent that the planners had imagined that students would show up, like factory workers, for classes in the morning and would leave in the afternoon, commuting many miles in each direction.

The existing higher education system was fragmented and consisted mainly of institutions whose scale made it impossible for them to operate effectively. A total college-age population of 84,000 students was being served by 23 public universities and 47 private institutions. The average undergraduate enrollment at private universities was slightly over 150 students. The average undergraduate enrollment at the public universities was slightly over 2,000. The vast majority of current and potential college students said that they wanted to study science and engineering at the university level. When asked to rank the factors that were most important, students chose curriculum quality, guarantees of employment, and the availability of modern facilities for recreation, health care, and transportation. Prestige was among the least important factors.

The disconnection between national needs and local higher education was profound. Existing public institutions were consumed with climbing the pyramid. They were chasing international recognition while the private schools—some of which charged high tuition—had no serious chance of assembling a critical mass of resources to carry out courses of study. Local universities of all kinds concentrated their offerings in business, liberal arts, and law—fields that were favored by a small number of students. On the surface, reaching out to an internationally recognized university for help made sense, although it became clear early in the discussions that the aim was not to create a new university—which might have been accomplished quickly and efficiently by, for example, consolidating science and technology into a polytechnic with a scale needed to succeed. It was to find a prestigious American brand that would agree to offer cheap undergraduate degrees so that the incumbent institutions could concentrate their resources on climbing the pyramid.

In the end, professors from brand-name American universities could not be convinced to participate. In a shifting and volatile political climate, national leaders refocused on low-cost, online delivery of degrees. While affordability had been a priority, online programs offered few of the mentoring opportunities that students demanded and virtually no value for graduates who wanted to compete in the global economy. On the other hand, it did allow existing institutions to continue operating much as they had before, forever climbing a hierarchy that they no longer understood and had little local value.

That is why the homogenizing effects of the Carnegie classification have had such significance. Philip Altbach, who has studied the course of research universities in developing countries, notes that this kind of homogenization is likely to be the fate for many regions of the world:

> Almost all contemporary universities, regardless of location, are European in structure, organization, and concept.... This trend means, for most developing countries, that higher education institutions are not integrally linked to indigenous cultures and in many cases were imposed by imperial rulers.[18]

Hierarchies of Élites

As we will see in the next chapters, research universities compete in many ways. One effect of homogenization might have been to create a large class of universities that were peers and had no need to compete. That did not happen. Pyramids abhor homogeneity, so there needed to be a way for the few institutions that reached the pinnacle to proclaim that fact to the world. Virtually all universities would like to have a reputation for being elite. Coveting elite status explains much of what happened in the United States.

An unanticipated effect of the Carnegie classification was the wholesale pursuit of prestige by the entire array of American colleges and universities. Kerr eventually acknowledged as much:

> The elite institutions in the United States remained elite; some even more elite in their admission standards. The rest of the system absorbed the impacts of this enormous historic development.... [T]he one-time teachers colleges became comprehensive colleges and universities with a vast added array of occupationally oriented programs. The community colleges and the comprehensive colleges and universities took on, even eagerly, the impacts of universal access to higher education.[19]

Proclamations came quickly. Hierarchies of Élite universities are nowhere more prominently on display than in national and international rankings. Some rankings, like the *USNWR*'s Rankings of Best Colleges or *Times Higher Education*'s World University Rankings, are backed by news organizations.[20] Others, such as the Shanghai Jiao Tong University's Academic Ranking of World Universities and Consejo Superior de Investigaciones Cientificas's Ranking Web of Universities, are the outcome of academic research projects.[21] An ill-fated effort by the National Research Council (NRC) of the US

National Academy of Science resulted in a ranking in which some other-wise highly regarded universities were surprised to find themselves with mediocre assessments, while other universities that had never previously been regarded as Élite suddenly were near the pinnacle.[22] Institutions that had gone out of their way to avoid mentioning their previous NRC rank-ings were quick to publish press releases bragging about their newfound status at the top of the pyramid.[23]

Accreditation

An influential industry has grown up around the idea of using data to mea-sure the quality of academic programs. Virtually every country in the world uses some form of regulatory power to determine what kind of organization deserves to be called a university. In the United States, unlike many coun-tries, that job is carried out not by the government but instead by six inde-pendent regional accreditors whose methods of assessment are approved by the Department of Education, and another forty or more specialized accred-iting bodies that examine specialized programs in fields like engineering, law, medicine, and business. The regional accreditors wield the most power in the US system. To be eligible for federal financial aid, for instance, a student must be enrolled in an accredited college. The loss of accredita-tion would cause enrollments to plunge at most universities, leaving them financially unable to continue operations.

It is part of scholarly culture around the world to submit to external assessment. It is too easy for academic programs to become insular and disconnected from both the needs of students and intellectual trends that make for vital academic discourse. Advisory panels, academic peer review of scholarly work, and a variety of program reviews, including accreditation, have long been part of that culture. But accreditors have over the years expanded their missions to include quantitatively and objectively compar-ing, assessing, and certifying quality, and they are not subtle about their intentions. The *Principles of Accreditation* manual for the Southern Associa-tion of Colleges and Schools (SACS) bears the subtitle *Foundations for Qual-ity Enhancement.*[24]

Nearly every region of the world has adopted an approach to accrediting their institutions of higher learning. The reasons are diverse. In the United States, accreditation grew from a genuine desire to protect the public from unscrupulous or incompetent operators along with a combination of three otherwise-unrelated interests: the wishes of industrialists like Carnegie, who imposed the discipline of the factory floor on quality in education;

the legitimate needs of the federal government to have a simple way of distinguishing legitimate academic programs from pretenders who might try to tap into government funds to support students in pursuing worthless degrees; and the realization among university leaders that third-party analysis of program strength and viability might be a useful counterweight to a system that otherwise relied solely on faculty judgment.

The European model is different. European universities are chartered by laws that govern both academic content and university operations. Nevertheless, European universities usually form boards of visitors to review and assess their programs, using the same standards as US accreditors. In Japan and most of Asia, the quality of higher education has acquired the same aura as industrial quality, giving rise to elaborate governmental agencies, and supporting organizations that define and administer quality standards. The immense variety and range of colleges and universities in Africa almost screams for organizations to assess their quality. In India, where twenty-five thousand small, affiliated colleges operate without the academic oversight of larger, more established institutions, there is a bureaucracy devoted to licensing and registration. There is little argument around the world that agreement about what constitutes a bachelor's degree would be helpful, and there is little controversy that standardization would improve transparency and portability, but accreditors worldwide have adopted different approaches.

Accreditors say that their job is to objectively assess the quality of institutions and academic programs, but what does that mean? When pressed, university presidents express dissatisfaction with almost every aspect of current accreditation practices, yet there are relatively few who, like Stanford's Hennessy, say what is really on their minds: "Accreditation is really broken." Stanford is an Élite institution, and there is no serious doubt about the quality of a Stanford education, but when the Western Association of Schools and Colleges notifies Stanford provost Etchemendy of a pending accreditation visit, dozens of professors and administrators drop whatever they are working on to help write a report addressing the nearly one hundred core requirements ranging from demonstrating "continuous, documented excellence in teaching" to providing "measures of financial health as requested by the Commission" as well as "evidence of improvement based on analysis of results." It is a system ripe for excess. School administrators are coached on the finer points of catering to the needs of the visiting accrediting committees and reminded that well thought out amenities like gift bags can help sway a committee's evaluation. Over and over again, accreditors have adopted the language of the factory floor—the language of statistical quality control—using phrases such as "continuous, comparative evaluation of quality." The data they demand are supposed to provide evidence that these requirements have been met.

In the thinking of regional accreditors, these are the kinds of data that can be used to assess the quality of a university or college, and indeed many of the core requirements can filter out fraudulent or incompetent institutions. An accreditor's seal may make all the difference in the world for many new institutions or those that cater to at-risk students who need to know that their dearly earned credentials are recognized by an independent, expert authority. Belle Wheelan, who runs the sprawling and powerful regional accreditor SACS, points out that while the public may not understand accreditation, "people know they don't want to go to a school without it."[25] That may be true, but assuring minimal standards is a far cry from the more expansive claims of the accreditation industry.

What sends many college presidents over the edge is the lack of any credible explanation supporting the idea that pressing universities for expensive, continuous evaluation has any impact at all on quality improvements. "Quality, from Washington, DC's standpoint, is job placements and loan payback," says Wheelan. "That's not our view of quality."[26] Accreditors like SACS wield enormous power, and even established institutions—under the theory that squeaky wheels are likely to draw unwanted attention—are reluctant to criticize too strongly. Hennessy is not shy, though. "Whenever I press someone who's an advocate for continuous, comparative evaluation, for how to do it, they have no ideas aside from standardized testing," he says. The kind of standardized testing used in elementary and secondary schools seems particularly ill suited to the kinds of skills that university courses try to impart. Hennessy believes that "the kinds of skills we are trying to teach are not testable. And besides, we would like those skills to peak ten or more years after college."

Wheelan seems to be arguing that tangible outcomes like completion and employability are not related to quality. There are others who push back strongly on the idea, arguing that rather than providing a sieve that separates reputable programs from those that are not, accreditation is an expensive and time-consuming waste of resources. As evidence, they point to the large number of accredited programs that fail to graduate students and other examples of plainly failed programs that routinely pass muster with accreditors. Kevin Carey, director of policy for Education Sector, a think tank, is more blunt: "There appears to be no graduation rate so low that colleges lose accreditation if they fall beneath it for any appreciable length of time, even when the rates in question are statistically speaking barely distinguishable from zero."[27]

It is hard to argue that accreditors' interventions actually improve quality when there appear to be no minimum standards. As many institutions that enroll minority students are quick to note, graduation rates do not account for part-time students, students who transfer to other schools, adult learners who never intend to graduate, or students who take seven or more years to graduate because of financial circumstances. Still, sixty accredited institutions in California and Hawaii reported 2008 graduation rates of 20 percent or less for full-time, first-time students, and according to Carey, "Most of these institutions report similar numbers year after year."[28]

There is one aspect of regional accreditation that draws almost universal acclaim for its effectiveness. Accreditors require institutions to develop a quality enhancement plan (QEP), a concrete proposal to make a specific improvement that affects student learning and performance. The enhancement plan is different from every other document that accreditors require. It is neither quantitative nor prescriptive, and for those who think that accreditors should set minimum standards and then allow institutions to design their own approaches with that framework, it is an example of how accreditors can make a positive difference by simply getting out of the way. For many, a QEP is a rarely granted license to experiment, and because accreditors want to see QEPs, institutions are inclined to promote—and fund—projects that result from QEPs. The development of a QEP has been the occasion for fundamental shifts within some institutions. Jackson State University, a HBCU that once struggled with ill-prepared students, declining applications, and low graduation rates, used a SACS QEP to structure a new strategic direction. The result was an immediate increase in enrollments, improvements in math and science scores, and a dramatic shift toward students with better prospects for on-time graduation. Accreditors are quick to capitalize on these successes and insist on prominent branding.

Paul LeBlanc thinks that technology will ultimately disaggregate the very concept of a university, thus presenting a problem for accreditors who are used to reviewing vertically integrated organizations and activities. What happens, say, when the control that accreditors want a school to demonstrate has been contracted out to third-party service providers?

Accreditation has been based on a review of an integrated organization and its activities.... [It] is now faced with assessing learning in an increasingly disaggregated world with ... new stakeholders and participants, various contractual obligations and relationships, and new delivery models.[29]

And what happens when new delivery models arise that are completely at odds with accreditors' assumptions? The entire superstructure of accreditation is based on the idea of students attending semester-long classes taught by instructors. LeBlanc has received permission from the Department of Education to offer credit for competency-based education, which does away with the idea of a class altogether: "Students demonstrate competencies through completion of tasks that are then assessed by faculty reviewers.... Students can't slide by with a C or a B; they have either mastered the competencies or not."[30]

As LeBlanc points out, the ingrained view that higher education is delivered by a vertically integrated entity is one reason that it is hard to draw connections between accrediting procedures and meaningful outcomes. Homogenization is rewarded; personalization is not. A student who receives a Pell Grant or Stafford Loan—two of the most common forms of federally backed financial aid—must use that money to pay tuition at an accredited university. The university combines that money with the tuition payments of every other student. That may not be the best use of federal funds, but there is no possible way for educators to tell. There is another approach.

Federally sponsored grants and loans might be made available to students in a kind of bank account, much like flexible health care spending accounts, to be used to purchase whatever educational services matter most. Many students may choose to use MOOCs or other inexpensive delivery methods for introductory courses, reserving most of their funds for later use. For some students, those services might include special advising, tutoring, and competency-based education testing, though not classroom instruction. For other at-risk or low-income students, approved spending categories might include family or nutritional counseling services, housing, or work-study subsidies. There are compelling public policy motivations behind this kind of disaggregation of federal aid. Federal officials, for example, gain visibility into what kinds of postsecondary spending actually affects learning outcomes.

Whatever solutions are eventually adopted, it is unlikely that accreditation in its current form will survive intact. Personalization, disaggregation, disruptions like competency-based education, and public resistance to continued spending with uncertain outcomes will certainly push accreditors away from the idea that they can affect quality improvements to more limited missions. As a result, the value of traditional accreditors is moving rapidly to the margins.

Pyramids and Homogenization

Approval by an accreditor is only an acknowledgment that program or institutional quality is acceptable, and that is a long way from ranking in the international pyramid of the Élite. Pursuing excellence sounds like a good aspiration for any institution—one that is hard for anyone interested in the health of higher education to oppose. But who defines excellence? In most of the world the answer lies in the pinnacle of the pyramid. No longer content with providing assurance that an institution meets certain minimal quality standards, accrediting organizations—public and private—are now engaged as advisers to help universities climb the pyramid.

For some, it is a matter of national priorities to meet the challenges of globalization by building world-class universities. Nian Cai Liu, who was a professor of chemistry when China's Project 985 for building world-class universities was launched, recalls how quickly the mission of accreditation was transformed into a ranking exercise:

During the [strategic planning] process I asked myself many questions: What is the definition of a world-class university? How many world-class universities should there be globally? What are the positions of top Chinese universities in the world's higher education system? How can top Chinese universities reduce their gap with world-class universities? In order to answer these questions, we started to benchmark top Chinese universities with world-class universities, which eventually resulted in a ranking of world universities.[31]

The solution for Liu and his colleagues was to begin with four groups of US universities that spanned the range of academic reputations from the elite to the lesser known, placing Chinese universities in that spectrum according to a wide range of indicators of academic quality.

Deane Neubauer, former University of Hawaii chancellor and founder of the East-West Center, which studies the effects of globalization on higher education, has compared Liu's experience to others in the Asia-Pacific region and come to the conclusion that rankings may serve a purpose that accreditation cannot: they create a kind of "currency" that economies can use to measure the effectiveness of their investments in higher education. In the process of doing so they may in fact devalue traditional accreditation. Neubauer's reasoning is that since accreditation and other similar approaches to quality assurance try to measure an institution's capacity and capability, they really only measure what the organization might do. He concludes that ranking efforts throughout Asia and the rest of the Pacific region "clearly shifts the focus on institutional assessment from what it is capable of doing to what it does do."

This reasoning is not unusual. It is reflected in virtually every region of the world: measurement of the progress of an academic institution has been replaced by rankings that show, to use Liu's terms, the "gap with world-class universities." In other words, regardless of where you are in the world, quality is measured in terms of the outcomes achieved by Élite institutions. The problem is, according to Stanford's Hennessy, "I have yet to see anyone who can tell me how to measure those outcomes."

Circulation of the Elite

Elitism is so ingrained in higher education that it tends to dominate discussions about the future. When university leaders get together to talk about the importance of various factors for the future of their universities, it is— regardless of location and mission—their elite status or progress toward elite status that is uppermost. Given the vast and heterogeneous nature of higher education institutions this seems incredible, but remember that homogenization has smoothed out many of the differences between colleges and universities. There are:

• research universities in the developed world that compete for recognition and resources
• research universities in developing or middle-income countries that imitate the research universities of the developed world with the hope of gaining recognition to lift them to higher ranks in the pyramid[32]
• primarily undergraduate or vocational colleges and universities with little hope of participating in global scholarship, which because they are staffed by professors from research universities whose professional aspirations demand access to graduate students and research projects, nevertheless establish graduate programs to complement their undergraduate programs
• institutions that play a more limited role, and have neither research aspirations nor faculty with any interest in research

Homogenization was in part a consequence of the Carnegie classification—the consequence that Kerr did not anticipate—and is the single thread that ties all fifty thousand of these institutions together. In this era of globalization, accreditation leads to a set of internationally accepted assessment methodologies. Institutions will inevitably be compared and ranked in a hierarchical pyramid, and in an effort to imitate the Élite institutions at the top of the pyramid, will start to behave alike. The culture of academic elitism will creep into every corner of the globe, because that is how academic institutions are measured.

Does the emergence of an elite imply that the most meritorious are members of it? This is an old and much-debated question among economists. The most compelling answer was given a hundred years ago by the

Italian economist and mathematician Vilfredo Pareto. Pareto was responsible for defining the power laws that govern economic choices that today are known to govern Internet economics as well.[33] Pareto was also responsible for the principle called the *circulation of the elites*, which states that regardless of how capabilities of an elite population are defined, their quality can only be maintained if there is a chance that nonelites can someday enter into the elite ranks.[34]

Hierarchies make that circulation nearly impossible. Presidents, provosts, and department chairs of prestigious academic departments receive their training at other Élite schools. The same institutions show up on lists of academic awards and prizes. Undergraduates who are admitted to Élite graduate programs are by and large graduates of other Élite undergraduate programs.[35]

It is oftentimes difficult in academic ranks to separate a generalized desire for excellence from the actions that are required to achieve it. Excellence is presented in the guise of prestige. What institutions in the Middle are left with is a pyramid that needs climbing. There are two consequences of what often seems like a mad rush to maintain a culture of elitism. The first is that the climb to the pinnacle is bound to fail for most institutions. For most, the game is rigged, and they will find there is no pathway to the Élite. The second is that elitism is no pathway to excellence. Even copying the actions of Élite institutions does not result in an academic culture that is best (or even good) for most students. In a technologically fueled revolution, hierarchies seem anachronistic, and the innovators know this. Climbing pyramids might be important, but LeBlanc is more concerned with the 80 percent of all college students who want a more direct path to a better job or higher salary. So are Ben Nelson and a dozen other innovators who are convinced that the excesses of accreditation, rankings, and incessant homogenization of higher education are the root cause of widespread dissatisfaction with higher education, and constitute the rationale for change.

8   Rankings

Universities are rewarded for behavior that has little to do with educational quality, while educational outcomes get lost in a shuffle of meaningless statistics. Reaching the pinnacle of the pyramid means better students and larger alumni donations. Faculty clamor to be hired by institutions at the top of the hierarchy, and corporations, believing their graduates are more talented, compete to hire their students. Parents and students alike know this and flood the top schools with applications. The universities at the top of the pyramid are winners. It is tempting to declare winners by reducing educational quality to a single score so that institutions can be ranked from best to worst.

With each improvement in rank, the quality of student applications improves and the number of applications for faculty positions from other top-ranked programs increases. Faculty members win more awards, and the volume of sponsored research grows. Upper administration rewards this kind of performance. That might not seem unusual to the casual observer. After all, these are surely indicators of quality, aren't they?

The amazing answer is "no," at least as far as the *USNWR* editors are concerned.[1] For example, the only thing that matters for a typical graduate program in computer science is what 31 of the administrators of the other 175 computer science programs around the country think about it, expressed on a five-point scale. The stakes are high considering how little thought goes into ranking the quality of US graduate programs.

The stakes are even higher for rankings of undergraduate programs, which draw enormous attention every year. Even a one-position change in the *USNWR* rankings can mean a 1 percent change in the number of applications, drowning out other indicators of academic quality.[2] Over a four-year period, Howard University fell from its 96th position in the rankings of national universities to 142—a breathtaking drop in quality that cost President Sidney A. Ribeau his job. What could have so decimated the academic ranks of Howard that in the time it took first-year students entering in 2010 to complete their studies, the same skills and knowledge that had in prior years been taught to congressmen, cabinet members, judges, authors, scientists, and executives simply evaporated? Was it possible for the same first-year students to systematically decrease the likelihood of future success for every year spent at Howard University? The *USNWR* editors reported that several factors led to Howard's decline. First of all, Howard declined to report several key statistics. So the newsmagazine simply used old data or made estimates. In other words, they made it up—a methodology that *USNWR* hangs around the neck of Ribeau: "Howard's decline in the most recent rankings was mainly due to its administrative inability or refusal to report its most recent data about itself to *U.S. News.*"[3]

"Parents and students actually make decisions based on the difference between eleventh and twelfth place rankings in *USNWR*," says Stanford president John Hennessy, "and it is totally meaningless." The stakes are high, and there are incentives to give the process a nudge. During the same 2010–2014 period, there was a spike in fraudulently reported statistics like acceptance and retention rates as well as alumni giving. Claremont McKenna, Emory University, Iona College, Bucknell, and George Washington University—all highly ranked—were caught rigging data. Quantifying quality seems like a noble pursuit, but it is riddled with problems. Do rankings indicate how well graduates do? Did students acquire skills that improve over their lifetimes? Were they well prepared for their chosen careers? These are the same questions that vexed the first person who tried to rank universities.

A Wide Net with a Fine Mesh

Sometime in late 1903, Edwin Slosson, a professor at the University of Wyoming, decided to leave what must have been a comfortable life teaching chemistry and psychology and occasionally lecturing on photography to become literary editor of the *Independent* magazine in New York. Slosson was using the teaching job at Wyoming to support himself while he completed his PhD in chemistry. Leaving academia altogether was something of a surprise, but it was a move that was not as far-fetched as it sounds. Slosson had been writing articles for the *Independent* for several years, and had spent the previous summer in New York working as what we would today call an intern. He managed to attract the attention of editor and publisher Hamilton Holt, who offered him a full-time position. He was a modestly successful professor, but Slosson's move to the New York magazine scene brought him acclaim as an expositor of science. His books and articles earned him respect as "easily the outstanding interpreter of sciences to the non-technical public."[4]

Perhaps because he himself had been a student only a few months before or because of his experience in the university town of Laramie, Slosson was keenly interested in higher education. It was an interest he carried to his new job. He decided it was time for someone to sort out the incredible but chaotic growth in America's colleges and universities. In just a few decades, the number of degree-granting institutions had literally exploded. A few dozen colonial copies of Oxford and Cambridge had almost overnight become thousands of universities, colleges, institutes, adult education programs, professional schools, and seminaries. The Morrill Act alone had resulted in dozens of new land grant universities, each of them with a unique mission to provide training above and beyond what might be expected from a classical European curriculum. Slosson wanted to have "a clear idea of their present condition and relative standing." Aware of the gap between college catalogs and annual reports to alumni, on the one hand, and actual conditions, on the other, he began writing articles to help his readers navigate the maze of new institutions by "finding out for [himself] what our leading universities are now doing."[5]

In 1910, Slosson collected his *Independent* articles into the first ranking of American universities.[6] It was the book that in all likelihood started the twentieth century's global obsession with world rankings of universities, but it started out on a different path. In fact, the array of world universities today would have been as incomprehensible to Slosson as we find the hodgepodge of institutions—large and small, research and instructional, public and private, secular and denominational, wealthy and hardscrabble, legitimate and frankly crackpot—that made up higher education at the dawn of the twentieth century. Public universities in the United States were wealthy, small, and elite. Private universities were far more numerous, but they were of variable quality, and often lived hand to mouth on whatever funds could be scraped together from friends, alumni, and in some cases strangers on the street.[7] Many were experimental in nature. The idea of a modern research university had not completely formed by 1910.

When Slosson looked at the combined influence of universities on American culture, he reckoned, for example, that Rensselaer Polytechnic Institute should rank higher than MIT among schools specializing in engineering and science because there were thirty-five prominent Rensselaer alumni, but only twenty-five MIT alumni, who had risen to positions of prominence. He thought that institutions with the highest expenditures were the most interesting due to their "novel features and unsettled problems." He took at face value the Carnegie classification, which classified universities according to how much money they spent for instruction, which he regarded as "a fairer criterion than any other objective standard."[8]

Slosson was so distrustful of academic marketing puffery and self-reported assessments of status and prestige that he ignored self-reported data completely, and only ranked a university once he had spent a week in residence, "living in some club or boarding house, attending classes and talking with as many of the faculty and students as [he] could."[9] He took into account how well a university was funded and how much it paid its professors. The size of the instructional staff was important as was how much was spent on instruction above what students paid for tuition. He threw Johns Hopkins University—which he otherwise regarded as under-funded—into his rankings because he considered research to be the wave of the future and did not think he could leave such an innovative university off the list. Prestige was conspicuously absent from his assessments. The colonial colleges had specialized in the circulation of the elite, but there were still unsettled social arguments dating back to Thomas Jefferson and Alexander Hamilton about where the governing class should be educated. Class held little sway for Slosson. The modern trappings of the Élite did not enter into his calculations.

Unlike modern-day ranking organizations, he did not take into account standardized test scores, selectivity, or self-reported admissions data about the grade point average of entering first-year students, or whether they attended public high schools. He did not poll an institution's peers for subjective reputational assessments, or objectively count research publications or faculty accolades as proxies for prestige. He ranked only fourteen universities—an approximately equal mix of public and private institutions—because he could describe firsthand what it meant to be a student there.

Slosson's path was not the one chosen by the organizations that rank universities today. They base their evaluations not on personal experience on campus but rather on carefully constructed models that aggregate data from many sources into a single figure of merit. Today's rankings are more concerned with quantifying prestige. The modern view is that selectivity—controlling the quality of incoming students—is more important than anything else. Typical of American rankings, *USNWR* Rankings of Colleges and Universities compile data not only on admissions but also on a mysterious quantity called yield, which measures how popular a school is by comparing offers of admission made with the number of first-year students who actually show up.[10] Also important are metrics like ratios of male-to-female students and how far students have to travel to actually show up on campus. The international rankings of world universities are obsessively focused on research and research universities. To make it to the top of the Shanghai Jiao Tong University's rankings, for instance, you have to be a research university with prestigious faculty members who win many awards.[11] The *London Times* THE-QS ranking is in many ways the gold standard for international comparisons, but is dominated by research universities that are highly regarded by other research universities—a subjectively assessed quality that is tied to test scores and entrance criteria, and therefore overly influenced by how selective an institution is.[12]

None of these have any relationship to how well students learn what the university is supposed to be teaching. In fact, education is nearly absent from today's rankings. "A useful measurement," according to former Yale University professor Roger Shank—one of the originators of modern cognitive approaches to learning—"would be to wait a year and then test students on what they had learned the year before," but no such data are gathered by any of the major rankings. Teacher-to-student ratios are significant for the rankings, although as I pointed out in chapter 3, these are numbers that have little impact on learning. The amount of money spent on education would be as intriguing today as it was in Slosson's time, but opaque university accounting so confounds spending, cost, and price—which as I will discuss later in this chapter, have virtually nothing to do with the quality of an educational experience—that it is impossible for most institutions to say exactly what they spend incrementally on classroom instruction.

There is little disagreement around the world about which universities belong in a list of the top one hundred. Many of the modern American Élites were highly regarded by Slosson himself. But the combined enrollment at these hundred institutions is barely 0.5 percent of worldwide college enrollments, so it is only natural to ask where the rest of the world turns, not only to answer Slosson's question, "What are our leading universities doing?" but also to find out which universities—outside the list that everyone agrees are Élites—should be classified as "leading." And if it should be too difficult to define the notion of a leading institution, can we at least say what it means to be a college or university in which the quality of education falls above a given threshold?

Accreditors are supposed to answer this latter question, but retired University of Hawaii chancellor Neubauer, who has studied the question of how rankings like Shanghai Jiao Tong, THE-QS, and *USNWR* influence accreditation decisions around the world, has concluded that the homogenization of higher education has encouraged accreditors to look to rankings as a guide to quality versus, say, "the fundamental role of universities—teaching and service to the community—which are not well taken into account by the rankings." As Neubauer says, "Ranking tables colonize others. They render the complexities of universities simple by creating that phenomenon to which all societies seem vulnerable—ordering by rank." Universities around the world define themselves by who is above them. "The result," observes Neubauer, "is that, despite disclaimers, the rankings come to stand for quality."

Slosson went to classes. He took up residence and spoke with both faculty and students, and in doing so isolated a set of iconic institutions whose complexities, problems, and possibilities were worthy of study as well as imitation by others. How different this is from today's methods, where a mathematically determined hierarchy that values prestige and the elite nature of a hand-selected student body above all else is what defines a university. To get to the top of the modern hierarchy, you have to cast a net through which many will slip. It is not what Slosson intended:

When psychologists become skillful enough to determine vocational ability by tests of reaction times and association of ideas, we may save money, time and metabolism of gray matter by confining higher education to the fittest. In the meantime it is best to throw out a wide net with a fine mesh.[13]

A university that defines itself by where it lies in a ranking of the fittest is playing a rigged game. To make it to the top of the ranking pyramid, a college cannot cast a net with a fine mesh, because ranking is tied to prestige. Prestige in turn depends on who is excluded. Students, administrators, boards, donors, employers, and the public are easy prey in this contest to quantify the educational experience and its value. The largest and most scientifically rigorous project ever conducted to quantify educational quality wrecked any hope of being able to do that.

A Resignation

Graduate education is in a category all its own among the world's universities. For one thing, graduate students, unlike undergraduates, are presumed to be well beyond the postadolescent years when parental stand-ins play a significant role.[14] The responsibility for learning is not the same for graduates and undergraduates, and the research reputation of professors—who are expected to incorporate research and scholarship in the graduate classroom—is a key determining factor in assessing institutional reputation.

Furthermore, graduate education is a test of intellect and resolve that prepares students for specialized—often high-pressure—careers of the kind that undergraduates are not typically equipped to handle. There is a different kind of societal interest in graduate training that justifies investment in individual professors (in the form of laboratories and attractive salaries) and students (in the form of scholarships, fellowships, and assistantships) that advance specific agendas.

Finally, graduate training is open-ended and indefinite to a degree that would not be tolerated in undergraduate settings. Students are not *entitled* to access to programs, professors, or even institutions, and once admitted, may toil for years only to find that they cannot fulfill the rigorous requirements of a degree. There are no guarantees and not much leeway for students who need extensive supervision or are otherwise not inclined to take charge of their own education.

There is little controversy about the desirability of matching students with graduate degree programs and providing as much information as possible about program quality, much of which can be reduced to facts and figures that academic communities understand, but how does a prospective graduate student find out which programs are good matches?

Graduate school applicants are rarely influenced by the quality of a school's athletic program or residential accountrements that might appeal to an eighteen-year-old looking for an extension of the high school experience. A campus that would be boring for a first-year college student might be just the thing that a first-year PhD student is looking for. Most graduate curricula are concentrated in a specific field, so reputation outside that field is not relevant. *USNWR* and world rankings such as THE-QS and Shanghai Jiao Tong are well aware of these differences, and effectively market their services as guides to the selection of graduate schools. Like the rankings of colleges and universities, these services have defined a hierarchy of prestige in graduate education. Every university that grants a master's or PhD degree wants to be in the top twenty in that field. There may be two hundred or more schools that compete for the same twenty "top" slots, so most graduate programs become second or third choices. A second-choice school rarely gets its pick of new faculty members and has a hard time selling its research. So even in graduate education, there is a Middle. Like everyone else in the Middle, second-choice graduate schools spend a lot of time figuring out how to climb the reputational ladder.

It is tempting to dismiss rankings like the *USNWR* ranking of graduate programs as crass commercialism, beauty contests where the votes either automatically go to the schools that graduate the most voters or, as is often alleged by schools in the Middle, programs that have long passed their peak but live year after year on reputations that are no longer warranted. It is a convenient construction for an up-and-coming program, but it is seldom true, and it is rarely a winning one. Perceived quality and reputation are highly correlated so there is no serious dispute about the quality of top-ranked graduate programs. Faculty in the Middle long ago realized their dilemma and began looking for an alternative: a ranking that was not only more objective and quantitatively supportable but also endorsed by a third party whose credentials and motivations were above reproach.

Conveniently enough, there is in the United States just such a third party: the National Academy of Science (NAS), an elite corps of scientists who are chosen for membership in an elaborate and exhaustive process designed to identify only the most accomplished candidates for membership. The NAS, as it is commonly known, was chartered by Abraham Lincoln to provide advice—unbiased and of unquestionable quality—to the federal government and others.

One of the branches of the NAS is the NRC, a research arm of the NAS that utilizes NAS talent to undertake studies when called on by the federal government. For several decades, the NRC has ranked graduate programs, and because its weight is so great, the NRC's rankings were widely regarded as an objective indication of program quality. Everyone from prospective students to university administrators to government research funding agencies agreed that the NRC ranking had some objective relationship to program quality. The biannual release of the NRC rankings was eagerly awaited. Careers, reputations, and research funding rose on the strength of an improved NRC ranking. But as the number of graduate programs increased and the widespread availability of other rankings made it a less urgent spending priority for the NAS, the intervals between the NRC rankings grew. There was a thorough refresh of the NRC rankings in 1994, and then nothing. For nearly a decade, the NRC was silent on graduate program quality, letting the *USNWR* have the field to itself, despite objections from the Middle that the commercial rankings were biased, subjective, and superficial, and should be ignored.

NAS leaders heard the call and in 2002 commissioned a radically new, data-driven assessment of PhD programs. Chaired by Princeton astronomer Jeremiah Ostriker, the Committee to Examine the Methodology for the Assessment of Research-Doctorate Programs was charged with making a fresh and uniquely scientific assessment of graduate schools:

The purpose ... is to provide common data, collected under common definitions, which permit comparisons among doctoral programs. Such comparisons assist funders and university administrators in program evaluation and are useful to students in graduate program selection. They also provide evidence to external constituencies that graduate programs value excellence and assist in efforts to assess it.[15]

Ostriker was the perfect person to lead this effort. He studies the cosmos, and is known on the Princeton campus as a fierce and aggressive advocate for data-driven science. For Ostriker, there could never be enough data.

The other major player in this project was Charlotte Kuh, a Yale-trained economist and head of the NRC's policy and global affairs division, which is responsible for gathering data and conducting studies. For Kuh, this was a chance to establish a research methodology and warehouse of information so rich that future generations of analysts would come calling just to get access to it. In fact, the methodology was so important to Kuh that she imagined a separate volume just to describe it. Independent of the rankings themselves, the methodology would be a unique and valuable contribution:

The methodology used to assess the quality and effectiveness of research doctoral programs will be examined and new approaches and new sources of information identified. The findings from this methodology study will be published in a report, which will include a recommendation concerning whether to conduct such an assessment using a revised methodology.[16]

There were others on the committee who were less zealous. Among them was former Columbia provost Jonathan Cole. Cole was deeply involved in higher education policy circles. He was writing a book on the nature of the research university and knew as much as anyone in the country about the forces at work in reshaping higher education in the United States. He was initially a strong supporter of Kuh's methodologically centered approach to assessing the nation's PhD-granting departments, but the NRC study gradually lost its luster in Cole's eyes. It eventually became an extraordinary battleground.

Beginning in 2004, the NRC sent email questionnaires to faculty members in every one of the five thousand departments, schools, and programs that it was going to assess. Often running dozens of pages, these questionnaires were intended to provide an unprecedentedly detailed picture of program quality that would once and for all settle the questions about not only who was at the top of the reputational pyramid of research universities but also how an institution in the Middle could climb to the top. Vast quantities of data poured in, yet for months—and eventually years—no information came out. A preliminary version of the NRC report was promised in 2006, but Christmas came and went with no feedback from the committee about when the analysis would be complete.

As questions mounted about the delays, the NRC was forced to explain what was taking so long. There were inconsistencies to be checked. Quality-control processes kicked in that required a new round of data gathering. Existing taxonomies of the fields of study were thrown out, and new definitions were invented that not only captured the range of study in US graduate schools but also allowed for newer disciplines to be represented. Above all, though, the data rolled in.

By 2007, rumors were flying that things were not going well. The committee had become uncommunicative, and rifts were appearing among the usually monolithic NRC staff members who supervised the entire effort. There were allegations that professional ambitions rather than objective science were driving many of the technical decisions. By 2009, there was open rebellion in professional societies and associations. A report that was already seriously late had slipped its schedule once again. The committee had begun another round of data gathering—this time inquiring about the nature of scientific publication in the various specialties that would be covered by the report. It was a little late to be asking those kinds of questions. Diplomatic missions were sent to brief the groups representing the research disciplines.

I was on the board of directors of the Computing Research Association (CRA) during much of this time. The NRC staff began visiting organizations like the CRA in 2009 to try to quell outright revolt. The first briefing to the CRA board was uncomfortable. There had been leaks about the closely held data sources that were being used to evaluate programs. Those sources included extensive catalogs of journals and periodicals that defined what it meant to be an acceptable publication in the various academic disciplines. There had been early grumbling about the new taxonomy of disciplines, but by this time the grumbling had turned to alarm because, incredibly, the journals and conferences that the committee had chosen to be representative of computing did not include many of the major research outlets for the field.[17] Furthermore, for computer science, the committee had chosen to include periodicals such as the *Journal of Slavic Languages*, in which no computing research could be found at all.

The first board briefing was tumultuous. The data badly underestimated the research productivity of the entire field, raising fears that computing research was going to be portrayed in a negative light relative to other sciences. Despite an explicit methodological goal to "assist funders and university administrators in program evaluation," the implications of flawed comparisons seemed to escape the NRC staff.

This was at the height of the economic recession, and public universities were taking every opportunity to cut costs by closing or consolidating underperforming programs. The University of Central Florida was using leaked NRC results to consolidate its computer science department out of existence. Several board members waved newspaper reports of just such actions at the University of Iowa that very week, but the briefers held fast. "It's better than nothing," Kuh told the board. The NRC staff seemed to be aware that the results might be misleading for some disciplines, yet claimed that administrators knew that the results would be revised in subsequent analysis and would take that into account. It sounded to me and many other board members that we were not being briefed on an eagerly awaited report on the status of American research universities but rather a research proposal for continuing to analyze the vast information warehouses that the committee had constructed.

The meeting exploded. A letter from CRA board chair Eric Grimson to MIT president Chuck Vest, who was also president of the NAS, "suggested that [the] NRC consider either excluding computing and related fields from the study altogether, or excluding the flawed citation counts, or including a disclaimer to accompany the flawed data and a promise to release a new report once the problems were fixed." There were other fields that were considering similar nuclear options. To avoid a complete breakdown of the process, Vest intervened and directed the committee to revise its publication list.

In 2010—nearly four years later than planned—the NRC released the first version of its assessment of research programs.[18] The first round of data had looked back four or five years. Much of the information reported in the 2004 questionnaires was already four years old, so by 2010 some of the data were a decade or more out of date, and could no longer claim to represent objective reality. Questions mounted about exactly what the NRC was assessing.

Even more important, the report was overly complex as well as riddled with errors and inconsistencies. Those were problems that could be fixed over time, but the NRC had also changed the rules of the game. Rather than ranking programs, it chose to present the complex data in two equally confusing views, each derived from a different methodology, and each accompanied by statistical error bars—some so large that the results were virtually meaningless—and confidence intervals that made interpretation difficult. Programs that were highly ranked in all other rankings found themselves suddenly demoted to also-ran status, and programs that had no discernible reputational advantage were promoted to the ranks of the Élite. The lucky institutions wasted no time in preparing press releases announcing that their time had come and—although they had known it all along—it was good to see their Élite status validated by the National Academy of Sciences.

Cole had composed his letter of resignation long before the report was released, but instead of bailing out on his colleagues, he continued to try to influence what he knew was a losing cause. When Cole did resign, he was public and explicit about why. His open letter of resignation said it was an inaccurate, misleading study, "not worthy of publication."[19] This was to be the rigorous ranking applying statistical methods to meticulously defined and validated data that would once and for all put to rest any reliance on the superficiality of commercial rankings. But it turned out to be a project that was doomed nearly from the start, riddled with errors and mistakes. Expectations had run high, and through all the years of data gathering, report preparation, and roiling dissatisfaction within the research community, the NRC did little to tamp those expectations down. "That made it virtually impossible for the committee or the academy to say: 'Unfortunately, we could not obtain meaningful results with our data set.'"[20]

I spoke with Cole just after he published his open letter, and he was characteristically calm about what had happened. He was even generous in attributing motives and failings. The NRC project failed, he said, "but it was not because of scientific misconduct." Rather, Cole contended, the failure resulted from "a false definition of the issues."

We talked in particular about the briefing to the CRA board and the idea that there would be subsequent studies and revisions of the analysis, more volumes of results that would further refine, revise, and sharpen our understanding of doctoral research, and that administrators, students, and funding agencies would fully understand this. "That," Cole said, "is not a reason for publishing a flawed report." As Cole pointed out in his letter of resignation, "Those volumes rarely appear—letting stand weak reports and unwarranted conclusions."[21] For Cole, the NRC ranking project was a failed experiment, valuable only if the experimenter recognizes and learns from the failure. Lack of intellectual courage, according to Cole, is the reason that the NRC did not admit failure, arguing against all evidence and experience that portents of quality, even if flawed, were better than nothing—better even than reputations that had been carefully constructed over years, decades, and sometimes generations of teachers and students:

> The majority of committee members, however, would not grant that reputations are real—and have real consequences. Students and faculty members take reputations seriously when making choices about graduate education or jobs. Reputations are not constructed out of whole cloth; they have been earned, for the most part over decades. They are, in a sense, a composite of the other variables in the study, like publication and citation information, as well as an indicator of some less-tangible variables, like the general intellectual tone of a university.[22]

Beyond Portents

See how high the hornet's nest, 'twill tell how high the snow will rest
—ancient portent[23]

The NRC study was a failure. If the NAS, using its most sophisticated analytic tools, cannot quantify program quality, how does anyone improve
on Slosson's simple methods, including what Cole calls gauging "general
intellectual tone," for identifying great universities? Perhaps the answer lies
in forgetting about defining the worth of a university by where it sits in
an elaborately constructed ecosystem—in effect, forgetting about who is
above you. Perhaps the answer lies in defining the value of an institution
by checking to see how well it does its job.

The NRC project was aimed less at answering the seemingly simple question "How well are you doing?" than at making a case for measuring portents of quality. One such portent is counting the number of citations to a
journal article. The number of times that a particular scientific article has
been cited tells you nothing directly about the value of a PhD granted by
the institution where the article's author is employed, yet over time, many
scientists came to believe that graduates of programs with professors who
publish many highly cited articles were more sought after than not.

Citation counts and the other data that the NRC collected are often
associated with good educational outcomes, but not always. In fact, one of
the persistent criticisms of the NRC ranking is that many programs in the
Middle actually became quite adept at producing many highly cited papers
with little scientific importance, and that data trumped the actual experiences and outcomes of students over many, many years. In effect, schools
in the Middle became good test takers because they knew the right answers
beforehand. It was precisely the approach that Slosson had rejected a hundred years before, but there was no one like Slosson to ask what was actually
going on—and it is easy to see why. It is absurd to think that the NRC could
take up residence in each of the five thousand programs under consideration just to see what they were like. But Slosson did his work a century ago.
It is possible to adopt his goals and use modern methods to achieve them.

The very idea of value in higher education is a surprisingly contentious
one, engaging with, on the one hand, those who say that the value of a
university education is self-evident and needs no further explanation or
justification, and on the other hand, those who say that it's all just numeri-
cal, and once you know the score, there is nothing more to be said about
the college experience. Justifying college on how well it prepares you for a

career or enhances your lifetime earning potential sounds utilitarian. It is almost not worthy of an institution of higher learning, some would say. What might the proponents of the intrinsic worth argument have said? The university is there for the cultivation of the intellect. It is a justification that stands in contrast to a purely utilitarian view. However, cultivation of the intellect comes with a price tag. When a college education is free or nearly free, the price tag does not play a significant role in the discussion. But in the United States, the price—even for mediocre institutions—is steep, and compared to the ability of American families to pay, getting steeper at an alarming rate. A course in English literature may be its own good, but in the world where students, parents, and taxpayers actually live, rationalizing the value of a university on intrinsic worth is not sustainable. It denies any economic merit for an activity while at the same time raking in money from those who want access to it.

What Will You Learn? What Will You Earn?

Throughout this book, we encounter the following questions over and over again:

1. Does an institution serve the people it is supposed to serve?
2. Are there among a university's graduates a sufficiently large number of successful and influential alumni to warrant a second look at what is being done to achieve those results?
3. Besides the visible success stories, what happens to most graduates once they get their degrees?
4. What, exactly, do students learn?
5. How important is an institution to the city or region?

Questions three and four are simply not addressed by published rankings. They cannot be answered by seeing who is above you in the pyramid. Both are *value* questions that can be answered by, like a modern day Edwin Slosson, taking a twenty-first-century look at what is actually going on.

It is entirely reasonable for a student who graduates with tens of thousands of dollars in loans to ask whether or not there will be a job waiting to pay it off. There are universities that consistently produce graduates who are in demand in the job market and, in effect, earn a financial dividend for having attended. These institutions have a uniquely well-defined value proposition for prospective students: "Study here and you will be well positioned to not only get a financial return on your investment of time and money but also, on average, earn more over your lifetime."

One of the innovations wrought by the Internet is the ability to track the long-term earnings potential of college graduates, and relate it to their majors and the institutions where they studied. Web sites like payscale.com make it simple to compare universities in this way.[24]

Economists have tracked the effect that a university's reputation has on graduates' earnings.[25] In 1982, there was an earnings differential of about 39 percent and it was attributable to Élite status. Graduates of private Élites were 13 percent better off than graduates of public Élites,—a difference that is in part due to the fact that public universities do not get to handpick their first-year class. Between 20 and 30 percent of the entering first-year students at large public universities in the United States never graduate, and the wage penalty for not graduating is between 2 and 6 percent of starting salaries and wages. While today the wage gap between graduates and nongraduates is as large as ever, the Élite premium has all but disappeared. The return on investment (ROI, calculated by comparing outlays for tuition and fees to a thirty-year income projection) is still high overall, but Élites are scarcely present in the top ROI schools, and as tuitions rise, more and more brand-name universities are displaced by lesser-known institutions offering degrees that are in higher demand. Two maritime colleges and seven engineering schools cracked PayScale's top ten for thirty-year ROIs.[26] Stanford is the only Élite on that list that is not an engineering school, although the strength of Stanford's engineering programs is surely an important factor in its current rank.

In fact, the choice of major is more predictive of earnings potential than the choice of institution. Petroleum engineers consistently rank number one in that regard. The top ten also includes computer engineering and computer science, electrical engineering, applied math, and statistics. A college graduate's chances of earning a significant premium over other graduates of the same institution are enhanced by simply choosing a technical major. Science, technology, engineering, and mathematics (STEM) accounts for fourteen of the top fifteen careers, and professionals with STEM degrees account for thirty-eight of the top fifty earning professions.[27]

The Lumina Foundation studied the state-by-state variation of earnings by institution and type of degree.[28] What apparently influences earnings the most are qualities associated with individuals. Grades are a major factor in long-term earnings, and so is innate talent. None of these factors have any relationship to the ranking of the university attended. Indeed, a Mellon Foundation report investigated the question of what happens to equally talented students who apply to the same school but end up attending different ones.[29] The surprising answer is that they end up earning about the same. In other words, where students attend college is less crucial than where they apply. The one thing that does seem to matter across all these studies is privilege. The more expensive the school, the better the earnings.

Even the most vocal opponents of assigning economic value to a college education admit that a school in which students fail to learn has not done its job. But surely the colleges and universities at the top of the reputational pyramid got there by graduating students who learn something. If so, then there might actually be a good reason after all for paying attention to the course catalogs of institutions that are highly ranked, because their students learn what course catalogs claim is being taught in the classroom. Slosson knew that course catalogs were no substitute for experiencing classroom teaching firsthand, and it was in this spirit that the American Council of Trustees and Alumni (ACTA) decided to grade a thousand colleges and universities based on what students actually learn.

It is the most basic obligation of a college to supply access to subjects like composition, literature, foreign languages, economics, science, and mathematics. A college curriculum should contain at least one course in history, provided it is a broad treatment of the subject and not a niche course on the history of a certain region or ethnic group. There should also be exposure to the sciences, but which science matters. A general laboratory science like physics or chemistry is a better introduction than nonlaboratory sciences such as astronomy or geology. It also matters who teaches a science course. Like history, science is sometimes narrowly taught by nonspecialists who do not provide an overview of the field.

These seven courses have a special place in a college curriculum. They are the courses that occupy 80 percent of the first- and sophomore year for 80 percent of all college students. They are sometimes called the general education or *gen-ed* requirement—a phrase that belies the scope of the national investment in making sure that proper attention is paid to how they are conducted. Because students frequently transfer from school to school in the first two years, institutions have a real interest in establishing that credits mean the same thing everywhere. Accrediting agencies are charged with checking this simple proposition; just because a college says it has a math or history requirement doesn't necessarily mean that students have actually studied those subjects. Accreditors, like ranking organizations, look for complex indicators of quality. Had they looked at what was being taught, they might have come to different conclusions.

ACTA used simple criteria: a college receives a letter grade on the basis of how many of the gen-ed requirements a student is required to successfully complete. To earn an A, a college has to require at least six of the seven required gen-ed courses. The exact grading standards are shown in table 8.1.

Table 8.1
What Will They Learn? Grading Scheme

Grade	Number of required gen-ed courses
A	6–7
B	4–5
C	3
D	2
F	0–1

Only twenty-one of the more than one thousand colleges surveyed by ACTA received an A. The immensity of this failure needs a moment to sink in: it is possible to graduate from 99.8 percent of all colleges and universities in the United States without writing a coherent paragraph, understanding what makes the seasons, or reading at least one of the world's great novels. There are graduates of highly regarded institutions who have no idea what a trillion means and therefore cannot understand the immensity of the 2008 mortgage crisis. Only 17 percent of college graduates know when the Battle of the Bulge took place.[30]

The schools on the A-list are not all that selective. Most of them would not be highly regarded in any of the published rankings because they admit most of the students who apply. Not a single school from the *USNWR* top twenty received an A in the 2012 ACTA study. No Ivy League schools received an A. The average tuition on the A-list is $16,300, well below the average tuition for all institutions, but some, like the military academies, charge no tuition at all. The largest public university on the A-list is the University of Georgia, whose $9,000 tuition is one of the lowest in the United States. A student actually can attend tuition free because Georgia offers the Hope Scholarship to residents who maintain a B average. A-list schools have mixed success in graduation: six-year graduation rates vary from a low of 27 percent at the San Antonio branch of the University of Texas to over 80 percent at the University of Georgia. St. John's College is an A-list school despite the fact that there are no majors and no departments. Its entire curriculum is based on the Great Books of the Western World.[31]

There is one HBCU on the A-list—Morehouse College in Atlanta—that counts members of congress, university presidents, CEOs, and a US surgeon general as well as actor Samuel L. Jackson and director Spike Lee among its alumni. Morehouse has managed to integrate medical and life sciences education into a serious undergraduate curriculum. ARCS Foundation, a nationwide philanthropic organization that provides awards to *graduate* students in the sciences, so highly regards the program at Morehouse that it makes awards to Morehouse *undergraduates*.[32]

What is common to all these schools is that their performance is not defined by their relative position in an arbitrarily defined rankings pyramid. None of them should care who is above them. Massachusetts Colleges and universities as a group are more highly ranked in major surveys than other states. Yet 59 percent of them are graded F by ACTA for allowing students to graduate with only two gen-ed courses on their transcripts. There are only eight Ivy League colleges, and they tend to be among the most highly regarded in the world, but three of them also require only two gen-ed courses. High tuition is no guarantee that students will learn what they should be learning either. Of the colleges charging $40,000 or more for tuition, nearly 60 percent receive Ds and Fs from ACTA.

No matter where you look for hierarchies that say something about the intrinsic worth of a college, you find a meaningless jumble of measurements that are in fact only portents—even measurements as basic as the venerable SAT scores.

There is substantial evidence that SAT scores are not predictive of anything except zip code.[33] Two former university presidents (Bowen of Princeton, and Bok of Harvard) examined the effect of SATs on admission and completion.[34] Only about 10 percent of the variation in first-year grades is explainable by SAT scores, which are intended to indicate how ready a student is for college. On average, SAT scores are tied to household income, which means that the population of students with high scores is less diverse. Income is tied to neighborhoods, and zip codes are assigned on the basis of neighborhoods, which with few exceptions tend to be homogeneous communities. Bowen firmly believes that high school grades are a better predictor even when admissions officers know little about the high school. Bates College, one of the most highly regarded liberal art colleges in the United States, abolished mandatory SATs in 1985, and later concluded that not only was there no negative impact but student quality actually improved.[35]

The production of students who are ready to enter graduate or professional schools seems like a quality that would have some relationship to published rankings, but that turns out to be incorrect, too. Tiny New Mexico Institute of Mining and Technology produces more graduates who go on to get PhDs than anyone else in the country.

Whatever the hierarchy, and no matter how quantitative and precise it seems, rank is meaningless. "Universities simply have to tell you how well they do with kids that are like your kid," says Stanford's Hennessy. "That's not a perfect measure, but it's pretty good." Information like that is what Slosson was after a hundred years ago, but it is seldom available today. College presidents who are obsessed with where their institutions fall in a ranking—about who is above or below them—engage in naked institutional envy; however, institutional envy is no basis for a sound academic strategy.

9 Institutional Envy

"Would you tell me, please, which way I ought to go from here?"
"That depends a good deal on where you want to get to," said the Cat.
"I don't much care where—" said Alice.
"Then it doesn't matter which way you go," said the Cat.
"—so long as I get SOMEWHERE," Alice added as an explanation.
"Oh, you're sure to do that," said the Cat, "if you only walk long enough."

—Lewis Carroll, *Alice's Adventures in Wonderland*

There are 128 colleges and universities of note in Great Britain. All but two of them publish their strategic plans, which are supposed to be their primary guides to how decisions will be made in the near and long-term future, how resources will be allocated, and what actions they are prepared to take. For the vast majority of the faculty, staff, and students at those institutions, the plans mean little. They are routinely derided by faculty members as further evidence of the corporatization of the academy and as unwarranted intrusions into academic life by faceless boards of trustees whose ranks are swollen with businessmen trying to force-feed short-term market ideologies on unwilling professors, or by accreditors and other bureaucrats enamored with planning. Sometimes it is the university administration—the ranks of which have broken free of their boundaries in recent years and, at many institutions, expanded dramatically—itself that comes under fire.[1]

There is some truth in all these criticisms, because prospective students do not find the plans particularly illuminating either. Applicants who have already decided to spend their undergraduate years in a particular locale or trade on a family legacy at a certain institution are not swayed at all by plans that deal with the content of curricula, nature of campus life, or promise of an innovative educational experience. Applicants who have real decisions to make find more often than not that a school's strategic plan is useless to them, given that one plan reads more or less like every other plan.

The other major use of a strategic plan is fund-raising, and the plans are careful to identify opportunities to advance the institution's agenda with major gifts, buildings, and industrial contracts. The plans are seldom successful in that regard. In fact, private donations to colleges and universities are affected more by the state of the economy than by any other single factor. For many, a university's strategic plan is an expensive exercise in irrelevance. It is a document that because it fails in its principle goal of differentiating one university from another, sits on a shelf and is notable only for the extent to which is ignored.

As we have seen already, higher education is hierarchical and competitive. Institutional behavior is determined as much by which other universities occupy coveted spots in the pyramid as by any concern. Rankings are to be improved, graduation rates increased, and endowments expanded. Strategic thought is frequently dominated by concerns like these, not by the value offered to students. Undergraduate universities want graduate programs so that they can move up in the Carnegie classification. Institutional envy can easily be mistaken for strategic direction. But what happens when a university uses a strategic plan for something completely different? This chapter is about the kind of innovation that takes place when an institution, strapped to a mission that is bound to lead to failure, decides to do something unique—to use its mission not as a straitjacket but rather as a launching pad. Nevertheless, before that story can be told, you have to understand why strategic innovation is so difficult to achieve in higher education.

The Myth of the Self-Managing University

There is an alarming tendency among university faculty to dismiss the very idea of a strategic plan. For some, a plan smacks of management, and management is the embodiment of everything that threatens the view that "people are hired to be on university faculties precisely because they can think for themselves and do not need managing. They are collectively self-managing."[2] It is a strange argument, for there is certainly nothing to suggest that university professors are so much more prudent, moral, or diligent than any other group of individuals. They are not so parsimonious and prudent in their allocation and use of funds, for example, that they therefore should be immune from the need to be accountable to authority.

For others, it is just one of many signs that things have gone to hell—largely, they assert, because of the rise of the administrator class within the university.[3] Benjamin Ginsberg, in his book *The Fall of the Faculty*, observes that before 1955, strategic planning within academia was rare and carried out at only ten of the largest universities in the United States, while today it is a rare campus of any size that does not have an office of institutional planning. This, Ginsberg notes, is in direct correlation with the growth in the number of administrators on college campuses.[4]

True, but it is also in direct correlation with the size of higher education in general, which in countries like the United States has grown by 800 percent since 1955. In 1955, there were 2.6 million students enrolled in American colleges and universities. By 2010, that number had grown by almost an order of magnitude to over 21 million.[5] In 1955, there were about 1,200 universities in the United States compared with over 4,500 today.[6] Personal spending for higher education amounted to about $2.8 billion in 1955, or less than 2 percent of the $180 billion spent today.[7] It is inconceivable that growth of that magnitude could be accomplished with no increased administrative effort, although it is always tempting to generalize from the simplicity of small enterprises to the needs of large, complex systems.

It is also inconceivable that once in place, academic leadership could not have a set of guiding principles for making decisions. In fact, most academic leaders have plans of some kind. They are just not very good.

Ambition Is Not Strategy

What Ginsberg and others actually object to is a bad strategic plan. I have participated in enough university strategic planning exercises to know that they invariably start badly with visioning statements and, frequently at the urging of a paid academic facilitator, brainstorming about aspirations. In academia, strategic plans are grand visions for the future and not very helpful when critical choices are rushing at you. Strategy is needed if you are facing choices, and if there are catastrophic consequences for poor choices, strategy looms large as necessary for survival. Strategy is all about competition. Universities prospered for generations with few competitive pressures and therefore little need for strategic choices. But today's competitive landscape is different than the relatively peaceful years of academic growth and expansion. How different was the 2012 inaugural address of MIT president Rafael Reif from other presidential inaugurals that talked about stewardship and preserving the past?

Yet just when the world needs us the most, we find ourselves at the threshold of a historical transformation. This technological transformation has the potential to reshape the education landscape—and to challenge our very existence. In deciding how to respond, universities stand at a crossroads of risk and opportunity.[8]

An incoming president of a major university whose first words promise historical transformation and choices is such a rare event that historical comparisons are hard to come by. It happened in 1869, when incoming Harvard president Charles Eliot, in his inaugural address, overthrew hundreds of years of European curriculum, eliminated virtually all required courses, and promised that Harvard at least would thereafter operate on a uniquely American model. Both Reif and Eliot ascended to their presidencies at a time in which the "very existence" of universities was being challenged by unexpected competition. In both cases, decisions had to be made, but academic decision making is easily undermined, oftentimes by the very culture that helps make a university successful.

Universities venerate culture. Sometimes academic culture is overpowered by great reverence for tradition. It is an attitude maintained by the symbols and trappings of academic life, from medieval academic garb worn at commencement ceremonies, to eating clubs and secret societies that mark exclusive domains. Culture, however, rarely serves a higher purpose. It is part of a faculty-centered view of what the university is for and how it operates, and it is frequently used to trump strategy,[9] but that is a false dichotomy. Without a culture that is aligned with strategy, the strategy will fail, yet allowing the self-interest of culture to dictate future decisions does not make sense either. History is filled with examples of how this false choice leads to ruin.[10]

The problem is that the strategic plans for most universities are just bad plans. When Antioch College died in 2011, it was a failure of a strategy that constrained by an inwardly focused culture, provided no guide for how to avoid the downward spiral of falling enrollments.[11]

Ginsberg rightly observed that most university plans are a cover for not planning at all. Fearful of an aggressive faculty culture, university leadership creates empty exercises that make people feel that they are being consulted while at the same time asserting authority over the future direction of the institution. True strategy is a coherent plan of action backed by argument.[12] Rather than a plan for action, a university strategic plan is often a substitute for it.

It should come as no surprise that university strategies promise excellence. Many are produced by institutions that are excellent already and compete successfully with the best universities in the world for international recognition as Élite. Many others are within striking distance of international acclaim, but most only have aspirations for that kind of recognition. Strategy cannot start with aspirations. It has to begin with what you have to work with—what makes you different—and like Reif's inaugural address, a clear statement of what competition threatens you.

A Strategic Planning Primer

The gold standard for analyzing the competitive needs of organizations is Michael Porter's 1980 masterwork *Competitive Strategy*.[13] Porter laid out forces that need to be managed in order to understand an industry. These include bargaining power, competitive rivalry, threats that new entrants pose, and the likelihood that customers will find a substitute for your products or services. At first sight, these forces seem far afield from the business of running a university, but the same forces that shape other industries also shape universities. Universities, for example, rely on suppliers of all kinds: from faculty members who supply course content to publishers who supply textbooks and journals. There is a large industry aimed precisely at supplying raw materials that a university can hammer into courses, programs, and degrees. The one thing that universities count on is maintaining the upper hand in bargaining with these content suppliers. A shift in that balance of power might affect prices or—as unionized faculty have already demonstrated—the ability to make merit-based decisions. Customers, competition, and alternative ways of doing things all have a potential impact on the way that higher education operates. There is no doubt that these are the forces at work on a global scale to change our conception of a university. In spare but powerful language, Reif laid out the challenge posed by those forces at his inauguration at MIT:

We must subsidize a deficit that no business could tolerate, a deficit that we may not be able to subsidize forever.... But today, this financial challenge is building to a crisis point. Why? Because the landscape is suddenly alive with credible low-cost alternatives: relatively new educational technologies that are making it possible for a great many more individuals to learn high-level skills and content at a minimal price.[14]

Who has power in this new landscape? Certainly not the producers of course content. The traditional suppliers of content are professors and textbook publishers, but for the most part their power is not concentrated. Any institution could easily adopt new, open content, thanks to the OCW revolution that was launched at Reif's own institution. The truly powerful forces shaping higher education are students, the rivalry posed by peer institutions that are now competing for both students and funding, and new entrants like the online content providers whose services are an increasingly attractive substitute for the traditional classroom. Table 9.1 shows who has the strategic advantage in today's universities.

Table 9.1
Who Has the Strategic Advantage in Higher Education?

Competitive force	Advantage	Characteristics
Professors and publishers	Low	• Power not concentrated • Many substitutes • Low cost of switching
Students	High	• Large and growing group • Undifferentiated universities • Tuition is large fraction of total revenue
Threat of substitution/new entrants	High	• Offer relatively low prices • Cost of switching declines • Plan to increase market penetration and capacity
Rivalry from peers	High	• Many peer competitors • Declining demand for undifferentiated services • Many barriers to leaving an institution once enrolled

The only strategic choices available to an academic institution are those that it uses to differentiate itself to students and gain an advantage over new entrants as well as existing, competing peers. Yet this one driving concern of strategic plans—the one thing that Reif chose to concentrate on at MIT, which is already in a dominant position relative to its competitors—is almost completely absent from the plans of most colleges and universities.

It is certainly absent from the plans of the 126 British universities that publish their strategic plans. A typical British plan describes:

Vision: to make the university a world leader

Values: we value diversity, inclusion, openness, creativity, and innovation. The university helps all students and staff to achieve their full potential. It not only helps in the creation of knowledge, it also acts as a custodian of knowledge. [Ours] is a plan that uses excellence, internationalization, inclusivity, and sustainability to prioritize the university's activities. Maintaining a high quality campus is important, as is a promise overall to define excellence.

In fact, 125 of the 126 plans in Great Britain promise to pursue world-class status. It is a rare university anywhere in the world that does not have its eye on world-class status. The lone British institution that does not mention world-class does promise to conduct world-leading research.

Higher education in the United Kingdom is facing unprecedented challenges. Much like the portrait painted by Reif for American universities, even the best of those institutions have to contend with falling revenues and mounting public pressure to make higher education an equal stake-holder in digging England out of social as well as fiscal problems, including high unemployment rates among college graduates, failure to serve the multiethnic communities that now dot the towns and villages of industrial England, and an unsustainably high number of colleges that are spending scarce resources climbing the prestige pyramid. Yet scant attention is paid in any of the published plans as to how to address these problems.

It is a textbook-perfect case study of how to make sure that strategic plans gather dust on shelves—documents that once written, do not guide future actions.[15] These are plans that:

- fail to face the problems confronting the institutions
- promise to make a leap in performance without so much as a hint of what key strength is being built on
- contain fuzzy, blue-sky objectives, which skip over the fact that no one knows how to get there
- are built around fluffy catchphrases like world-class

There is nothing unique about the schools in Great Britain. It is hard to find a strategic plan anywhere that, for instance, addresses the question of how an institution is going to differentiate itself, or by what magical transformation a middle-of-the-road university is going to transform itself to compete with the most prestigious in the world. These plans are not only interchangeable in the abstract; in many cases, they can be literally interchanged with only minor modifications.

Copying from Your Neighbors

In 2006, a rash of plagiarism allegations hit Southern Illinois University at Carbondale, prompted in part by the firing of a faculty member named Chris Dussold who allegedly copied the teaching philosophy statement of another professor during his tenure review. The case galvanized an informal network of unhappy faculty members who had mounted various legal challenges to the university and used the Dussold case as a justification for examining speeches and administrative documents, including the university's strategic plan, which contained identical passages to the 1999 plan of Texas A&M University, where the chancellor of Southern Illinois had been previously employed. Significantly, both plans contained the same list of "critical concerns" and "gaps." The similarities that seem to have enraged the Dussold supporters involved, for example, Texas A&M's use of the phrase "Achieving a Culture of Excellence," compared to the Southern

Illinois plan's "The Next Step: Excellence at Work." There must have been something more than the use of the word excellence that fired up the critics of the Southern Illinois administration, because universities everywhere use the phrase liberally. There are hundreds of similar plans in the United States, Japan, and the Middle East that are virtually indistinguishable from each other.

There was one thing that did not attract criticism: although Southern Illinois defined a goal of making the university one of the top seventy-five public research universities, there were few indications of exactly how that might happen. Southern Illinois graduates about 26 percent of its entering first-year class—a graduation rate that places it well below the 34 percent national average for public universities and nearly 20 percent below the average for the cohort of the top seventy-five public research universities that it hopes to join. By the time the university decided to scrap its plan in late 2012, its enrollment had fallen 5 percent in one year and had been in decline for eight consecutive years—a competitive challenge that was never addressed in the plan.

There are, however, a handful of academic strategic plans that aim to set the world on fire. They never mention world-class aspirations. They define success in their own terms and explain exactly the decisions that will be taken to meet their challenges.

These are plans that address existential questions, and they look startlingly different than the plans of other universities. If they succeed, they will change the higher education system in ways that are every bit as profound as the high-tech Silicon Valley crusaders. For one of those plans, the difference lies in embracing a mission that others have abandoned.

Not a Failure of Mission

Diminutive, effusive Carolyn Meyers nearly bubbles with optimistic enthusiasm, except when you start throwing around what she calls meaningless statistics. Then she bristles, especially when the conversation turns to completion rates. The percentage of enrolled students who earn a degree in six years or less is used like a battering ram in college rankings, and no institutions in the United States are more vulnerable on that score than the 105 colleges, medical schools, and research universities that constitute the HBCUs. Meyers is the tenth president of Jackson State University in Jackson, Mississippi, an HBCU whose graduation rate is 20 percentage points below the national average for white students. Meyers stops the conversation cold and asks, "Does it matter if it's six years?" She is an engineer with a doctorate from Georgia Tech. "Look at our students," she says, referring to the large number of part-time students, who cannot pay full tuition. "These aren't students who flunk out. They can't afford to stay." It is a compassionate argument, but Meyers is, above all else, a realist. She sees what is happening at other HBCUs, and is determined that Jackson State not slip into the downward spiral of falling enrollments, cuts in funding, and decreased academic expectations that is hollowing out the once-special mission of these institutions. "That dynamic will change," she asserts.

For Meyers and her small band of lieutenants, it is not a failure of mission; it is a failure of strategic thinking that plagues HBCUs and other schools with specialized missions. She knows how to correct that. "We are changing the equation," she says.

HBCUs were established for former slaves in the US South in the aftermath of the Civil War. They were a combination of public and private institutions with names like Natchez Seminary, State Normal College for Colored Students, and Howard Normal and Theological School for the Education of Teachers and Preachers. Higher education in the South was segregated, so these new schools concentrated on producing the teachers and clergy who were needed in black neighborhoods, towns, and communities.

When the Morrill Act created land grant universities in 1862, students of color were for the most part excluded from the ambitious congressional plan to provide "training in the agricultural and mechanic arts to the industrial classes."[16] Most of the new universities excluded black students by enforcing racist admissions policies, either explicitly, as in the segregated South, or more subtle means in those states in which black students were found for various reasons to have applications that disqualified them from admission. A second Morrill Act was passed in 1890 that established land grant universities for black students who had been excluded from existing land grant colleges.

Some existing schools changed their names to match their missions. Howard Normal and Theological School for the Education of Teachers and Preachers became Howard University, and established a reputation as a selective, challenging institution in the style of the Ivy League schools. Howard's alumni include American firsts—like Thurgood Marshall, the first black US Supreme Court justice, and Edward Brooke, the first black US senator—and Nobel laureates such as Toni Morrison. Martin Luther King Jr., a graduate of Atlanta's Morehouse College, recruited people like Howard alumnus Andrew Young to the cause of civil rights.

For over a century, HBCUs served populations that were underserved by white society. They became pathways for teachers. Some, like Louisiana's

Grambling State University, became national football powers. Some became pathways to advanced degrees. "If you were a person of color in graduate school, the probability was very high you had an undergraduate degree from an HBCU," explains Jackson State provost James Renick. "HBCUs have been a bridge, up and out," says Meyers, but after a generation of reversals and unexpected competition, that is a difficult role to play today. Paradoxically, advances in civil rights have taken their toll on institutions like Jackson State.

The desegregation that began with the landmark Supreme Court decision *Brown v. Board of Education* also started eroding the special position that HBCUs had enjoyed.[17] Places like Jackson State began losing their most desirable prospects to Mississippi's larger public universities, where there were suddenly communities of black students who could support and nurture each other while also enjoying the expanded facilities and enhanced reputation of a big-time college campus. Jackson State became, increasingly, the school of last resort for students who had the kind of uneven preparation that would have doomed them at larger, more prestigious schools, or nontraditional students who were not tied to a schedule for degree completion and were content to plod along for years, taking courses that may or may not lead to a degree. The story at HBCUs for the last fifty years is one of decline.

The share of undergraduate degrees earned by black students started to drop from its high of 35 percent in 1976 to 21 percent in 2001. Success rates for black students, which had been rising modestly for decades, also declined. The recession was an incentive for states to cut funding. In some cases, 50 percent or more of state allocations were slashed.

Circumstances were already dire at schools like Grambling State University, but the recession made things much worse. State-mandated cuts that seemed to fall most heavily on the HBCUs pushed Grambling to the edge of catastrophe. University leadership chose to protect athletics at the expense of academic programs. By 2013, half of Grambling's state allocation was budgeted for athletics. Between 2008 and 2013, a 61 percent tuition increase was needed just to keep some academic programs alive amid furloughs and increased teaching loads. When the school's football team protested athletic budget cuts by staging a walkout, the university's response was to forfeit what was supposed to be Jackson States's homecoming game—an annual celebration that draws thousands of supporters to the Mississippi campus for a weekend of football. It was a blow to Grambling's football legacy, but it was particularly unfair to Jackson State, which had not contributed anything to Grambling's woes, yet now faced steep financial penalties.

But Grambling's problems were not unique. Even famed Howard University came under national scrutiny. The vice chair of its governing board warned that competition for students from less expensive public universities along with a familiar combination of fiscal problems and bad strategic choices may mean that "Howard will not be here in three years."[18]

The recession also undermined support in black communities for the HBCU message of opportunity. Black unemployment was double the national average—a statistic that Renick spoke to me about openly: "Everyone has aspirations to be gainfully employed, but for our kids it's a risk. Most people think of college as an opportunity, but I speak to parents all the time, who say, 'I'm going to borrow more than my car costs? I don't think so!'" For Renick, recruitment is as much about risk reduction as making the most of opportunities. For many families of Jackson State's freshmen, it's a risk to send a child to college and delay income for a later promise of something better.

Like every other university in the Middle, the sustainability of HBCUs is tied to forces beyond their control, and that sustainability is in doubt. Meyers and Renick both know what is happening to higher education: the vicious cycle of increased costs, declining family incomes, and increased expectations. "In order to survive, JSU has to do a lot of things differently," says Renick. The trick, he notes, is "respecting the role of the past and recognizing we have to change. If you focus on change, then you run a risk, but if you focus too much on history, you are out of touch with profound changes in the environment."

Jackson State's strategic plan begins with a single, new thought about what it has to do differently. "Our reputation was enough in previous years to draw freshmen," says Meyers. That is no longer sufficient. "We cannot simply imitate Ole Miss. We have to offer something unique." Mississippi is a state with huge problems. Only 20 percent of its high school graduates go on to college, but it needs educated citizens to solve its problems. So strong was Myers's commitment to solving Mississippi's problems that in an era of shrinking academic programs, contracting to fit smaller budgets, she decided that Jackson State needed to *grow*.

"Because of our historic mission, students come to us less prepared," explains Renick. Some black colleges have tried to address this issue by straying from their roots, and expanding racial and ethnic diversity in ways that undermine the unique character of an HBCU. That was not Jackson State's approach. "The mission can become a straitjacket. It doesn't allow you to grow and develop," Renick acknowledges. "Instead ... we decided to use the mission as a launching pad." To begin with, Jackson State needed more diversity among black students. "In addition to our current students, we wanted more students who are top scholars. We wanted more full-time students who are financially prepared to fund their education, because there is a correlation between ability to pay and achievement."

"It's not just enough to admit them," says Meyers. "You have to retain them. What we've added to the mix is a commitment to graduation." Meyers set money aside so that every student who is academically eligible can stay in school. HBCUs have grown accustomed to confining the search for students to a pool of prospects that is being whittled away by competition. The Jackson State strategy is to create the bell-shaped curve that will result in low achievers rubbing elbows with high achievers. Some of those students will be people with different expectations than eighteen-year-old high school seniors because the fastest-growing group of learners in Mississippi is between the ages of twenty-five and thirty-five.

To reach enough new students who qualify for admission—the new high achievers—Jackson State has to be a presence where those students are. Meyers opened a branch location in Madison, Mississippi, a suburb of Jackson whose high-achieving students have been served in the past by a branch of Tulane University. Jackson State tuition is a fraction of Tulane's. There has been a fierce battle aimed at keeping Jackson State out of the neighborhood. "That's where our students are going to be," says Meyers.

Jackson State also has started creating aggressive partnerships with local community colleges. The university established a new office for community college relations. As Renick points out, "They have a great track record in enrolling students of color, but have been less than stellar in their completion rates." His problem is to figure out how to motivate those students to stay in the community college to get a degree and then move to a four-year college.

"It's more than an articulation agreement," says Renick.[19] "We teach engineering courses on-site at their campuses," he explains. "Instead of building a lab at JSU, we will put the lab on the community college campus." It sounds like a philanthropic gesture that ultimately costs Jackson State money, but in Renick's view, "It's not all altruism on our part. Sure, they get better labs, but that only improves the quality of the students that they send to us."

It is not the same thing, though, to get students in the door and to do something interesting with them in classrooms. I was skeptical that there was anything in this plan that made Jackson State unique until I was introduced to Robert Blaine, Renick's special assistant for cyberlearning. As we wandered through the hollow shell of what once were library stacks, I asked

Blaine what the inevitabilities were for a university like Jackson State. "It's ubiquitous content," he said. "A lot of our students don't start out with foundational skills, like reading, writing, speaking, and listening, so that's where we want them to spend their initial effort. And we want them to learn how to do those things in their discipline."

To Blaine, that means sociology students should start thinking like sociologists from their first day on campus. They should write like sociologists, read critically like sociologists, and begin using the tools and lexicon of sociologists. This was a profound idea. I had heard physicist Carl Wieman explain to teachers the importance of *thinking like a scientist* in STEM disciplines where undergraduates often know nothing about physics.[20] "Acquiring expert competence in any field—the field does not matter, it could be science, chess, or sociology—requires a new way of thinking about the subject matter that can only be achieved by many hours of a special kind of intense learning." In effect, learning to think like a sociologist means that teachers have to become cognitive coaches who help students exercise their brains through hours of deliberate practice. Wieman's science classroom gathers data from hundreds of research studies that involve active learning, formative assessment, and context-rich problems. If Blaine was as successful as Wieman, the brains of Jackson State first-year students would change as result. It was an inescapable consequence of cognitive science. What Blaine wanted to achieve was an idea that connects to the deepest levels of how students learn and achieve.

"This side over here is called INNOVATE. It's where faculty members build the tools that will be used by students over there." Blaine pointed to the other side of the room. "It's called CREATE. It's where students create their own primary source material." In the core of the Jackson State curriculum, information is everywhere, so education should not be about how to access that information but rather how to use it to create value for someone else. "That means using information to create new information. We want to build tools so that students can do that the first day they hit campus." He described INNOVATE as a kind of educational machine shop. "It's impossible to teach a traditional course in this kind of environment," Blaine said.

To be effective, a professor would have to change the conception of a course. No longer able to get by with giving speeches to passive audiences, professors at Jackson State would have to become Wieman's cognitive coaches—active participants in a learning process, making the tools that students will use for higher-level reasoning skills. Jackson State teachers would, among other things, alter their student's perception of a field. Students who create their own course content will no longer be able to get by memorizing isolated pieces of information handed down from an authority. According to Wieman, a novice thrown into that learning environment actually becomes *more* of a novice. Creating a coherent structure for concepts and solving widely applicable problems quickly alters perceptions. Wieman has tried this approach with novice physics students. He found that "a seven-minute, first-day survey is a better predictor of who will end up majoring in physics than first-year course grades." Above all, says Blaine, "professors will have to become fluent digitally. INNOVATE will be filled with technology and the JSU faculty has to become skilled at using it."

The CREATE space was going to be used for digital collaboration. It is an acute problem for HBCUs that incoming students cannot always afford laptops and tablets. CREATE bridges that digital divide. "It's where students will literally create their own textbooks," says Blaine. It does not make economic sense to demand that incoming students who have lived most of their lives below the poverty line have to buy books that cost two or three hundred dollars. In a flipped classroom, students watch videos and read books outside class, but at Jackson State, "students have to create that material as well," explains Blaine. "You can't do that in sociology without thinking like a sociologist. Or like a historian in a history class. If the professors have done their jobs well, these students will have to acquire skills they didn't have before."

I had seen this approach work at Temple University. Temple is one of Pennsylvania's public universities. Temple, Penn State, and the University of Pittsburgh are what Pennsylvania calls *state-affiliated* universities, which means that as large research institutions, they have more freedom to chart their own way than public institutions in most states. It also means that Pennsylvania provides a smaller share of Temple's operating budget. Temple is located in North Philadelphia, not far from the hard-edged neighborhoods where the action in Sylvester Stallone's *Rocky* movies took place. Temple students tend to be poorer than the students at the University of Pennsylvania on the other side of town or nearby Drexel, both of which are private institutions. When former Temple chief financial officer Tim O'Rourke announced plans to convert a seventy-five-thousand-square-foot Verizon data center into the TECH Center for Temple students, I was skeptical. Concentrating information technology in a facility was a risky move, and one that I thought would not serve students well. Among other problems, I thought that turning fluid, mobile information technology into bricks and mortar like a library was a sure recipe for high costs and eventual obsolescence.

TECH stands for Teaching, Education, Collaboration, and Help. The first thing that you notice when you enter the center is the buzz. Students are everywhere and they are in constant motion, plugging laptops into the hundreds of flat-panel displays that dominate the open space, commandeering conference rooms or video production labs, or spread out in Silicon-Valley-like collaboration alcoves. I had been in libraries that were fitted with personal computers and had never been impressed. I always felt they were still libraries, with librarians ready to "shhh" rambunctious undergraduates who might disturb others engaged in more serious work. TECH was a different kind of facility. It was designed for the kind of serious work that creative collaboration inspires. It was also a bridge over the digital divide for Temple's bread-and-butter students.

I was curious about the kind of investment that Temple was willing to make in TECH. That was where O'Rourke's financial background was obvious. TECH had been designed to be manageable and sustainable, with state-of-the-art operations centers and a strategic plan for refreshing the technology. But most of all, TECH was the kind of learning space that forced its users to behave differently. The space that Blaine showed me had the same potential, and I thought that the Temple financial model would work equally well at Jackson State.

There is a pedagogical reason for creating new source materials. It keeps incoming students interested because it *concerns them*. The history books that Jackson State students would otherwise have to buy do not include the history of black people to any appreciable degree. Blaine tells first-year Jackson State students that they are going to create the history of "New Peoples." To get that into primary source materials requires an act of creation. It is the same for literature, economics, and the fine arts. "No matter where you look, our students are going to have to bring *New Peoples* into a conversation that would have ignored them otherwise."

The concept of New Peoples is a metaphor for the entire Jackson State strategy. New Peoples populate Renick's bell-shaped curve with high achievers who would not have access without Jackson State. There are new peoples in Madison, Mississippi, and a dozen local community colleges. The commitment to fund the education of underserved Jackson State students keeps new Jackson State students in school and returns them to their communities.

Commitment to Act, Supported by Argument

In less than six months, Meyers and Renick had begun to lead a traditional HBCU in a direction that did not depend on vague aspirations of being world-class, meaningless measures of quality, or me-too promises of becoming someone else. Getting it done is a challenge. "The faculty are a huge chasm in the middle of it all," Renick told me. "They are the mechanism for getting it all done." He worries about the ones who are moving slowly, augmenting what they are currently doing, and others who stand outside looking in with no particular plans to join. On the other hand, the Jackson State plan is based on growth. "We are hiring new faculty," promises Meyers. "We are moving new people in because we are growing."

It is too soon to know for sure, but Jackson State seems to be benefiting already. In fall semester 2013, the first-year class was the largest ever—and the majority of them were the kind of full-time students who are more likely to complete degrees. Thirty percent were eligible for the honors program, and 37 percent were enrolled in STEM fields. "We used to worry about losing students to the big public universities," confides Renick, "but that has changed. At least, that's what the anecdotal evidence shows." For the present at least, Jackson State seems to be taking students away from its predominantly white competitors, Mississippi State and Southern Mississippi.

At its core, the Jackson State strategy is to spend money on game-changing ideas that distinguish the university from its peers and competitors. Much of that money will come from growth, and the university has a small endowment to draw on. Like other HBCUs, it also has access to funds that give it a unique edge. Part of the Education Act of 1964 that recognized HBCUs was a provision that gave them direct access to federal funding to augment their own resources. It is a built-in advantage that Meyers and Renick know how to use. They are taking direct aim at the university's mission. "I don't think the mission has changed in more than a century," says Renick. "There will always be an underserved segment that needs a nurturing, supportive environment to succeed. I just don't think you have to aim down to reach those people."

Like Crow at Arizona State University, Meyers's Jackson State is looking for unpolished gems to carry their college experience back to their communities to add value. She explains it this way: "We will change the brand of HBCUs from a school that minorities can get into to a school that polishes the gems."

III   Ramparts

10 Brands

Resistance started to rise in early 2013. edX, which had a certain obsession with partnering only with Élite institutions, rejected many dozens of requests from institutions that believed they could benefit by an association with the MIT and Harvard names, but not all top-tier universities wanted to associate their names with the consortium. Amherst would have been a perfect partner for edX. It is prestigious and small, and its seminar-like classes emphasize the liberal arts. Highly regarded Duke was also an ideal partner for edX. After all, Duke was also a liberal arts university. It had been a Coursera partner and had a substantial financial commitment to the technology. Within weeks of each other, both Amherst and Duke said "no." Not only did Amherst reject an offer to join edX; it did so with some fanfare. "Would we join some sort of agribusiness company that was taking over family farms and producing junk food if they offered us some incentive to do it?" said Amherst professor Steven George, who led the opposition to an edX proposal that was supported by university president Biddy Martin.[1] Duke publicly worried that despite the lure of MIT and Harvard, there was much in the edX agreement that would dilute its own brand. Seventy-five Duke faculty members signed a letter rejecting edX. They objected, for example, that "while paying Duke tuition, students will watch recorded lectures and participate in sections via webcam—enjoying neither the advantages of self-paced learning nor the responsiveness of a professor who teaches to the passions and curiosities of students." If determined resistance to the Revolution was going to materialize, universities would seize on branding as a first line of defense.

There are universities whose very names call to mind images and feelings that are unique and enduring. These institutions each have a presence that attracts people from all corners of society with a fierce loyalty unlike any other. A commercial enterprise might spend millions of dollars on advertising campaigns, and still more millions on internal controls to ensure consistency of themes and messages—on *branding*—only to see its market presence undermined by a lawsuit, errant executive, or botched product release. Commercial brands are fragile. University brands are in a different category; they are difficult to establish and hard to damage. To illustrate, I want to tell you a long story about a brand that should have been destroyed—but instead emerged largely unscathed by events and actions that were totally under its control—and an as-yet incomplete story about an audacious attempt by a new kind of university to shoulder its way into the crowded field of academic brands.

Fallen

When Jerry Sandusky, a former assistant to Penn State University's football coaching legend Joe Paterno, was dragged away by police in late 2011, the allegations of sexual abuse that in other circumstances might have been evidence of nothing more than personal depravity and a shocking ability to betray trust, quickly swirled out of control, threatening the reputation of the storied, 150-year-old institution. Swept up in the ensuing scandal were coaches, programs, and the panoply of administrators who for more than a decade had allegedly covered up twenty or more incidents of child abuse. In fact, Sandusky—who despite complaints and warnings about inappropriate behavior had been honored with the title "coach emeritus"—was helped by Penn State. He was even given access to the university facilities where the abuse took place.

Paterno, whose statue guarded the entrance to Beaver Stadium and enshrined forever the glories of seasons long past, was sick with lung cancer. He successfully avoided the media for days, but when he finally faced the press, he appeared to be an especially broken man. The reporters crowding his front door demanded to know when he became aware of Sandusky's attraction to young boys, and how he could have overlooked years of warning signs and troubling reports of inappropriate behavior.

Paterno was eighty-five years old and looking forward to his final season as head coach. He was used to answering the aggressive questions of a postgame press conference, but this was not the leader of old, and it was not that kind of press conference. This was a type of interrogation—personal, probing, and accusative—that he had never faced before. Paterno stared, uncomprehending through thick glasses, resentful, bitter, and uncharacteristically unsure of himself. There had been stories, and Paterno must have been replaying the meetings and encounters in his mind, trying to recall his reaction to reports by eyewitnesses to Sandusky's behavior, and trying to make sense of the now-shattered but clearly blind trust he had placed in Sandusky.

In January 2012, cancer finally killed Paterno, hastened no doubt by the effects of his firing, the scandal, and the prospect of facing criminal charges. His statue came down. President Graham Spanier and other administrators were indicted for concealing child abuse. An independent review panel led by former FBI director Louis Freeh found structural failures that protected intercollegiate football from the kind of scrutiny that would accompany most other $70 million ventures. Among the findings in the 270-page Freeh report was a nearly complete disregard for Sandusky's victims in the doomed, headlong rush to protect the Penn State brand:

Our most saddening and sobering finding is the total disregard for the safety and welfare of Sandusky's child victims by the most senior leaders at Penn State. The most powerful men at Penn State failed to take any steps for 14 years to protect the children who Sandusky victimized.[2]

In the aftermath, the university would pay $60 million to victims' families and the National Collegiate Athletic Association (NCAA). Eleven wins were removed from Penn State's football record. A football scandal and the personal failings of Sandusky had besmirched the university's reputation, and there were predictions that student applications and donations would drop precipitously, imperiling an already-grave financial plan to cope with massive cuts to the university's budget. The scandal and its cover-up were a blot on the brand of a once-great institution. In fact, protecting the Penn State brand had been at the heart of its failure as an institution: "Bad publicity affects a panorama of different events including the brand of Penn State, including the university, including the reputation of coaches, including the ability to do fundraising. It's got huge implications."[3]

Protecting Penn State's brand was the furthest thing from the minds of the committed reformers who used the Sandusky scandal as evidence of the rot of intercollegiate sports and the NCAA. Sports analyst and lawyer Jay Bilas characterized Penn State's actions as a "conspiracy of cowards."[4] Brands rarely survive this kind of damage. The energy company Enron was a $60 billion giant, whose shares were trading at seventy times its earnings, when it was forced into bankruptcy. Its business model, which relied on inflated statements of revenue and profits, collapsed amid a 2001 investigation by the US Securities and Exchange Commission of fraudulent accounting practices. Enron's founder, Ken Lay and its chief operating officer, Jeffrey Skilling were both indicted on federal charges, convicted, and sentenced to prison. The pensions of thousands of employees were wiped out.

The damage to the brand of Arthur Anderson, the fabled auditing and consulting firm whose reputation had been compromised by Lay and Skilling, was so great that it too went out of business. The Enron bankruptcy was the largest in US history—a distinction that would be held for exactly one year.

In 2002, Bernie Ebbers, CEO of the telecommunications company World-Com, was found to have used fraudulent accounting practices to maintain the share price of stock in a company whose value was actually declining. WorldCom was fined over $2 billion. The company moved its headquarters to Virginia, changed its name to MCI, and hired former Hewlett-Packard executive Michael Capellas to guide the company through Chapter 11 reorganization. In 2005, Verizon Communications purchased MCI. In the aftermath, the US government passed sweeping legislation, the Sarbanes-Oxley Act, which imposed new rules for financial reporting and auditing on every publicly traded company in the United States.[5]

There are hundreds of examples of brands that were transformed, enhanced, or damaged by products, events, or changing customer tastes. Honda, once known as a peddler of lawn mowers, motorbikes, and cheap cars, became the brand most associated with the rapid rise in Japanese quality and design. In the 1990s—when cell phone conversations were frequently affairs that were shouted over static-filled connections—Sprint urged new customers to imagine hearing a pin drop and became the brand associated with quality. Coca-Cola's plan to replace its iconic soft drink brand with "New Coke" was derailed by massive public outcry. IBM's once-innovative Selectric typewriters and Xerox's futuristic office equipment were made obsolete by their own research laboratories.

University brands work differently. Within months of the publication of the Freeh Report and imposition of crippling sanctions by the NCAA, rumors began to surface from within the Freeh investigation that the report was flawed, and in fact Paterno and Penn State had been wrongly accused and convicted in the press.[6] Despite the humiliating national scandal, criminal indictments and tragic circumstances for Sandusky's victims, many on the university's board of trustees placed the blame for damaging Penn State's reputation not on the underlying facts but on Freeh himself. A vocal minority demanded that the board repudiate the Freeh Report and call for a fresh investigation. "We need to defend Penn State," said one alumni-elected trustee at an October meeting of the board, to applause from the audience.[7]

A group of Penn State faculty members publicly protested the unfair treatment of the university and its reputation by both Freeh and the NCAA.[8] Student support for Penn State football was strong. It helped that the NCAA chose to restore scholarships that had been stripped in the wake of the

Sandusky scandal, but that does not explain the increased popularity of the university's academic programs. Enrollments at the main campus had increased by 2013. Within months of paying a $60 million penalty to the NCAA, donations from alumni and other supporters increased dramatically. Donations to Penn State totaled $208 million in 2012.[9] Two years after the university's name had been ignominiously dragged through the mud, the long-term effect of the scandal is unclear. The NCAA has moved on to new battles; Penn State emerged embarrassed but operational under new management. There are reformers who place the blame squarely on big-time intercollegiate athletics, which they say turns universities into entertainment companies, yet they are no closer to their stated goal of decoupling academics and athletics.

Mottoes and Reputations

The Penn State scandal illustrates not that it is impossible to damage a university's reputation but rather that in the academic world, the brand—the relationship in the public mind between name and reputation—of a university is much more complex than in the commercial world of products and services. As ephemeral as the concept of a brand might be, reputations are real and have real consequences.[10] Reputations determine who applies for admission, which faculty candidates are hired, and how much effort corporate recruiters put into on-campus interviews. But there is no marketing strategy that can establish or even improve a university's brand in the absence of a reputation that has been earned over many decades versus constructed in an advertising campaign.

There is an entire category of management consultants who specialize in academic branding, and descend on college campuses to sell complicated packages of advertising, slogans, consulting services, and organizational tools to better tell the story of brand vision and values. In the previous chapter, I outlined the reasons for discounting the vision as a useful basis for strategic plans. For the same reasons, brand vision also has limited usefulness for universities: in the absence of decisions, vision is meaningless. Brand vision is frequently summarized by a motto of some kind. Thomas Hackett in his 2007 essay on university slogans claims that mottoes matter less for universities whose brand needs no introduction.[11] Everyone knows what Yale stands for: "Yale does have a motto—Lux et Veritas or 'Light and Truth'—but its slogan might as well be 'Yale.'"

There are occasional examples, like MIT, where a school's motto is actually a perfect institutional description of how decisions are made. MIT's motto is *Mens et Manus*, or "Mind and Hand"—a phrase that reflects the essence of an MIT education: knowledge for practical purposes.[12] In 2004, Arizona State University adopted the "New American University" as a descriptive tagline, reflecting its operating principles aimed at providing accessible, affordable education at the highest possible levels of quality. Arizona State's inclusiveness was in such sharp contrast to the direction of American higher education, which equated quality with the selectiveness of elite institutions, that it warranted its description as a new kind of American university.[13]

But does that mean lesser-known institutions might need a motto to help establish their brand identity? I cannot find a single compelling case that might illustrate such a need. Lesser-known universities that have established a comfortable niche by providing value to their stakeholders find that brand-marketing campaigns add little or nothing to their reputations. Institutions battling fundamental challenges to their value propositions are not helped at all by their branding:

• Antioch College proudly bore the motto bestowed in 1852 by its first president Horace Mann, "Be ashamed to die until you have won some victory for humanity," right to the moment it shuttered its doors in 2007—a victim of dwindling interest in the kind of education that the college offered.[14] Antioch's brand was always strong and associated with progressive causes, and to the end it was an apt declaration of Antioch vision and values.

• When an audit revealed that 97 percent of the Chinese students who graduated from Dickenson State had not really completed degree requirements, the university soon acquired a reputation as a diploma mill for foreign students. It would have been even more embarrassing if the school motto had promised to uphold excellence, but fortunately, the university's motto is "Once a Hawk, Always a Hawk," which did not even hint at academic reputation.[15]

• The University of Southern New Hampshire, on the other hand, has excelled during the largest budget cuts in the nation—a resurgence that has more to do with President LeBlanc's redefinition of the institution as a center for online learning and competency-based assessment than its bland "The Greatest and the Best" motto.

• The once high-flying for-profit University of Phoenix has seen enrollment and revenues drop precipitously, despite its "Thinking Ahead" motto. The university's problems have less to do with its branding strategy than its inability to anticipate the disruptive nature of new online technologies like MOOCs and its perceived refusal to respond effectively to student complaints about low success rates and excessive debt.

The Sudden Importance of Brand

University faculty members have been by and large indifferent to the idea of institutional marketing and downright hostile to the tone and sensibilities of branding experts. But the MOOC revolution changed all that. Critics of MOOCs around the world adopted the view that courses that were massive and open would damage a university's reputation. In an open letter to Michael Sandel, a Harvard professor who taught an edX MOOC on social justice called JusticeX, members of the San Jose State University Department of Philosophy said that—despite their admiration for Sandel's course—JusticeX was damaging to the "departments across the country [that] possess unique specializations and character, and should stay that way." The edX model, they claimed, was "spearheading the creation of two social classes in academia [and] thus amounts to a cruel joke."[16] The San Jose State letter was anything but unique. Objections boiled down to these three:

- Rejection of the MOOC "model" in favor of the locally popular model of instruction.
- Homogenization of subject matter and viewpoint, undermining the uniqueness of the local brand while promoting the interests of elite (and in some cases corporatist) brands.[17]
- Fear that the ranks of professors will be thinned or constrained, or that their value will be undermined by the economies of scale that are possible with online instruction.

Objections like these rely on the critical assumption that there are distinctive features, laudable reputations, and compelling value propositions that need protection. The validity of these concerns about the branding of their institutions assumes there is brand value to be protected.

There is a fourth line of argument. By exposing their courses and instructors to an audience of hundreds of thousands of students, universities' every misstep and hiccup is magnified by the Internet lens. This was the case when a Georgia Tech course (ironically titled Fundamentals of Online Education) was suspended in February 2013—at first for a few days and then indefinitely as more courses on the same topic became available—because of inadequate quality controls. Critics were quick to pile on, some using the occasion to point out that MOOCs are immature and will take time to improve, but many more raising shrill warnings that the sheer size of MOOC-like courses makes it more probable that university reputations will be damaged by badly designed or implemented courses.

Fundamentals of Online Education was predicted by many to be an object lesson on how easily a university's brand could be sullied by a MOOC. Exactly the opposite occurred. In February 2013, I was the director of Georgia Tech's Center for 21st Century Universities, the internal think tank that launched the university's digital education initiatives, including MOOCs. It was painful to watch the instructor's public struggle with the medium, yet we pressed on with the development of at first twenty and then forty MOOCs. Enrollment in the university's MOOCs did not slow at all. On February 1, 2013, there were almost a hundred thousand students enrolled in Georgia Tech MOOCs. As I write this paragraph in spring 2015, enrollment in Georgia Tech's MOOCs has risen to over a million and shows no sign of slowing down.

It takes generations to establish a university's reputation. An institution's reputation is built layer on layer by the value it provides to its students, the surrounding community, and its internal stakeholders. Bonds of trust grow and surround institutions and those who see them as important. Once established, a reputation is so hard to destroy that even a concerted effort by people of ill will cannot do it. On the other hand, hollow value is not so hard to damage.

Inheriting Trust

In the academic world, reputation is tied to trust. Parents trust that their postadolescent offspring will be safe and well cared for; students trust that their hard work will be rewarded with a distinctive position in society, and that being known as an alumnus of a particular institution will have a positive personal and professional impact later in life. Communities trust that the universities operate in the best interests of citizens. University brands by and large reflect trust. Except for a relatively few universities that are so well known, their names alone instantly establish a trust relationship, universities around the world inherit trust from some larger system. In even sophisticated college towns, the reputation of the local institution is based on inherited trust.

I have wandered university towns like Hanover, Kyoto, Daijon, Singapore, Vienna, and Doha asking waiters, hotel clerks, fellow train passengers, colleagues, acquaintances, and complete strangers about the local colleges. Invariably, local perceptions had been shaped somewhere else. "Well, you know this is an Ivy League school," said one passerby. I asked someone whether they knew how the local schools stacked up internationally, and was told, "Our traditions go back hundreds of years." A stranger reminded me that "we are a Big Ten school," as though no more explanation was needed. "Of course, it's accredited," said someone who did not know exactly what that meant. Education City in Doha, Qatar, is home to a half-dozen American universities, and the chief attribute that locals know about those campuses is that they are branches of prestigious American universities. Parents trust rankings: "I want to be sure that my daughter gets a degree from a highly ranked university." Local leaders trust that being "just like a major research university" brings economic good fortune. Sometimes simply a desire to be in a different group is enough: "I know that [these kinds of universities] are usually not very good, but we are actually more like [another kind of university]."

Inheriting trust from somewhere else—effectively putting a university's brand in the hands of someone else—is seldom a good idea, especially when it is used as a substitute for reputation. It did not, for example, work out well for universities that have their roots in medieval Europe.

The European Middle Ages were a great contradiction. Out of the political and cultural ferment from Turkey to Spain that marked the years 800 to 1499 grew unbelievable misery in a dark world that William Manchester describes as "lit only by fire."[18] Superstition, disease, brutal inequality, and senseless war wrecked medieval towns and cities, whose populaces would sometimes fluctuate by 30 percent as large-scale dislocation, famine, and plagues worked their will. God played a central role in how people viewed nature, history, literature, and even themselves. The tension between reason and faith could not always be accommodated, and gave rise to persecution on the flimsiest excuses.

Learning was tempered by dogma, politics, and fear. But somehow, in the middle of the chaos of medieval Europe, the idea of a university managed to take root. First as the tentative gatherings of scholars to learn from the likes of Peter Abelard and Thomas Aquinas, then as organized operations at Bologna, Barcelona, and Paris appeared, students from across Europe gathered by the thousands to pursue studies in law and medicine. Out of beginnings like these, grew higher education: "The university is one of the great creations of the middle ages. It became stabilized as a corporative institution linked to the expansion of the cities and destined to become what we now call higher education."[19]

Yet a mere three hundred years after they were founded, the great universities of the Middle Ages were in financial and intellectual ruin. Their reputations lay in tatters. They were regarded by the public as "conservative homes of outmoded knowledge," obsessed with teaching Aristotle to middle-class sons—future surgeons, lawyers, and clergy whose ambitions stopped short of wealth, political power, or scientific ferment—when the real action was elsewhere.[20]

The middle class had been redefined by the wealth and privilege of the Renaissance, and the children of the merchant class were far more likely to be modern. Scientific and literary revolutions had bypassed the old universities. Italian universities were willing collaborators in the persecution of Galileo. The University of Paris played a shameful role in the trial of Joan of Arc. The Reformation did not help either. Exactly which version of Christianity was to be served by universities was suddenly unclear. The whole of England reckoned that Oxford and Cambridge were all that the empire needed to supply bureaucrats and ambassadors to the world. They had become tools of the establishment, in the view of many, and it was no longer possible to simply cast oneself as a university in the mold of a great European university in order to acquire a form of inherited legitimacy.

The invention of the modern research university with its emphasis on science and mathematics, first in Germany, then throughout northern Europe, was a break from the past because it prioritized meritocratic societies of scholars, knowledge creation, and the organizational trappings needed to help it succeed above all else. Another break from the past happened right under the noses of the traditional institutions. A community of Jesuits in Rome set up an experimental college that stressed teaching. The response was so overwhelming that this new Collegio Romano was packed within a year and had to immediately relocate to more spacious quarters to accommodate the demand. It was not long before a global network of Jesuit colleges and universities challenged traditional state-run universities for academic supremacy, at least for the undergraduate education of the masses of young students whose parents demanded a different experience. Nor did it take the New World long to throw off the trappings of a classical European education.

When Thomas Jefferson founded his own university in Virginia, it was not with an eye toward Oxford and Cambridge, despite the dozens of copies of those institutions that had been imported to the colonies. Reformers like Jefferson knew that training political and social leaders for America had little in common with the compulsory core curriculum in Europe, and more in common with the academies of northern Europe that had been built on the model of Jesuit colleges. By the end of the nineteenth century, hundreds of new experiments in higher education were under way in the United States. The vast majority of them bore no resemblance to the European forebears—or to each other, for that matter. Many of them had adopted no models at all, and were making up curricula and degree standards as well as modes of operation that had little grounding in sound educational practice. It was not always easy to tell proper universities from idiosyncratic schools that, at best, offered vocational training, but all too often were simply fronts for religious indoctrination or moneymaking schemes for bilking an uneducated, frequently non-English-speaking working class.

It did not help that some of the confusion was sown by the likes of Harvard, which in 1869 began to divest itself of all traces of a classical curriculum when incoming president Eliot announced in his inaugural address that Harvard would soon dispense with all required courses.[21] It had only been a few years before Harvard started dismantling its European heritage that the US Congress passed the Morrill Act, which created the land grant colleges, further tipping America away from the European model, and creating a whole new class of educational institutions by combining agriculture and engineering with scientific and classical studies "in order to promote the education of the industrial classes."[22]

If there had ever been hope of inheriting a reputation from one's peers or trust from overarching systems of higher education, it had been abandoned by the time Slosson began writing his essays for the *Independent* in a bold attempt to offer examples of great universities whose practices might be adopted. But Slosson's approach to making sense of American higher education was high-minded and decidedly not prescriptive. At about the same time, money was pouring into the construction and operation of new schools and colleges, and money demanded something a little more concrete than Slosson's fourteen examples.

There was a massive outpouring of philanthropy to institutions of higher learning at the beginning of the twentieth century. Shocked by the dismal state of university administration and accountability, philanthropist-industrialists demanded minimal standards as a condition for institutions that wanted grants and gifts. Then there was the question of how money was being spent. Massive increases in enrollments in the mid-twentieth century threatened to overwhelm the nation's colleges, which had never been too concerned about the efficiency of their operations. Efficiency in post–World War II America meant factory efficiency, and so colleges and universities adopted the methods of the factory floor. Accreditors were the quality control department of the factory. It was a role they adopted enthusiastically.

Quality stamps from accrediting bodies, league tables, and informal associations were once trusted by the public. They were how individual institutions transferred trust and established their brand. Élite universities did not need the quality stamps of a third party, but for most universities in the Middle recognition was needed to establish their brands. In the minds of many Americans, there has been a dramatic fracturing of trust in those brands.

Starting with a Clean Slate

We are in the midst of a continuing decline in public confidence in higher education. When asked how they would rate the job that the higher education system is doing in terms of providing value for the money spent by students and their families, a large majority of respondents said that colleges and universities were doing a poor or only fair job. The public's view is in stark contrast to the opinions of university presidents who by a wider margin thought that they were doing an excellent or good job, and the even wider majority of college graduates who felt that their education was a good investment.[23] A college diploma evidently buys admission to a club of satisfied members, but—continuing a twenty-year trend—a declining share of the American public thinks that the average person can afford to pay the price of admission. And more than one-third of the American students who can afford it will fail to complete the requirements for their degrees— a completion rate that is among the lowest of the twenty most developed countries in the world.[24]

Ben Nelson knew these dismal data, and thought about what they meant for the future. He was a thirty-eight-year-old Silicon Valley entrepreneur. Nelson had just sold his photo-sharing company, SnapFish, to Hewlett-Packard, and had time and energy to spend on larger causes. Higher education was not a natural choice. His only prior experience in education was to have graduated from an Ivy League university, but he had watched as the value of universities that were once highly regarded was being hollowed out. It seemed to Nelson the brand of higher education was being damaged for no good reason. Some institutions, like Penn State, had suffered self-inflicted wounds, but most were the subject of what Nelson saw as daily, withering, unrelenting criticism. He had an idea about how to change all that. Nelson wanted to build an elite, challenging university around students, and wanted it to be affordable.

"What if," he reasoned, "we simply concentrated on the problem of getting a student from Point A to Point B?" Point A could be any time that a student actually started learning college-level material, but Nelson wanted to keep it simple. "Let's suppose that Point A is already pretty advanced," he

said. "Maybe Point A corresponds to acquiring basic skills like reading critically and writing effectively, and maybe also mastering enough basic content, so that teachers can concentrate on more advanced material." That
corresponds to the first two years of college—a part of the undergraduate
curriculum called the gen-ed requirements. Most schools spend a disproportionate amount of time and money moving unprepared or unmotivated
students through gen-ed requirements. Many of them fail at this stage. This
was the same problem that preoccupied James Renick and his colleagues at
Jackson State University, and Nelson had just said he was going to sidestep
it altogether. "But we want to be an Élite university," he commented. "If I
have to spend a lot of time with you on basic material, you are simply going
to fail with the more advanced material the way I want it to be taught."

He then asked, "What is Point B?" As it turns out, point B can be whatever you want it to be, provided it is based on some definite educational
outcome. "As opposed to completing credits or semesters? Of course!" He
wanted to know what a university would look like if it focused only on supporting the intellectual development of students along that path. "What if
everything else was subordinate?" With a handful of exceptions, universities were concentrating on something else altogether. They were building
winning football programs, hiking tuition to close budget gaps, or siphon-
ing money from classroom instruction. They were enhancing prestige—all
the while expensively maintaining a "college experience" that had nothing
to do with the intellectual development of students.

Nelson thought that if you want to create a brand in education that
was about getting from point A to point B, there were no current models
to build on. "The few places, like Olin, that try cannot operate at the scale
that is needed.[25] There is literally nothing to start with," he said quietly. He
stared across the empty loft that he hoped would be filled with students in
the coming months. "You might just as well start with this. You might as
well start with a clean slate."

I had heard Ben's clean-slate pitch before. We had talked about it in a San
Francisco bar, one late autumn afternoon in 2011, before he had concrete
ideas about how to make it happen. "People will invest in education." That
was the first thing Nelson said to me. "Harvard is the number one brand
in the world. There are thousands, tens of thousands of kids, who do nothing but dream of getting into Harvard. But," he added, "Harvard's brand
is based on prestige. We will be about brand, and that's something hugely
different."

The "we" he was talking about was called the Minerva Project, which
at that point was little more than a spreadsheet, a conviction about how

people behave, and a plan to create a university that is comparable to the Élite brands of higher education. It was not clear to me why he was so focused on Harvard and the Ivy League universities. There were after all many different ways to invest in education, and with the sudden interest of Silicon Valley entrepreneurs, the time seemed to be right to look at as many alternatives as possible.

In any event, this plan seemed just as full of rosy optimism as a dozen others I had seen in recent weeks, and I said so. Minerva students were going to only pay for value that ended up on their degrees, and since this was a for-profit venture, Nelson needed a critical number of paying customers or else the fixed expenses of running the business would turn into unsustainable losses that would make it impossible to continue operations. I was most interested in the line on his spreadsheet that represented enrollment growth—*student acquisition* is what people in the education business call it. Minerva needed ten thousand students just to break even. Where were they going to come from? I imagined it was possible to compete with other for-profit businesses like the University of Phoenix for price-sensitive students or community college students who were interested in converting associate degrees into bachelor's diplomas. This was a growing population. Unless Nelson was willing to set his sights on this kind of student, I believed that student acquisition would be Minerva's downfall.

But Harvard was on Nelson's mind, because Minerva had just scored a big win. Former Harvard president Summers had just agreed to chair Minerva's advisory board. Nelson had called Summers—"out of the clear blue sky." Summers is a former treasury secretary in the Clinton administration and economic adviser to Obama. I was intrigued that he would buy into Nelson's dream of affordable, Élite education for the masses. Summers had a controversial tenure at Harvard, but he presumably knew something about the Harvard brand. "When we met, he had no context on Minerva, which was just a concept," recalls Nelson, "but at the end of an hour and a half meeting, he volunteered to chair the board." Summers evidently thought that there were ten thousand students in the world capable of doing academic work at the level of a Harvard undergraduate and that they would be attracted to a school like Minerva. Nelson agreed. "Larry was excited about bringing high-quality education to people who are locked out of the system."

Minerva was unlike anything being planned in Silicon Valley at the time. For example, it was going to be a real university with classes, degrees, deans, and campuses. There were high expectations for point A, so it would be difficult to be admitted—in many ways, more difficult than to gain admittance to Harvard, although for different reasons. "The Ivy League curates its freshman class," explained Nelson. "They are trying to create a totality that is statistically picturesque: one concert pianist, but not two and also a concert violist." But there is only room for sixteen hundred in a freshman class that is handpicked from tens of thousands of applications. The Ivy League might be concentrating on the wrong statistics. "When you are Élite and have to be a certain size, sometimes you make decisions that make it hard to get students from point A to point B."

When I asked what he meant by that, Nelson told me about helping to recruit an entering class for an actual Élite. "I was given a huge computer printout," he said. "Dozens and dozens of names with GPAs and test scores next to them." They had all been admitted, but not all of them had agreed to attend come September. Nelson's job was to call everyone on the list and try to convince them to accept their offers. Almost everyone was a top student. "They all seemed to have graduated first or second in their class, and had unbelievable test scores." Except that every once in a while, one entry seemed just a little bit off. "Rather than first or second in their classes they were one-hundredth." It took a few minutes, but it eventually sunk in. These were the children of alumni. "They were rich legacies and sports recruits. It didn't matter how well prepared they were or even whether they could handle the coursework. They were going to be admitted and—point B or no point B—they were going to graduate." This is how a curated freshman class is assembled. "When you curate a class you are assembling a portfolio, not searching for all the students who should be in your program."

In the process, Ivy League schools reject students who can succeed. Minerva turns the concept of Élite on its head. Élite is not defined by who is rejected but rather by what students have accomplished. It does not matter to Minerva where you live, what language you speak, how old you are, or whether you can pick up stakes and move seven thousand miles away to attend classes. "We handpick our freshman class, too," Nelson said. "We are handpicking all those who are qualified to attend because we do not have a concept of slots to be filled with students. All that matters is whether a student is above or below the cut. If they are above, we will accept them."

He did some rapid arithmetic. "There are at least five hundred thousand students worldwide who can succeed here. We will not get all of them, which is good, because that's a number that would break the bank." But Minerva is betting that the educational experience it offers will attract 2 percent of that market.

It was an idea that had also been tried by President Crow at Arizona State University, and had led to rapid growth at that public university. Crow's *New Gold Standard* for American public universities was a decade-long project to rebrand the research university. In Crow's view, higher education had, for several generations, valued prestige over other outcomes. The correlation between rising reputational ranking and selectivity in admissions was a sign of a public system gone seriously awry. His reaction was to push for an admissions policy that would offer a place in Arizona's freshman class to any student who would have qualified for admission to Berkeley in 1960—an era before rampant grade inflation in which high school grades of B or better in challenging courses would have qualified a student for entry to virtually any public university in the United States. Nelson, too, understood the Arizona State model. "Publics have that [access obligation] as a moral obligation to society. But most are running away from it because they are chasing prestige."

What makes the Minerva brand unique is Nelson's insistence on jettisoning anything that was only relevant to prestige. In the process, many trappings of the college experience fail to make it past the company's financial scrutiny. First to go are the courses that, in Nelson's view, are simply there to transmit information. "We are raising the bar," he observed. Arriving students are expected to not only demonstrate fluency in gen-ed courses but also must know at least one foreign language. These are required courses for graduation at Minerva and elsewhere, but there are no introductory courses of any kind, and Nelson thinks that makes it "harder to get through Minerva than an Ivy League university." Although technology made that an easy step, it is not simply a matter of replacing lectures with MOOCs. "Forget lectures," Nelson asserted. Forget also the idea of stand-alone courses that have no connection to each other. "We want," he continued, "to create something that develops a student over time." Minerva is there to move a student from point A to point B.

Media coverage was intense, and although he is generally happy with the company's press, Nelson was not prepared for the attention. He seemed almost surprised that public discussion about Minerva has been rational. "That has helped our branding." Maybe this is because Minerva is so odd that it poses no obvious threat to existing institutions. In fact, the endless stream of visitors from traditional universities seems to regard Minerva as a sort of laboratory. Nelson told me that he has been impressed with the senior university officials who have visited Minerva. They tell him, "We have curriculum envy," and want to know whether Minerva would be willing to offer temporary sabbatical positions to their faculty. Many say, "We would love for you to teach them how to teach, because they don't know." Minerva would be happy to be co-opted in this way.

The story that won over Larry Summers also resonated with others. Former US Senator Bob Kerrey, who had most recently been president of the New School in New York, joined Summers on the board right after it was created. Like Summers, Kerrey was a controversial university president, whose prickly encounters with New School faculty were highly visible. A month later, former Carnegie Foundation president Lee Schulman—another reform-minded insider—also joined. So did Wharton School dean Patrick Harker. Princeton's Ann Marie Slaughter, who was Hillary Clinton's director of policy and planning in the US Department of State, joined in late 2013.

That was enough to get the attention of the White House and Senate leaders like Lamar Alexander and Tom Harkin, whose Health, Education, Labor, and Pensions Committee had spent several years wrestling with the problem of accreditation of low-quality, for-profit universities. Minerva's approach to accreditation has been to steer a middle course. Minerva accepts no Title IV funding from the federal government, so the university is under no obligation to seek accreditation from one of the six regional accrediting agencies. Nelson is suspicious of accreditation because it has stepped beyond its traditional role of setting minimum standards. On the other hand, Minerva would like its graduates to be on a level playing field when it comes to highly competitive graduate school admissions. In mid-2013, Minerva announced an incubation partnership with the Keck Graduate Institute (KGI) of the Claremont Colleges. KGI and Minerva would also share courses, curricula, and facilities. As Nelson explained, "The Minerva Schools will be incubated within KGI and in a few years may spin off as an independent entity. It's the way KGI itself got started." In return, Minerva would submit its curriculum for accreditation by the Western Association of Schools and Colleges.

Minerva was designed to be a fable. Its founding dean, Stephen Kosslyn, connects Minerva to the first European university at Bologna. "Students arrived, and they said 'teach me,'" observed Kosslyn. "Bologna was an association of foreign scholars; it was a student-centered university." But the model that took over in Paris and elsewhere in Europe was a faculty-centered one. "We are student centered," said Kosslyn. "We want to become more like the original universities." It is not just a rebalancing of power; it is a re-centering of the university experience. "Our goal is to create the premier student-centered experience," said Nelson. "If a student pays tuition, you can't say 'Thanks for the money. I will now use it for something you don't want, like football or research.' If you do that, your brand suffers and you eventually lose in the marketplace." Nelson's view is that universities have been operating this way for a long time. They survive only because there is no alternative. But suppose, Ben wondered, if you declare what you want to be and offer that to a global classroom. Minerva's experience so far is that what you declare is what you are compared to. For Nelson and Minerva, that is a student-centered university that helps high-performing students to excel by training them for success. In fall 2014, Minerva enrolled its first class. It was a little smaller than Nelson had hoped for, and his costs were somewhat higher, but his intentions as its founder remain clear and largely unchanged. "You build what you are. If we are not great, then we will not open, but there is no incentive for adding a feature that is different from what we want to be."

The Minerva brand will be highly valued only if Minerva students do well. Then it doesn't matter that Minerva has a short history or does not have the usual badges of acceptance by academic peers. "If we are successful," Nelson maintains, "our graduates will have a field day with the graduates of any other university. They will demolish them in the marketplace."

11   Ivory Towers

It brings a dramatic image to mind. The Revolution is an assault on the Ivory Tower—and its noblest ideas like scholarship, tenure, and academic freedom—that must be defended at all costs by holy warriors. In reality, the Ivory Tower represents strengths and contradictions. Society wants institutions that are ethical beacons, but political leaders do not necessarily want them to be socially engaged. Scholars want the prerogatives of untrammeled inquiry, but they also seem like an entitled minority to those who pay the bills. Institutions that might otherwise eschew materialistic trappings find themselves enmeshed in base commerce designed to enhance the bottom line. While decrying short-term thinking and a trade school mentality, universities are constantly looking for new ways to be relevant. They aspire to larger goals, but they behave like corporate entities.

If higher education is remade, then it is hard to imagine how the rituals of the Ivory Tower will survive intact. Tenure might be the first to go, but it is the notion of a university as a place apart from society that is the real target. In what seems like a uniquely modern headlong rush toward relevance and economic impact, the Ivory Tower has come under full assault, yet in reality critics have been at it for centuries. If you are inclined to believe that the modern university is disengaged and out of touch, you might attribute it to walls that European professors began erecting around their institutions in the thirteenth century, almost immediately after the founding of the first universities.

The University of Bologna, which is widely believed to be the first Western university, was organized at the instigation of the students who came from across Europe to study there. Their needs were paramount. Everything from paying for classes to dealing with local politicians was organized around student needs. Bologna and the universities like it were centered on students. Shortly thereafter, priorities shifted away from student-centered universities to master universities, which were organized around professors—the masters—who taught in them. Professors—stable and well connected—were a more effective force in shaping institutions than poor, transient students, but professors were also more concerned with their own needs. Almost from the start, the masters began the process of severing ties with most of society. Whether to protect their own prerogatives or provide a safe space for scholastic life, the result was a sacred structure, a tower made from ivory, the world's most precious material, from which inhabitants could survey the world from fortified heights. Fortifications turned out to be a good idea.

Academic Freedom

Advancing knowledge—the only function of the Ivory Tower about which there is agreement—requires disengagement. However romantic the notion of a lone scholar pursuing knowledge for its own sake, Ivory Towers do not look the same from the outside. Disengaged scholars appear to talk only to themselves and frequently have little concern for the practical consequences of their work. They do not run with the herd and oftentimes radiate a sense of entitlement that annoys the very people on whose generosity they depend for survival. What scholarly inquiry promises is change (another contradiction, since what scholars despise most is change in their own circumstances). Scholars therefore are prone to attack by the established order, which has few reasons to consider change. Attacks on the freedom of intellectuals to pursue scholarly inquiry began almost immediately after the first universities were formed.

The eleventh-century priest and teacher Peter Abelard had attracted the attention of the church hierarchy by exposing inconsistencies in doctrine.[1] That he did so for audiences of hundreds of enthralled students did not stand him in good stead with his sponsor and protector, Canon Fulbert, whose niece, Héloïse, Abelard was supposed to tutor. That Abelard and Héloïse became lovers and that their affair produced a child, did not help Abelard's cause either. She was banished, and he pursued, tortured, and imprisoned, but Abelard's example greatly influenced the formation of European universities and emboldened the first academic scholars to pursue knowledge, putting aside fear of consequence.

Caught up in the debate over the church-sanctioned teaching and proof by Copernicus that the earth revolved around the sun, in 1631 Galileo, a professor at the University of Padua, published a book titled *Dialogue concerning the Two Chief World Systems* refuting the idea of an earth-centered universe.[2] A year later he was declared a heretic. Galileo was brought before the inquisition on charges that he had violated a 1616 injunction against advocating Copernican theory. He was forced "even with the threat of torture" to renounce his work—"I affirm, therefore, on my conscience, that I do not now hold the condemned opinion and have not held it since the decision of the authorities"—after which he was placed briefly in formal custody before being allowed to retire to a farmhouse in Arcetri, where he grew blind and, nine years later, died. Throughout the Reformation, Counter-Reformation, and over the following centuries into modern times, persecution of various sorts slowed but did not halt academic inquiry.

In 1894, a University of Wisconsin professor named Richard Ely was put on trial for political bias for "teaching socialism and other vicious theories to students at the University." The case was tried before the Wisconsin Board of Regents and drew national attention. To the dismay of Ely's chief antagonists, the board refused to evaluate his work, but instead issued a stirring endorsement of academic freedom, today called the Wisconsin Magna Carta: "Whatever the limitations which trammel inquiry elsewhere we believe the great state University of Wisconsin should ever encourage that continual and fearless sifting and winnowing by which alone truth can be found."[3]

A few years later, Stanford economist and sociologist Edward A. Ross was fired for his progressive views, which included condemning the railroad companies for exploiting Chinese immigrant laborers. Leland Stanford, the founder of the university, had amassed his fortune in railroads, and his widow, who eventually had all she could stand of Ross's public antagonism toward the Stanford family, arranged for Ross to be dismissed.

Attacks on academic freedom accelerated in the twentieth century with the growth of research universities. Psychology professor James McKeen Cattell's resistance to conscription during World War I offended Columbia president Nicholas Murray Butler. Cattell was widely regarded as the "dean of American science," but Butler had him dismissed from his position at Columbia for his uncompromising antiwar stance. The 1941 firing of Robert Cocking, the University of Georgia's dean of education, revolved around Cocking's alleged support of integrated schools and association with a progressive Jewish foundation in New York. The affair had been orchestrated by Georgia governor Eugene Talmadge, an ardent segregationist. The McCarthy-era blacklisting of intellectuals was in part intended to silence the inquiry of wayward professors, and J. Edgar Hoover's FBI carefully prosecuted investigations of anyone who might strike him as odd—or at least at odds with American interests—including the likes of John Kenneth Galbraith and J. Robert Oppenheimer, the Berkeley physicist who led the wartime Manhattan Project. Professors who protested American involvement in Vietnam were harassed during the 1960s, and the Iraq War rekindled sensitivities about academics supporting un-American causes. Jonathan Cole's defense of academic tenure catalogs the attempts to pressure Columbia to fire professors for antiwar comments or supporting Palestinian causes.[4] Ward Churchill, a professor at the University of Colorado, was investigated, stripped of his tenure, and fired after making incendiary comments following the September 11, 2001, attacks on the World Trade Center.

Modern assaults on the prerogatives of the Ivory Tower have not been limited to the United States. The Nazis pushed Jewish scientists out of German universities, and during the height of the Cold War, academic freedom in Eastern Europe was replaced by a corrupt oligarchy that determined not only political orthodoxy but also how strictly academics had to adhere to it. Chinese universities during Mao's Cultural Revolution purged faculty ranks of dissenters and troublemakers. The Muslim world is filled with institutions whose faculty members must adhere to strict Islamic principles as a condition of employment. Despots and corrupt bureaucracies around the world regularly purge universities of economic and social theorists that do not support government policies.

The history is not all bleak. Through most of the last two centuries, Great Britain has been a magnet for independent thought. Even the polymaths among the American founders were products of colonial colleges that operated as replicas of Oxford and Cambridge. Among the forty-eight research universities in England, Oxford and Cambridge merge into public consciousness as a single Ivory Tower—*Oxbridge*—where Oxford's Hawksmoor Towers and Cambridge's Kings College Chapel converge even though they are separated by a hundred miles.

What the Ivory Tower stands for—disengagement to free the individual intellect in the creation of knowledge—is the very thing that makes universities great, say, defenders of academic freedom. It is the argument that E. M. Forster used in his 1939 *Atlantic Monthly* counteroffensive to those who "would pull down all Ivory Towers." As far back as history stretches, we can see intellectuals trying to "retire into their Ivory Towers and there to resist or modify the instinct which they possess as members of the herd—and to decry and resist the inevitable assaults."[5]

Quality, Control, and Freedom

When, in late 2013, the twenty members of the philosophy department of San Jose State University published an open letter to Harvard philosopher Sandel, they made special note of the "great peril" facing their university, and as if to confront the "criticism of the traditional lecture model," enumerated the principles behind their refusal to participate in an experimental edX version of Sandel's course on social justice. They were concerned that Sandel's course would reflect "the largely white student population from a privileged institution" rather than "[their] own diverse faculty, who bring their varied perspectives." It was a "scary" prospect, they argued, aimed at "replacing faculty with cheap online courses." It was part of a "renewed attack [on the liberal arts] in public universities," and partially advanced by administrators at "our own California State University System," whose primary concern was "financially driven and involves a compromise of quality."[6] The philosophy faculty rejected the course, but Sandel continued to offer and refine it through edX to an ever-larger audience of students. The open letter made its way quickly through the national media, prompting calls for a full-scale retreat from the idea of using MOOCs in public universities.

The San Jose State comments about diversity struck many as hard to understand. The student body there is 25 percent white, which is indeed more diverse than Harvard's, which is 48 percent white, but the intellectual heritage of the San Jose State philosophy faculty members is virtually identical to far less diverse universities; they come mainly from privileged institutions like MIT (40 percent white), Boston University (48 percent white), Stanford (47 percent white) and the University of Rochester (51 percent white).

The open letter seems to be about three concerns: quality, control, and freedom from interference. These themes dominate critical barbs thrown at higher education today. Like the San Jose State philosophy department, academia—at least that part of it for which the idea of Revolution holds no appeal—sees in the development of technologies like MOOCs an assault on the quality of education. Signing agreements with companies like Coursera and edX are part of an attempt to wrest control of course content from the faculty. It is an assault on academic freedom, according to the philosophy department; it is an attempt to replace "interaction with professors engaged in … research" with the start of a process designed to "replace professors and dismantle departments."[7]

The San Jose State letter is reminiscent of a 1913 open letter from Johns Hopkins University professors to colleagues at other Élite institutions. It was a call to arms for defenders of the Ivory Tower. There had been withering attacks on academic institutions in 1913. "Everything about the college is under the fire of its critics—its government, its ideals of social life, its right to exist at all," wrote former MIT president Henry Pritchett, head of

the Carnegie Foundation.[8] The Johns Hopkins letter urged the formation
of an "ecumenical society" aimed at protecting institutional and societal
interests that "were not being adequately cared for."[9] It was a call that was
answered by 650 professors who were acknowledged leaders in their fields.
When they convened in January 1915, it was with an eye toward three concerns that hung ominously over major institutions:

Quality: "Debasement of academic standards" fueled by rapid growth
Control: The "undue power" that growth had given to administrators
Freedom from outside interference: The likelihood that "wealth and worldliness" had
"made academic freedom more vulnerable than before to covert aggression"[10]

The 1915 convention marked the beginning of the ecumenical society
that the Johns Hopkins faculty members had imagined: the AAUP. The first
order of business was to adopt the "Declaration of Principles on Academic
Freedom and Academic Tenure," a sweeping document that not only outlined cases of abridged academic freedom, like the ones in the previous section, but also the purpose of unfettered inquiry itself along with the nature
and governance of the institutions in which that inquiry takes place.[11] The
declaration had, in fact, been in the works since 1913, when a group of nine
academics led by Johns Hopkins philosopher Arthur Lovejoy began to craft
a statement that would guide the growing number of research universities
to once and for all adopt policies for protecting academic freedom. By coincidence, Lovejoy, an author of the Johns Hopkins letter, had been a member of the Stanford University faculty when Ross was fired—an action that
prompted his resignation. Lovejoy would, along with the famous American
educator John Dewey, be the inaugural president of the AAUP.

On the subject of inquiry, the declaration makes a powerful case that
the university is an ivory tower—"an inviolable refuge" from tyranny however it arises, whether from uninformed public opinion or entrenched plu-
tocracy. An academic institution exists, says the declaration, not only to
instruct students and promote the development of experts for society as a
whole but also "to promote inquiry and advance the sum of human knowledge."[12] The inviolable nature of this free inquiry is to be guaranteed in
practical terms by academic tenure—a concept that AAUP committees on
academic freedom returned to repeatedly over the years, culminating in a
1940 revision of the declaration to include specific provisions for granting,
denying, and removing tenure.

The declaration is much more circumspect about the nature of governing boards. The framers of the declaration acknowledge that universities are
"controlled by boards of trustees" and that "upon them it devolved to determine the measure of academic freedom," but they also view universities

with suspicion, allowing only that boards hold a "public trust." Members of such boards "have no moral right to bind the reason or the conscience of any professor," the declaration determined.[13]

It is no accident that Ross and Ely are among the authors of the declaration, or that the events that led up to the document seemed to have been perfectly set up for the betterment of college professors. Ross was indeed fired by Stanford University for repeated and publicly tweaking Mrs. Stanford on matters ranging from free silver to advocating socialist causes, including union strikes against the very railway industry on which the Stanford family depended. Ross, for his part, had apparently planned to annoy the Stanford family, test the idea of academic freedom, and make himself the central figure in a national crusade: "If I got cashiered, as I thought would be the case, the hollowness of our role as 'independent scholar' would be visible to all," Ross admitted in his autobiography.[14] Ely, on the other hand, had already seen how the public might respond to the summary firing of a professor whose only transgression seemed to be arriving at the truth by "sifting and winnowing."[15] In Wisconsin, the particularly inept Oliver Wells, a political unknown who had been appointed director of public education, pursued Ely. Wells let an internal dispute about unionization mushroom inexplicably into the national scandal that propelled Ely's rise as a defender of academic freedom, and prompted the famous sifting and winnowing statement on behalf of academic freedom at the University of Wisconsin.

The origins of the AAUP and its continuing appeal to university faculty are rooted in the 1915 call for an ecumenical organization that cut across disciplinary boundaries in pursuit of a moral cause. And because there would always be a ready supply of scholars to test the patience of administrators, boards, and the general public, the AAUP believed it could always arrange for an existential conflict that would test whether the Ivory Tower could withstand assault from outside.

The Crumbling Tower

World War II brought a fall from innocence for much of academia. University scientists on all sides had been deeply involved in the war effort, but none more so than the British and Americans as well as the veritable army of refugee scientists who, fearing the worst in continental Europe, flooded into places like Princeton, Cambridge, and Berkeley. The same academic research that was responsible for the atomic bomb and breaking enemy codes cut both ways, however. Manhattan Project alumni published the

Bulletin of Atomic Scientists, complete with a doomsday clock counting down the minutes to nuclear annihilation. MIT professors founded the Union of Concerned Scientists, whose mission included devising "means for turning research applications away from the present emphasis on military technology toward the solution of pressing environmental and social problems."[16]

The door was nevertheless open. In the United States, Vannevar Bush's letter to President Franklin Delano Roosevelt made the case that "basic scientific research is scientific capital," and outlined the advantages of maintaining a peacetime capability in scientific research, which led directly to the establishment of the NSF. The NSF along with the National Institutes of Health, departments of defense and energy, and an array of federal agencies poured money into American universities during the 1950s. Europe was slower to recover from the war and slower to make these kinds of investments. But by the 1980s that had changed, and the new European Union was investing in large-scale research projects and facilities. The difference was that European research was centrally controlled, which may have benefited corporations and research laboratories, but did not have an appreciable impact on higher education.

American universities, on the other hand, were responsible not only for a massive increase in spending but also a massive increase in research output in the form of patents and the formation of new, capital-intensive industries. University presidents like California's Clark Kerr restructured their institutions and how they were managed. It was Kerr who coined the term multiversity to describe a new kind of enterprise in which many competing interests were served by a complex organization with departments, schools, laboratories, and disciplines, each poised to serve different stakeholders. This was a crack in the Ivory Tower. Teaching colleges aspired to become research universities, and research universities aspired to become multiversities, which Kerr conceived to be "a mechanism held together by administrative rules and powered by money."[17]

That was not the mission imagined at the 1915 convention that adopted the declaration. The Ivory Tower was supposed to have a unifying mission and be impervious to the demands of the marketplace, but the multiversity was not so disengaged. It existed to serve society. "It lacked a unifying mission." It was, in the words of critics, a "service station," an "educational General Motors."[18] The "Declaration of Principles on Academic Freedom and Academic Tenure" anticipated that the voices of the faculty would hold sway in matters related to academic strategies, hiring, and firing. Kerr closed departments that he thought were not helpful to the university's goal of ranking sixth among all American universities. He removed department heads whose performance was subpar, and he overruled 20 percent of all tenure decisions made at lower administrative levels.[18]

Tenure

Tenure is one of the outward trappings of the Ivory Tower that is hardest to explain to the rest of society. The AAUP was founded on the idea that tenure guarantees academic freedom, but for a growing minority, tenure is simply one mechanism, and one that is better left behind. It is according to some "the single most important factor preventing change in higher education."[19] It drives up college costs, and "professors who possess it have no reason to improve their teaching."[20] Few of the critics have anything to back up their claims, yet they know that simply calling tenure a lifetime guarantee of employment is enough to get the public on their side.[21] Presidents see the value in long-term job security to provide a measure of freedom to pursue inquiry and avoid the kind of short-term thinking that plagues private industry, but even offering to replace tenure with long-term contracts meets with resistance. Former US senator Kerrey, when he was president of New York's New School, was met with howls of protest for suggesting that faculty members be given twenty-year contracts in place of tenure. Kerrey's proposal was denounced as just another attempt to corporatize the academic workplace.

The AAUP, faculty unions, and a wide variety of on-campus organizations are vigilant in exposing any attempt to further corporatize the faculty workforce. The institution of tenure is their Maginot Line, but the fortifications may already have been overrun. By some estimates, 20 percent of four-year undergraduate institutions operate without tenure at all. New institutions consider the Kerrey proposal for long-term contracts to be an option. Florida Polytechnic University was designed to operate without tenure, and Minerva, Nelson's attempt to create high-quality education for the masses, will not offer tenure. According to Nelson, "The faculty who approach us, frankly have no interest in it." Some traditional institutions, like the highly regarded Olin College, have never felt the need for tenure. Others, like otherwise-traditional Bennington College in Vermont, have abolished it altogether. In fall 2013, New Jersey's Kean University denied tenure to two-thirds of the candidates presented to the president's office for approval. Kean's board of trustees backed the president's decision. Faculty in community colleges may unionize, yet few community colleges offer tenure. The majority of all college professors are part-time or contingent faculty. Many are employed semester by semester on short-term teaching contracts. The percentage of tenure-track positions has shrunk to 25 percent of the university workforce in the United States.

European universities followed a different path. Faculty members at public universities are civil servants who therefore have job security, but that did not have much effect on the development of the revered research universities in England and the rest of Europe. They made uniquely European decisions. Oxbridge represents to Cambridge president Leszek Borysiewicz "a particular culture, values, and ethos." One that is "not beholden to short term goals." It is, according to Borysiewicz, "able to maintain a focus on long-term objectives that may take a decade or more to realize."[22] It is hard to argue with Oxbridge's success with this culture. Cambridge and Imperial College, the other major institution that Borysiewicz has led, together account for more innovation than the rest of the research universities in Great Britain combined. Oxbridge is a culture based on an elite brand that attracts a particular kind of research talent from around the world, though it is hardly inwardly focused. At least in the sciences, the major research initiatives at Oxbridge are collaborative, and motivated as much by creating societal value and economic growth as by sheer intellection.

It is as if a dividing line had been drawn between traditional universities that were, on the one hand, "defective institutions, isolated, inwardly focused, and overly concerned with the affairs of their faculty," and on the other hand, a new generation of universities, filled with socially and economically engaged scholars who climbed down from their ivory towers to work with university technology transfer offices or provide advice to business executives. Kerr's multiversity was "driven more by necessity than by voices in the air."[23]

Introspection and Individualism

Harvard historian Steven Shapin recalls a description of Ivory Tower thinking:

Shut up in his ivory tower, each writes for himself alone. Having little or no function to fulfil in the social world of his time, he has lost touch altogether with an audience, and retreats into seclusion, where introspection sets in, and often a distorted individualism results.[24]

Today, although "almost no one has anything good to say about the Ivory Tower and specifically about the university in its supposed Ivory Tower mode," American and British academia still rally around a romanticized notion of ivy-covered walls and the lone, independent scholar, pursuing truth for its own sake.[25] Academics are unwilling to abandon the crumbling tower. The rise and fall of Duke's English department is a tale of how, with determined and skilled leadership, Ivory Towers can spring up in the modern university, but it is also a story of how quickly introspection sets in—and distorted individualism results.

In 1984, Duke University was a university with elevated aspirations. Like many southern institutions, it had a loyal following. It had been only sixty years since John B. Duke had turned Trinity College into Duke University with a $40 million endowment and plans to build a Gothic campus in the style of Princeton near the original college. The university had a research operation and was a member of the exclusive American Association of Universities (AAU). Duke's president at that time was former governor and US senator Terry Sanford, a man with a deep-seated belief in education. Sanford had twice been a Democratic candidate for US president and was a phenomenally successful fund-raiser. The people who gave money to Duke during the Sanford years were counting on him to bring Élite status to the university on a scale that would match the grandness of the campus itself.

It is not recorded exactly when in the Sanford administration the decision was made to turn Duke's English department into a national powerhouse, but the climb to prominence began in earnest in 1984 when Sanford hired Frank Lentricchia, a Duke alumnus and influential critical theorist. Lentricchia had a simple plan: build a distinguished faculty and turn them loose. The person he hired to execute that plan was Stanley Fish, head of the English department at Johns Hopkins, and someone who had a carefully cultivated public image—a rare combination of academic accomplishment and media showmanship. Fish was an example, said a *New Republic* profile, of someone who "turned careerism into a philosophy."[26] He was a major literary catch for Duke, but he also brought with him another eminent scholar, his wife, Jane Thompkins, a professor at Temple University in Philadelphia. That turned out to be the key to Fish's approach to building the reputation of English departments.

Hiring stars was nothing new. Fish had seen the star system work at Berkeley. It had worked for him at Johns Hopkins. But he had another secret. He knew how to turn a weakness of academic hiring into strength. Certainly adding elite scholars would be helpful in building the reputation of an entire department, but elite scholars were also the most difficult to hire. How could a rising department convince stars to pull up stakes, bundle up their best graduate students, and homestead at a middle-of-the-road academic department? It meant starting over—maybe in a less sophisticated institution with administrators who would be less appreciative of celebrities. At the very least, building a department would mean hiring, fund-raising, mentoring, curriculum committees, and other distractions— less time for pursuing research. Fish's solution to this problem was inspired by his own situation: he was one-half of a star couple. There were plenty of couples in similar circumstances—professors who were excellent in their fields, though could never manage to find simultaneous academic appoint- ments in the same city. The predicament is so common in academic life that there is a name for it: the two-body problem. Two-body problems are so dif- ficult to resolve that star-quality couples often find themselves employed in institutions that are thousands of miles apart. I have married friends who work in the same field at universities on opposite coasts and schedule their trips to professional conferences strategically so that they can be together, even if only for a few days. Universities that make it easy for couples to find suitable appointments together, especially couples of the caliber of Fish and Thompkins, have a competitive advantage in the academic marketplace.

Fish was a master of university politics. He even writes a column about it for the *New York Times*. He knew how to arrange senior positions for cou- ples, but in order to do so he would have to expand the breadth of Duke's English department by expanding into high-profile, arcane, and socially controversial areas. In the hands of someone less capable, this would have been difficult at a conservative, southern school like Duke. Fish would have to hire quickly and in areas that would bring an immediate payoff to the department. Furthermore, the department would have to cater to the needs of the stars, removing from their shoulders administrative and other time- consuming responsibilities. That was one of Fish's special talents. Despite nervous donors and alumni, Duke went along with the idea, and it kicked off a wave of celebrity hiring in the English department.

In rapid succession Duke hired husband-wife teams from Maryland, Penn, Amherst, and Johns Hopkins. One of the highest-profile scholars was Henry Louis Gates. Gates was, next to Fish, the best-known English professor of his day. Like Fish, Gates was an academic superstar, an expert cultivator of media attention, and not at all shy about staking out extreme, usually quot- able positions on an array of issues, especially related to race. So it did not surprise anyone that Gates made Duke a stop on his journey from Cornell to Harvard. Like Gates, most of the new arrivals were capable of rattling the nerves of deans and presidents, but that too was familiar territory for Fish. While most of his colleagues wrote jargon-laced articles that were more or less incomprehensible to the general public, Fish wrote cleanly and simply, leaving little doubt where he stood on a particular topic. His stances were often attention grabbing—like, "Why there is no such thing as free speech."[27]

Fish made his academic reputation during the rise of the postmodernist movement in the arts and humanities. He was the most visible advocate of reader-response criticism, which holds that the meaning of a text can only be discerned in the response it provokes in a reader. Among well-known English departments, the deconstructionist approaches like reader-response theory provoked divisive arguments. Fish counted on this reaction, and had made it a centerpiece of his academic career. His book *Is There a Text in This Class?* hammers the point home to students.[28] The answer is always "no." Importing this kind of controversy to Duke was part of the strategy.

Other academic troublemakers were also being recruited. There were Marxists and scholars who specialized in gender and sexuality, including several who specialized in theories based on gay sexuality that had been advanced by Eve Kosofsky Sedgwick and Michael Moon. The appearance of such material in the course catalog of one of North Carolina's best-known universities probably caused some consternation among the university's socially conservative friends. The English department at Duke may have become a department of stars, but it was also developing a certain kind of notoriety. Notoriety attracted graduate students.

By the early 1990s, Fish was firmly in control. The governance of academic departments occupies a special place among the concerns of professors. Decision-making responsibilities that are shared among faculty and administrators had been a firm principle of American academic life since it was articulated by the educational philosopher Dewey at the turn of the twentieth century. But shared governance had little impact on how decisions were made at Duke. Fish had a reputation for an authoritarian style that would have rattled colleagues who were not as self-confident as Duke's faculty. In most departments, professors comb through academic details of curriculum and classroom teaching, looking for crannies into which their opinions can be inserted, yet Duke's stars did not mind that faculty meetings were infrequent. When Fish joked that most decisions did not really require their attention, he could get away with it because they, for the most part, agreed with him. Based on his success in selling English to Duke University and turning the investment into academic gold, he was the darling of both the upper administration and his colleagues. There had rarely been a more dramatic rise in academic quality.

However successful Fish was at building Duke's Ivory Tower for literary theory, English courses were, for the majority of Duke students, only a means to an end. For most people, an English department is charged with teaching required courses to wave after wave of undergraduates who regard composition or poetry as obstacles to be overcome. At Duke's stratospheric heights, English was transformed into something else. Duke had become the vanguard of academic critical thought. Those with Duke PhDs were in demand, and began populating English departments around the country as assistant professors who, in turn, sent their best students to enroll in the Duke PhD program. Curricular issues that would occupy lesser departments did not seem to matter much at Duke. There was nothing like a core of required courses for majors, and survey courses were scarce.

Of Duke's graduate program, a 1992 external review committee would later say that its curriculum was a "hodgepodge."[29] Faculty members seemed to revel in the ad hoc nature of the PhD program. "There is no curriculum," they reportedly told the review committee. "We simply teach what we want to."[30] But the graduate program had become famous, and the sheer talent of Duke's faculty dazzled the committee. Whatever problems there were, the external reviewers claimed, could be addressed.

But like most universities, Duke reviews its programs every five years. The 1998 edition of the English department review was less generous. The review committee found a department in shambles. The graduate program had not made any progress toward what would be considered a regular curriculum, and an air of irresponsibility had infected the undergraduate program as well. The committee was careful to point out that the "department still finds itself without anything we would be disposed to describe as an undergraduate or a graduate curriculum."[31] As if to confirm the fate of ivory towers as places where introspection sets in and distorted individualism results, Duke's English department had turned from the analysis of literature to memoir writing and a particularly vicious form of intellectual attack that aims to undermine a fellow professor's personal relevance.[32] Mariana Torgovnick, a protégé of Fish's, had become department head in 1996—the first woman to head a department at Duke. Her tenure exaggerated existing tensions and ideological biases.

David Yaffe, who had access to the department members in 1998, "paints a dark picture of intolerance and hostility," citing the findings of the review committee:

The dissatisfaction with the chair ... is deep and widespread. There was unanimous feeling that the present chair's term should not be extended beyond next year when her current three-year term ends.... More than a few of the faculty favored immediate change at whatever emotional and professional cost.[33]

What was seductive in Fish's hands became malevolent in the Torgovnick administration, which according to a *New York Times* article, adopted "Mr. Fish's authoritarian style without his charm."[34] Sedgwick, in apparent retaliation for an "increase in anti-intellectualism," began to exert what Yaffe characterizes as undue influence on the hiring process.[35] The exodus from Duke started that same year, as seven tenured faculty members either left Duke or moved to administrative positions. Lentricchia left the department and denounced the field. Fish's wife had quit teaching. When Fish left Duke to accept a deanship at the University of Illinois in Chicago and the management of the day-to-day affairs of the department was placed in the hands of a committee handpicked by the administration, the collapse of the Duke Ivory Tower was complete—an event that was chronicled on the front page of the *New York Times*.[36]

The growth and decline of the Duke's English department is a story of contradictions, all of them tied to Ivory Tower thinking. If you believe in the inevitability of the Ivory Tower's fate—to lose touch altogether with an audience and retreat into seclusion—then the collapse of the English department is not much of surprise. After all, it abandoned its duty to teach critical reading and writing skills, in favor of bolstering a risky agenda. "[Having] made little effort to foster a sense of collective purpose or identity among its members, stressing their value as individuals instead," any other outcome would have been remarkable.[37]

The star strategy that began with the hiring of Lentricchia could only be maintained by an overpowering figure like Fish who was somehow able to anticipate collective decisions of faculty without actually hearing their opinions. Nor could it have thrived without a kind of hive behavior that systematically devalued undergraduate instruction.

Shifting Battles

Almost no one today uses the term "Ivory Tower"—most insiders are well aware that ivory towers are not held in high esteem—but many university faculty members nevertheless believe that the attributes of tower culture can be recast in romantic terms and still form the basis of academic life.

But what about the institutions of academia that still rely on the Ivory Tower? Tenure is already rare enough to be an oddity in much of higher education. Universities that have tenure cling to the grueling ritual of evaluating the suitability of young scholars for lifetime employment contracts, but even at universities with large tenured faculties, there may be more faculty members who do not have tenure. As a tool for ensuring academic freedom, many presidents believe that tenure's value has not caught up to other changes taking place. Tenure forces a dedicated instructor to abandon the classroom for the research laboratory, and many new PhDs are not interested in the life choices that go with an academic research career. They are easy targets for Minerva or Olin. Humanities professors who once ridiculed the remote and ineffective medium of the MOOC find themselves increasingly drawn to the sheer magnitude of the open classroom.

Even the organizations that are dedicated to maintaining the Ivory Tower seem to be casting about. Faculty unions appear to be more concerned with contracts and working conditions than with the nature of academic scholarship. The AAUP, whose membership peaked at a hundred thousand—nearly one in five professors—in the early 1970s went into a decade of rapid decline in the 1980s and never recovered. Today the AAUP enrolls just 7 percent of all full-time, tenure-track faculty members. That may help explain why the AAUP has shifted its focus from the Ivory Tower issues like academic freedom to moral crusades, which are much easier to explain. In 2009, the AAUP launched a campaign to "alert faculty members to the growing danger that ... federal court decisions are undermining First Amendment protections for public university faculty members speaking out about campus governance."[38] Defenders of the Ivory Tower have always been willing to engage in battles, but as often as not, these are skirmishes that do not register outside academia. A fight over who has the moral high ground might turn out to be more than a local skirmish. It might set forces of good and evil against each other. A holy war is a different matter altogether and much more difficult to ignore.

Holy Wars

The success of the Revolution is intimately connected to the successes and failures of *faculty governance*. At universities where faculty preoccupation with governance is the strongest, self-interest and the intrusion of organized labor make conversations about the future confrontational and infused with the us versus them fervor of holy wars. Faculty governance is a contradiction—a blend of shared responsibility and entitlement that drenches many academic conversations. The very idea combines noble aspirations with base opportunities for unchecked authoritarianism. Nevertheless, this extraordinary principle lies at the heart of the modern university. Striking at faculty governance is a direct assault on what it means to be an academic institution, because—in the minds of many—the only question that matters is, "Who is in charge?" Just raising this query can derail change, stop strategy in its tracks, and defeat reasoned discourse. It is interesting that the central figure in the saga of Duke's English department was Stanley Fish, a person who saw the fundamental contradictions in faculty governance. As an administrator, Fish was autocratic in a way that should have provoked concern among defenders of faculty governance, but it never did. "I would announce changes and see if anyone said anything," he told a *New York Times Magazine* interviewer in 1992.[39] He is a defender of the Ivory Tower but is also openly dismissive of the particular brand of university governance that has dominated academia for the last century.

The term faculty governance is misleading. There are few universities that embrace the idea that faculty members actually govern the institution. Colleges and universities have adopted a principle called *shared governance*: the idea that decision-making authority and responsibility is distributed among professors, administrators, and governing boards, although anyone who has spent time with college faculty members might easily get a different impression: "A faculty leader … [said] that shared governance means that professors, who are the "heart of the university," delegate the governance of their universities to administrators, whose role is to provide a support network for the faculty."[40]

Survey after survey of faculties and administrators paint two contradictory pictures.[41] On the one hand, most professors do not care about issues like governance. Elected governing committees frequently have to scrape together a slate of candidates from the faculty ranks. It is a rare professor who can name the members of the university governing board. Some claim that they are not even aware of who the president or provost are. In the Ivory Tower collegiality reigns, and decisions are made by discussion and consensus. Even the idea that there is a decision-making hierarchy is foreign to many professors. On the other hand, among governance zealots, there is a feeling that faculty voices are not being heard when important decisions are made, and that the situation is growing steadily worse. This is a firmly held opinion despite a wealth of data to show that across a wide range of institutions, the involvement of ordinary professors in the governance of their institutions has increased over the last thirty years.[42]

Shared governance is a flame kept alive largely through concerted action. No institution wants to be accused of trampling academic freedom, so the influence of organizations like AAUP on American campuses looms large. Each new slate of officers elected by the AAUP seems intent on moving the organization closer to labor union status. In 2012, the candidates for the top offices ran on a platform stating that "the single most effective way to protect academic freedom and shared governance is through collective bargaining." They soundly defeated their opponents.[43] Whenever there is a dispute involving faculty participation in running an institution, or real and perceived attacks on faculty prerogatives, AAUP teams descend on a campus to investigate, analyze, and ultimately produce reports that support faculty rights. The AAUP paints itself in a slightly different way. It is not organized labor but rather a vigilant protector of justice for higher education—justice that is secured when academic decision makers dominate.

Former University of Michigan president James Duderstadt, who ran one of the most effective and complex administrations in the country, speaks for a broad consensus of college presidents: "Universities must develop the capacity to move rapidly. This will require university leaders to occasionally make difficult decisions and take strong action without the traditional consensus-building process." Strong action is "demanded by the government, the media, and the public at large," maintains Duderstadt, because of "increased complexity, financial pressures and accountability." The twenty-first-century university demands "stronger management than in the past."[44] The very mention of strong management is often enough to raise alarms that higher education is under siege from corporations and corporatists that want to dismantle its structure. Fish said in a *New York Times* essay that academics desire to "have it both ways" by working in large organizations while still proclaiming themselves to be their own bosses. True believers in shared governance, according to Fish, are "less interested in parceling out the roles on the basis of competence, training, and organizational hierarchy than in affirming what they take to be a point of morality." It is an opportunity, he adds, to mount "a holy war, waged by the forces of good and evil."[45]

Grievance and Investigation

Because accreditors demand it, nearly every institution publishes a "Statement on Shared Governance." Some of the statements are simply a listing of standing committees along with their members and administrative homes, with pointers to the committee charters. Many others, however, bear the marks of battle; they are less statements of governance than truth and reconciliation plans prepared for mediation:[46]

The problem is that this climate of mistrust has built up over such a long period of time that it will take a corresponding period of time to build it up, if everyone is interested in doing that. I do not think everyone is. Even now, I have the feeling that this effort was paid for by the school merely to maintain accreditation. If accreditation were not an issue, this would not have happened.

Some seem to be part of a much longer search for the meaning of governance:

The study was guided by a framework in which President [Deleted] was asked the following questions: (1) What is our common (or not common) understanding of what governance means and what shared governance is, ... (2) What does shared governance mean from a cultural perspective, [and] ... are there areas of agreement regarding what shared governance is and how [it] is carried out?

Others display the grievances that justify articles of war, like this one:

There is a feeling among political leaders, boards of governors (regents or trustees), and top administrators (chancellors, presidents, and the like) that any sharing of authority impedes their "right" to make the big decisions.

Or this one that holds out hope for some compromise:

This understanding of shared governance incorporates two suppositions: (1) when it comes to important issues, final decision-making power belongs to the president, and (2) all subordinate campus constituents are pretty much equal, regardless of function and expertise (the insidious implication of the term "stakeholder"). This brand of shared governance, which resembles corporate quality-improvement programs like Total Quality Management (TQM), is certainly preferable to tyranny or dictatorship. In fact, on many campuses—especially those on which presidents routinely make decisions without consulting anybody—the implementation of the stakeholder understanding of shared governance would constitute a great leap forward.

The AAUP is often called on to offer an opinion when there are disputes that involve faculty rights. At one time, these investigations were confined to complaints about tenure and academic freedom, but as in the case of the closing of Antioch College in 2007, investigations frequently spill over into matters related to how a university is organized and how administrative decisions are reached. Here are some examples of the disputes that the AAUP has investigated:[47]

Idaho State University: The Idaho State Board of Education [suspended] the operation and bylaws of the faculty senate at Idaho State University and [directed the] ISU president to "implement an interim faculty structure" ... in order to preserve the university's teaching and research mission.... The available evidence carries no suggestion that the ISU faculty senate's activities were destructive of the ends for which the university exists.

Miami-Dade Community College: The administration [abolished] the existing systems of academic government following a faculty vote in favor of collective bargaining.... Whatever the achievement of [the current administration,] they have been accomplished in large part through a substantial erosion of the faculty's role in the governance of the college.

Elmira College: [This report] deals with a welter of episodes that have contributed to a situation with no obvious beginning, middle, or end.... [T]he investigating committee sought to depict the tone and implications of what will be seen as very poor governance relationships at Elmira College rather than to describe individual episodes in great detail.

Lindenwood College: Current conditions for academic governance are truly deplorable.

The University of Virginia: The board of visitors and its rector [initiated on June 8, 2012] the effort to force the president's resignation. The events resulted from a "failure by those charged with institutional oversight to understand the institution over which they presided and to engage with the administration and the faculty to be well informed." The episode resonated well beyond the confines of the University of Virginia. It triggered intense national press coverage and drew the prompt attention of the regional accrediting agency. The AAUP expressed interest almost from the start. The Association's annual meeting issued a resolution in support of the senate on June 16.[48]

Corporatists

It is a peculiar interpretation of academic freedom that asserts the right for college professors to conduct themselves largely without external accountability. Academic careers are often boosted by promising to reverse a long-term trend toward a corporate style of management. The word corporate is a particularly common epithet among academic insiders, and one that is prone to be hurled at offending administrators, boards, and universities. Fish pointed out the AAUP's use of the term "corporate style of management" in a report criticizing administrative decisions at Idaho State University. "The phrase ... is freighted with scorn and contempt usually reserved to tyranny and dictatorship," wrote Fish. To the AAUP, Fish claimed, every dispute between administrators doing their jobs and "a faculty that insists not only on doing its job without being monitored but on its ... right to monitor everyone else's job" is a titanic struggle for the soul of academia.[49]

Among promoters of shared governance, there is an obsession with the idea that the corporate management of universities undermines governance. The language at a 1996 AAUP Shared Governance vs Corporate Management conference was mordant with images of the "infusion of corporate language, processes and values into academic decision-making," and revulsion that the emerging "hero cult of the 'manager' are norms seeping like swamp gas into the hallowed halls of ivy."[50] Such language is today thrown about casually:

The classic strategy, documented by many campuses, is what might be termed a stealth attack on governance launched under cover of summer vacations and faculty inattention.... [I]n fact, senior administrators pursue other avenues of consultation, including hand-picked committees. A wide variety of campuses, from private to public, are experiencing the gradual displacement of regular faculty governance in favor of a hierarchical, corporate decision-making structure.[51]

Larry Gerber, the chair of AAUP's committee on university governance, is one of those who beats a drum, as alarm, whenever a corporate or "hierarchical" style of management is detected on a college campus. To Gerber and others at AAUP, these are signals not of differing approaches:

Liberal education is today coming under increasing attack. It is no coincidence that many of those who seek to reduce higher education to a form of narrowly conceived job training are also in the forefront of efforts to replace shared governance with a corporate model of management. Advocates of a top-down management style who want to transform faculty from professionals into "employees" and students into "consumers" tend to see liberal education as a waste of time and resources, because they fail to see the immediate "payoff" of the liberal and fine arts and because they are willing to allow the "market" to determine what should and should not be taught.[52]

It is a message that is echoed dozens, and perhaps hundreds, of times whenever those who believe that faculty governance is under siege get together, usually with language that becomes more extreme with each passing year:

But whether it involves contesting the tyranny of neo-liberal agendas that are eroding the tenure process, fighting against the capricious interference of governmental agencies that deny individuals the resources they need and deserve to function adequately, or working to make higher education bureaucracies less corporatist and more fair, the commitment you have made to the preservation of academic freedom you make on behalf of all of us ... regardless of one's particular institutional affiliation or location.[53]

Public and private universities have very different views on these matters, and there are many highly regarded institutions that are inclined to have the least tolerance for what many presidents see as irresponsible meddling in internal affairs. In MIT's unique governance model, for instance, there is no faculty senate. Instead, a dozen standing committees with faculty, administrative, and staff representation handle the affairs of the institute.

Minerva's Ben Nelson deliberately chose a governance model that avoids all traces of shared governance. "We chose Caltech's model," he says: "We have sections not departments. Section heads and the provost make all the decisions. No senate. No president interferes. That is our governance model. Deans of two schools and four divisional deans make all the decisions. They run the academic affairs of the university. A completely separate group runs the student experience. They operate independently with different decision structures."

It is not that Caltech is indifferent to academic freedom and the AAUP's goals. There has been a chapter on campus since 1930 when William

Bennett Munro, who founded Caltech's Division of Humanities and Social Sciences, was also named national president of the AAUP, and the faculty thought it would be unwise for Caltech not to have a local chapter. Caltech economics professor Horace Gilbert had just joined the new division, and recalls that except for its support of academic freedom, Caltech did not see the AAUP in the same light as other institutions:

I was always pleased that the top people were professional, and I hope this continues, because if it becomes a labor union I think it will be the end of the AAUP as we have known it.[54]

This was no doubt a result of the relationship between the Caltech faculty and administrators. "At Caltech there was no squaring off, no confrontation between the faculty and the administration."[55] Even during a 1931 pay cut, a source of financial stress that might have prompted that kind of confrontation, there was relative calm. There was no thought of consulting the AAUP. "So far as I know, there was no objection," Gilbert recounts. "Nobody liked it, but there was no objection." Even the AAUP role in tenure cases was not appealing to Caltech, where the faculty committee on tenure "took the place of any kind of action that the AAUP might have taken here [at Caltech]."[56]

The AAUP chooses its battles wisely. It does not investigate low completion rates, which it regards as the fault of secondary schools, or decreased affordability, which can be remedied by restoring state funding for public universities.[57] Careers are derailed by the exercise of hierarchical authority, but the AAUP does not intervene. It did not choose to raise cries of corporatist management style when Fish, a capable defender of the idea that "in every phase of its operation, the university is in fact a commercial enterprise," was building the Duke English powerhouse.[58] It was not until Togovnick took over as department chair that grievances began to be lodged that might have triggered a response from the AAUP.[59] Then, in a reversal that Fish would not have tolerated, the Duke faculty members turned on their chair, much as an inflamed mob turns on a victim.

12 Governing in the Age of Internet Empires[1]

Walled City is of the Net but not on it. There are no laws here, only agreements.
—William Gibson, *Idoru*, 1996

The last rampart is the mob. In April 2014, Brandeis University, bowing to an orchestrated Internet campaign, withdrew its invitation to women's rights activist Ayaan Hirsi Ali to speak at commencement, where she was also to have been awarded an honorary degree. Some days later, Christine Lagarde, managing director of the International Monetary Fund—the first woman to hold that position—withdrew in the face of social network protests as 2014 commencement speaker at Smith College. At about the same time, former US secretary of state Condoleeza Rice responded to outrage fueled by online media by withdrawing from the spring commencement ceremony at Rutgers University. Robert Birgenau, former chancellor of the University of California and champion of the rights of undocumented immigrant students, preempted Haverford College's plan to revoke his commencement invitation by declining it. Birgenau's treatment of Occupy Wall Street protesters had been widely criticized in blogs, online newsletters, and email petitions. Inexplicably, the very Haverford student leaders who had the most to gain by confronting Birgenau guaranteed that he would not have to face hostile questions. When Birgenau withdrew, students declared it a "small victory."[2] The iconoclastic comedian Bill Maher was scheduled to give the fall 2014 commencement address at Berkeley—the birthplace of the free speech movement in the 1960s—when the Muslim Student Association, protesting televised comments concerning fundamentalist Islam, mounted a campaign to bar him from campus. Notre Dame resisted calls to revoke Barack Obama's invitation to speak at its 2009 commencement because of his stand on abortion rights, but not before a petition bearing three hundred thousand names was presented to university leaders. All were targets of special interest groups that swarmed in mob-like fashion, mounting petitions and smear campaigns to bully university administrators.

It is ironic that the same technologies the Revolution promotes can, in other circumstances, be turned on reformers and legitimate governing bodies alike. In the age of social networks, rules matter less than the informal understandings that cross geographic and political boundaries and create and empower unaccountable mobs in ways that were unimaginable only a few years ago.

A Way of Governing

Hirsi Ali, a native of Somalia, was subjected as a young girl to ritual genital mutilation and nearly forced into marriage against her wishes—experiences that fired her lifelong battle to combat the mistreatment of Muslim women. She moved to the Netherlands, where she was elected to Parliament. Her 2004 film *Submission* was harshly critical of Islam, and in Amsterdam, a radical Islamist who threatened to also kill Hirsi Ali murdered the film's director, Theo van Gogh. Bloggers first noted her anti-Islamic writing. The cause of barring Hirsi Ali from campus was picked up by American Islamic advocacy groups, which began email and social media campaigns to label her "a notorious Islamophobe."[3] Lagarde, Rice, and Birgenau were also attacked by online petitions and social media campaigns aimed at overturning institutional decisions that many thought were controversial, but had no bearing whatsoever on the universities' academic programs.

Groups often find allies to support campaigns to silence unpopular views on campus, or coerce faculty and administrators whose actions put them out of favor; accreditors and unions, for example, can choose to challenge the way boards control costs or evaluate presidents. Like villagers storming the gates of a castle, organized labor, political activism, and vested self-interest can easily coalesce into an unelected, unappointed, and unaccountable mob that can effectively make decisions about business issues, such as real estate, institutional assets, and partnerships with service providers and corporate sponsors. Tactical control of these groups may be in the hands of Twitter users. Strategy is frequently worked out on Facebook pages and communicated by WordPress blog postings that are reposted on the *Huffington Post*. Within hours, tens of thousands of activists can swirl to force the hands of authority.

At other times, shadowy influence controls events. In late 2014, a Palestinian American professor of American Indian studies named Steven Salaita was offered a faculty position at the University of Illinois. As is usual in such situations, Salaita resigned from his faculty position at Virginia Tech and prepared to move to Champaign, Illinois, to begin a new chapter in his career. That was when he was told that the university had withdrawn the employment offer, leaving him unemployed and his reputation in shambles. Apparently one or more trustees objected to his biting criticism of Israeli policies in Gaza, turning a routine appointment of an eminent scholar into a public spectacle that had nothing to do with his qualifications, but did serious damage to his career.[4]

These are not merely cases of enterprises run amok. They represent a way of governing. The power of a mob to hijack rational decision making is great. The well-honed procedures and culture of academia—the institutions of the Ivory Tower—amplify voices that are not accountable to anyone, but they are voices that can work their will nevertheless. Much as our small band of innovators uses online technology to remake higher education, creating vast communities of new learners and experimenting with new business models, mobs form easily in the era of the Internet, and a mob that grows without limits or accountability can just as easily become a governing force of its own.

Milton

Early in the movie *Office Space*, the hapless, hopeless character known only as Milton is moved from his cubicle among the other employees of a spirit-crunching company called Initech to the basement, where entombed in a wire cage, he sits alone in the dark, unpaid, protecting the one material possession that gives him status—a red stapler.[5] A soulless manager and the administrative legions that work for him have decided that this is the course of action most appropriate for Milton's unstated transgressions. Milton is literally unable to communicate. He is ridiculed and excluded from all social interaction. His coworkers are completely indifferent. Milton's fate is a picture-perfect instance of a phenomenon called workplace mobbing: "an impassioned, collective campaign by co-workers to exclude, punish, and humiliate a targeted co-worker."[6]

Like Milton, Maria Togovnick and Robert Birgenau were also mobbed. So were hundreds of others, who accused of disloyalty, aberrant scholarship, or political insensitivity have been pursued, harassed, and driven out of academic life. What happens when an academic mob—moved by the morality of its cause and convinced that it has chosen the right side in a holy war—clashes with legitimate authority? Are such battles likely to have enduring impact? Will the institutions that submit to the rule of a mob find themselves marginalized as bypass economies form and other, newer institutions take over?

Mobs search for victims to persecute, but of course not everyone who feels persecuted is actually a victim. The Ivory Tower by design excludes some who think of themselves as worthy for inclusion. Academic life is supposed to be a meritocracy, and not everyone is of equal merit when it comes to scholarship. There are countless lawsuits by professors who, denied tenure, argue with all sincerity that theirs was the instance in which a system designed to guarantee academic freedom actually denied it. Emotions often run high in such cases, and it is easy to see how being turned down for promotion can spiral into charges of personal bias, institutional unfairness, or simple incompetence on the part of promotion committees. In fact, universities are governed in ways that seem to invite that kind of abuse.

At most universities, important decisions like hiring, firing, promotion, and tenure frequently hinge on outrageously subjective judgments. Promotion committees solicit recommendations from—typically anonymous—peers, who comment on the significance or relevance of a candidate's research along with other qualities, like reputation and personality. Reputations are often assessed in comparison to other individuals. Speculation about the future course of a candidate's career may stand in equal measure with an objective record of accomplishment. Student evaluations—sometimes laced with personal animosity and often lacking perspective—can undo a promotion as surely as a negative recommendation from a respected peer. Faculty rights organizations are frequently asked to intervene, but with few exceptions courts have held that academic personnel decisions may follow the internal logic of university governance. According to this logic, the academic workplace should not be capricious and ad hoc, but it does not need to be fair. Much of this work of managing the academic enterprise is in the hands of professors, who operating under the righteous banner of faculty governance may be able to direct power against their individual colleagues without personal accountability.

Academic Mobbing

University of Waterloo sociologist Kenneth Westhues has cataloged hundreds of cases of academic mobbing by bullying supervisors and spontaneous academic mobs. In both situations, says Westhues, mobbing is often an unintended by-product of prerogatives such as tenure and academic freedom: "Tenure is supposed to protect scholars from outside control, but it does a lousy job of protecting them from one another."[7]

The pattern could have been copied from the inquisition.[8] An unlucky victim—someone who stands out from the crowd—is singled out, and under threat of public humiliation is pressed to either recant or quit. In many cases the victim hands the instruments of torture to the tormenters by committing real or contrived offenses. Colleagues, either out of fear for their own safety or as payback for past conflicts, abandon the individual— sometimes by ritualized shunning, and sometimes by participating in trials and tribunals.

Ruth Tucker claimed that her sin was to be the only woman at tiny Calvin Seminary. Her attempts to fit into an all-male culture drew the attention of a new administration, which mounted a three-year campaign to deny her the full professorship and tenure that had been promised when she was hired. When she appealed, her colleagues turned against her. "I remained apart from the faculty, feeling depressed, excluded and isolated," she recalls.[9] A special panel of mediators recommended immediate redress, but the trustees apparently disregarded that report. Tucker left shortly after that.

The academic mobbing of Herbert Richardson is unusual because he has been both the accuser and accused. Richardson's story plays out over forty years, and involves a great many characters and events, but its essence is this: since the 1960s, Richardson had been the only Protestant professor in the otherwise all-Catholic St. Michael's College, a subsidiary of the University of Toronto.[10] When in 1989 the previously ecumenical St. Michael's College took a sudden, conservative turn, a newly installed college administration demanded that faculty members pledge in writing to adhere to Catholic orthodoxy in their teaching and other scholarly activities. Richardson refused. It was not the first time his behavior had attracted attention.

Richardson was an idiosyncratic scholar in many respects, but he came under special scrutiny because he founded and owned Edwin Mellen Press, a publisher of monographs, dissertations, and, sometimes, controversial manuscripts—including an enthusiastic theological defense of Scientology. There were detractors and critics who claimed that Mellen was a vanity publisher of second-rate material. Richardson replied that he had always insisted on strict vetting requirements to ensure academic quality. Nonetheless, Mellen Press grew in size and scope. Richardson did his best to keep his academic responsibilities separate from his commercial activities, often working weekends to avoid taking time from his teaching schedule at St. Michael's College. An unfortunate classroom incident, a medical leave gone awry, a disgruntled Mellen Press employee, and Richardson's well-intentioned but ill-timed founding of an alternative university called

Edwin Mellen University all led to a demand by St. Michael's president J. Robert S. Prichard that Richardson either resign or face a public tribunal for gross academic misconduct.

In 1994, Prichard launched a seventeen-day trial—at an estimated cost to St. Michael's College of $500,000—aimed at terminating Richardson. The grounds for dismissal included not only the classroom incident and murky circumstances surrounding the Edwin Mellen enterprises but also charges that Richardson cost the university money by leaving windows open in winter, that he failed to wash blackboards, and that he played favorites with students. The Internet was in its infancy in 1994, but it was effective enough to help launch a media campaign to discredit Richardson as a scholar, claiming among other things that he was a "fascist Scientologist." The charges that he misused his medical leave and improperly engaged in commercial activities stuck, and Richardson was dismissed.

For much of the next decade, Richardson pursued critics in an attempt to regain his reputation. In 2010, a McMaster University librarian named Dale Askey published a blog post describing an exchange with Richardson during which Askey was accused of academic mobbing. As Askey reports, "I had publicly called [Mellen] a junk publisher, so name-calling was certainly in play."[11] In 2013, Richardson filed a $4 million lawsuit against Askey and McMaster. The Internet, which had played a part in Richardson's 1994 tribunal at St. Michael's College, now lit up with blog and Twitter postings along with all the power of modern social media. There were hundreds of heated exchanges on both sides of the Richardson matter, asserting on one side that Richardson was trying to interfere with Askey's academic freedom, and on the other that Askey was part of a decades-long persecution based on Richardson's unpopular views. The conflict continues with no resolution in sight.

Internet Amplifications

Mobbing requires an ability to isolate and reinforce polarized points of view, but the ability of a single perspective to dominate a discussion has always been limited by how many interested parties could be drawn into a conflict. Social media changed that. A Twitter posting is only 140 characters long. It is intended to be easily and quickly consumed and passed on. A tweet that is broadcast to a sufficiently large number of followers can propagate exponentially and become a call to battle on a scale and with a speed that would have been impossible to achieve previously. The recent history of academic mobbing parallels the development of social media. Maria Togovnick was virtually helpless in the face of verbal assaults that were circulated to only a few people. Likewise, there were only a few people who needed to gang up on Ruth Tucker to seal her fate. Richardson's battle has moved to the Internet and is still raging. There are sociologists who study the effect of technology on this kind of group behavior.

Sarita Yardi and danah boyd, a scientist at Microsoft Research, call this phenomenon *group polarization*: "Opinions have been shown to become more extreme simply because their view has been corroborated, and because [those who hold those opinions] grow more confident after learning of the shared views of others."[12]

The Internet amplifies this effect, making it easier to consume information that reinforces shared values and interests within small groups. When members of a deliberating group move toward extreme views, the result is group polarization. Technologies like Twitter make it possible to transmit a small amount of information— public and available to anyone who chooses to look—to draw large numbers of people into a group. Yardi and boyd note, for example, that religious beliefs—at least among college students—are easily activated in this way. When the source of information is a trusted organization dedicated to protecting the principled morality of a cause, even college professors can behave like the true believers of a fundamentalist sect. It is one of the ways that academic holy wars are waged, and it is how academic mobbing gets started in the age of the Internet.

Professors congregate in academic departments in which decisions about hiring, promotion, and firing take place. Professors make value judgments. They file and investigate grievances, and petition third parties to take sides in their otherwise-internal disputes. And when existential threats to the nature of their enterprise are detected, professors are prone to mount a group attack, often with a conviction that has been reinforced by years of talking only to each other. If the principles that underlie shared governance are vulnerable to mob rule, what happens when academic mobbing is backed by powerful organizations and directed against the legitimate exercise of authority? That is what happened to Hirsi Ali. It is also what happened in the Column Culture of the University of Virginia in summer 2012.

Column Culture

At the University of Virginia, Column Culture refers to the white-columned Rotunda that dominates the Lawn, the focal point of the academic village that Thomas Jefferson designed. The Rotunda so occupies the thoughts of generations of Virginia students that white-haired alumni make annual pilgrimages just so that they can remind themselves what it feels like to look at the world through the double columns in the Dome Room. The columns represent a kind of disengagement from external affairs. To outsiders it seems like an insular culture, a place where the single most dominant architectural feature is a sort of blind through which the outside world is filtered. To insiders—and the many thousands who want to be insiders—it is the intellectual heart of campus life—a campus where students and faculty alike talk about Jefferson in familiar but hushed tones, as if he had just stepped away for a few minutes and would shortly return to evaluate the state of their stewardship. It is a strength that seems to influence everyone from student members in Virginia's nineteenth-century secret societies to classroom teachers. It even influences the administrators and governing bodies responsible for the less romantic details about how the university should be run.

It was into Column Culture that Teresa Sullivan was dropped one August afternoon in 2010. Sullivan had been cultivating the skills of an academic administrator since her undergraduate days at Michigan State University. She had been the provost at the University of Michigan, and before that had held a similar position for the sprawling University of Texas system. Sullivan was reputed to be a meticulous, disciplined manager with a knack for controlling costs. She had no prior connection to the University of Virginia. In fact, she had never been on the Charlottesville campus before her appointment as president there. Sullivan was a scholar, and some thought she might be viewed as "the faculty's president." Others believed that although she was not necessarily a visionary leader, she was someone who could put on "green eyeshades." After John Casteen's twenty-year tenure as president, it was probably time for someone who could take a fresh look at the somewhat-creaky organization of the University of Virginia.

The university was weathering financial and political storms caused in part by the lingering effects of the recession along with a decline in state support. The university was also feeling pressure from a newly discovered energy among peers and competitors around technology-enabled ways of conducting business. Everything about how a public university operates— from how to generate revenues and control costs to the kind of pedagogy used in classrooms—seemed to have become an opportunity for innovation. Talk of disruptive change was in the air among academic insiders, and it seemed unlikely that an institution like the University of Virginia, which was virtually founded on the idea of disrupting an older, classical European style of university education, could stand on the sidelines of such a global conversation. A new president would necessarily be drawn into that discussion and would be required to make some decisions. Whatever course the new president set, there would be risks. There were bound to be critics waiting, ready to undermine the tough stances that a strong leader would have to take. A too-aggressive change agenda would draw protests from those who venerated the past and suspected that the new president—an outsider—would not. An approach that was too timid—or worse, did not display the university's leadership on the international stage—would certainly invite questions from the public about the university's commitment to providing affordable excellence for the citizens of the Commonwealth. Setting an intermediate course did not seem wise either. Such a strategy was bound to irritate several constituencies at once and would certainly give ammunition to those who were less enthusiastic backers. Someone more familiar with campus and state politics might have been able to weave her way through this obstacle course, but challenges were inevitable for any new president, especially for an outsider who was not steeped in Column Culture. In August 2010, Sullivan became the eighth president, an outsider without strong constituencies internally or externally, successor to a long-serving and popular president. She would be the first female to lead an institution that might soon be looking for reasons to reject her leadership should she make a misstep. Failed presidencies often turn on such matters, but Sullivan would soon declare her loyalty to the status quo—the venerated University of Virginia past. She would call herself an "incrementalist."[13] It was insurance, a life preserver that in Virginia's column culture might someday be used to rescue a presidency.

Like most universities, the job of hiring a new president at the University of Virginia falls to a governing board. In Virginia that board—the Board of Visitors—is appointed by the governor and led by an elected rector, who functions as a sort of board chair. In 2010, the membership of the Board of Visitors was in transition. John O. "Dubby" Wynne, the rector who had been an internal champion for Sullivan's appointment, was going to be replaced by longtime board member Helen Dragas, a Virginia Beach real estate and construction developer and member of Virginia's Council for Higher Education. Dragas had been appointed to the board by a liberal Democratic governor and then reappointed by a conservative Republican four years later.

There are some idiosyncrasies dating from the university's founding, but for the most part there is nothing special about the structure and authority of the university's Board of Visitors. Except for certain privately owned companies, all organizations over a certain size are governed by such boards. In the private sector, they are called boards of directors. Public sector organizations have boards of trustees. Government-run enterprises report to oversight committees. Museums, foundations, churches, and professional societies all operate under the guidance of boards that hire and fire senior leadership, oversee finances, set policies, and determine whether or not they are being carried out. The Board of Visitors delegates duties to senior administrators at the University of Virginia, and in turn is accountable to the Virginia legislature, governor, and the people of the Commonwealth. The relationship between the board, university administration, and the Commonwealth is complicated, but there is nothing unprecedented about the complexity of higher education in Virginia.

With Casteen's retirement in 2009, Wynne launched a search for a new president. A presidential search for a public university is an exercise in balancing public and private information. Candidates with the most desirable credentials are often sitting presidents or others whose current positions would be compromised should their names be made public. On the other hand, names cannot be kept confidential indefinitely. Recommendations must be solicited, and serious candidates need to meet with faculty, students, administrators, alumni, and others—both on and off campus—whose opinions matter to the board. Oftentimes, a board decides quickly on a single prospect and uses the search as an extended courtship, wooing a candidate who has already signaled a willingness to accept an offer. The Board of Visitors concluded its search, and on January 11, 2010, announced that Sullivan had been unanimously elected president. Wynne called her "an extraordinary talent, who brings to the university enormous depth and breadth of experience."[14] To all appearances, Sullivan's presidency was launched with the full support of the Board of Visitors. If board members harbored doubts about Sullivan's abilities, no one talked about it in public. Yet no veil of secrecy in public life is perfect, and it was well known that Sullivan had both supporters and detractors on the Board of Visitors.

Presidential Derailments

Every presidency comes to an end—sometimes involuntarily—like Sullivan's did on June 8, 2012. Except in rare cases of misconduct, public information about failed presidencies is usually hard to come by. When the president of the confusingly named California University of Pennsylvania was fired after anonymous complaints were made about the school's financial problems, the public announcement was factual and spare. The decision was made by Pennsylvania's higher education commission. The university's governing board was notified of the action the day before the termination was made public. Even high-profile presidential departures like Ohio State's Gordon Gee are accompanied by relatively little information. Gee's retirement in 2013 was widely assumed to be a result of a series of public gaffes, but official comments mentioned only that he was "loved by the university."

It may come as a shock to the public, which is generally shielded from the details of personnel management, but fired presidents are frequently not tuned in enough to current board thinking to know when they are in trouble. For example, Georgia Perimeter College president Anthony Tricoli sent an upbeat email about an award he had won to the Georgia Board of Regents on the evening before he was fired: "I am the first individual from a two-year college to receive this award since 2001. Pretty exciting. Some good news among the weird of late."[15]

The weird news of late had to do with rumblings from the regents that Georgia Perimeter College was in financial trouble, but Tricoli had reasons for thinking that things were going well. He was tuned in to other voices. In 2011—a year before—the AAUP had given him the Ralph S. Brown Award for Shared Governance. Modeled after the AAUP award for academic freedom, the Brown award is "reserved for those occasions when some accomplishment in the area of shared governance is identified as so outstanding as to merit being singled out."[16] What was Tricoli's shared governance accomplishment that was so outstanding as to merit being singled out? Tricoli was a rising star when he was nominated. According to the nominating letters, his accomplishment was a "passionate commitment to shared governance, teamwork, and collaboration."[17] He was a president who knew how to establish "a model of inclusivity and transparency."[18] He had created an environment in which faculty found themselves "more than at any time in recent years, dealing as professionals and equals in a cooperative and consultative process."[19]

Less than a year later, Tricoli was removed as Georgia Perimeter College president, leaving behind a financial disaster.[20] The college would end the year with a $20 million deficit, largely the result of unconstrained spending. A four-year analysis of revenue and expenses showed that by 2009, there was a $7.3 million shortfall that would continue into the future. "Employment levels are far higher than they should be," said a letter from the system office to Tricoli. The Georgia Perimeter College student newspaper published a time line leading to Tricoli's departure, along with both positive and negative emails about his tenure. One email message in particular caught my eye: "When we lost our Lawrenceville campus and its 7,000 students in 2007, Dr. Tricoli was told he would have to cut 350 jobs

... and not a single person lost his or her job."[21] The writer sent the email not to complain about fiscal mismanagement but rather to praise Tricoli as a "dynamic leader [whose loss] at such a time would cripple the college."[22] SACS, the regional accreditor, sanctioned Georgia Perimeter College. Layoffs and programmatic cuts would be needed to bring the college's financial situation to an acceptable state. The AAUP issued a statement of "retrospective regret" for its selection of Tricoli for the Brown award that was titled "Departure of Georgia Perimeter College President a Mixed Blessing."

In August 2013, Norfolk State University's board voted to remove its president in a move that most observers, including the president himself, called "sudden and unexpected."[23] A few months before that, Arcadia University's board fired President Carl Oxholm without warning, giving him the news in a closed meeting that lasted for hours. Oxholm said he was stunned. The list of presidents who were shocked by their board's decision to terminate them is long, but it is not surprising that so many firings seem to creep up on their targets. Stephen Trachtenberg, Gerald Kauvar, and Grady Bogue, in analyzing derailed presidencies, note that "board-president relations are a major factor in presidential derailments. While some presidents overlook this obvious point, others find themselves with a different board than the one that hired them."[24]

The confidentiality of personnel actions is often entangled with legal practicalities. Even in states with sunshine laws that are supposed to promote open disclosure, access to details of personnel actions may be limited by legal requirements. But just as frequently it is a matter of prudence: advance warning gives both sides in a personnel dispute time to line up supporters for public spectacles aimed at changing a decision. When the University of Oregon voted in public to terminate President Richard Lariviere's contract, chaos ensued. Signatures had been gathered by supporters and opponents, both sides predicting that confidence in the state's flagship university would be shattered. The governor himself weighed in, using unusually blunt language. Even the football team got into the act.

It is no wonder that University of Virginia's board kept the extent of its differences with Sullivan under wraps until the last minute, when in an email dated June 10, 2012, Rector Helen Dragas and Vice Rector Mark Kingston announced that the president would be stepping down effective August 15. The fact that Sullivan was given two more months to wrap up her presidency was a signal that there were no financial disasters, terrible scandals, or matters of gross incompetence awaiting disclosure. Sullivan's departure was apparently the end result of long-simmering problems, but it was not, by recent standards, going to be a particularly rancorous one.

Getting the Language Just Right

A *New York Times Magazine* article describes the early events from the viewpoint of Larry Sabato, a popular political science professor with University of Virginia roots extending to his undergraduate days when he served as student council president. The *Times* portrays Sabato as incredulous that Sullivan "had been pushed aside with so little evident justification." After all, Sabato reasoned, there had been no hint of a scandal. He predicted a "P.R. disaster of national proportions."[25] If so, it would be a precipitated one. It was not because there was something unusual about Sullivan's firing.

Sabato has many opinions on matters internal and external to the university. He is a favorite of cable news shows and also has a certain status as a campus opinion maker. Andrew Rice, the author of the *Times* piece, goes to great lengths to capture Sabato's sense of unease over what everyone would soon discover to have been Sullivan's firing by the board. It was, according to Rice, unease that woke "the slumbering college town of Charlottesville," as "students and faculty condemned what they saw as a coup." That is where most published accounts veer wildly off track. It was not outrage within the Column Culture that roiled the University of Virginia in spring 2012 but rather an orchestrated, high-tech, academic mobbing of Helen Dragas, the Board's Rector, and the person on whom wrath was rained.

Dragas was not prepared for the weapons that were trained on her. The attack was led, according to the *New York Times*, by Wynne, the former rector who had been Sullivan's champion when she was hired.[26] Dragas did not know it at the time, but there was already a well-tested battle plan in place. "Corporatism" and "corporate management" became the convicting charges, repeating nearly word for word the specter of "the infusion of corporate language, processes and values into academic decision making" that drenched the 1996 AAUP Conference on "Shared Governance vs. Corporate Management."[27] Building on such narratives there was a coordinated social media campaign to demonize Dragas. An anti-Dragas Facebook page was launched. Insiders say that Sullivan's own communications, fund-raising, and alumni relations teams set up a war room to enlist supporters and orchestrate their responses. When a wealthy alumnus published a defense of the board's actions, it also was seized on as evidence of corporate control.

Repeating the corporate control war cry, *Huffington Post* bloggers Zach Carter and Jason Linkins described the dire situation at the University of Virginia.[28] Their blog post drew 5,901 comments—many of them dripping with personal animus toward Dragas—and was tweeted 470 times. Another blogger questioned whether Sullivan was being attacked for not being corporate enough. Dragas (who was variously misidentified as a provost, chairman, and Wall Street financier) is a corporatist, said other bloggers. A high-profile University of Virginia professor was so moved that he published an open letter of resignation that was emailed to thousands of influential academics. Thousands of emails, Facebook postings, tweets, blogs, online comments, and other social media messages, most of them taken directly or indirectly from the writings of AAUP's Gerber,[29] and alarmist talk about corporate take-overs were what woke Charlottesville from its slumber.

The first press announcements said that Sullivan was being released because of a failure in strategic planning. In response, "strategy" was attacked as a "weasly little phrase." There was a call for the AAUP, which did not have a chapter on campus, to "articulate a democratic alternative to neo-corporatism." With considerable justification, the University of Virginia styles itself as an Élite public university. But it also has ambitions to become private and even more elite. Commenters assailed the very schools that the University of Virginia wanted to compete with, calling them "hyper-capitalist Stanford/MIT."[30] Dragas was "steeped in a culture of corporate jargon and buzzy management theory"[31] when she "secretly engineered a coup." The word *coup* was used many times, but never was there an explanation of how a lawfully constituted board exercising its statutory authority could constitute a coup. And as if on cue, a popular University of Virginia blogger repeated one of Sullivan's own sound bites: "Corporate-style, top-down leadership does not work in a great university."[32]

Messages like these reverberated throughout cyber space. The closed faculty mailing list at my Center for 21st Century Universities logged hundreds of separate emails, many of them quoting or re-quoting attacks on "corporatism" and hierarchical management styles. I was traveling in Europe in late June 2012, and was able to follow events in the international press, largely enabled by a steady stream of social media postings decrying the situation.

Members of the Board of Visitors made no secret that they had been frustrated by Sullivan's "outright refusal to develop a meaningful strategic plan." If true, that would have been a crisis in governance serious enough to provoke action from most boards. Nevertheless, the AAUP quickly authored a report condemning Sullivan's firing "reportedly without previous or subsequent explanation."[33] SACS, the regional accreditor for the University of Virginia—in an action that shocked many experts on university governance—jumped into the fray, alleging that the decision had been made by a minority of the board, when in fact a super majority had supported Sullivan's resignation. The president of the Association of Governing Boards, which often sides with the AAUP on such matters, would say only that Dragas engaged in "top-down management," conceding that "she had the authority to do so."[34]

Insiders argue that virtually none of what the AAUP alleged in its initial report had a basis in fact. Prolific University of Virginia faculty blogger Siva Vaidyhathan gathered online support for the idea that "universities do not have business models," and likened the board actions to "21st century robber barons try[ing] to usurp control of public universities."[35] Private emails between board members made passing reference to a David Brooks column in the *New York Times* titled "The Campus Tsunami" that threw support to technology-enabled modes of instruction like MOOCs. When those emails were made public, newfound campus resistance to MOOCs and for-profit MOOC providers like Coursera jumped into the action.[36]

Social media played a central role in amplifying the controversy. Sabato had 71,000 Twitter followers in the summer of 2012. His tweets normally run toward political commentary. Yet in the *New York Times Magazine* profile, Rice characterized Sabato, whose $300,000 salary is paid for by the president's office, as the fair-minded, objective observer and conciliator. Sabato's Twitter stream in late June was actually a running commentary that evokes play-by-play coverage of the Arab Spring uprisings. At the height of on-campus protests, Sabato tweeted:

This Board has done more damage to the University I love than the 1895 Rotunda fire.

He marshaled forces,

The BOV 16 are flummoxed but 2,000+ ppl on Lawn & big majorities of faculty & alumns see obvious solution—put Sullivan back.

He urged them to fight on in the face of long odds:

1000s working together, everyone vital, to encourage BOV to do the right thing Tuesday. It's OK: Failure of New Coke made original even better.

When it was clear that the ordeal was almost over, Sabato was there:

WaPo report is true—Some BOV members want to reinstate Sullivan. But can they get to majority of 9 in time?

And once the board announced it was going to reverse itself, Sabato was with the cheering crowds in the University of Virginia's version of Tahir Square:

Dragas & Sullivan met just before mtg. "Time to bring UVA family back together."

Finally, victory was won:

Dragas supports reinstatement of President Sullivan. IT'S OVER! REASON WON....
YES, IT'S PRESIDENT SULLIVAN AGAIN!

A team of AAUP investigators subsequently criticized Dragas and the
board, claiming the decision to remove Sullivan was arbitrary and without cause.[37] The AAUP investigators failed to interview Dragas, but their
report nonetheless labels the rector as "headstrong, imbued with a belief
in 'engaged trusteeship,'" and says that her actions were undertaken "with
single-minded zeal ... without informing herself of the essentials in the
underlying matters." It is a harsh report filled with assertions that according to some of the principals have yet to be established. Dragas responded
simply that the report contained "multiple errors of fact."

The attacks on Dragas and the Board of Visitors were an academic mobbing. The AAUP had staked out a position within hours of Sullivan's firing
and well before any facts were known, so there was probably no evidence
that could have dissuaded the investigating committee from echoing
the organization's long-standing opposition to what it sees as corporate
approaches to university governance.

While events were still unfolding, Dragas and the Board of Visitors
received support from other boards of trustees and the conservative ACTA.
ACTA president Anne Neal wrote in an email to Dragas, "Brava to you and
your fellow board members for taking courageous action. We need more
trustees to understand that these are challenging times that require [bold]
and innovative leadership."

ACTA later explained its stand in a response to the AAUP's call for
"greater communication between faculties and governing boards"—a position that ACTA supports, although it sees things a little differently:

[The] AAUP would undercut the authority trustees must have if they are to exercise
their role as the ultimate governing body. It complains that boards have increasingly
adopted "top-down decision-making strategies." ... Decisive leadership to deliver
significant change will seem "top-down" to those who resist change—but colleges
must change if they are to deliver better education at a price families can afford....
Faculty advice is vital as needed changes are planned—but ultimately setting strategic and academic priorities are top-level board decisions.[38]

Dragas is not interested in relitigating the Sullivan dismissal or discussing what she calls "the back stories behind the published back stories,"
which she believes made it easy to isolate her from many of the other board
members. But the personal nature of the assault weighs on her. "I am disappointed by the attacks from faculty," she says, "over the removal of a

president that a supermajority of the board believed was not fulfilling the best and highest leadership for UVA." Where was the faculty concern for fairness, she wants to know, "when the president proposed to cut financial aid for low-income students?"

In the aftermath of her dismissal and reinstatement, Sullivan called for a drastic reshaping of the university's aid program for low-income students, which required them to take out loans. Charlottesville was once again roiled—this time with opposition to the new rules. A petition with over nine thousand signatures asking the board to reinstate the no-loan policy was presented to the administration. There was a chorus of students opposed to the change. Protests were organized. This time the faculty were silent.

The highest priority for Sullivan after her reinstatement was a $65 million budget increase for raises for her faculty. She argued before the board in an open meeting that the raises were needed to avoid squandering the university's distinction "due to hopelessness, cynicism, resentment, and anger" among faculty over their own compensation. Large raises were necessary, she said, to make the university competitive, so "supplementing faculty salaries through endowments and raises must be the highest priority for the Board of Visitors."[39]

If Dragas was the target of an academic mobbing, she must have given her opponents openings beyond missteps surrounding the Sullivan dismissal, but many trustees around the country are openly concerned that the Sullivan case is a wake-up call. They worry that college administrators seek boards that are cheerleaders. "Board input is treated like an invading virus," according to many trustees I have spoken with. Many experts believe that Dragas and the Board of Visitors, "however awkwardly, [were] within the charge established by Thomas Jefferson himself to choose the leader who would best direct the school."[40]

Choosing between Mobs and Corporations

What we are left with is the question of how a traditional university can be governed in an age of the vast but unaccountable Internet Empires like Twitter and Facebook. This is an age in which group polarization amplifies the effect of divisive forces. Governing boards have a responsibility to monitor the actions of presidents and ensure that decision making is consistent with the best interests of the university. We have already seen how corporate governance gone awry can irrevocably damage reputations and brands. The same thing can happen when university governance is derailed.

The AAUP founders were aware that shared governance by definition includes boards of trustees and other governing boards, but in its zeal to counter corporate and hierarchical approaches to university management, today's AAUP runs the risk of catering to an increasingly inwardly focused audience—one that like medieval universities, places the desires of professors and their profession ahead of students and the larger society that institutions are supposed to serve. That was not John Dewey's intention when the AAUP was formed and the 1915 declaration established the concept of academic freedom. The declaration described the university as a "public trust," and Dewey himself valued the needs of society above narrow interests. The declaration's framers recognized "there are no rights without corresponding duties."[41] A 2007 article in the *Chronicle of Higher Education* catalogs the many ways that the AAUP has strayed from this path, taking a turn toward collective bargaining and burnishing its "image as a stodgy faculty club … that is no longer relevant to young professors, many of whom have never even heard of it."[42]

Boards can be as slow to innovate as the institutions they govern. Although organizations like the Association of Governing Boards and ACTA publish regular magazines offering advice to boards, there are no real guidelines for what it means to be an effective governing board. Many, like Virginia's Board of Visitors, seem to have evolved to avoid the possibility that board members will actually be aware of thorny problems that might pose difficulties for the president. Penn State's board, for instance, recently expanded to thirty-eight members, nearly three times the size that experts recommend for effective governance and so large that, during open meetings to debate the highly critical Freeh report on the Sandusky affair, some members admitted that they had never been involved in board discussions of the matter.[43] Many private university boards are even larger—so large, in fact, that it is structurally impossible to keep the entire board aware and engaged. In an age when Internet-enabled mobs can spring to life overnight to undermine governance on a wide scale, disengaged boards are dangerous.

Unlike most of the world, there is no Ministry of Education in the United States. American universities (especially public ones) were conceived differently with appointed governing boards that are accountable to society. In the US system, boards have ultimate legal authority to choose top administrators, approve faculty appointments, and guarantee academic freedom. Institutions are then given considerable autonomy in day-to-day matters. Autonomy is so ingrained that shared governance is sometimes willfully, almost comically misconstrued to mean that administrators work for the faculty and that governing boards are at best irrelevant to a university's mission.

In normal times it probably does not matter much, but these are not normal times for higher education. Changes are needed, but as former University of Michigan president Duderstadt has pointed out, change will be slowest at the institutions where shared governance, the last rampart in the Revolution, is strongest.

Who has the interest of society uppermost? Presidents are accountable, but most have careers to advance. They have powerful incentives to behave like stewards for those who have fared well under the status quo. Not faculty. They are often deluded about the need for someone to be in charge at all. Not students themselves. They have even narrower interests and lack perspective. The press routinely confuses legitimate board actions with campus coups. The AAUP itself acknowledges that governing boards are responsible for the social contract that binds universities to the people they are supposed to serve. Not all boards are good at that, but it is hard to argue that the long-term interests of society are served by polling unaccountable mobs.

The contract that universities have with society is strong in this country, and it has been renewed every generation. But it is diminished every time a mob is rewarded for undermining legitimate authority. There is nothing corporatist about vibrant governance. There is no sport in using Internet Empires that operate with their own rules and without boundaries to amplify personal attacks on trustees and administrators. It is a celebration of mob rule.

IV A Social Contract

He is sometimes called patient zero. At age twenty-one and less than a hundred days after he enrolled, Zach Sherman earned an associate degree from the College for America; he is the college's first graduate. "I chose CFA, because my employer ConAgra Foods, said I wouldn't have to pay for it," he says. "But I also thought it was pretty cool that there were no due dates involved."[1] That was important, because there were weeks when Zach logged as many as fifty-six hours as a sanitation worker for ConAgra, the food conglomerate that makes Hunt's Ketchup, Hebrew National Hot Dogs, and hundreds of other products. A traditional college experience in which years are divided into semesters and semesters are divided into courses that require attendance would have been impossible for Zach. He had tried that once, but family responsibilities changed his circumstances. His goal is now a better job at ConAgra.

"Zach looks a lot like most other college students," Paul LeBlanc told me. The College for America is a branch of Southern New Hampshire University and part of LeBlanc's plan to use a different kind of university to reach such students. "The bottom 10 percent of wage earners is large," says LeBlanc. "I'd say a very strong sense of mission informs SNHU. We serve people for whom attending college is not a guarantee." In less than a year, College for America attracted a thousand students who, like Zach, considered cost to be a barrier. But there were others as well. "A single mom juggling work and kids, and an education." LeBlanc begins to list his inaugural class. "An international student whose family pooled all their wealth to send their kid to America. Their future is pinned to his success." The list goes on: "A first-generation student who has few models for college success."

The degree that Zach earned is in every respect a college degree, but setting up a university in this way was not easy. Leblanc managed to convince the US Department of Education to try something called competency-based education in place of the standard Carnegie credit hour. In College for America, students do not take regular courses but rather complete projects to demonstrate 120 competencies defined in the Lumina Foundation's Degree Qualification Profile.[2] "It's a fundamental shift from the credit hour, where time is fixed and learning is variable," explains LeBlanc, "to a model where learning is fixed and time is variable." Shifting to the new model was a feat of innovation. In the first place, the current system is set up to favor the 20 percent of all college students who attend traditional residential campuses. But from 1999 to 2000, community colleges enrolled more new students than all other institutions combined.[3] "The Élites have an influence on our policy debates and images of higher education far out of proportion to their actual size," he adds.

LeBlanc does not like to be called a Revolutionary. "I am an innovator," he says. He admires MOOCs, but is skeptical of their ultimate impact and thinks that evolution is the most likely prospect for many public universities. He is the first in his family to attend college. "We have experienced the transformational power of education in our lives," he explains. The University of Alberta's Jennifer Chesney, who joined with George Siemens and his colleagues to enable the first MOOCs—like so many who have no problem seeing Revolution as the inevitable outcome—also feels a strong sense of social responsibility. "Universities have a social contract to democratize knowledge," she told me. In fact, everyone in the small band of innovators describes the same mission. LeBlanc says his own college experience is "increasingly out of reach of far too many people. Social inequality is growing." I had asked LeBlanc the question that Slosson asked a hundred years ago: "Who are you important to?" His response was passionate: "People like Zach. There is an enormously important social contract between higher education and society."

Competency-based education may not be a revolution, but in LeBlanc's hands it is hard to tell the difference. "It is part of a movement," he says. And the movement is growing—and not just at MOOC start-ups or struggling community colleges. Experiments are under way at Purdue University and the University of Michigan, for example. The University of Wisconsin system, including the large research campus in Milwaukee, launched its Flexible Option program in fall 2014. President Obama described what it might mean for average families: "Higher education cannot be a luxury. Every American family should be able to get it."[4] It is an idea deeply rooted in a revolutionary concept that was planted in Wisconsin over a century ago.

Who Are You Important To?

Camp Randall Stadium at the University of Wisconsin overpowers the senses when on cool autumn Saturdays, eighty thousand football fans start screaming. That a mere game should provoke such a display would have been incomprehensible to John Sterling, who presided over the university during the Civil War, when Camp Randall was a military training camp and prison, a place of discipline and misery in equal measure.[5]

To Sterling and the next seven presidents of the university, democracy was palpable, a thing not to be taken for granted. They were young men in the 1860s and remembered the war. For the people of the state of Wisconsin, democracy was something to be nourished by this new kind of university. The University of Wisconsin still bears Sterling's mark. When President Charles van Hise was inaugurated in 1903, he made special mention of a vision that connected the modern university to its founders: "I shall never rest content until the beneficent influences of the university reach into every home in the commonwealth, and the boundaries of our campus are coextensive with the boundaries of the state."[6] It was an echo of Horace Mann. The principle that knowledge and education would be used to ensure democracy became known as the Wisconsin Idea, but it was more than a mere idea. It was a contract.

The contract is under assault. Public confidence in colleges and universities is declining. Corporate and government intrusion into the affairs of higher education is on the rise. Financial support is being withdrawn, respect is diminished, and many wonder whether it matters if the compact is broken. One result of the Revolution might be permanent fracturing, as institutions break apart and corporations, government, and the general public sphere each absorb the pieces. Another possibility is that the social contract will be renewed, this time by Revolutionaries who are convinced that the idea of a university cannot survive without it.

Who Is Served?

Who exactly does a university serve? One line of reasoning is that universities should prepare graduates for jobs that will exist in the future. In the United States, there is an unbroken stream of studies and exhortations to policy makers all urging colleges and universities to produce more graduates in fields that serve national economic needs.[7] It is not only an American phenomenon. A significant fraction of citizens in most countries suffered losses during the global financial crisis, raising fears about future global competitiveness, and prompting governments around the world to reexamine the roles of colleges and universities. Even the wealthiest countries, like the oil-rich kingdoms in the Middle East, wondering whether their citizens will be prepared for a global knowledge-based economy, have convinced major research universities to set up local campuses to teach engineering, science, and business.

But universities have a role beyond producing engineers and entrepreneurs. Universities, for instance, foster values. They graduate literate individuals with analytic skills who can serve the common good, engage in ethical behavior, and be functional participants in democracies.

These two lines of thought are often at odds with each other, especially when there is public money involved. If a university exists to serve a public good, such as promoting economic development that benefits everyone, how do you explain to society why it should also invest in the benefits that having a college degree gives to individuals, which is clearly a private good? Maybe society should only invest in that part of a university that benefits everyone. On the other hand, a university equips its graduates with marketable skills and opportunities that are difficult to achieve otherwise. That sounds to many like a private benefit that is best funded by private sources. If so, what obligation does an institution have to the public good?

One possible way to resolve this problem is to acknowledge the different classes of universities that serve specific needs. Perhaps, for example, it is the job of public research universities to fuel economic growth—say, by producing highly skilled PhDs—while the production of liberally educated good citizens is the responsibility of smaller, private, liberal arts colleges. California's Harvey Mudd College is such an institution. It enrolls slightly less than eight hundred undergraduates, thirty-seven times fewer students than the University of Wisconsin in Madison. Yet in 2010, equal numbers of undergraduate degree-holders from Wisconsin and Harvey Mudd earned doctorates in computer science.[8] A similar pattern holds across all science and engineering (table IV.1). There were nearly thirty-two thousand science and engineering PhDs awarded in 2006. US research and nonresearch universities were each responsible for about one-third of their undergraduate degrees (the other third came from universities outside the United States). So clearly society benefits from the private investment that individuals make when they pay tuition to institutions that promise private benefits.

The same is true for virtually every attempt to tease apart the benefits that accrue to a particular class of stakeholder in higher education. Seminaries produce clergy but they also graduate gifted teachers. Graduates of

Table IV.1

Science and Engineering Doctorate Recipients, by 2005 Carnegie Classification of Baccalaureate Institution, 1997–2006

Year	All institutions	Research universities	Other doctorate-granting institutions	Master's colleges and universities	Baccalaureate colleges	Other/ unclassified Carnegie group	Foreign institutions	Unknown baccalaureate institutions
1997	28,650	8,277	3,034	2,640	2,461	290	8,129	3,819
1998	28,772	8,592	3,148	2,716	2,663	263	8,255	3,135
1999	27,338	8,368	3,033	2,754	2,636	262	7,675	2,610
2000	27,557	8,386	2,997	2,662	2,586	206	7,832	2,888
2001	27,069	8,226	2,920	2,784	2,576	220	7,980	2,363
2002	26,262	7,686	2,905	2,748	2,503	268	7,661	2,491
2003	26,914	7,784	2,926	2,677	2,541	254	8,343	2,389
2004	27,995	7,675	2,897	2,831	2,617	262	8,970	2,743
2005	29,774	7,830	3,077	2,873	2,602	263	10,464	2,665
2006	31,760	8,074	3,093	2,960	2,735	318	11,657	2,923

Notes: Research universities are the Carnegie group doctorate-granting universities, with high research activity. Other doctorate-granting institutions include the two other such Carnegie categories: high research activity and doctoral/research universities. Other/unclassified Carnegie groups includes associate's colleges, special focus institutions, and tribal colleges.

Source: National Science Foundation 1997–2006.

historically black colleges and universities may return to leadership positions in their communities but many also go on to elite professional careers as lawyers, bankers, and politicians. Ivy League alumni often slide into lives of privilege. But Sudanese orphan Paul Lorem, armed with a degree from Yale University, will return to his village in South Sudan to help rebuild it.[9] His classmate Brooke Levin worked on an *Innocence Project* team to secure the release of a man who had been wrongfully convicted of murder and spent seventeen years on California's death row.[10] Many more people than anticipated actually benefit. It is impossible to analyze an institution to determine exactly who it serves. It is in the nature of what it means to be a university. Universities are *platforms*. They provide services to diverse stakeholders, who often have competing interests. A university serves *all* of them.

Some people are troubled by this. Even the simple question of whether there is value in a college diploma—a proposition that for most of the twentieth century provoked overwhelmingly positive responses—now divides public opinion. This is how a crisis of confidence is brewed. Just like the global concerns of the roles that governments and businesses played in the Recession, "fear and anxiety among the citizenry have stimulated ... rethinking the values that underpin the workings of ... universities."[11] As I will show later, there is a way out of this dilemma. A university could declare who it intends to serve.

How Important?

It is not enough to simply issue a declaration. The path that an institution takes has to be important to the people it serves. Bypass economies make it possible for society to choose different ways to meet its needs. PayPal cofounder Peter Thiel is well educated. He has degrees in philosophy and law from Stanford, but he is not so sure that it is a good idea for everyone to follow in his footsteps. Convinced that higher education was in an economic bubble in which demand and prices far outpaced value, Thiel and fellow PayPal cofounder, Luke Nosek, announced in 2010 a competition to identify twenty promising students under twenty years of age, and award them $100,000 each to drop out of school and do something else. The "something else" part was important. In order to be interesting, a proposal had to explain why pursuing an alternative to a traditional education would be better than simply staying in school. The program was called 20 under 20, and when it was announced, the criticism was immediate, intense, and widespread.

"Devaluing education!" was the most common complaint. Jacob Weisberg's *Newsweek* review of the project called it a "nasty idea," but not everyone in higher education was as negative.[12] MIT's director of admissions featured the two MIT students who had received grants in his blog, explaining not only why they were good choices for Thiel but also why they had been good choices for MIT. The university promised the students that they would be readmitted if they ever wanted to come back. The 20 under 20 program is now called the Thiel Fellowship and is administered through the Thiel Foundation.

Two years later, Dale Stephens wrote an editorial for the *Wall Street Journal* arguing in part that a student who had the cash to attend Harvard Business School would be better off keeping the money and moving to where people are starting businesses:

If you want a business education, the odds aren't with you, unfortunately, in business school. Professors are rewarded for publishing journal articles, not for being good teachers. The other students are trying to get ahead of you. The development office is already assessing you for future donations. Administrators care about the metrics that will improve your school's national ranking. None of these things actually helps you learn about business.[13]

A few days after the editorial was published, I was speaking to the governing board of a large public university. A board member stopped me in midsentence, threw a copy of the *Wall Street Journal* on the table, and said society had no business at all spending money on universities that offer degrees because better outcomes could be achieved by dropping out.

How important is a college? Would anyone notice if an institution simply disappeared? Hundreds of institutions have already failed that test. When in 2010 New Mexico legislators began debating whether or not some of the state's 25 public colleges and universities should be shut down, there were few defenders of the local campuses that were most in jeopardy.[14] Over the last 150 years, 27 colleges and universities in the state of Alabama have disappeared. East Alabama Female College, a Baptist college in Tuskegee, was founded in 1852 and operated for 12 years before a fire destroyed it. It was never rebuilt. The Masonic East Alabama Female Institute in Talladega closed in 1858, five years after being founded. In California alone, nearly 170 institutions have been sold, merged, or simply closed without a trace.

The Contract

Higher education sometimes seems like a system adrift as change swirls around it. Simple knowledge delivery to distant parts of the globe is now cheap and effective. Abandoning van Hise's promise to reach into every home, many public universities have reached instead for a higher position in a hierarchy of the Élite that excludes the people they are supposed to serve. Other institutions have lost their privileged status. The Ivory Tower has—if not crumbled—been replaced by Clark Kerr's multiversity. The academic workforce is being restructured, and futurists now talk openly about new modes of learning and new kinds of institutions. A university that survives must serve the people it was intended to serve. It must be important to someone. A university only makes sense if it is a valued entity. Universities need contexts that help define them.

Contexts can be local. There will always be a need for culturally proficient citizens who understand and respect local value systems, preserve history that would have otherwise been lost, and are prepared to address the local economic needs.[15] Some problems, like energy and the environment, transcend often-fluid political boundaries. These are regional contexts that invite collaboration among universities, provided that governments permit it. There is also a global context for higher education. The principle values of higher education—the nature of scholarship, preservation of academic freedom and independent governance, and duty to address the public good—bind together all institutions. Contexts allow society do ask, How will we judge you? Are you here to serve this physical village or a global community?

The contract is this:

Universities agree to a context to provide educated members of society, economic benefits, and a community committed to the institution's success. In return, society supplies funding, respect and protection for academic processes, and trust in the ethical nature of the academic enterprise.

To hold up their end of the bargain, universities have to play three roles. A university's main role is the education of graduates who can be productive members of civil society. Universities are safe spaces, but they are also ethical beacons. New ideas are frequently the most challenging ones and they would not be explored at all but for the existence of objectively transparent institutions that afford protection for inquiry. Universities as economic engines is another role, although it is the one that is most often cited as a motivation for investing in higher education. Universities deliver ideas, inventions, and innovations in return for payment. They also train the workforce: above and beyond the needs that society has for a generally educated citizenry, there are some needs that can only be met by graduates with certain skills that must be produced in certain numbers. Doctors, farmers, lawyers, architects, teachers, and engineers must all be produced, and the rate of production is determined by society. Finally, universities are enterprises with members like students, professors, and financial supporters, and there are tertiary roles, responsibilities, and duties that revolve around them.

Actually structuring a contract along these lines might seem like a symbolic exercise— an unlikely, elaborate, utopian scheme. But it is not so farfetched to imagine that contracts like this one may become more explicit and more common. A contract just like this was one of the first things that occurred to the founders of the American republic.

It Shall Be the Duty

John Adams occupies a space in US history that is sometimes hard to explain by modern standards. He was not the first president, and served only a single term as the second. It is Jefferson, not Adams, who is usually associated with the Declaration of Independence. He was prolific, but Adams is not an author whose writings are as widely read in school as *The Federalist Papers*. He was central to the American Revolution, but did not cut a dashing revolutionary figure. He did not have the dominating stature of George Washington, for instance. Yet it is John Adams's intellect that suffuses US democracy. Adams was barely forty-four years old the day that "A Constitution or Form of Government for the Commonwealth of Massachusetts" was published. Adams was the sole author. The Massachusetts Constitution is today "one of the great, enduring documents of the American Revolution.... [It is] the oldest functioning written constitution in the world"[16]

Tucked away in chapter 6, in a paragraph innocuously titled "The Encouragement of Literature, Etc." was a declaration "startling in its originality, unlike any other, to be found in any constitution ever written until then, or since."[17]

Wisdom and knowledge, as well as virtue, diffused generally among the body of the people being necessary for the preservation of their rights and liberties; and as these depend on spreading the opportunities and advantages of education in various parts of the country, and among the different orders of the people, it shall be the duty of legislators and magistrates in all future periods of this commonwealth to cherish the interests of literature and the sciences, and schools and seminaries of them, especially in the university at Cambridge.[18]

Adams had defined the social contract between the citizens of Massachusetts and its schools and universities—"especially" Harvard. It is hard to miss Adams's intent: government had a *duty* to "inculcate" virtues for the common good, including "humanity and general benevolence." Education was to be the foundation of society, teaching principles like "public and private charity, industry and frugality, honesty and punctuality, ... sincerity, good humor, ... and generous sentiments among the people."[19]

"I was curious," said Arizona State University president Crow, "about what had happened to the idea that the spread of knowledge was important to maintaining liberties." After all, the Adams "duty" paragraph appears in none of the founding documents of the American republic, "so I decided to examine the presidential State of the Union Addresses delivered between 1790 and 2012.... There is a two-hundred-year gap with no mention at all of national educational goals," Crow said. "The only mention of specific national goals is Barack Obama's 2012 speech."

There were, of course, national initiatives in the United States that furthered Adams's social contract. The Morrill Act of 1862 empowered states to form land grant universities to "promote the liberal and practical education of the industrial classes in the several pursuits and professions in life," and after a twenty-eight-year delay, a provision for the establishment of the HBCUs and "such institutions for colored students shall be entitled to the benefits of this act and subject to its provisions, as much as it would have been if it had been included under the act of eighteen hundred and sixty-two."[20] Other expansions of the land grant mission came much later, but there was nothing to match the moral force of Adams's vision of education—especially public education—until 1877.

The Wisconsin Idea

The next time Adams's duty clause made an appearance in American higher education was nearly a century later, in the plains of the US Midwest. But this time it changed the course of public education in the United States. In 1874, the University of Wisconsin appointed John Bascom, a political philosopher from Williams College, as its president. Bascom was a graduate of Andover Theological Seminary and follower of the Social Gospel Movement, which preached that it was a moral obligation of Christians to build a society that improved conditions here on earth for all. He was a powerful presence, delivering his moral message "with sledge-hammer blows."[21] So it is no great surprise that the address that Bascom gave to Wisconsin's 1877 graduating class is called a "sermon."[22]

Bascom began by listing the reasons for tying universities to society, noting that even in the best of the sectarian colleges, education "is poorly supported by surrounding conditions, and does not rest on a foundation from which it can reach the entire community." The University of Michigan was, in Bascom's view, an example of "the only way in which a truly commanding university can be built up among us." As for duty, Bascom took the state of Ohio to task for consigning education to a "voluntary effort," neglecting its obligations, and subdividing its efforts "to the last degree of weakness."

The colleges of Ohio have been founded under the conviction that higher education is to be entrusted to voluntary effort. She is a wealthy, powerful State, with every advantage of position, and a relatively homogeneous and educated population. What is the result of the voluntary principle operating under these favorable conditions without check? She has nine universities and thirty-three classical colleges. Of these forty-two institutions scarcely one can be said to have a national reputation, and the most of them are not known beyond their own immediate vicinity. Harvard alone exerts far more general influence than they all combined.[23]

Having subdued the idea that society could somehow be a passive bystander, Bascom's sledgehammer blows defined the three ideals that would guide American public universities for a hundred years, beginning with wisdom, which Bascom said "is the principle thing" for men and for states.

First, it is wisdom that "gives a mastery over physical forces, the insight which discloses the constructive laws of mind and society" and equips citizens with character. Second, every citizen should have access to "all inquiry and all truth," which is a "common possession." Third, a citizen educated in a public institution has received a great gift, "pledged to the action of intelligent, patriotic citizens," and intended to benefit both the individual and the state. "The two things are not in conflict, but they can only be harmonized by a noble life. To such a life, at least in its social bearings," graduates are "pre-eminently bound."[24]

The idea that there is a mutual obligation between the state and university that "the university should improve people's lives beyond the classroom" became known as the Wisconsin Idea.[25]

Members' Code

If society has an obligation to the members of a university, then a contract should also demand that the members obligate themselves as citizens of both society and the academy. The Wisconsin Idea was guided by Bascom's deep belief in ethical concepts and values, like self-governance, integrity, egalitarianism, truth, and interpersonal trust. David Watson from the University of London's Institute for Education translated this belief system into an institutional code that guides the university's obligations: care in establishing truths, fairness, willingness to explain, keeping promises, sustaining communities, and establishing a culture of respect.[26]

There is a strong commitment to ethical concepts and values in the Wisconsin Idea—a commitment that defines the responsibility that the state has to the members of the university and also the obligations that the members of academic communities have to society.[27] There are universal values like academic honesty and respecting ownership of the work of others, social norms such as proper academic behavior and manners, cultural values like respect for the physical environment, personal qualities like self-motivation, and the adherence to principles such as respect for governance and submission to external assessment that are unique to the scholarly life.

The Mission

It has been three years since the start of the Magic Year when a half-million learners around the world signed up to take free Stanford and MIT courses online, and started a movement that gathered momentum and joined with others to eventually engulf higher education. Coursera—now a consortium of over a hundred universities—is the largest provider of what are recognizable university courses. Udacity and edX have shifted strategies, but their courses still draw students in ever-increasing numbers.

A small band of innovators set out to transform higher education. Even if they did not always agree on what that would look like, they did know that a new social contract would be defined by a singular idea: the Revolution would enable higher education to directly reach people around the world, bypassing governments and states, if necessary. Chuck Vest did not see why knowledge should be closely held and vowed to use his influence to make his university's course content available for the asking. Daphne Koller's vision is to "teach the world," and she feels so strongly about it that the phrase was for many months the password that instructors used to log in to the Coursera Web site. Paul LeBlanc's vision is to use technology for self-paced competency-based education, drawing a line between traditional semesters and credits (which he says are at the heart of MOOCs), on the one hand, and "the areas that adult learners need to be successful." Michael Crow does not believe that prestige is conferred by selectivity, and Zvi Galil's ideal is affordable education in a rapidly growing field with many jobs. Carolyn Meyers wants to lead an institution that offers something unique. The innovators do not even agree that a Revolution is under way, but all agree that there are irresistible forces shaping and remaking colleges and universities. Those forces started long before the Magic Year. If there is a Revolution, it began quietly, without grand gestures or decisive battles.

Saint Ignatius sent his Jesuits priest out into the world with the charge to "set the world on fire." Bascom had promised that knowledge was a "community possession." Adams said the state had a "duty." Today, innovators who wear their convictions in conspicuous fashion are remaking higher education. They are innovators who, like LeBlanc, see "a perfect storm that is driving enormous change." They are attacked, but in their view, the attacks are the flailing of incumbents. In the age of the Internet, innovators have learned that what the incumbents think about change is irrelevant. What matters is whether society finds value in what these innovators are trying to do. If the incumbents lack an organized, coherent, and opposing argument, they will fail. What unites the small band of innovators is a mission to make higher education accessible, affordable, excellent, and fair. That is the contract they believe society has with its universities.

It is a mission that has attracted converts. Former Yale University president Rick Levin now leads Coursera. I asked John Doerr, Coursera investor and partner at the Silicon Valley venture capital firm Kleiner Perkins, "Why is Kleiner so interested in this? This seems like a long-term project."

"It's a family project," he responded. When she found out that Salman Khan was using family savings to run his one-person academy for tens of thousands of students, Doerr's wife, Ann, sent Khan a text message: "You need to support yourself. I am sending a check for $100,000 right now."

"Have I told you about the Mission?" Coursera cofounder Andrew Ng asked. I shook my head: "No." He moved the keyboard to the side and leaned over the table like he was going to let me in on a secret. "Whatever else happens with Coursera, we will continue offering free courses," he whispered.

"Who else knows?" I asked. "Everyone," he said. "That's why we call it the Mission. Everyone who works here knows that," he said, pointing to the chaotic tumble of black fleece pullovers, hoodies, and worn blue jeans rushing back and forth in the Coursera suite outside the conference room. A senior engineer at Coursera looks vaguely like an undergraduate in my computer science courses—quite young, in other words, to someone my age.

I asked several of them at lunch, "Do you know about the Mission?" Between mouthfuls of burritos and rice in the Coursera cafeteria, they all nodded. "Yes, the Mission," someone replied. Then they all nodded again.

I was reminded how moved Sebastian Thrun had been by the emails he had received. "I cannot go back," he had said at the time. "If you educate the most people in the world," he later told me, "you become the most important university in the world." I asked Anant Agarwal if there was a Mission for edX. "Of course," he answered. "How can you resist the social challenge? This will improve people's lives." LeBlanc's Mission at Southern New Hampshire University is "the social good that higher education does when it does its job well." When you mention Ng's Mission to modern-day Revolutionaries, they all react the same way: there is a quiet moment and then, almost as if they all recognize the same signal, a nod of acceptance. This will improve people's lives.

In early 2014, Andrew Ng joined Baidu, the company that dominates online search in China. For Ng, it is a return to his roots in artificial intelligence and a chance to lead fundamental brain research. He is still chairman of Coursera's board, but I wondered how his departure from day-to-day activities affected the Mission. Recently I asked Koller about it. She smiled, leaned back in her chair, and quietly said, "Yes, the Mission."

New Charter

A month later, I received an unexpected email from Michael Crow. "Lacking a new Land Grant Act and losing patience waiting for the arrival of the urban focused land grant discussed occasionally over the last few decades, we went ahead and created a new charter for a new kind of research university," he wrote. When I reached him by phone, he said, "This university has never had a charter. I wanted something simple so it would be hard to misinterpret our intention."

It is a promise, he told me to be "measured not by whom we exclude, but rather by whom we include." "The university," he said, "will assume fundamental responsibility for the economic, social, cultural, and overall health of the communities it serves." I asked him if he was renewing the Adams social contract. "We looked at his beautiful prose and asked ourselves how would that moral commitment be made today," Crow replied. "It would not be a commitment to an outmoded system," he said, "it would be a completely different mission."

Epilogue

One by one, Revolutionaries filed into the meeting room on the thirty-first floor of the Madison Avenue headquarters of the Carnegie Corporation and took their seats at the gleaming new conference table, until there were no seats left unfilled. When Andrew Carnegie established his foundation in 1911 to "promote the advancement and diffusion of knowledge and understanding," he undoubtedly had in mind assemblies like this, and as an October rain fell in New York, everyone entering the building seemed to be aware of the significance of where we were meeting. Like a war council, a small band of innovators was first to arrive. I reminded Sebastian Thrun of the cold Palo Alto morning three years before—we shared breakfast and discussed his plans to remake universities. Seated next to me were Zvi Galil and Anant Agarwal. Daphne Koller was not there, but she had dispatched her new chief academic officer, Vivek Goel, to represent Coursera.

It was apparent that the Magic Year had faded, and what was once a small band of innovators had grown. Jason Palmer represented the Bill and Melinda Gates Foundation, and Lumina Foundation had sent Dewayne Matthews. Former University of North Carolina president Molly Corbett Broad, who was now president of the American Council on Education, was delayed by weather, but she would be seated directly across from me. And there were two traditional universities. Provost Nathan Urban spoke for Carnegie Mellon University. Georgia Tech provost Rafael Bras had called the group together.

Interspersed were representatives from national news organizations. For the first time in as long as I could recall, members of the press sat silent, waiting to find out who would speak first. Everyone knew the Revolution's agenda. This was going to be an assessment of status.

It had been a tumultuous year for Thrun and Udacity. Euphoria surrounding the launch of the Georgia Tech degree had given way quickly to talk of failure when a hastily arranged trial of a MOOC-based math course at

San Jose State University was called off after students apparently performed much worse than expected. A clearly dejected Thrun had announced that his product was "lousy for undergraduates" and Udacity was going to turn its attention to vocational training, where students were better motivated and prepared. It was an announcement that made sense in Silicon Valley—where start-ups are always revising their products and rewarded for "pivots" that reshape their strategies—yet it was an easy target for holy warriors whose barely concealed glee at Udacity's shifting fortunes was only enhanced by San Jose State's "pause."

But if any of this had cowed the assembled council, it was not apparent. "It is hard to square the SJSU experience with ours," said Galil. Thrun had been mobbed, but it did not change his zeal for remaking higher education. On this rainy Wednesday, there was not going to be a retreat from the goals of the Revolution. In the end, the stories tumbled on to the table—stories of success, shifting motivations, surprising alliances, and unexpected defeats. Bras was struck by the intensity of feeling surrounding the social contract. There were fears that the Ivory Tower would derail change. There was recognition that economics does not favor the status quo, yet also that simply giving everyone access to education does not mean they will be able to take advantage of it.

"Indira Gandhi University, the largest in the world, already enrolls more than three million students. Imagine what an MIT or Carnegie Mellon for a million students would be like," said Gates Foundation executive Palmer. "That would mean redefining university missions." It was the conversation that started the Revolution.

Then Sebastian's voice, so quiet you had to strain to hear: "I have a dream that we will truly democratize education—make it accessible to everyone." Everyone else was silent. It was the same riveting tale of spiritual conversion he had told an audience long ago in Munich. "Great universities compete on how many people they exclude," he said. "If the measure of success suddenly shifts to inclusiveness, it will change the face of humanity."

Appendix

The World's Universities

There are tens of thousands of universities in the world. The exact number is hard to pin down. Some are hundreds of years old, and count among their faculty and alumni celebrated presidents, authors, saints, artists, and scientists as well as notorious scoundrels and tyrants. Sixty-one of them were in existence before 1520 and operate today in much the same way they did before the Renaissance (table A.1).[1]

Others, like all American universities, are relative newcomers, and have by virtue of good fortune and inspired leadership managed to elbow their way to international recognition. Among them are many that are now regarded as the best in the world. That kind of greatness is not the fate for the rest. They serve more limited purposes. Some are smaller institutions, focused on the needs of their communities. They pass on the skills that the local economy needs most. They teach agricultural, mechanical, and military arts. They educate farmers, teachers, engineers, lawyers, and clergy. Still others are experiments. Some are virtual ones—a type of institution we think of as modern, but that in fact has been around for many generations. Most have campuses, faculties, and classrooms. Between these extremes are thousands of institutions. They are the ones that enroll most of the world's university students. They are often underfunded and under severe pressure to deliver more with fewer resources. They are the least able to take risks. It is these institutions that will have the most difficulty finding their way in times of change, although they have much in common.

Despite the vastness of this diverse landscape, higher education seems somehow familiar, regardless of where you are in the world. It is a common fiction that universities are somehow unique to cultures and nations, and therefore ways of doing business in one part of the world are hard to transfer to other parts. There are differences, but they have always been

Table A.1
Enduring World Universities

Before 1200	Before 1300	Before 1400	Before 1500	Before 1520
Bologna	Cambridge	Cologne	Aberdeen	Halle
Modena	Coimbra	Ferrara	Aix-Marseille	Madrid
Oxford	Lisbon	Florence	Barcelona	Santiago de
Paris	Macerata	Grenoble	Basel	Compostela
Parma	Montepellier	Heidelberg-	Bordeaux	Urbino
	Naples	Kraków	Caen	
	Padua	Orlean	Catania	
	Salamanca	Pavia	Copenhagen	
	Siena	Perugia	Freiburg	
	Toulouse	Pisa	Genoa	
	Valladolid	Prague	Glasgow	
		Rome	Griefswald	
		Tours	Leipzig	
		Vienna	Louvain	
			Mainz	
			Munich	
			Nantes	
			Poitier	
			Rennes	
			Rostock	
			Saragossa	
			SevilleSt.	
			Andrews	
			Tubingen	
			Turin	
			Uppsala	
			Valencia	

exaggerated, and even those differences are disappearing before our eyes. Universities are organized into departments, faculties, and colleges. The academic year is marked by semesters or quarters and vacations. Periodic visits by accreditors and review teams hold nearly identical yardsticks up to measure quality. Details vary, of course. More or less technology, the political influence of governing officials, and the amount of bureaucracy that governs day-to-day activities are all determined by local factors, but there are worldwide rules, and everyone seems to know what they are, even if it's less clear how to apply them.

A student who is plucked from a community college in California and deposited in one of Japan's many private colleges, a small college in rural India that is affiliated with one of the larger Indian universities, or a new technical institute in the Sudan would, aside from language, comforts, and accoutrements, find life within the classroom walls rather unchanged.

Degrees, courses of study, titles of classes, and textbooks are either exactly the same or vary only in minor ways. Day-to-day academic life is also similar. Teaching is the primary activity for professors, but even at the remote outposts that make up the hinterlands known as academic Siberia, professors regard themselves as scholars.[2] Professors read similar journals and attend conferences devoted to the same topics. And of course in most universities, they teach the same facts, concepts, and skills.

Even Africa—many of whose universities are ignored internationally—is dotted with enterprises that are recognizable as institutions of higher education. Faculty salaries are meager, facilities are poor, and teaching loads—which may involve hundreds of students crowded into windowless classrooms and thousands of exams each term—are large, but many aspirations are shared with Western institutions. The Abaarso School of Science and Technology in Somalia was founded in 2008 as a graduate business school by investor Jonathan Starr. Despite desperate conditions in Somalia, the Abaarso faculty is mainly composed of professors who were trained at American universities, including Harvard and George Washington University. Remarkably, there are a number of professors from Minnesota. The dean of the school of computing was trained at the Red Sea University in Sudan, which has a world ranking of near sixteen thousand, making it a more prestigious institution. A senior administrator at the Red Sea was in turn trained at the Future University in Sudan, which ranks in the top ten thousand and thus is a destination to which an ambitious scholar might aspire.

Élites

A tiny fraction of the world's universities are the *Élite* institutions that have the resources, brands, and political support to chart their own courses. In the United States, there are perhaps a hundred elite academic brands. These are institutions that are known for the quality of their programs and graduates. Most of them have either amassed large endowments (over a billion dollars) or are government-backed institutions with ample resources. They are able to control their own destinies. Élite universities have every reason to believe they are immune to change, and they act like it. At the other end of the spectrum are colleges and universities that are *emerging*.

Emerging

Emerging institutions are resource poor, and it shows in the quality of their offerings. Their faculty are poorly trained and poorly compensated. These institutions tend to be overcrowded and beset with political problems that prevent any real progress. But an emerging institution has a mission, a compelling reason for existing. An emerging university has aspirations, but lacks the assets to create real value for its stakeholders. For an emerging university, any change that increases its ability to use meager resources, to tap into a worldwide network of scholars who can offer a higher quality of instruction, is welcome. A changing landscape helps an emerging university. Between the Élites and the emerging institutions lies the *Middle*, where most of the world's colleges and universities can be found.

The Middle

Published estimates of the number of colleges and universities in the world vary wildly. Most people would have no difficulty agreeing that there are at least ten thousand degree-granting schools, colleges, and universities globally, but no one is responsible for tracking the exact number. The Spanish Cybermetrics Lab gathers data from online sources to identify and rank just under twelve thousand institutions.[3] There are nearly that many universities in the United States and Europe alone, so the actual number is much larger than that.

United States: The integrated database of postsecondary schools maintained by the US Department of Education lists over seven thousand officially recognized institutions of higher learning in only the United States.[4]

India: Taking into account all institutes from its complicated system of state, private, and corporate colleges, it would appear that India operates at most six hundred universities. But that ignores India's "affiliated colleges," a system of perhaps twenty-five thousand degree-granting institutions operating in towns and villages that are too small or isolated to participate directly in the Indian higher education bureaucracy.[5]

China: Chinese authorities report there are about two thousand universities that are licensed to offer courses and issue diplomas, but there is a network of hundreds of specialized schools like the China University of Post and Telecommunications (中国邮电大学), Beijing Institute of Civil Aviation (北京民航学院), and China Normal University (中国师范学院), which have names that have never before been translated from Chinese and about which little is known outside China.

Japan: The Japanese government charters 745 *daigaku*, but Japan's higher education sector is overbuilt, and there could easily be another thousand schools and colleges that should be counted.[6]

Africa: Africa is home to at least a thousand colleges and universities, although in some countries decades of civil war and social conflict have decimated infrastructure and communications, so the only institutions that are visible are the large national universities and relatively wealthy religious colleges that do not rely on government support.

Latin America: Another four thousand universities in Central and South America operate programs and grant degrees that are recognized internationally.

Europe and the Middle East: Counting Russia, continental Europe from Scandinavia to the Mediterranean, the United Kingdom, and the Middle East from Indonesia to North Africa, there are six thousand institutions or more—a number that is growing rapidly, as outmoded state-run schools are challenged by an array of new public and private universities as well as institutes, many of them focusing on technological and business skills that planners believe are better suited to coming economic challenges.

Others: There is also a difficult-to-classify array of for-profit, open, online, specialized, industrial, or distance education colleges whose number can only be guessed at. The McDonald's fast-food company operates a training facility just outside Chicago called Hamburger University. New York celebrity executive and sometimes presidential candidate Donald Trump founded Trump University to offer online training in entrepreneurship, but when it came to light in 2010 that the company was under investigation for illegal business practices, the name was changed to the Trump Entrepreneur Initiative.[7] Futurist Ray Kurzweil founded Singularity University—a name inspired by his 2006 book *The Singularity is Near*—that offers graduate training in managing technology disruptions.[8] Albert Schweitzer University, despite its imposing name, has no classes and grants no degrees, preferring instead to promote pacifism and humanism.[9] The rector of official-sounding European University, a private institution in Belgrade that "operates within the standards of the Nation, as well as the European Union, United States and the Bologna Process," is also president of the European Academy of Science—a Serbian organization aimed at legitimizing the works of its president, and whose name is easily confused with the actual academy of sciences in Europe, the European Academy of Sciences.[10]

Combining all estimates, there are as many as fifty thousand enterprises around the world that deserve to be called colleges or universities, and most of them are neither Élite nor Emerging. They are in the Middle.

The numbers would swell considerably were we to count as universities the thousands of religious schools, hermitages, monasteries, and other places for study whose sole purpose is contemplation of a single text, doctrine, person, or culture. These institutions may attract students in large numbers, but they usually fail tests—like employing a faculty with recognized credentials—that universities in modern times must pass to be worthy of the title. If these organizations offer degrees at all, they are typically not accredited, and their curricular are seldom widely recognized. They often refuse to recognize the existence of a social contract. There are, of course, many universities with religious affiliations—the global network of Catholic universities established by the Jesuits along with the schools of Islamic studies that dot the Near and Middle East are just two examples—that serve both secular and religious goals.

Notes

Preface

1. DeMillo 2011.

Introduction

1. See the appendix.

2. Gilman 1885.

3. Anderson 1978.

4. Brademas 1971.

5. Cheit 1971.

6. Stoke 1937.

7. Rudolph 1962, 97.

8. Ibid., 54.

9. Thelin 2013.

10. Remarks by US secretary of education Arne Duncan (US Department of Education 2012).

11. Moody's Investor Services 2013.

12. Blumenstyk 2014.

13. Bowen 2012.

14. Federal Education Budget Project 2013.

15. Pew Research Center 2011.

16. Sinclair 1935.

17. Eidiger 2011.

18. Gladwell 2008.

19. Pew Social and Demographic Trends 2012.

20. DeMillo 2011.

21. Gilman 1885.

Chapter 1: Map of the World

1. See chapter 14.

2. Widdom 2012.

3. Thrun 2012b.

4. Thrun 2012a.

5. DeSantis 2012.

6. Salmon 2012.

7. Lewin 2011.

8. Brooks 2012.

Chapter 2: Shifting Landscape

1. Carlsmith 2002.

2. See chapter 11.

3. Franklin 1749.

4. DeMillo 2011.

5. Amy Gutmann, inaugural address, University of Pennsylvania, October 15, 2004.

6. Morrill Act of 1862 7 U.S.C §304.

7. DeMillo 2011.

8. For a description of the Threads Program and its genesis, see ibid., chapter 9.

9. Delta 2012.

10. Thrun 2012c.

11. See http://www.augmentedtrader.wordpress.com/2013/11/20/a-comparison-of-online-mooc-versus-on-campus-course-delivery (accessed December 29, 2014).

12. Most public universities or university systems in the United States budget on a per credit hour basis, using a fixed formula to reimburse institutions based on the total number of graduate or undergraduate credit hours taught. For example, the Interactive Distance Education Alliance, a consortium of twenty public universities, publishes a common price per credit hour; see http://www.gpidea.org/students/costs (accessed December 29, 2014).

13. Seamans and Zhu 2011.

14. Ibid.

15. Tuitions are also kept relatively low at private research universities, except that instead of state subsidies, private donations and endowments are used.

16. National Center for Education Statistics 2005.

17. Ballou, Mishkind, Mooney, and van Kammen 2002. A PI is the lead scientist on a sponsored research proposal. The PI's signature is required for virtually all hiring and firing related to a research project, and it is the PI who is ultimately responsible for delivering research results on time and within the project budget. A PI is usually a member of the faculty but not an administrator.

18. Ballou, Mishkind, Mooney, and van Kammen 2002.

Chapter 3: Levity, Brevity, and Repetition

1. Hilton 1934; Weir 1989.

2. Dettmer 2014.

3. Hilton 1934.

4. William Torrey Harris, US commissioner of education, 1889–1906.

5. Bransford, Brown, and Cocking 2000.

6. Reductionists attempt to explain complex phenomena in terms that are simpler and more fundamental, even if those explanations are too complex and unwieldy to be put to practical use. Antireductionists counter with a demand that their necessarily more intuitive explanations of the world cannot be swept away without explanation. "Why is the reductionist view more valid than ours?" they would argue.

7. Hook and Farah 2013.

8. Bransford, Brown, and Cocking 2000.

9. Miller 1994.

10. This is the portion of the frontal lobe of the brain, often called the cerebral cortex and thought to be the location of many of the higher functions of the brain.

11. Fried et al. 2001.

12. Walker and Stickgold 2004.

13. Rait 1912, 142–143.

14. They rescinded it two hundred years later. For a discussion of the role of faculty-centered universities, see DeMillo 2011.

15. Weimer 1993.

16. The question of lapses of attention in the classroom is still unsettled. For many years and over many studies, the prevailing opinion was that the typical attention span was ten or fifteen minutes, but a 2007 literature review found no direct evidence of this, although allowed that there may be a pattern of decline during a lecture. This scenario is based on the most recent study involving direct observations of attention lapses; see Bunce, Flens, and Neiles 2010.

17. Khan Academy, n.d.

18. Rojstaczer and Healy 2012.

19. See http://www.knewton.com (accessed December 30, 2014).

20. Quoted in *Scientific American* 2012.

21. Mitra and Rana 2001.

22. Wang, Haertel, and Walberg 1993/1994.

23. Bloom 1984.

24. Ibid.

Chapter 4: Technology Curves

1. See http://en.childrenslibrary.org (accessed January 2, 2015).

2. Kurzweil 2006.

3. Pirsig 1974.

4. University of Iowa Libraries, n.d.

5. http://www.ted.com/talks/philip_zimbardo_on_the_psychology_of_evil?language=en (accessed March 16, 2015).

6. Lambert 2012.

7. Taleb 2010, 336.

8. Stobart 1929.

9. Ibid.

10. Alan Clive Jones, "Speaking of Science: BBC Science Broadcasting and Its Critics, 1923–64," Unpublished thesis, Department of Science and Technology Studies, University College London, 2010.

11. Jones 2010.

12. Cafferty 2011.

13. Hattie 2009.

14. Ibid.

15. Ibid.

16. Ibid.

17. Ibid.

18. Wieman 2009.

19. For all Lipton and related comments on his GLL blog, see http://rjlipton.wordpress.com/2010/08/08/a-proof-that-p-is-not-equal-to-np (accessed January 4, 2015).

20. Edmundson et al. 2013.

21. Carlson and Berry 2008; Hsiao and Bruisilovsky 2010.

22. Snow et al. 2008.

23. Hattie 2009.

24. Robinson 2001.

25. See chapter 5.

26. DeMillo 2011.

27. Carlson et al. 2013.

28. Thille 2012.

29. See cra.org/ccc/docs/init/bigdatawhitepaper.pdf (accessed January 3, 2015).

30. See http://www.gtisc.gatech.edu/doc/emerging_cyber_threats_report2014.pdf (accessed January 3, 2015).

Chapter 5: Internet Scale

1. For a more complete discussion of the cost disease and role of faculty productivity in college tuition, see chapter 6.

2. Mead 2013.

3. See http://platohistory.org (accessed January 7, 2015).

4. Oppenheimer 1997.

5. Stanford education professor Larry Cuban, quoted in ibid.

6. Ibid.

7. ibid.

8. Watters 2011.

9. Quoted in ibid.

10. DeMillo 2011. The evolution of writing surfaces includes erasable whiteboards, projectors for acetate transparencies, and even new technologies for projecting PowerPoint™ presentations, but these are all just minor variations of the original black chalkboard—an invention that itself was an innovative use of small slate tablets that had been common—though expensive—student accoutrements since the Middle Ages.

11. Bernstein 1841.

12. Ibid.

13. Ibid.

14. The term hype cycle was coined by the information technology consulting company the Gartner Group to describe the acceptance process for technological innovations in which expectations are grossly inflated after the introduction of a technology trigger. According to Gartner, rapid disillusionment follows the peak of inflated expectations, but when an innovation manages to survive the "trough of disillusionment," there is a much slower "enlightenment" period that plateaus into a much longer period in which the productivity gains of the technology are finally realized.

15. Moore 2001.

16. Grossman 2013.

17. Carlyle 1850.

18. cf. Oppenheimer 1997.

19. Odlyzko 2012.

20. Quoted in Lenzner and Johnson 1997.

21. Ibid.

22. Hoxby and Avery 2012.

23. Jaschick and Lederman 2014.

24. Gomez et al. 2013; http://collegeforamerica.org/site_images/Reduced_College_for_America_Public_Version.4.16.13.pdf (accessed January 9, 2015); http://catalog.flatworldknowledge.com (accessed January 9, 2015); Hoxby and Avery 2012.

25. Adams, n.d.

26. Ibid.

27. Ibid.

28. Jergen 1974.

29. Eliot 1869.

30. See http://nces.ed.gov (accessed January 11, 2015).

31. American Association of University Professors 2009.

32. Braverman 1974; Zuboff 1989.

33. Institute of Medicine 2013.

34. Ibid.

Chapter 6: Accessibility

1. Given spending trends for 1998–2012, state investment in higher education for the following states will reach zero by 2052 (ordered by the year in which state allocations disappear): Colorado, Alaska, South Carolina, Rhode Island, Arizona, Vermont, Montana, Massachusetts, Oregon, Minnesota, Virginia, New York, Wisconsin, Washington, New Hampshire, Texas, and California. At the current rates of spending, Indiana, Wyoming, Oklahoma, Connecticut, Nebraska, Georgia, Kentucky, Louisiana, New Mexico, and Arkansas will continue to invest in higher education well into the next century. Postsecondary Education Opportunity, http://www.postsecondary.org/topicslist.asp?page=1&od=&search=State%20appropriations# (accessed January 11, 2015).

2. Taylor 2012.

3. Jaffelin 2012.

4. Piketty 2014.

5. See, for example, Ginsberg 2013.

6. Downs 1967.

7. Ibid.

8. McCauley 1982.

9. Newman 1891.

10. Willson and Lacey 1957.

11. Newman 1891.

12. Selingo 2013.

13. Bennett 2013.

14. US Government Accountability Office 2011.

15. Ibid.

16. Blumnestyk and Richards 2010.

17. "U.S. Public University Medians for Fiscal Year 2009 Show Tuition Pricing Power Amidst Rising Challenges" is available only to Moody subscribers, but the results are summarized in Blumenstyk 2010.

18. Ibid.

19. According to the 2013 *US News and World Report* national university rankings.

20. Bowen 2012.

21. Ibid.

22. Schumpeter 1911.

23. Zuboff and Maxim 2002.

Chapter 7: Pyramids

1. James 1903.

2. Ibid.

3. Hoffman 1976.

4. Kerr, Gade, and Lawakoa 1994.

5. Maslow's hierarchy of needs also describes the needs of college students. These are needs that change with demographics and geography. In this sense, there is nothing metaphoric about the Maslow hierarchy. Students who are hungry or fear for their physical safety will not be effective learners, and conditions in which basic freedoms do not exist also discourage full participation in the learning process. These are considerations that influence program and course design.

6. Gilman 1885.

7. Weber 1918.

8. Berube 2013.

9. Association of American Universities 2004.

10. Sokal 1996.

11. The foundation of the medieval liberal arts was called the trivium and was composed of three subjects: grammar, logic, and rhetoric. The four subjects that comprised the quadrivium were arithmetic, geometry, music, and astronomy, and together with the practical arts (medicine and architecture) were preparation for further study.

12. Gilman 1885.

13. Carnegie Commission on Higher Education 1971.

14. Ibid.

15. Ibid.

16. Thurgood, Golladay, and Hill 2006, 5.

17. McCormick and Zhao 2005.

18. Altbach 2007.

19. Kerr 2001, 116–117. Kerr was in many ways the twentieth century's Newman. Just as Newman struggled throughout his latter career to continuously refine "the idea of a university," Kerr refined his valedictory *The Uses of the University* at least four times.

20. *US News and World Report* 2013; *Times Higher Education* 2013.

21. Shanghai Jiao Tong University 2013; Consejo Superior de Investigaciones Cientificas 2013.

22. National Research Council 2010.

23. For a more detailed description of the NRC ranking fiasco, see chapter 8.

24. Southern Association of Colleges and Schools 2009.

25. Ibid.; Kelderman 2013. Like most regional accreditors, SACS has separate commissions that focus on precollege and postsecondary education.

26. Ibid.

27. Quoted in Western Association of Schools and Colleges, n.d.

28. Ibid.

29. Ibid.

30. Ibid.

31. Liu 2011.

32. These institutions realize that they cannot match top institutions, but most countries can support at least one research university that can carry out high-quality research relevant to national needs.

33. DeMillo 2011.

34. Pareto 1961.

35. This rule, though, is less firmly established than the others. For the NSF annual studies of where undergraduates in successful graduate program receive their degrees, see Burrelli, Rapoport, and Lehming 2008.

Chapter 8: Rankings

1. *US News and World Report*, 2013.

2. Luca and Smith 2013.

3. Morse 2013.

4. Howe 1935.

5. Slosson 1910.

6. Ibid.

7. DeMillo 2011, 260.

8. Ibid.

9. Ibid.

10. *US News and World Report* 2013.

11. Shanghai Jiao Tong University 2013.

12. *Times Higher Education* 2013.

13. Slosson 1910.

14. The need for institutions to assume some of the functions of parents was formalized in a legal doctrine called in loco parentis, which required colleges and universities to exert reasonable control over student activities by establishing curfews, restrictions on behavior, and other rules that would otherwise be rejected by adults. The formal idea of in loco parentis has all but disappeared from American higher education.

15. Ostriker and Kuh 2004.

16. Ibid.

17. This could not have come as a surprise to the NRC team. Many engineering research specialties move so quickly that relying on journals—which often take years to review and publish a paper—would slow the pace of scientific and technical discovery. These fields use highly regarded conferences as their primary publication outlet. MIT's Eric Grimson, the CRA board chair at the time, recalls that "[the] CRA had taken a clear position on this a decade earlier, and had pointed this out to Charlotte and the NRC staff as early as 2002. Our offer to provide input on key publication venues were rebuffed."

18. Ostriker and Kuh 2010.

19. Cole 2011.

20. Ibid.

21. Ibid.

22. Ibid.

23. An ancient portent is usually included, along with winter thunder, the quantity of twigs gathered by pigs, and the girth of wooly caterpillars, in almanacs and oral folktales as one of the signs of an impending severe winter. Portents like these may over time be associated with calamitous events, but they are not predictors.

24. PayScale 2012.

25. Brewer, Eide, and Ehrenberg 1999.

26. PayScale 2012.

27. STEM is also generally assumed to include computer science.

28. Schneider 2013.

29. Stavey Berg Dale of the Mellon Foundation and Alan Krueger of Princeton.

30. OMNITEL Roper 2012).

31. Gathering the sixty volumes that today comprise the Great Books of the Western World was a project initiated at the University of Chicago by Mortimer Adler. It was eventually adopted and commercialized by Encyclopedia Britannica CEO William Benton. The idea behind the series was to identify those books of such enduring value that they will over generations contribute uniquely to national discussions and be worthy of rereading.

32. See http://www.arcsfoundation.org (accessed January 22, 2015).

33. Baron and Normal 1992. The SAT is redundant when good measures of past performance are available, such as standardized achievement tests and especially class rank (which is useful in predicting other outcomes aside from grades).

34. Bok and Bowen 1998.

35. Bradley et al. 1990.

Chapter 9: Institutional Envy

1. Ginsberg 2013.

2. McCauley 1982.

3. Ginsberg 2013.

4. Ibid.

5. Carter et al. 2006.

6. Ibid.

7. US Department of Commerce: Bureau of Economic Analysis, n.d.

8. Reif 2012.

9. The phrase "culture eats strategy for lunch" is usually attributed to management expert Peter Drucker, although it has found common use in many places.

10. Military examples abound. In the corporate world, CEO Lou Gerstner's dramatic turnaround of IBM is a good illustration. Gerstner 2003.

11. DeMillo 2011.

12. Rumelt 2011.

13. Porter 1980.

14. Reif 2012.

15. Rumelt 2011.

16. Act of July 2, 1862 (Morrill Act), Public Law 37–108, which established land grant colleges, 07/02/1862; Enrolled Acts and Resolutions of Congress, 1789–1996; Record Group 11; General Records of the United States Government; National Archives.

17. Brown v. Board of Education 347 U.S. 483, 490 (1954).

18. Anderson 2013.

19. An articulation agreement is an understanding between colleges about how courses from one institution will be incorporated into the curriculum of another. Agreements like this are common between four-year institutions and community colleges because they give community college graduates an opportunity to enter a four-year degree program without repeating required courses.

20. For a fuller explanation of Wieman's approach to improving STEM education, see chapter 4.

Chapter 10: Brands

1. http://www.insidehighered.com/news/2013/04/19/despite-courtship-amherst-decides-shy-away-star-mooc-provider#ixzz367RAhdcN (accessed January 24, 2015).

2. Freeh Sporkin and Sullivan 2012.

3. Ibid.

4. Quoted in McCarthy 2011.

5. Sarbanes-Oxley 2002.

6. Web site of Record for Truth in the Sandusky Scandal, n.d.

7. Susan Snyder, philly.com, October 30. 2014, http://articles.philly.com/2014-10-30/news/56292071_1_board-chair-keith-masser-richard-dandrea-anthony-lubrano (accessed March 16, 2015).

8. *Centre Daily Times* 2013.

9. Wolverton 2012).

10. Cole 2011).

11. Hackett 2007).

12. MIT president Reif used the imagery of Mens et Manus in his October 17, 2013, letter announcing a new innovation initiative—an example of alignment of action and values. http://web.mit.edu/newsoffice/2013/letter-regarding-mit-innovation-initiative-1017.html (accessed January 25, 2015).

13. DeMillo 2011, chapter 19.

14. Ibid.

15. Associated Press 2012.

16. Members of the Philosophy Department of San Jose State University 2013.

17. Meister 2013.

18. Manchester 1992.

19. Janin 2008, 1.

20. Ibid., 149.

21. Eliot 1869.

22. Morrill Act of 1862 7 USC §304.

23. Pew Research Center 2011.

24. Organisation for Economic Co-operation and Development 2004.

25. Franklin W. Olin College of Engineering is a private university in Needham, Massachusetts. Founded in 1997, it has resisted growth, despite recognition as one of the best engineering programs in the United States. Olin's small size enables student-centered, project-based learning to be integrated into its curriculum, which revolves not around courses but instead around a portfolio of designs that students must complete in order to advance.

Chapter 11: Ivory Towers

1. I use Peter Abelard as a metaphor for the pure scholar. He has a legitimate claim on being the first university professor. See DeMillo 2011. He was a member of a small group of independent thinkers including Aquinas and Saint Anselm of Canterbury who taught and lectured just as Western Europe was emerging from the Dark Ages and entering a time of intellectual ferment. It is ironic that these figures worked on their own, unprotected by institutions.

2. Galilei 1632.

3. http://www.library.wisc.edu/text/wirereader/Contents/Sifting.html (accessed January 27, 2015).

4. Cole 2010.

5. Forster 1939.

6. Members of the Philosophy Department of San Jose State University 2013.

7. Members of the Philosophy Department of San Jose State University 2013.

8. Metzger 1965.

9. AAUP 1989.

10. Ibid.

11. American Association of University Professors 1915.

12. AAUP 1989.

13. AAUP 1915.

14. Ross 1977.

15. Herfurth 1949.

16. Union of Concerned Scientists 1968.

17. Kerr 2001.

18. Soo and Carson 2004.

19. Taylor 2010.

20. Hacker and Dreifus 2010.

21. In fact, these kinds of claims contradict most of what we know about academics. Salaries of tenured professors rise much more slowly than entry-level faculty salaries, so tenured professors actually contribute proportionately less to cost increases. Furthermore, professors are, as a group, much more self-motivated than society as a whole, so the desire to improve teaching is completely unrelated to the granting of tenure.

22. Borysiewicz's actual title is vice chancellor, which in the British public system is the equivalent of a university president.

23. Kerr 2001.

24. Shapin 2012, 7.

25. Ibid.

26. Jacoby 2013.

27. Fish 1993.

28. Fish 1982.

29. Yaffe 1999.

30. Ibid.

31. Ibid.

32. Shapin 2012.

33. Yaffe 1999.

34. Scott 1998.

35. Yaffe 1999.

36. Scott 1998.

37. Yaffe 1999.

38. Nelson 2009.

39. Begley 1992.

40. Olson 2009.

41. Leach 2008.

42. Ibid.

43. Schmidt 2013.

44. Duderstadt 2009.

45. Fish 2011.

46. These anonymized excerpts of internal discussions are taken from publicly available faculty discussions of shared governance.

47. DeMillo 2011; American Association of University Professors, n.d.

48. The AAUP took the extraordinary step of passing a resolution in support of the president's side of the dispute at the University of Virginia while events were still unfolding and a full six months before an investigation could actually be launched. The investigating committee eventually took the liberty of commenting on the rector's "mindset": "*The rector's rhetoric reflects a mindset of entrepreneurial control common in small and medium-sized business enterprises.*" The investigating committee discerned the rector's mind-set without actually speaking with her. See AAUP's Committee on College and University Governance 2013.

49. Fish 2011.

50. Scott 1996.

51. Ibid.

52. Gerber, n.d.

53. Epstein 2008.

54. Gilbert 1978.

55. Ibid.

56. Ibid.

57. http://www.aaup.org/news/statement-president%E2%80%99s-proposal-performance-based-funding (accessed January 28, 2015).

58. Fish 2007.

59. Scott 1998. Most of them seem to be petty disagreements over Togovnick's administrative style. Among them: Togovnick scheduled separate faculty meetings for senior and junior faculty—an entirely common practice that increases dialogue. Professors circulated a petition opposing the idea. She also selected a student to attend a conference with her despite student demands that the student be elected.

60. Soo and Carson 2004.

Chapter 12: Governing in the Age of Internet Empires

1. The phrase "Internet Empires" was used by researchers at the Oxford Internet Institute to illustrate the global dominance of the most visited Web sites. It is in turn borrowed from the popular computer game *The Age of Empires*. Google, Facebook, Baidu, and Yahoo! are dominant. These empires control communication and information access around the world. They cross geographic, religious, political, and corporate boundaries, and their citizens often set up nation-states, controlled not by laws but by agreements. http://geography.oii.ox.ac.uk/?page=home (accessed March 16, 2015).

2. Lederman 2014.

3. Ali 2004.

4. Chen 2014.

5. Judge 1999.

6. Westhues 2004.

7. Gravois 2006.

8. Westhues in fact noted this analogy to religious inquisitions and purges. Westhues 2005.

9. Tucker, n.d.

10. Among the twists and turns of the Richardson story is the unique status of the publisher, Edwin Mellen Press, a controversial academic publishing company founded and owned by Richardson himself. Mellen Press and Richardson's relationship to it became one of the points in the indictment against him by his employer, St. Michael's College. Westhues 2004.

11. Askey 2010.

12. Yardi and boyd 2010. The spelling of danah boyd is not a misprint; it is deliberately spelled out in lowercase letters.

13. Rice 2012.

14. http://news.virginia.edu/content/teresa-sullivan-extraordinary-leader-and-respected-scholar-become-eighth-president-uva (accessed March 13, 2015).

15. Schick 2012.

16. On the concept of shared governance, see chapter 11.

17. American Association of University Professors, 2011.

18. Ibid.

19. Ibid.

20. Downey 2012.

21. www.collegiannews.com/2012/08/dismissed-what-they-havent-told-you-about-tricolis-resignation (accessed January 29, 2015).

22. Ibid.

23. "Ousted NSU president: Termination was 'sudden, unexpected and disappointing,'" *Richmond Times Dispatch*, August 25, 2013, http://www.richmond .com/news/state-regional/ousted-nsu-president-termination-was-sudden-unexpected-and-disappointing/article_2720eeee-29af-58e9-989b-e879952872aa .html?mode=jqm (accessed on March 13, 2015).

24. Trachtenberg, Kauvar, and Bogue 2013.

25. Rice 2012.

26. Ibid.

27. Scott 1996.

28. Carter and Linkins 2012.

29. Gerber, n.d.

30. Diamond 2012.

31. Carter and Linkins 2012.

32. "Message from President Sullivan to the Board of Visitors," once available at http://president.virginia.edu/speeches/12/message120618.html, has since been removed from the university's Web site.

33. AAUP press release, June 16, 2010, http://www.aaup.org/AAUP/newsroom /2012PRs/UVA.htm (accessed January 29, 2015).

34. Carter and Linkins 2012.

35. Vaidyhaathan 2012.

36. Brooks 2012.

37. AAUP's Committee on College and University Governance 2013.

38. American Council of Trustees and Alumni 2013.

39. http://www.virginia.edu/bov/meetings/12nov/12NOVBOARDMINUTES.pdf (accessed January 29, 2015).

40. American Council of Trustees and Alumni 2013.

41. American Association of University Professors 1915.

42. Wilson 2007.

43. http://news.psu.edu/story/332349/2014/11/13/administration/board-trustees -meeting-be-streamed-live-online (accessed on March 13, 2015).

Part IV: A Social Contract

1. http://collegeforamerica.org/videos/entry/cfa-student-stories-conagra-foods -zach-sherman (accessed January 30, 2105).

2. Lumina Foundation 2014.

3. Delta Project 2010.

4. Associated Press and *Journal Sentinal* Staff 2013.

5. Sterling succeeded Henry Barnard, Wisconsin's second president, whose tenure was cut short by chronic illness.

6. Burke 1971.

7. Committee on Prospering in the Global Economy of the 21st Century2007.

8. One of the critical areas noted in ibid.

9. Kristoff 2012.

10. Yadidi 2013.

11. Garba and DeMillo 2013.

12. Weisberg 2010.

13. Stephens 2013.

14. Monteleone 2010.

15. DeMillo 2011.

16. McCullough 2001.

17. Ibid.

18. "The Encouragement of Literature, Etc.," in A Constitution or Form of Government for the Commonwealth of Massachusetts, chap. 6, sec. II.

19. Ibid.

20. 7 U.S.C. §304; 7 U.S.C. §322.

21. Drury 2011.

22. Bascom 1877.

23. Ibid.

24. Ibid.

25. Ibid.

26. Watson 2007.

27. Ibid.

Appendix

1. Kerr, Gade, and Lawakoa 1994.

2. DeMillo 2011, 61.

3. Consejo Superior de Investigaciones Cientificas 2013.

4. US Department of Education 2013.

5. *India Education Review* 2011.

6. There is no real agreement in Japan about what a daigaku is. Originally meant to apply to government-chartered degree-granting institutions, it could refer to any kind of postsecondary school, including new, experimental, private schools that seem to spring up without any regulation at all. As a consequence, the number of daigaku has grown in recent years, and now includes junior colleges (*tanki diaguku*), schools of design, and other entities that are outside the control of government regulators.

7. *Huffington Post* 2011.

8. Kurzweil 2006.

9. Albert Schweitzer University, n.d.

10. European University, n.d.

References

AAUP's Committee on College and University Governance. 2013. College and University Governance: The University of Virginia Governing Board's Attempt to Remove the President. Association of American University Professors. http://aaup .org/reports-publications (accessed May 8, 2015).

Adams, Henry. n.d.. History of the United States: Life in 1800. American Studies Hypertext Project, University of Virginia.

Albert Schweitzer University. n.d. http://www.albertsc.com/menus/menuwhoarewe .htm (accessed January 31, 2015).

Ali, Hirsi. 2004. *Submission*. Produced by Theo van Gogh and Gijs van de West-elaken. Dutch Public Broadcasting Company (VPRO).

Altbach, Philip G. 2007. Peripheries and Centres: Research Universities in Developing Countries. *Higher Education Management and Policy* 9 (2):111–134.

American Association of University Professors (AAUP). 1915. Declaration of Principles on Academic Free and Academic Tenure. http://www.aaup.org/NR/rdonlyres/ A6520A9D-0A9A-47B3-B550-C006B5B224E7/0/1915Declaration.pdf (accessed January 28, 2015).

American Association of University Professors (AAUP). 1989. 75 Years: A Retrospective on the Occasion of the Seventy-fifth Annual Meeting, American Association of University Professors. *Academe* 73 (3).

American Association of University Professors. 2009. Characteristics of Part-Time Faculty Who Would Not Prefer Full-Time Position at Current Institution. July–August. http://www.aaup.org/article/characteristics-part-time-faculty-who-would-not -prefer-full-time-position-current#.Uw9yO4W6nk0 (accessed January 11, 2015).

American Association of University Professors. 2011. Dr. Anthony S. Tricoli Receives AAUP's Ralph S. Brown Award for Shared Governance. June 10. http://www.aaup .org/AAUP/newsroom/prarchives/2011/brown.htm (accessed January 29, 2015).

American Association of University Professors. n.d. College and University Governance Reports. http://www.aaup.org/reports-publications/aaup-policies-reports/college-and-university-governance-reports (accessed January 28, 2015).

American Council of Trustees and Alumni. 2013. Two Cheers for the AAUP. June 4. http://www.goacta.org/the_forum/two_cheers_for_the_aaup (accessed January 29, 2015).

Anderson, Nick. 2013. Howard Trustee Says University in Trouble. *Washington Post*, June 7. http://articles.washingtonpost.com/2013-06-07/local/39811315_1_howard-s-colleges-board-chairman (accessed January 24, 2015).

Anderson, Polly. 1978. College Enrollment Decline. *Illinois Issues*, February 17. http://www.lib.niu.edu/1978/ii780215.html (accessed March 16, 2015).

Askey, Dale. 2010. The Curious Case of Edwin Mellen Press. September 22. http://web.archive.org/web/20110630153231/http:/htwkbk.wordpress.com/2010/09/22/the-curious-case-of-edwin-mellen-press/ (accessed January 29, 2015).

Associated Press. 2012. Chancellor L. Dickinson St. Will Repair Reputation. WADZ 8 television, ABC, February 14. http://www.wdaz.com/event/article/id/12266/ (accessed January 25, 2015).

Associated Press and *Journal Sentinel* Staff. 2013. Obama Unveils College Aid System, Touts UW's Flexible Option. *Milwaukee Journal Sentinel*, August. http://www.jsonline.com/news/education/obama-touts-uws-flexible-option-degree-program-in-college-speech-b9981598z1-220689121.html (accessed January 30, 2015).

Association of American Universities. 2004. *Reinvigorating the Humanities: Enhancing Research and Education on Campus and Beyond*. Washington, DC: Association of American Universities.

Ballou, Janice, Matthew Mishkind, Geraldine Mooney, and Welmoet van Kammen. 2002. National Science Foundation Report on Grand Size and Duration: Principal Investigator FY 2001 Grant Award Survey and Institutional Survey. Arlington, VA: National Science Foundation. http://www.nsf.gov/pubs/2004/nsf04205/mathematica_nsfrptfinal6.pdf (accessed December 29, 2014).

Baron, Jonathan, and M. Frank Normal. 1992. Achievement Tests and High School Class Rank at Predictors of College Performance. *Educational and Psychological Measurement* 52 (4): 1047–1055.

Bascom, John. 1877. Education and the State: Baccalaureate Sermon. University of Wisconsin at Madison, June 17.

Begley, Adam. 1992. Souped-Up Scholar. *New York Times Magazine*, May 3.

Bennett, William J. 2013. *Is College Worth It? A Former United States Secretary of Education and a Liberal Arts Graduate Expose the Broken Promise of Higher Education*. Nashville, TN: Thomas Nelson.

Bernstein, Josiah F. 1841. *The Black Board in the Primary School: A Manual for Teachers to Illustrate Some Valuable Methods of Interesting and Instructing Young Children.* Boston: Perkins and Marvin.

Berube, Michael. 2013. The Humanities, Unraveled. *Chronicle of Higher Education,* February 18. http://chronicle.com/article/Humanities-Unraveled/137291 (accessed January 16, 2015).

Bloom, Benjamin. 1984. The 2 Sigma Problem: The Search for Methods of Group Instruction as Effective as One-to-One Tutoring. *Educational Researcher* 13 (6): 4–16.

Blumenstyk, Goldie. 2010. Public Colleges Turn to Tuition Increases to Offset Budget Squeezes. *Chronicle of Higher Education,* August 31.

Blumenstyk, Goldie. 2014. At 2 Conferences, Big Claims Are Staked on Higher Education's Future. *Chronicle of Higher Education,* May 12. http://chronicle.com/article/At-2-Conferences-Big-Claims/146461/?cid=at&utm_source=at&utm_medium=en (accessed December 22, 2014).

Blumenstyk, Goldie, and Alex Richards. 2010. 149 Nonprofit Colleges Fail Education Department's Test of Financial Strength. *Chronicle of Higher Education,* August 11.

Bok, Derek, and William G. Bowen. 1998. *The Shape of the River.* Princeton, NJ: Princeton University Press.

Bowen, William G. 2012. The "Cost Disease" in Higher Education: Is Technology the Answer? Tanner Lectures, Stanford University.

Brademas, John. 1971. The Financial Crisis in American Higher Education. *Journal of Student Financial Aid* 1 (1): 46–52.

Bradley, D. R., W. Hiss, M. Bruce Datta, M. Kinsman, S. Provasnik, and J. Smedley. 1990. The Optional SAT Policy at Bates: A Final Report. Lewiston, ME: Bates College, Committee on Admissions and Financial Aid.

Bransford, John D., Ann L. Brown, and Rodney R. Cocking. 2000. *How People Learn: Brain, Mind, Experience, and School.* Washington, DC: National Academy of Sciences Press.

Braverman, Harry. 1974. *Labor and Monopoly Capital: The Degradation of Work in the Twentieth Century.* New York: Monthly Review Press.

Brewer, Dominic J., Eric R. Eide, and Ronald G. Ehrenberg. 1999. Does It Pay to Attend an Elite Private College? Cross-Cohort Evidence on the Effects of College Type on Earnings. *Journal of Human Resources* 34 (1): 104–123.

Brooks, David. 2012. The Campus Tsunami. *New York Times,* May 3. http://nyti.ms/KIfEdC (accessed March 16, 2015).

Bunce, Diane M., Elizabeth A. Flens, and Kelly Y. Neiles. 2010. How Long Can Students Pay Attention in Class? A Study of Student Attention Decline Using Clickers. *Journal of Chemical Education* 87 (12): 1438–1443.

Burke, Jack. 1971. Accent on the News. *Milwaukee Journal*, June 27.

Burrelli, Joan, Alan Rapoport, and Rolf Lehming. 2008. *Baccalaureate Origins of S&E Doctorate Recipients*. Arlington, VA: National Science Foundation Directorate for Social, Behavioral, and Economic Sciences.

Bush, Vannevar. 1945. Science the Endless Frontier: A Report to the President by Vannevar Bush, Director of the Office of Scientific Research and Development. Arlington, VA: National Science Foundation.

Cafferty, Jack. 2011. The Cafferty File. January 3. http://caffertyfile.blogs.cnn.com/2011/01/03/technology-replacing-personal-interactions-at-what-cost/ (accessed January 3, 2015).

Carlson, Patricia A., and Frederick F. Berry. 2008. Using Computer-Mediated Peer Review in an Engineering Design Course. *IEEE Transactions on Professional Communication* 51 (3): 264–279.

Carlson, Ryan, Konstantin Genin, Martina Rau, and Richard Schienes. 2013. Student Profiling from Tutoring System Log Data: When to Multiple Graphical Representations Matter. In *Proceedings of the 6th International Conference on Educational Data Mining*, ed. Sidney K. D'Mello, Rafael A. Calvo, and Andrew Olney. Memphis TN: International Educational Data Mining Society.

Carlsmith, Christopher. 2002. Struggling toward Success: Jesuit Education in Italy, 1540–1600. *History of Education Quarterly* 42 (2): 215–246.

Carlyle, Thomas. 1850. Latter-Day Pamphlets. Part I: The Present Time.

Carnegie Commission on Higher Education. 1971. *New Students and New Places*. Hightstown, NJ: McGraw-Hill.

Carter, Susan B., Scott Sigmund Gartner, Michael R. Haines, Alan L. Olmstead, Richard Suth, and Gavin Wright. 2006. *Historical Statistics of the United States,* Millennial Edition Online. Cambridge: Cambridge University Press.

Carter, Zach, and Jason Linkins. 2012. UVA Teresa Sullivan Ouster Reveals Corporate Control of Public Education. *Huffington Post*, June 24. http://www.huffingtonpost.com/2012/06/24/uva-teresa-sullivan-ouster-_n_1619261.html (accessed January 29, 2015).

CBS Worldwide Inc. 2000. The Scuffed Halls of Ivy. *60 Minutes.* Edited by Catherine Olian. July 23.

Centre Daily Times. 2013. Penn State Faculty Members Urge Others to Support Paterno-NCAA Lawsuit. August 8. http://www.centredaily.com/2013/08/08/3726024/penn-state-faculty-should-support.html (accessed January 25, 2015).

Chang, Victoria, Kimberly Elsbach, and Jeffrey Pfeffer. 2006. *Jeffrey Sonnenfeld: The Road to Redemption*. Palo Alto, CA: Stanford Graduate School of Business.

Cheit, Earl Frank. 1971. *The New Depression in Higher Education*. New York: McGraw-Hill for the Carnegie Commission on Higher Education.

Chen, Jodi So. 2014. Professor Who Lost U. of I. Job Offer Lashes out against Administrators. *Chicago Tribune*, October 7. http://www.chicagotribune.com/news/local/breaking/ct-salaita-speaking-tour-met-1007-20141007-story.html (accessed February 15, 2015).

Cole, Jonathan. 2010. Why Academic Tenure Is Essential for Great Universities. *Huffington Post*, November 5. http://www.huffingtonpost.com/jonathan-r-cole/why-academic-tenure-is-es_b_779440.html (accessed January 27, 2015).

Cole, Jonathan. 2011. Too Big to Fail: How "Better Than Nothing" Defined the National Research Council's Graduate Rankings. *Chronicle of Higher Education*, April 24. http://chronicle.com/article/Too-Big-to-Fail/127212 (accessed March 15, 2015).

Colvin, Geoffrey. 2000. The End of the Affair: Jeffrey Sonnenfeld's Battle with Emory University Is Finally Over, but the Question Remains: Why on Earth Did Emory's President Accuse Sonnenfeld of Vandalism? *Fortune*, September 4. http://money.cnn.com/magazines/fortune/fortune_archive/2000/09/04/286828/ (accessed January 29, 2015).

Committee on Prospering in the Global Economy of the 21st Century: An Agenda for American Science and Technology. 2007. *Rising above the Gathering Storm: Energizing and Employing America for a Brighter Economic Future*. Washington, DC: National Academies Press.

Consejo Superior de Investigaciones Cientificas. 2013. Ranking Web of Universities. July. http://www.webometrics.info/en (accessed February 15, 2015).

Delta. 2012. Udacity Statistics 101. Angry Math, September 10. http://www.angrymath.com/2012/09/udacity-statistics-101.html (accessed December 29, 2014).

Delta Project. 2010. *Trends in College Spending, 1999–2009*. Washington, DC: Delta Project.

DeMillo, Richard A. 2011. *Abelard to Apple: The Fate of American Colleges and Universities*. Cambridge, MA: MIT Press.

DeSantis, Nick. 2012. Stanford Professor Gives Up Teaching Position, Hopes to Reach 500,000 Students at Online Start-Up. *Chronicle of Higher Education*, January 23. http://chronicle.com/blogs/wiredcampus/stanford-professor-gives-up-teaching-position-hopes-to-reach-500000-students-at-online-start-up/35135 (accessed December 26, 2014).

Dettmer, Kevin J. H. 2014. *Dead Poets Society* Is a Terrible Defense of the Humanities. *Atlantic*, February 19. http://www.theatlantic.com/education/archive/2014/02/

-em-dead-poets-society-em-is-a-terrible-defense-of-the-humanities/283853 (accessed February 15, 2015).

Diamond, Stephen. 2012. Was the Firing of UVA President Sullivan Legal? June. http://stephen-diamond.com/2012/06 (accessed March 15, 2015).

Downey, Maureen. 2012. Tricoli Out as Perimeter President; College Faces a $16 Million Shortfall. ajc.com, May 7. http://blogs.ajc.com/get-schooled-blog/2012/05/07/tricoli-out-as-perimeter-president-college-faces-a-16-million-shortfall/ (accessed January 29, 2015).

Downs, Anthony. 1967. *Inside Bureaucracy*. New York: Scott Foresman and Company.

Drury, Gwen. 2011. *The Wisconsin Idea: The Vision That Made Wisconsin Famous*. Madison: University of Wisconsin.

Duderstadt, James. 2009. *A University for the 21st Century*. Ann Arbor: University of Michigan Press.

Edmundson, Anne, Brian Holtkamp, Emanuel Rivera, Matthew Finifter, Adrian Mettler, and David Wagner. 2013. An Empirical Study on the Effectiveness of Security Code Review. In *Lecture Notes in Computer Science*, ed. Jan Jurgens and Riccardo Scandriato, 7781: 197–212. Berlin: Springer-Verlag.

Eidiger, Jason David, Eric B. Bailey, William Martin Bachman, Alan C. Cannistraro, Michael John Nino, Kenjiro Fukuda, and Elbert D. Chen. 2011. US Patent No. 13/274274.

Eliot, Charles W. 1869. *Address at the Inauguration of Charles Wilson Eliot as President of Harvard College*. Cambridge, MA: Server and Francis.

Epstein, Irving. 2008. Introductory Remarks for the Illinois AAUP Fall Meeting. http://www.ilaaup.org/fall201008.asp (accessed January 28, 2015).

European University. n.d. http://www.eu.ac.rs/images/Simpozijum%202014/SEPARAT.pdf (accessed March 13, 2015).

Federal Education Budget Project. 2013. Federal Student Loan Default Rates. July 10. http://febp.newamerica.net/background-analysis/federal-student-loan-default-rates. (accessed August 10, 2013).

Fish, Stanley. 1982. *Is There a Text in This Class?* Cambridge, MA: Harvard University Press.

Fish, Stanley. 1993. *Why There Is No Such Thing as Free Speech*. New York: Oxford University Press.

Fish, Stanley. 2007. Shared Governance: Democracy Is Not an Educational Idea. *Change*. http://www.changemag.org/Archives/Back%20Issues/March-April%202007/full-shared-governance.html (accessed January 28, 2015).

Fish, Stanley. 2011. In Academia, Who Works for Whom? *New York Times*, June 6. http://opinionator.blogs.nytimes.com/2011/06/06/faculty-governance-in-idaho/?_r=0 (accessed January 28, 2015).

Forster, E. M. 1939. The Ivory Tower. *Atlantic Monthly*, January, 51–58.

Franklin, Benjamin. 1749. *Proposals Relating to the Education of Youth in Pennsylvania*. Philadelphia: B. Franklin, Printer.

Freeh Sporkin and Sullivan. 2012. Report of the Special Investigative Counsel regarding the Actions of the Pennsylvania State University Related to Child Sexual Abuse Committed by Gerald A. Sandusky. State College: Trustees of Penn State University.

Fried, I., C. L. Wilson, J. W. Morrow, E. D. Behnke, and L. C. Ackerson. 2001. Increased Dopamine Release in the Human Amygdala during Performance of Cognitive Tasks. *Nature Neuroscience* 4 (2): 201–206.

Galilei, Galileo. 1632. Dialogue concerning the Two Chief World Systems. Ed. S. E. Scioritino. Trans. Stillman Drake. http://law2.umkc.edu/faculty/projects/ftrials/galileo/dialogue.html (accessed January 27, 2015).

Garba, Precious Kassey, and Richard DeMillo. 2013. Social Contract and the Future of Universities. Draft of presentation to the World Economic Forum, Global Agenda Council on Future of Universities.

Gerber, Larry G. n.d. Inextricably Linked: Shared Governance and Academic Freedom. http://old.suny.edu/powerofsuny/transformationteam/sharedgovernance/files/Inextricably%20Linked.pdf (accessed January 28, 2015).

Gerstner, Louis V., Jr. 2003. *Who Says Elephants Can't Dance? Leading a Great Enterprise through Dramatic Change*. New York: Harper Business.

Gilbert, Horace N. 1978. Interview with Mary Terrall, February 10, 14, 21, and 28. Caltech Archives, Pasadena, California.

Gilman, Daniel Coit. 1885. *The Benefits with Society Derives from Universities: An Address*. Baltimore: Johns Hopkins University Press.

Ginsberg, Benjamin. 2013. *The Fall of the Faculty: The Rise of the All-Administrative University*. New York: Oxford University Press.

Gladwell, Malcolm. 2008. *Outliers: The Story of Success*. New York: Back Bay Books.

Gomez, Stephen, Holger Andersson, Julian Park, Stephen Maw, Anne Crook, and Paul Orsmond. 2013. *A Digital Ecosystems Model of Assessment Feedback on Student Learning*. Canadian Center of Science and Education.

Gravois, John. 2006. Mob Rule. *Chronicle of Higher Education*, April 14. http://chronicle.com/article/Mob-Rule/36004 (accessed February 15, 2015).

Grossman, Sara. 2013. Survey Finds Only Limited Public Awareness of MOOCs. *Chronicle of Higher Education*, June 26. http://chronicle.com/blogs/wiredcampus/survey-finds-only-limited-public-awareness-of-moocs/44549 (accessed September 10, 2013).

Hacker, Andrew, and Claudia Dreifus. 2010. *Higher Education? How Colleges Are Wasting Our Money and Failing Our Kids—and What We Can Do about It*. New York: Macmillan.

Hackett, Thomas. 2007. Your (Lame) Slogan Here. *Chronicle of Higher Education*, November 23. http://chronicle.com/article/Your-Lame-Slogan-Here/31449 (accessed January 25, 2015).

Hattie, John A. C. 2009. *Visible Learning: A Synthesis of over 800 Meta-Analyses Relating to Achievement*. New York: Routledge.

Herfurth, Theodore. 1949. *Sifting and Winnowing: A Chapter in the History of Academic Freedom at the University of Wisconsin*. Madison: University of Wisconsin.

Hilton, James. 1934. *Goodbye, Mr. Chips*. New York: Little, Brown and Company.

Hoffman, Nicholas von. 1976. Universities Impervious to Change. *Montreal Gazette*, March 20, 9.

Hook, Cayce J, and Martha J. Farah. 2013. Neuroscience for Educators: What Are They Seeking, and What Are They Finding? *Neuroethics* 6 (2): 331–341. http://link.springer.com/article/10.1007/s12152-012-9159-3 (accessed January 2, 2015).

Howe, Harrison. 1935. *Dictionary of American Biography*. Vol. 17. New York: Charles Scribner and Sons.

Hoxby, Carolyn, and Christopher Avery. 2012. The Missing One-Offs: The Hidden Supply of High-Achieving, Low-Income Students. Working paper. Cambridge, MA: National Bureau of Economic Research.

Hsiao, I-Han, and Peter Bruisilovsky. 2010. The Role of Community Feedback in the Student Example Authoring Process: An Evaluation of AnnotEx. *British Journal of Educational Technology* 42 (3): 482–499.

Huffington Post. 2011. Trump University: No Longer a University? *Huffington Post*, May 25. http://www.huffingtonpost.com/2010/04/19/trump-university-no-longe_n_542469.html (accessed January 31, 2015).

India Education Review. 2011. India Needs More Universities: Kapil Sibal. *India Education Review*, November 16. http://www.indiaeducationreview.com/news/india-needs-more-universities-kapil-sibal (accessed August 8, 2013).

Institute of Medicine. 2013. *Delivering High-Quality Cancer Care: Charting a New Course for a System in Crisis*. Washington, DC: National Academy of Sciences.

Jacoby, Russell. 2013. Stanley Fish Turned Careerism into a Philosophy. *New Republic*, August. http://www.newrepublic.com/article/114224/ (accessed January 28, 2015).

Jaffelin, Emmanuel. 2012. Pourquoi Harvard ne fait pas rever? *Le Monde*, May 28. http://www.lemonde.fr/idees/article/2012/05/28/pourquoi-harvard-ne-fait-pas-rever_1707618_3232.html (accessed February 15, 2015).

James, William. 1903. The Ph.D. Octopus. http://en.wikisource.org/wiki/The_Ph.D._Octopus (accessed January 16, 2015).

Janin, Hunt. 2008. *The University in Medieval Life: 1179–1499*. Jefferson, NC: MacFarland.

Jaschick, Scott, and Doug Lederman. 2014. *Inside Higher Ed Survey of College and University Chief Academic Officers*. Washington, DC: Inside Higher Ed.

Jergen, Herbst. 1974. The First Three American Colleges: Schools of Reformation. In *Perspectives in American History*, ed. Donald Fleming and Bernard Bailyn, 7–8. Cambridge, MA: Charles Warren Center for Studies in American History, Harvard University.

Jones, Allan Clive. 2010. Speaking of Science: BBC Science Broadcasting and Its Critics, 1923–64. PhD diss., University College London.

Judge, Mike, dir. 1999. *Office Space*. 20th Century Fox, United States.

Kelderman, Eric. 2013. Accreditors Now Find Themselves under Critical Review. *Chronicle of Higher Education*, December 2. http://chronicle.com/article/Accreditors-Now-Find/143325 (accessed February 15 2015).

Kerr, Clark. 2001. *The Uses of the University*. Cambridge, MA: Harvard University Press.

Kerr, Clark, Marian L. Gade, and Maureen Lawakoa. 1994. *Higher Education Cannot Escape History: Issues for the Twenty-First Century*. Albany: State University of New York.

Khan Academy. n.d. http://khanacademy.org (accessed January 2, 2015).

Kristoff, Nicholas D. 2012. From South Sudan to Yale. New York Times, March 28. http://www.nytimes.com/2012/03/29/opinion/kristof-from-south-sudan-to-yale.html.

Kurzweil, Ray. 2006. *The Singularity Is Near*. New York: Penguin Books.

Lambert, Craig. 2012. Twilight of the Lecture. *Harvard Magazine*, March. http://harvardmagazine.com/2012/03/twilight-of-the-lecture (accessed February 15, 2015).

Leach, William D. 2008. *Shared Governance in Higher Education: Structural and Cultural Responses to a Changing National Climate*. Sacramento: California State University,

Sacramento Center for Collaborative Policy. http://ssrn.com/abstract=1520702 (accessed January 28, 2015).

Lederman, Doug. 2014. The Substitutes Speak Out. *Inside Higher Ed*, May 9. https://www.insidehighered.com/news/2014/05/19/substitute-commencement-speakers -say-everyone-lose-out-protests (accessed March 16, 2015).

Lenzner, Robert, and Steven S. Johnson. 1997. Seeing Things as They Really Are. *Forbes*, March 10. http://www.forbes.com/forbes/1997/0310/5905122a.html (accessed January 9, 2015).

Lewin, Tamar. 2011. MIT Expands Its Free Online Courses. *New York Times*, December 19. http://www.nytimes.com/2011/12/19/education/mit-expands-free-online -courses-offering-certificates.html (accessed February 15, 2015).

Lewin, Tamar. 2013. Master's Degree Is New Frontier of Study Online. *New York Times*, August 18. www.nytimes.com/2013/08/18/education/masters-edgree-is-new -frontier-of-study-online.html/?pagewanted=all (accessed December 29, 2014).

Liu, Nian Cai. 2011. The Phenomenon of Academic Rankings of World Universities Model: Future Directions. Paper presented to the Conference on Quality in Higher Education: Identifying. Developing, and Sustaining Best Practices in the APEC Region, Honolulu, August 4–6.

Luca, Michael, and Jonathan Smith. 2013. Salience in Quality Disclosure: Evidence from the U.S. News College Rankings. *Journal of Economics and Management Strategy* 22 (1): 58–77.

Lumina Foundation. 2014. *The Degree Qualification Profile*. Indianapolis, IN: Lumina Foundation.

Manchester, William. 1992. *A World Lit Only by Fire: The Medieval Mind and the Renaissance—Portrait of an Age*. New York: Little, Brown.

McCarthy, Michael. 2011. ESPN's Bilas on Penn State: "A Conspiracy of Cowards." November 9. http://content.usatoday.com/communities/gameon/post/2011/11/ espns-bilas-on-penn-state-a-conspiracy-of-cowards-joe-paterno-graham-spanier -jerry-sandusky-jay-bilas/1#.UnN3YBCc_74 (accessed January 25, 2015).

McCauley, Robert N. 1982. The Business of the University. *Liberal Education* 68 (1): 27–34.

McCullough, David. 2001. *John Adams*. New York: Simon & Schuster.

Mead, Walter Russell. 2013. Is the MOOC Hype Dying? *American Interest*, November 19. http://www.the-american-interest.com/2013/11/19/is-the-mooc-hype-dying (accessed February 15, 2015).

Meister, Robert. 2013. An Open Letter to a Founder of Coursera. *Chronicle of Higher Education*, May 21. http://chronicle.com/blogs/conversation/2013/05/21/

can-venture-capital-deliver-on-the-promise-of-the-public-university/ (accessed January 25, 2015).

Members of the Philosophy Department of San Jose State University. 2013. An Open Letter to Michael Sandel from the Philosophy Department at San Jose State University. April 29. http://www.documentcloud.org/documents/695245-san-jose-state-u-open-letter.html#document/p3 (accessed January 25, 2015).

Metzger, Walter P. 1965. Origins of the Association. *AAUP Bulletin* 51(3) (Summer): 229–237.

Miller, George. 1994. The Magical Number Seven, Plus or Minus Two: Some Limits on Our Capacity for Information Processing. *Psychological Review* 101 (2): 343–352.

Mitra, Sugata, and Vivek Rana. 2001. Children and the Internet: Experiments with Minimally Invasive Education in Rural India. *British Journal of Educational Technology* 32 (2): 221–232.

Monteleone, James. 2010. N.M. Legislators: Too Many Colleges. *Albuquerque Journal*, October 23. http://www.abqjournal.com/news/state/2302544state10-23-10.htm (accessed January 31, 2105).

Moody's Investor Services. 2013. Moody's: 2013 Outlook for Entire US Higher Education Sector Changed to Negative. January 16. https://www.moodys.com/research/Moodys-2013-outlook-for-entire-US-Higher-Education-sector-changed--PR_263866 (accessed January 16, 2013).

Moore, Cathleen. 2001. Comdex: E-Learning Touted as Next Killer App. *Computerworld*, November 15. http://www.computerworld.com/s/article/65737/Comdex_E_learning_touted_as_next_killer_app (accessed September 10, 2013).

Morse, Robert. 2013. Why Howard University Fell in the Best Colleges Rankings. *U.S. News and World Report*, October 7. http://t.usnews.com/bF030 (accessed February 15, 2015).

National Center for Education Statistics. 2005. 2004 National Study of Postsecondary Faculty. nces.ed.gov/pubs2005/2005172.pdf (accessed December 29, 2014).

National Research Council. 2010. *A Data-Based Assessment of Research-Doctorate Programs in the United States*. Washington, DC: National Academy of Sciences, National Academy of Engineering, Institute of Medicine.

National Science Foundation. 1997–2006. Survey of Earned Doctorates. Arlington, VA: National Science Foundation. http://www.nsf.gov/statistics/srvydoctorates (accessed January 31, 2015.)

Nelson, Cary. 2009. The AAUP: A View from the Top. *Chronicle of Higher Education*, December 1. http://chronicle.com/article/The-AAUP-A-View-From-the-Top/49301/ (accessed January 28, 2015).

Newman, John Henry. 1891. *The Idea of a University*. London: Longman, Green & Co.

Odlyzko, Andrew. 2012. *The Railway Mania: Fraud, Disappointed Expectations, and the Modern Economy*. Minneapolis: Railway and Canal Historical Society.

Olson, Gary A. 2009. Exactly What Is "Shared Governance"? *Chronicle of Higher Education*, July 23. http://chronicle.com/article/Exactly-What-Is-Shared/47065/ (accessed January 28, 2015).

OMNITEL Roper. 2012. American History Literacy Survey 2012. GfK Custom Research North America. http://whatwilltheylearn.com/public/pdfs/Roper_GfK _History_Questions.pdf. (accessed October 13, 2015).

Oppenheimer, Todd. 1997. The Computer Delusion. *Atlantic Monthly*, July. http:// www.theatlantic.com/magazine/archive/1997/07/the-computer-delusion/376899 (accessed February 15, 2015).

Organisation for Economic Co-operation and Development. 2004. Education at a Glance.

Ostriker, Jeremiah, and Charlotte Kuh. 2004. *Assessing Research-Doctorate Programs: A Methodology Study*. Washington, DC: National Academy of Sciences.

Ostriker, Jeremiah, and Charlotte Kuh. 2010. *An Assessment of Research Doctoral Programs*. Washington, DC: National Academy of Sciences.

Pareto, Vilfredo. 1961. The Circulation of Elites. In *Theories of Society*, ed. Talot Parsons, Edward Shils, Kaspar Naegele, and Jesse Pitts, 551–557. New York: Free Press of Glencoe.

PayScale. 2012. 2012 ROI Rankings: College Education Value Compared. http:// www.payscale.com/college-education-value-2012 (accessed January 22, 2015).

Pew Research Center. 2011. *Is College Worth It? College Presidents, Public Assess Value, Quality, and Mission of Higher Education: Social and Demographic Trends*. Washington, DC: Pew Research Center.

Pew Social and Demographic Trends. 2012. *The Digital Revolution and Higher Education*. Washington, DC: Pew Research Center.

Philosophy Department of San Jose State University. n.d. An Open Letter to Professor Michael Sandel from the Philosophy Department at San Jose State University. http://www.documentcloud.org/documents/695245-san-jose-state-u-open-letter .html#document/p3 (accessed January 31, 2015).

Piketty, Thomas. 2014. *Capital in the Twenty-First Century*. New York: Belknap Press.

Pirsig, Robert M. 1974. *Zen and the Art of Motorcycle Maintenance: An Inquiry into Values*. New York: William Morrow.

Porter, Michael E. 1980. *Competitive Strategy: Techniques of Analyzing Industries and Competitors*. New York: Free Press.

Rait, Robert S. 1912. *Life in the Medieval University*. London: Public Domain.

Rankin, Bill. 1999. Emory Chief Had Vendetta, Court Told. *Atlanta Journal and Constitution*, September 11: B1.

Reif, Rafael. 2012. Inaugural Address of MIT President Rafael Reif. September 12. http://president.mit.edu/speeches-writing/inaugural-address (accessed January 23, 2015).

Rice, Andrew. 2012. Anatomy of a Campus Coup. *New York Times Magazine*, September 11. http://www.nytimes.com/2012/09/16/magazine/teresa-sullivan-uva-ouster.html?pagewanted=all (accessed February 15, 2015).

Robinson, Ralph. 2001. Calibrated Peer Review: An Application to Increase Student Reading and Writing Skills. *American Biology Teacher* 63 (7): 474–480.

Rojstaczer, Stuart, and Christopher Healy. 2012. Where A Is Ordinary: The Evolution of American College and University Grading. *Teachers College Record*. www.gradeinflation.com/tcr2011grading.pdf (accessed January 2, 2015).

Ross, Edward Alsworth. 1977. *Seventy Years of It: An Autobiography*. New York: Arno Press.

Rudolph, Frederick. 1962. *The American College and University: A History*. Athens: University of Georgia Press.

Rumelt, Richard. 2011. *Good Strategy/Bad Strategy: The Difference and Why It Matters*. New York: Crown Publishing.

Salmon, Felix. 2012. Udacity and the Future of Online Universities. Reuters, US ed. January 23. http://blogs.reuters.com/felix-salmon/2012/01/23/udacity-and-the-future-of-online-universities (accessed December 26, 2014).

Sarbanes-Oxley. 2002. 116 STAT. 745—Corporate Fraud Accountability Act of 2002. Sarbanes-Oxley Act of 2002.

Schick, David. 2012. Tricoli: Some Good News among the Weird of Late. *The Collegian of Georgia Perimeter College*, May 24. http://www.collegiannews.com/2012/05/tricoli-some-good-news-among-the-weird-of-late (accessed March 15, 2015).

Schmidt, Peter. 2013. AAUP Names Julie Schmidt, a Veteran Labor Organizer, as Its Executive Director. *Chronicle of Higher Education*, August 13. http://chronicle.com/article/AAUP-Names-Veteran-Labor/141105 (accessed February 15, 2015).

Schneider, Mark. 2013. *Higher Education Pays: But a Lot More for Some Graduates Than for Others*. College Measures. http://www.air.org/sites/default/files/Higher_Education_Pays_Sep_13.pdf (accessed January 22, 2015).

Schumpeter, Joseph. 1911. *The Theory of Economic Development*. New Brunswick, NJ: Transaction. Translated 1934.

Scientific American. 2012. The Flynn Effect: Modernity Made Us Smarter. August 20. http://www.scientificamerican.com/podcast/episode.cfm?id=the-flynn-effect -modernity-made-us-12-08-20 (accessed January 2, 2015).

Scott, Janny. 1998. Discord Turns Academe's Hot Team Cold. *New York Times*, November 21. http://www.nytimes.com/1998/11/21/arts/discord-turns-academe-s-hot-team-cold.html?pagewanted=all&src=pm (accessed February 15, 2015.

Scott, Joanna Vecchiarelli. 1996. The Strange Death of Faculty Governance. *PS: Political Science and Politics* (December): 724–726. http://www.jstor.org/stable/420802 (accessed January 28, 2015).

Seamans, Robert, and Feng Zhu. 2011. Technology Shocks in Multi-Side Markets: The Impact of Craigslist on Local Newspapers. Econ Papers: Working papers, NET Institute. October 5. http://EconPapers.repec.org/RePEc:net:wpaper:1011 (accessed December 29, 2014).

Selingo, Jeffrey. 2013. Presidents and Professors Largely Agree on Who Should Lead Innovation. *Chronicle of Higher Education*, September 30. http://chronicle.com/ article/PresidentsProfessors/141893 (accessed February 15, 2015).

Shanghai Jiao Tong University. 2013. Academic Ranking of World Universities since 2003. http://www.shanghairanking.com/ (accessed January 18, 2015).

Shapin, Steven. 2012. The Ivory Tower: The History of a Figure of Speech and Its Cultural Uses. *British Society for the History of Science* 45 (1): 1–27.

Sinclair, Upton. 1935. *I, Candidate for Governor: And How I Got Licked*. New York: Farrar and Rinehart.

Slosson, Edwin Emery. 1910. *Great American Universities*. New York: Macmillan Company.

Snow, Rion, Brendan O'Connor, Daniel Jurafsky, and Andrew Ng. 2008. Cheap and Fast—But Is It Good? Evaluating Nonexpert Annotations for Natural Language Tasks. In *Proceedings of the Conference on Empirical Methods in Natural Language Processing (EMNLP '08)*, 254–263. Pittsburgh: Association for Computational Linguistics.

Sokal, Alan D. 1996. A Physicist Experiments with Cultural Studies. *Lingua Franca*, May. http://www.physics.nyu.edu/faculty/sokal/lingua_franca_v4/lingua_franca_v4 .html (accessed January 16, 2015).

Soo, Mary, and Cathryn Carson. 2004. Managing the Research University: Clark Kerr and the University of California. *Minerva* 42 (3): 215–236.

Southern Association of Colleges and Schools. 2009. *The Principles of Accreditation: Foundations for Quality Enhancement.* Decatur, GA: Southern Association of Colleges and Schools.

Stephens, Dale. 2013. A Smart Investor Would Skip the M.B.A. *Wall Street Journal,* March 1. http://www.wsj.com/articles/SB100014241278873238843045783282433 34068564 (accessed January 31, 2015).

Stephenson, Neal. 1994. *The Diamond Age.* New York: Random House.

Stobart, J. C. 1929. Wireless in the Service of Education. British Association for the Advancement of Science: Report of the Ninety-Sixth Meeting, 629–630.

Stoke, Stuart M. 1937. What Price Tuition. *Journal of Higher Education* 8 (6):297.

Taleb, Nassim Nicholas. 2010. *The Black Swan: The Impact of the Highly Improbable.* 2nd ed. New York: Random House Trade.

Taylor, Adam. 2012. It's Time to Start Watching the Giant Student Protests in Quebec. *Business Insider,* May 30. http://www.businessinsider.com/quebec-protests -montreal-students-casseroles-2012-5 (accessed January 28, 2015).

Taylor, Mark C. 2010. *Crisis on Campus: A Bold Plan to Reforming Our Colleges and Universities.* New York: Knopf.

Thelin, John R. 2013. *The Rising Costs of Higher Education: A Reference Handbook.* Santa Barbara, CA: ABC-CLIO.

Thille, Candace. 2012. *Changing the Production Function in Higher Education.* Washington, DC: American Council on Education.

Thrun, Sebastian. 2012a. DLD 2012—University 2.0. January 23. http://www .youtube.com/watch?v=SkneoNrfadk.

Thrun, Sebastian. 2012b. Homepage Sebastian Thrun. January 26. http://robots .stanford.edu/personal.html (accessed December 26, 2014).

Thrun, Sebastian. 2012c. Sebastian Thrun: Statistics 101 Will Be Majorly Updated. September 11. http://blog.udacity.com/2012/09/sebastian-thrun-statistics-101-will-be.html #sthash.X7YRxFmR.dpuf (accessed December 29, 2014).

Thurgood, Lori, Mary J. Golladay, and Susan T. Hill. 2006. *U.S. Doctorates in the 20th Century.* Arlington, Virginia: National Science Foundation.

Times Higher Education. 2013. The World University Rankings. http://www .timeshighereducation.co.uk/world-university-rankings (accessed January 18, 2015).

Trachtenberg, Stephen Joel, Gerald B. Kauvar, and E. Grady Bogue. 2013. *Presidencies Derailed: Why University Leaders Fail and How to Prevent It.* Baltimore: Johns Hopkins University Press.

Tucker, Ruth. n.d. My Calvin Seminary Story. http://www.ruthtucker.net (accessed January 29, 2015).

Union of Concerned Scientists. 1968. Founding document. Available at http://www.ucsusa.org/about/founding-document-1968.html#.VN0z53ahzP4 (accessed March 16, 2015).

University of Iowa Libraries. n.d. What Was Chautauqua? http://www.lib.uiowa.edu/sc/tc/ (accessed January 3, 2015).

US Department of Commerce: Bureau of Economic Analysis. n.d. Personal Consumption Expenditures: Higher Education. Washington, DC.

US Department of Education. 2012. Presentation at the Symposium on Innovation to Drive Productivity in Postsecondary Education, Washington, DC, September 10.

US Department of Education. 2013. Integrated Postsecondary Education Data System. http://nces.ed.gov/ipeds (accessed January 31, 2015).

US Government Accountability Office. 2011. *Federal Student Loans: Patterns in Tuition, Enrollment, and Federal Stafford Loan Borrowing up to the 2007–08 Loan Limit Increase.* Washington, DC: GAO.

US News and World Report. 2013. College Rankings and Lists. http://colleges.usnews.rankingsandreviews.com/best-colleges (accessed January 18, 2015).

Vaidyhaathan, Siva. 2012. Strategic Mumblespeak: UVA's Teresa Sullivan Was Fired for What? *Slate,* June. http://www.slate.com/articles/news_and_politics/hey_wait_a_minute/2012/06/teresa_sullivan_fired_from_uva_what_happens_when_universities_are_run_by_robber_barons_.html (accessed March 16, 2015).

Walker, Matthew P., and Robert Stickgold. 2004. Sleep-Dependent Learning and Memory Consolidation. *Neuron* 44 (1): 121–133.

Wang, Margaret C., Geneva D. Haertel, and Herbert J. Walberg. 1993/1994. What Helps Students Learn? *Educational Leadership* 51 (4): 74–79.

Watson, David. 2007. The University and Its Communities. *Higher Education Management and Policy* 19 (2): 21–30.

Watters, Audrey. 2011. Steve Jobs, Apple, and the Failure of Education Technology. October 8. http://hackeducation.com (accessed January 10, 2015).

Weber, Max. 1918. *Science as a Vocation.* Munich: Duncker and Humboldt.

Website of Record for Truth in the Sandusky Scandal. n.d. http://www.framingpaterno.com (accessed January 25, 2015).

Weimer, Maryellen. 1993. *Improving Your Classroom Teaching.* Thousand Oaks, CA: Sage Publications.

Weir, Peter, dir. 1989. *Dead Poets Society*. Touchstone Pictures, Los Angeles

Weisberg, Jacob. 2010. What's Wrong with Silicon Valley Libertarianism. *Newsweek*, October 18. http://www.newsweek.com/whats-wrong-silicon-valley-libertarianism-73877 (accessed January 31, 2015).

Western Association of Schools and Colleges, Senior College and University Commission. n.d. Concept Papers: Redesigning WASC Accreditation. http://www.wascsenior.org/redesign/conceptpapers (accessed January 18, 2015).

Westhues, Kenneth. 2004. *Administrative Mobbing at the University of Toronto: The Trial, Degradation, and Dismissal of a Professor during the Presidency of J. Robert Prichard*. Queenston, ON: Edwin Mellen Press.

Westhues, Kenneth. 2005. *The Pope versus the Professor: Benedict XVI and the Legitimation of Mobbing*. Queenston, ON: Edwin Mellen Press.

Widdom, Jennifer. 2012. From 100 Students to 100,000. February 24. wp.sigmod.org/?p=165 (accessed December 26, 2014).

Wieman, Carl. 2009. Why Not Try a Scientific Approach to Science Education? March 10. http://www.science20.com/carl_wieman/why_not_try_scientific_approach_science_education (accessed January 3, 2015).

Willson, Meredith, and Franklin Lacey. 1957. *The Music Man*. New York: G. P. Putnam's Sons.

Wilson, Robin. 2007. The AAUP, 92, and Ailing. *Chronicle of Higher Education*, June 8. http://chronicle.com/article/The-AAUP-92Ailing/3053 (accessed January 29, 2015).

Wolverton, Brad. 2012. Penn State Enrollment and Gifts Seem Unaffected by $20-Million Scandal. *Chronicle of Higher Education*, November 2. http://chronicle.com/article/Penn-State-Enrollment-and/135550 (accessed January 25, 2015).

Yadidi, Noa. 2013. Exonerated Convict Speaks to Criminal Law and Advocacy Students. *Harvard Westlake Chronicle*, January 21. http://www.hwchronicle.com/news/exonerated-convict-speaks-to-criminal-law-and-advocacy-students (accessed March 16, 2015).

Yaffe, David. 1999. The English Department That Fell to Earth. *Lingua Franca*. http://linguafranca.mirror.theinfo.org/9902/yaffe.html (accessed January 28, 2015).

Yardi, Sarita, and danah boyd. 2010. Dynamic Debates: An Analysis of Group Polarization over Time on Twitter. *Bulletin of Science, Technology, and Society* 30 (5): 316–327.

Zuboff, Shoshana. 1989. *In the Age of the Smart Machine*. New York: Basic Books.

Zuboff, Shoshana, and James Maxim. 2002. *The Support Economy*. New York: Penguin Books.

Index